John Waggoner
(1751-1842)
and
Margaret (Bonnett) Waggoner

ANCESTORS, FAMILIES
AND DESCENDANTS

Crystal V. Wagoner

HERITAGE BOOKS
2007

HERITAGE BOOKS
AN IMPRINT OF HERITAGE BOOKS, INC.

Books, CDs, and more—Worldwide

For our listing of thousands of titles see our website
at
www.HeritageBooks.com

Published 2007 by
HERITAGE BOOKS, INC.
Publishing Division
65 East Main Street
Westminster, Maryland 21157-5026

Copyright © 1995 Crystal V. Wagoner

Other books by the author:
CD: The People of Lewis County, (West) Virginia in 1850

All rights reserved. No part of this book may be reproduced or transmitted in any form or by any means, electronic or mechanical, including photocopying, recording or by any information storage and retrieval system without written permission from the author, except for the inclusion of brief quotations in a review.

International Standard Book Number: 978-0-7884-0218-0

Dedication

To my Granddaughters:

Sherie Lynn
Julie Ann
Amanda Lucille
Claire Elizabeth

Contents

List of Illustrations v
List of Photographs vii
List of Abbreviations ix
Preface xi

Part One 1
    The Port of Philadelphia Pennsylvania 3
    Hans Martin Wetzel Family 5
    Jacque (Jacob) Bonnett Family 7
    Wilhelm Waggoner Family 9

Part Two 13
    Wetzel and Bonnett Families in Maryland 15
    Bonnetts and Wetzels in Virginia 19

Part Three - South Branch of the Potomac, Virginia 23
    Wilhelm Waggoner Massacre 25
    Johannes Peter Waggoner 31
    Conrad Lutts 33

Part Four - Moving West, Dunkard Bottom 37
    Bonnett, Wetzel and Six Families 39
    John and Barbara (Waggoner) Lantz 45

Part Five - Hacker's Creek Settlement 53
    Samuel Bonnett 55
    Peter Hardman 77
    John & Margaret (Bonnett) Waggoner 89
    Elizabeth (Waggoner) Hardman 97
    Peter Waggoner 105
    William Waggoner (1816-1903) 109

The Virginia Stalnakers 118
Perry Green Waggoner 123

Part Six 137
    John and Susannah (Richards) Waggoner 139
    Paul Waggoner 147
    Henry Waggoner 155
    Elijah Waggoner (1804-1899) 161
    John Waggoner (1805-1879) 175
    Jacob Waggoner (1810-1847) 181
    Catharine Waggoner (1809-ca 1879) 185
    George Waggoner (1812-1877) 187
    William Waggoner (1813-1895) 189
    Susannah Waggoner (1814-   ) 191
    Mariah Waggoner (1818-1905) 193
    Samuel Waggoner (1821-   ) 195

Part Seven 197
    The Allman Family in West Virginia 199
    Samuel Oliver (1752-1819) 231
    Jonathan Boyles 235
    Nicholas Jones (1789-1878) 239
    George Scott 243
    David Watson (1806-1889) 247
    Philip Dunkel 259
    Charles T. G. Steffen (1836-1927) 261

Part Eight - Early Settlers at Hartford Connecticut 263
    Thomas Burnham (1617-1688) 265
    William Fry 273
    The Soloman Family 275
    Selbitz Family 283

Index 289

List of Illustrations

Map of old Philadelphia	2
Map of Virginia - 1748	14
Map of the Monongahela River	54
Harmony Cemetery Stones - Eliza Bonnett and Charlotte Hardman	75
Hewn Logs - Peter Waggoner's Cabin	108
Tombstones - Henry Waggoner (1802-1886) and Susan Waggoner	156
Lewis W. Ferrell - War Memorial	174
Emma Amelia (Steffen) Watson's Garden	257
St. Bonifacius Church Gorsleben, Germany	282
Map of Germany, Gorsleben	287

List of Photographs

Old Harmony Church	96
Peter Waggoner (1787-1879)	104
William Waggoner (1816-1903)	116
Susan (Cosner) Waggoner	122
Margaretha Johanna Pohlmann (Germany)	132
Johann Konrad Pohlmann (Germany)	132
Margaretha Christian Polhmann (Germany) with sisters	135
Paul Waggoner (1800-1877)	148
Peter Waggoner and Family	150
Elijah Waggoner (1804 - 1899)	160
John Calhoun Waggoner's cabin	170
John Calhoun and Emma Cornelia (Starcher) Waggoner	172
Four generations of The Jones Family	242
The David Watson Family	252
Children of Emma Amelia (Steffen) Watson	255
Grandchildren of Emma Amelia (Steffen) Watson	256
Charles T. G. Steffen and family	262
Inez Lucille Solomon - baby picture	264
William (Bill) Fry and Annie (Lane) Fry	272
Christian Frederick Solomon and Sara Jane (Selbitz) Solomon	278

Abbreviations

ae.	-	age
b.	-	born
bro.	-	brother
bp.	-	birth place
bpt.	-	baptized
ca.	-	circa (about)
Capt.	-	Captain
ch.	-	children
Co.	-	County
d.	-	died
d/o	-	daughter of
d-y	-	died young
D.A.R.	-	daughter of American Revolution
dau.	-	daughter
g.dau.	-	grand daughter
Ger.	-	Germany
g.son	-	grand son
h.	-	husband
Jr.	-	Junior
m.	-	married
Rev. War	-	Revolution War
sis.	-	sister
s/o	-	son of
(Sic)	-	copied as found (not a mistake)
Sr.	-	Senior
un.	-	un-married
wid.	-	widow
w.	-	wife
yrs.	-	years

Preface

None of this story could have been accomplished by researching just one member of any family. I have tried to research as many families as possible -- all have added to the overall story and have helped me to move this line along through the years. Quite often I was able to pick up a lost line through some other member of the family.

If a history is a past chronological record of events, as of the life or development of a people, it has happened and been written or recorded by someone, and can be their personal version of what happened and is seldom without bias.

I begin my story with a brief history of early Pennsylvania. I hope it will be easier to realize the kind of life our ancestors lived in the early days. Life was not easy or always happy, but they lived the best they could and survived, we are the proof.

I have tried to name places, according to the time and place when the events occurred. Example: In 1792 the place was Harrison Co. (W) Va. -- but in 1816 new county lines were drawn, and a new county, Lewis Co., was formed. Therefore if I were to document an event that occurred in 1792, I would use Harrison as the county, but if the event were after 1816, I would use Lewis as the county.

I want to thank the many people who have contributed to this history, and to those who have submitted their lines. I hope I have given credit, where credit was due. Great care has been taken to copy all information precisely, resulting in many misspelled words, and surnames.

I have searched for the original records of the events, told in this book, and tried to keep personal opinion and judgment out of records. There will be mistakes, for this I am truly sorry, I hope this book can be enjoyable to those who have ancestors and family in these records.

Part One

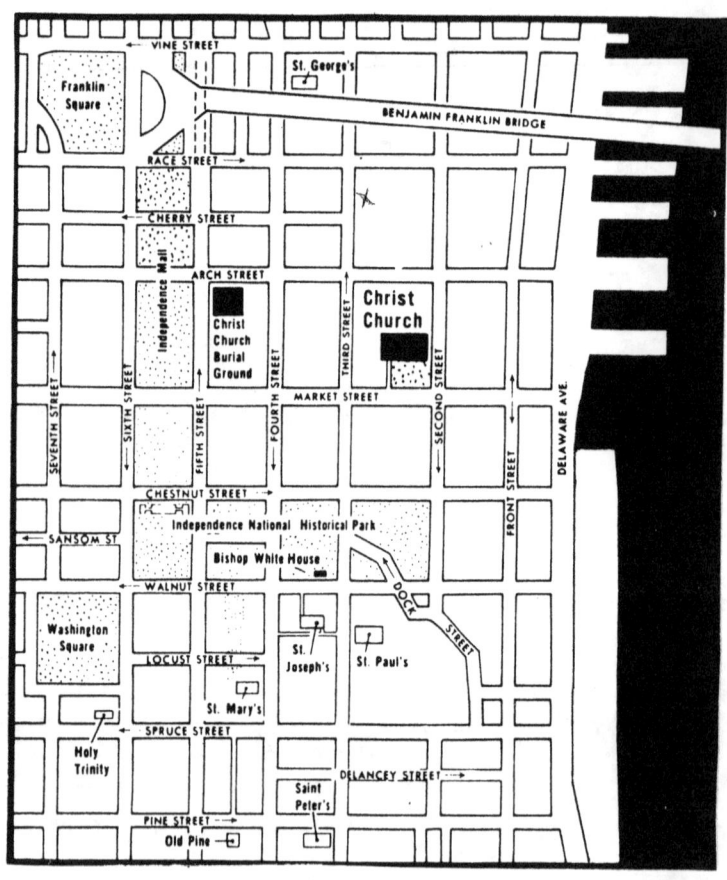

A map of old Philadelphia showing the historic churches that are still in use.

The Port of Philadelphia Pennsylvania

1681 - Over three hundred years ago King Charles II of England repaid a debt to Mr. Penn, father of William Penn, in the form of a land grant. The land grant was 45,000 square miles of land -- from the Delaware River, between southern New York and northern Maryland.

William Penn named the heavily wooded area Sylvania, from the Latin word for "woods". Then King Charles II added the prefix "Penn" - so we have Pennsylvania, and the beginning of the city in 1681.

Penn knew the land would support agriculture and commerce, but it had to be developed. So he became a real-estate promoter and developer on a grand scale. William needed to find people to emigrate and settle in this new land across the ocean. He had Quaker agents in Holland, and contacts in England and Wales, to sell the idea of freedom of religion and suffering from persecution. Land bonuses were offered to those who would buy sizable acreage, as he needed to convert his real property into usable cash.

The city was to be named Philadelphia, or the City of Brotherly Love. Wm. Penn arrived in 1682, after three months at sea, with three ship loads of colonists. The area on the banks of the Delaware River was already settled with Dutch and Swedish settlers, in small river towns. Penn welcomed all settlers, made them citizens of Pennsylvania, and gave to them the ownership of their land.

The original grid plan of 1863, for Wm Penn's central city, Philadelphia, is almost unchanged today. The city plan was laid out with wide streets running from the Schuylkill River to the Delaware River, some two miles in length and one mile in breadth. The new city was dotted with squares, parks, and alleys, and was divided into counties (Buck, Philadelphia, and Chester), townships, and lots. The building started on the banks of the Delaware River and moved slowly westward, certainly not as planned but it grew. The caves hollowed from the banks of the river, with roofs formed by bark and sod, chimneys of stone were evidently ruled out.

By 1700 the town had several hundred brick houses and businesses, with the dock area busy with incoming sailing ships. The growing city needed tradesmen of all types: Bakers, Printers, Tailors, Blacksmiths, brick layers, shoemakers, candle makers, etc. Settlers came for many reasons, but most likely for a better life. They came from Germany, England, Wales, and many other European countries.

William Penn's Charter of Liberties: "No people can be truly happy tho under the greatest enjoyment of civil liberties, if abridged of the freedom of their consciences as to their religious profession and worship".

Meeting Houses, (Quakers) Churches, and Synagogues sprung up all over the area. By 1733, the first Roman Catholic chapel appeared -- which the Provincial Council of Pennsylvania had to defend before the Governor of the province and won.

The Quaker Meeting House was built in 1682, Old Swedes Church (Gloria Dei) in 1698, Christ Church in 1695, and St. Joseph's Church (Roman Catholic) in 1733.

By 1708 Wm. Penn was in London battling political enemies, who sought to deprive him of his province.

Thus we have a picture of the city. Among the tens of thousands of Germans who came to Pennsylvania to escape religious persecution we have the first of our related families.

Hans Martin Wetzel Family

1731 Sept 21. Friday. The Britania, of London, Master Michael Franklyn, from Rotterdam, last from Cowes, England docked at the Port of Philadelphia, Penn. (Rupp - pg 70)

Among the 269 Germans we find the Hans Martin Wetzel Family, under the leadership of Johannes Bartholomew Rieger (this is the spelling in both the ship records and History of Lancaster Co. Pa. by Rupp), (1707-1769) an early Reformed pastor (Lutheran). As one Immigration list gives Hans Martin Wetzel age 31 - born Germany about 1700, wife Maria Barbara Wetzel age 33 - (b about 1696-7) and three children, Hans Martin Jr. - age 6 years, Nicholas age 4 years and Katharine age 3 years.

I can find no record of Hans Martin Wetzels Family for the next few years. They may have settled in Chester County or Lancaster County, Penn. The Rev. Rieger was elected pastor of the Reformed congregations in Philadelphia and Germantown where he served until 1734 - then moved to Amwell, New Jersey until 1739 - then to Lancaster Co. Penn while at Lancaster, he visited Reformed Church in Monocacy (Md.) and Virginia. 1739 - Next we will find the Hans Martin Wetzel family in the upper German settlement in Maryland. Records give two more children born after they arrived in America. John Wetzel b., ca 1733. b possible in Lancaster Co. Penn. and Henry Wetzel, b., ca. 1735. Lancaster Country was created in 1729 from Chester County, an original county created in 1682.

Jacque (Jacob) Bonnett Family

1733 Aug. 27 - Thursday the sailing ship Elizabeth of London, Master Edward Lee from Rotterdam, last Dover, reached the Port of Philadelphia. With 190 passengers in all, 58 males above 16 years, 50 females, 41 males under 16 years and 41 females under 16 years.

We find the family of Jacque (Jacob) Bonnett (Bonet), spelling on ship list) arriving two years after the Wetzels and fifteen years before the Wilhelm Waggoner family. These three families will meet and play an important part in each others lives. I have researched the land records in Chester Co. Penn. for Bonnett, the only record found was so faded and difficult to read, that it gave little or no proof of this family-.

(Rupp. on page 87 - gives Pennsylvania Emigrants,). From Friedrichstal in Baden to a town, founded in the year 1699, by the Margrave of Baden, Durlach, specifically for Huguenots refuges. (also Yoder, Rhineland, Em, pg. 89)

1733 Aug. 27 - Jacques (Jacob) Bonnett (spelled Bonet & Bunett in the list) age 32 years (b ca 1701) wife Mary Bonnett, age 32 (b ca 1701) with four children.

1. Margaret Bonnett age 8 years (b ca. 1725)
2. Susanna Bonnett age 4 years (b ca. 1729)   both listed as
3. Christina Bonnett age 2 years (b ca. 1781)   died on voyage.
4. John Simon Bonnett age 9 months (b ca. 1732).

I've always wondered if this could have been Samuel, who took over the family when the parents died in Maryland. I believe the Bonnetts lived in Paoli, Chester County, Penn. for several years.

We know Lewis Bonnett was born in 1737 in Paoli, Chester Co. Penn. from his sons letters to Draper in 1849 Ohio. We must also place

Catharine, Mary and Elizabeth in this family, as they were mentioned in Maryland records.

Draper's Mss. - Maj. Lewis Bonnett confirms his three Aunts & one Uncle, besides his father, for the family.

There were several Bonet, (Bonnett) Families around this time, and many children names, Mary, Elizabeth, Catharine, & etc., that there could have been a small mistake on the part of the scribe, or the part of some one copying the information. Because we know there was a Catharine, Mary & Elizabeth Bonnett who belonged to the Maryland family and married, we know their Families.

Wilhelm Waggoner Family

1748 Oct. 25 - Friday the sailing ships Patience and Margaret, captained by John Goven, late of Rotterdam, last of Leith, docked at the port of Philadelphia After a trip across the North Atlantic Ocean, at least a month, and two days sailing up the Delaware River from the Delaware Bay entrance, the view of their destination must have been a prayer answered. October would have been a colorful month with the wooded areas along each bank of the Delaware River. The captains list # 123-A- read - seventy-one men, twenty-nine women and six children. Wilhelm Wagoner age 42 years (not naming women) on the B-list Wilhelm (X) Wagner.   Jacob Lantz age 30 years - on B list signed Johannes Lantz and Baltzar Fliescher 20 years - same spelling on the B-list. They were at the mercy of the scribe if they could not read or write, so we have different spellings of the name, made in different places by different scribes.

All the above on the A list were located in Germantown churches, later on and in White Marsh near by (some fourteen miles to the north west of the city of Philadelphia.) If a friend, relative or member of the German colony met the Waggoners, I have no record of such. Many new immigrants were sponsored by the German society that helped new people get settled and into the churches and in an area where they spoke a language they understood.   There is no way the Waggoners could have met the Wetzels or Bonnetts in Pennsylvania, as both the Wetzels and Bonnetts were named in land deals in the upper German settlement in Maryland. (Maryland became a state in 1788, Frederick County was created in 1748 from Prince George County that was created in 1695.)   Large groups of Germans came south out of Pennsylvania and settled the north western part of Prince George, which enabled them to create Frederick County in 1748.

The Wetzels and Bonnetts were in Maryland by 1739 to 1740; long before the Waggoners came to Pennsylvania in 1748. We know Wilhelm Waggoner was 42 years in 1748 (on the ship list), he would have been born around 1706 in (Dutch Flanders) Germany. His wife Anna Elizabeth with two known children Mary about 6 years (b ca. 1743) and John Peter around 3 years (b ca 1746). (Both Mary & John Peter's ages are estimated by several items, although I've never found a date for either).

The Waggoners followed by both Johannas Lantz and Baltzar Fliescher, located in or near the Germantown area as all are found in church records in the next seven years. Germantown, was settled by thirteen German families in 1683 and by 1748 had a heavy German populous. It is some fourteen (14) miles to the north of the city of Philadelphia in 1748. Just to the west of Germantown was located White Marsh, also a German settlement.

Saint Michael's Evangelical Lutheran Church, established in 1728, served all the surrounding area of Germantown, Pa. Today the Third St. Michael's, built in 1895 stands on the original site at 6671 Germantown Avenue, in Germantown, Pa. The old cemetery began some 266 years ago, is at the back of the Church, with a more recent cemetery at the front area.

The old Germantown Pike, now Germantown Avenue, cuts through the northern part of Philadelphia Co. Pa. Aided by the Old Pike Road for travel, the Waggoner family may well have lived in nearby White Marsh, (Montgomery Co. in 1748) and attend St. Michael's Church.

From 1746 to 1757 the Rev. Michael Schlatter (1716-1790) was the Pastor of the Philadelphia and Germantown Congregations. The early St. Michael's Church records for 1749, Apr. 24 show the baptism of Anna Elisabeth, daughter of Wilhelm Wagner and Anna Elisabeth Wagnerin, bpt. age four weeks, makes her birth on Thursday 27 March 1749, just five months and two days after the families arrival in America. God parents were Baltzar Fliescher and Anna Elisabeth Dammerin. (In my first manuscript, Hackers Creek Journal, Vol. II Issue 2 - Jan. 1984 - I then stated " adding to the name of a female in early German usually indicates the single status of a woman. I wonder if Anna Elisabeth's maiden name was Wagner".)

As I'm not researching the Waggoner Family before the date of Immigration, the record will be copied as I found it in the church records, in the hand writing of the pastor. The church record in German reads: *"1749 April 24, baptised Anna Elisabeth, tochler des,*

Wilhelm and Anna Elisabeth Wagnerin. God parents Baltzer Fleischer und Anna Elisabeth Dannerin." This record would seem to give us the name of Wilhelm Waggoner's wife and the mother of the child Mary and John Peter, as well as Ann Elisabeth.

NOTE: Around 1753 the two churches-reorganized, and becoming larger, separated, thus our church became St. Michael's Lutheran Church of Germantown. Therefore, it's baptismal register begins in 1741.

Some time between April 1749 and Dec. 1750 the name Anna Elisabeth was replaced with the name Agnesa Waggoner. I have found no marriage date for Wilhelm Waggoner nor a death date for Anna Elisabeth Wagnerin.

In 1983 I searched the St. Michael's Church records in the Historical Society of Philadelphia, Pa., at 1300 Locust St., and also the Church Records at the Lutheran Church Record Library at Germantown, Pa.

On the 18th Sept 1750 Baltzar Fliescher married Hanna Catharine Wietmannin in Philadelphia, Pa. Records of St. Michael's' Lutheran Church, Philadelphia, Pa baptismal records start in 1742, Children of Balthasar and Anna Catharine Fleischer. Anna Elisabeth, bpt.. 6 Sept. 1751, Anna Catharine, bpt.. 29 Sept. 1753, Johannes, b 13 Dec. 1755, Johann Henrich, bpt.. 17 July 1788, and Anna Maria bpt.. 25 Nov. 1760.

In the records of St. Michael's Lutheran Church baptismal records at the Historical Society of Philadelphia, in the hand written records in German I found *"1752 April 26 Johannes, sohn des William Wagener und Agnesa, seine frau born 24 November 1751, Godparents Johannes Lentz und Maria Margaretha Benderin Ref."* (Johannes) John Waggoner was born Wednesday 24 Nov. 1751 (White Marsh, Penn.) and baptized some five months later on Wednesday, 26 Apr. 1752. His parents being Wilhelm (William) Waggoner and his wife Agnesa. Godparents Johannes Lentz (who came over on the ship with the family in 1748), and Maria Margaretha Benderin - this gives our John Waggoner a birth date as well as a baptism date, names his parents and gives the first name of Wilhelm's second wife.

The above record states the name of the Godfather as Johannes Lentz and the Godmother as Marie Margaretha Bendiren "Reformed". We find appearing in Christopher Sower's Germantown newspaper on Wednesday 1 Nov. 1752 this advertisement. *"Marian Johanne Benderin, widow, arrived in America, five years ago (1747) with three daughters, Maria Margaretha, Apollonia, and Christina. The daughters have served their time (indenture time) and Maria, who is with Henrich Zimmerman, Conestoga (Lancaster Co. Pennsylvania) seeks her mother."*

This ad appeared one month and twelve days before the marriage of Johannes Lantz and Maria Margaretha Benderin at St. Michael's on the 12 of December 1752. The record is in German *"Johannes Lantz un jung, wit Wilhelm Wagener und Maria Margaretha Benderin eine ledige person, ref Relig so bein Richard Wahl, in White Marsh, geherruil und nam mehr friest to Pfarrer - Handschurch".* Translated into English as follows: *"1752 Dec. 12 - Johannes Lantz a young person, lives with Wilhelm Wagener, and Maria Margaretha Binderin as a single, unmarried person, of Reformed religion, has been with Richard Wahl in White Marsh, completed her indenture, and is free to marry."*

This adds to the belief that Wilhelm Waggoner lived in White Marsh, Penn. and that Johannes Lantz who immigrated with them stayed with them until 1752, some five years. The name John (Johannes) Lantz will be found on through their lives when they move to Va. and later on when their youngest daughter marries. One can but wonder if its the same person or a coincidence. After living in the area for seven years or so, the Waggoner family and the newly married Lantz couple disappeared from all records of old St. Michael's'. Some time after 1753, Wilhelm Waggoner, his second wife Agnesa Waggoner and children Mary, John Peter, Anna Elisabeth and Johannes migrated to the South Branch of the Potomac, Hampshire County (later Hardy Co.) Virginia. It would seem Johannes Lantz and wife Maria Margaretha traveled along, as other records show them there also.

Part Two

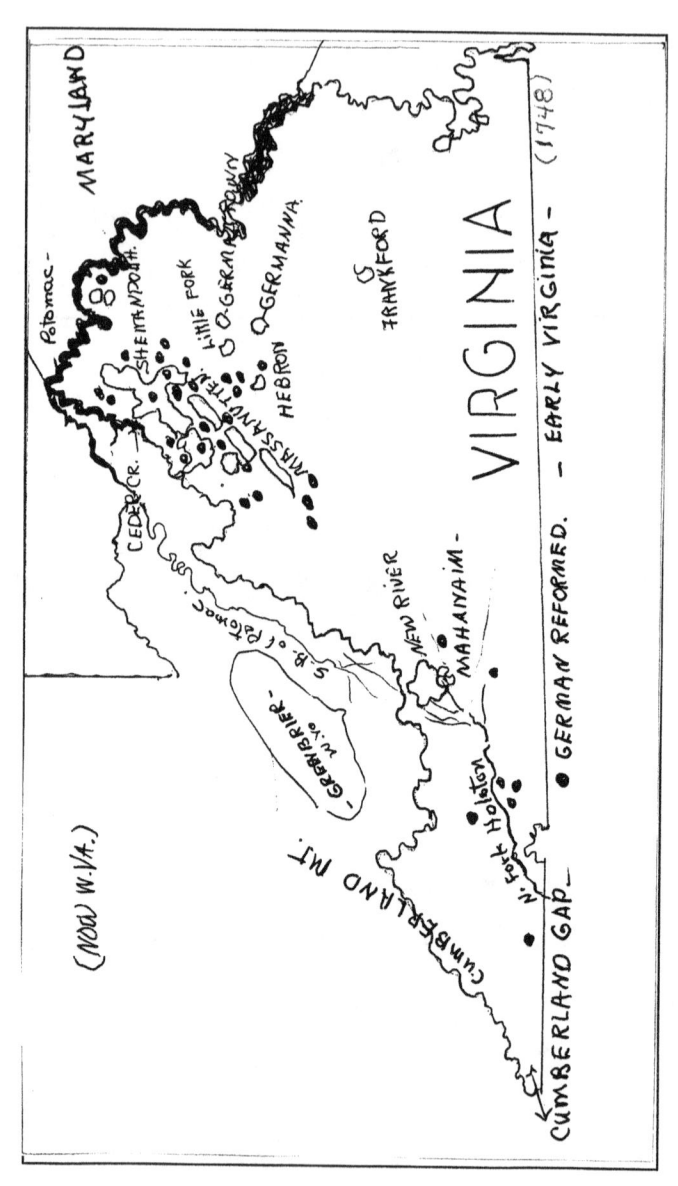

Map of Virginia - 1748

Wetzel and Bonnett Families in Maryland

We already know, the Wetzels came to America, in 1731 and were in the Chester Co. area of Pa. (Lancaster County created in 1729 from Chester Co.) The Bonnetts came in 1733 and surely met up with the Wetzels around Paoli, Chester Co. Pa., because they were in Maryland in five or six years. We find both families in the Upper German Settlement in Maryland by the year 1739.

After much thought, I must agree with <u>Pioneers of Old Monocacy;</u> (Early Settlement of Frederick County, Maryland.)1721 - 1743 by Grace L. Tracey and John P. Dern. (pg 207), we find Martin Wetzel Sr. and wife Maria Barbara as sponsors for the baptism of John Bernhardt Wiemmar (Wymer) in 1739 April 15, son of Bernhardt Wiemmar (Wymer) on one of Rev. John Casper Stoever's visits to Monocacy. The Wetzels were active in the early Lutheran Church of Monocacy and helped build the first one.

The Upper German settlement was located in the northern area of what is now Frederick County Maryland. If Hans Martin Wetzel born ca 1700 in Germany and his wife Maria Barbara (age 33, b ca 1798 in Germany) came; 21 Sept. 1731 with three children, Hans Martin Wetzel Jr. age 6 six years (b ca 1725 Germany), Nicholaus Wetzel age 4 years (b ca 1727, Germany) and Katherine Wetzel age 3 years (b ca 1728, Germany). The other two children would have been born in Lancaster Co. Penn.; John Wetzel, born ca 1733, and Henry Wetzel born ca. 1735, all were in Upper German Settlement by 1739.

Martin Wetzel Sr. had 100 acres surveyed on 25 Nov. 1741, he called the "Mill Place". The land was located near the German Monocacy Road, some two miles north of present day Lewistown.

On 28 May 1743, Daniel Dalany assigned the certificate of survey for his "Wine Garden" to Martin Wetzel's neighbor Jacob Bonnett who

15

on the same day reassigned it to Wetzel. Wetzel received the patent. In 1743 Wetzel also received the Patent for "Bonnett's Resolution", which had been surveyed by Daniel Dalany on 11 Nov. 1742. Wetzel enlarged this patent in 1752 to 400 acres and in 1753 conveyed it Daniel Lefever. In March 1748 Martin Wetzel was one of those Germans being overcharged by the sheriff in his Quit-rent collections.

So there is proof the Wetzels and Bonnetts were in the Upper German settlement together. I believe it also proves Jacob Bonnett and his wife did not die in Chester County Penn. None of his children would have been old enough to deal with land transactions.

Upper German settlement was in Prince George County up until 1748 when Frederick County was created.

In 1747 father Martin Wetzel Sr. and sons Martin Jr. age 22 yr. and Nicolaus age 20 yr. all signed Muhlenberg's articles in the Frederick Lutheran Church book. (Pioneers of Old Monocacy pg. 209)

The Wetzel family, according to family records no longer available, give these records:

Martin Wetzel Jr. m. Elizabeth Cromerston, between 1744 to 1749 four children Johann Jacob, (b 22 Dec. 1744), George Michael, John Friedrich and Maria Catharine Wetzel and in 1751 Magdelena Elisabeth Wetzel was baptized in Frederick Reformed Church.

Nicholas Wetzel m. Elizabeth Bonnett, 3 Apr. 1749, John Wetzel m. Mary Bonnett, sister of Elizabeth. Other Wetzel children were Catharine and Henry.

In 1748 Martin Whetzell (Wetzel) and George Saltner jointly purchased lot # No. 6D in Fredericktown. In 1756 Martin Wetzel (age 31) appeared on Peter Butler's Muster call at the start of the French and Indian War.

Luckily we have Lyman C. Draper's (1815-1891) Manuscripts, (nearly five hundred volumes), and they recorded and preserved much of America's early history. In Draper's series E. and S. we find histories of both the Wetzels & Bonnetts.

There are many people who have researched the Bonnett line, and there are some 40 Bonnet Immigrants listed in the Passenger and Immigration list Index. (pg 179). Again I find Pioneers of Old Monocacy by Tracey and Dern to be the most believable and their records seem to fit in with family records. (pg 214-215) There Jaques "Jacob" Bonet

(Bonnett) matches the Yoder Rhineland Emegrants. (pg 89) records for the Bonnetts.

Jacob Bonnett was 32 years old (b. ca. 1701) wife Mary Bonnett age 32 yr. (b. ca 1701) and four children:
- Margret (age 8)
- Susanna (age 4, listed dead on the voyage)
- Christina (age 2, also listed as dead)
- Johan Semon (age 9 mo.)

I wonder if there could have been a mix up on the ship list. If there were two families with children by the same names, that died, or if the scribe simply made an error. It is also possible that their children did die on the voyage, and that they used the same names for children born later in America.

Tracey & Dern mention family records on the Bonnett Family, from the notes of Professor J. Clarke Sanders of Kasper W. Va, but these records were not passed on to the Historical Society of Carroll Co. with other Tracey papers. This family would have been related in some way to the author Grace L. Tracey. So I'm putting quite a bit of faith in what records I find in "Pioneers of Old Monocacy".

After her father's death in 1960, Dr. Grace L. Tracey was joined in the research by John P. Dern.

I believe this note concerning the research of the Bonnett family, pertained to land records as Dern suggest more research needed to be done on these early land records.

Most of the Bonnett information checks out and the Draper Mss. letters from Maj. Lewis Bonnett clear up everything about the family.

Perhaps there were two families that immigrated near the same time with similar family names and an error was made in the immigration records. Because we know there were 3 sisters and only 1 brother of Lewis Bonnett Sr.

We have proof of the Jacque (Jacob) Bonnetts in Maryland before 1743. When on 28th of May 1743 Daniel Dulany assigned the certificate of survey for his "Wine Garden" to Martin Wetzels neighbor Jacob Bonnett and also in 1743 when Bonnett transferred the patent for "Bonnetts Resolution" to Martin Wetzel.

"Wine Garden", "Bonnetts Resolution" and Wetzel's own patent "Mill Garden" all bordered on to the west German Monocacy Road. "Piney

Neck" was patented, 28 Nov. 1741, to Henry Six and was due south of Wetzel. Jacob Bonnett moved to his third place, "Battleham" located on the west bank of Hunting Creek below the fork of the creek; the 26th of May 1744. (Today this parcel is located between Lewistown and Creagerstown). By 1753 the land had been resurveyed from 100 acres to 250 acres for Jacob Bonnett, who assigned it to John Hoofman. I believe both Jacob Bonnett and wife Mary died in Maryland around 1753. These land deals would have been to early for Samuel or Lewis to handle.

Maj. Lewis Bonnett Jr. (grandson of Jacob Bonnett) writes to Draper in 1849, "My Father Lewis Bonnett Sr. had only one brother, Samuel by name, who took charge of the family and moved to Virginia settling on the South Branch." He also writes, "my father had three sisters." According to family records (pg 215 of Old Monocacy) Jacob Bonnett was twice married. Of his children, Catharine married John Six (Sechs, or Sykes), Mary married John Wetzel, Elizabeth married Martin Wetzel Jr., and Lewis married Elizabeth Waggoner. Most of the Bonnetts moved on to Rockingham Co. Va. (They credit Professor J. Clarke Sanders of Keyser W. Va)

I have never found any record of Jacob Bonnett having been married twice. I think these land records pretty much prove the parents were in Maryland, though the land dates place the family there some time around 1740-1753.

Lewis Bonnett was born in Feb. 1737 - Paoli, Chester Co. Penn. His sister Mary (ca 1735-June 1805) was also born in Paoli, Chester Co. Penn.

I have seen the name Margareth Catharine Bonnett (ca 1725) who married John Conrad Six (Sechs, Sykes) (ca 1731-1786). Thus we have confirmation that the first child, Margaret age 8 years, born Germany, married John Conrad Six.

Bonnetts and Wetzels in Virginia

1757 - John Conrad Six and Catharine (Bonnett) Six were on the Shenandoah River area by 1757, where their first child Henry was born on 12 Feb. 1757.

They moved west, with the Bonnetts, Wetzeks, and Waggoners around 1770, as far as Dunkard Creek, where they remained. Tenmile Country and it's Pioneer Families; by Howard L. Leckey, (pg. 675-676).

Children of John Conrad Six and Catherine (Bonnett) Six were: Henry Six (1757-1842) m. Barbara Selsar, John Six (1758-ca. 1825), Phillip Six, Daniel Six, Mary (Garrison), Barbara (Knotts), Christina (Munger), Lewis Six, m. Catharine Lemley, Jacob Six, and Edward Six.

Mary Bonnett, second child of Jacob and Mary Bonnett, was born in Paoli, Chester County Penn. in 1737. The family was in Maryland by 1741, and had land dealings with the Wetzel family. Their lands lay side by side in the upper German settlement (now Frederick Co.), and they probably attended the same Lutheran Church in Maryland.

It is not clear where Mary Bonnett married John Wetzel (1733-1786) ca.1755-56. Their first child was born in 1757 in The South Branch (Rockingham County Va.)

Rockingham Co. was created in 1778 from Augusta Co. Va. Frederick Co. was created in 1738 from Augusta, and, Hampshire Co. in 1753 from Frederick Co. Va. I agree with the Draper's Mss. where Maj. Lewis Bonnett Jr. (their cousin) writes "'I'he children were born on the South Branch of Cedar Creek (in Shenandoah Co. Va.) -- all except the last son who was born at the mouth of Dunkard." Shenandoah Co. was created in 1772 from Frederick Co.

I have records referring to Old Field and Moores Field, both are located in now Hardy Co. Va., the area known as South Branch. Some of the references name counties that were not created by 1757; yet they refer to the place as "the South Branch" which is the south branch of the Potomac River in Hardy Co. Va..

John Wetzel and Mary (Bonnett) had seven children, five sons and two daughters:

- Martin Wetzel (1757-2 Oct. 1829) m. ca. 1782 -- Mary Coffield (Coffelt)
- Christiana Wetzel (ca 1759) m. Jacob Wolfe (1754-1834) Preston Co.
- George Wetzel (1761-1833) d in Ohio ae 72 yr. (Draper record: George Wetzel shot by Indians around 1777)
- Lewis Wetzel (Aug. 1763-ca. 1808) (Famous Indian fighter)
- Jacob Wetzel (16 Sept. 1765) m. 8 Dec. 1795 Ruhana Shepard. 1803 sheriff two years. 1807 moved to Indiana
- Susannah Wetzel (1676) m. Nathan Goodrich (Gattery)
- John Wetzel Jr. (1770) m. Eleanor Williams

Susannah Bonnett, the third daughter of Jacob and Mary Bonnett, never married, at least that is what was said by Maj. Lewis Bonnett Jr. "that she lived to be an old maid and died in Shenandoah Co. Va." Yet Leckey (Timmile County and It's Pioneer Families pg 675) lists Susannah, wife of Hezekiah Stewart. Three sons are listed on page 442:

- Jacob Stewart m. _____ Mason.
- Jesse Stewart (1 Oct. 1794-3 Dec. 1885) m. Rachel Smith Huffman (1 Feb. 1797 - 14 Sept. 1873) -- Both are buried at White's Church. He secured a patent for land on Pursley Creek on 23 Feb. 1837.
- David Stewart m. Elizabeth _____ went to Tyler Co. Va.

One record gives the birth date of Susannah Bonnett as being before 1741, if this is correct then she would have been 53 years old when Jesse was born. If this birth date is correct, then perhaps she was a second wife.

There are records in the Lutheran Church of Upper German settlement of an Elizabeth Bonnett, who married Martin Wetzel and they give baptism records for several children.

Lewis Bonnett Sr. would have, been the youngest son of Jacob and Mary Bonnett, born Feb. 1738 -- Paoli, Chester Co. Penn. He is mentioned in the Maryland settlement, and it states his only brother took over, when the parents died, and moved the family to Virginia.

Lewis Bonnett would have been around 33 years old in 1770 or 1771 when he married Elizabeth Waggoner. Elizabeth was born 27 March 1749 in Montgomery Co. Penn. She was not married, when mentioned in her step-fathers Conrad Lutts' will, 27 Jan. 1770. They were married ca. 1771, probably at her step-mother's, Agnes (Waggoner) Lutts, home in Romney, Virginia. Their first child was born in 1773.

Part Three

South Branch of the Potomac, Virginia

Wilhelm Waggoner Massacre

Sometime during the year of 1754 the Waggoner Family left Montgomery County, Pennsylvania and traveled south to Virginia. I find no records of this Waggoner family being in Frederick County Maryland with the Bonnetts' or Wetzels. They would have traveled on the German Monocacy Road, en route to Old Field Virginia in 1754 or 1755. The three families had to meet fairly early as their children married later on.

There are references to Wilhelm Waggoner near Old Field Virginia, but to date, I have no land records for him living near Moorefield, Hampshire County, Virginia (now Hardy county West Virginia).

Wilhelm Waggoner and wife Agnes came with a family of four children; Mary born ca 1743 Germany, about 12 years old in 1755. John Peter born ca 1746-7 Germany about 9 or 10 in 1755. Anna Elizabeth born 27 March 1749 (5 months after they arrived in Philadelphia, Pa.) would have been around 6 years old. Johannes Waggoner born 24 Nov. 1751, Germantown, (Montgomery County) Pennsylvania. This was a young family to bring into the South Branch Frontier.

We now know Barbara their youngest was born ca 1756 after they had arrived on the South Branch. I found Barbara (Waggoner) Lantz death date Feb. 1850 ae 94 yr. Wetzel Co. (W) Va of old age. She was blind and living with her son Alexander Lantz.

No land record for Wilhelm Waggoner has been found in either Hampshire or Hardy Co.'s between 1750 and 1770. Perhaps they had a quick claim deed or never filed. Yet he built a log house, fort style, for protection, and cleared land. These were times of great trouble with the Indians along the "Wappacoma" or South Branch. The Wilhelm Waggoner Fort like home is not to be confused with Fort Waggoner, later called Fort Buttermilk, which was commissioned by George

Washington around 1756 and under the supervision of Captain Thomas Waggoner of the French & Indian War. There is no relation between these two Waggoner families, that I can find.

There seemed to be a naming patterns for German families as follows:
> 1st son named after the Father's Father,
> 2nd son named after the Mother's Father,
> 3rd son named after the Father,
> 4th son named after the Father's eldest brother
> 1st daughter named after the Mother's Mother,
> 2nd daughter named after the Father's Mother,
> 3rd daughter named after the Mother,
> 4th daughter named after the Mother's oldest sister.

In some cases this seems to work, but up until 1800 you can be sure each generation has some of the same names as the generation before with new names being added for more children. We will find many named, William, John, Peter, Mary, Elizabeth, and so on. So many times generations are mixed up due to the similarity in names.

To tell of the first Tragedy of the Waggoner Family on the South Branch one must research both the Bonnett and Wetzel lines.

Draper's Mss. of the State Historical Society of Wisconsin, Madison Wisconsin (on loan, on film through Inter Library Loan), and Lewis Wetzel (Indian Fighter) by C. R. Allman. This is where one realizes there were two Indian massacres, the first generation, Wilhelm Waggoner on the South Branch ca 1758 to 1764. The second John Waggoners on Hacker's Creek 7 May 1792.

The names are the same, Mary, Elizabeth, and Peter in both generations.

I find no mention of the Wilhelm Waggoner tragedy on the South Branch other than the two references above and now <u>Virginia Germans</u> by Klaus Wust. Lyman C. Draper corresponded with Maj. Lewis Bonnett Jr. (1778-1863) in 1848 and 1849; (when he was a very old man living in Marysville, Union Co., Ohio) and a personal visit in 1845 in Ohio. Maj. Lewis Bonnett Jr. was the son of Lewis Bonnett (1737-1808) and Anna Elizabeth Waggoner (1749 after 1816). Lewis Jr. would have been a nephew of John Waggoner (1751-ca 1842) and Barbara (Waggoner) Lantz (1756-1850). We know John & Barbara were step-brother and step-sister to Anna Elizabeth (Waggoner) Bonnett, if a referance to this relationship states that they were family, same father but different mothers.

The best account of the Wilhelm Waggoner and Mary and Peters tragedy is from Draper's Mss., Vol. 11-E-124, in the correspondence between Lyman C. Draper and Maj. Lewis Bonnett Jr. in Marysville, Union Co. Ohio, 24 Jan. 1845 some ninety years later.

"My Mothers ancesters emmigrated, from what was than called Dutch Flanders about the same time and settled on the South Branch and there her Father built a small Fort and one day the old man being out in the field at work, a piece from the Fort with two of his children, a boy whose name was Peter and a girl named Mary.

The Indians came upon them killed and scalped the old man taking the boy and Mary who was then a young women captive, the Indians brightly judging that they would be followed by the Whites divided their party, each party had a prisoner and when the Whites pursued they happened to take the track of the party which had Mary and two or three horses.

The Whites came upon early in the morning and fired upon the Indians. Whilst around the fire. Killing one and wounded another. But unluckily one of the balls proved fatal to poor Mary.

She was shot through the body and died the next day. A young man that was to been married to her in a few days was along and warily lamented poor Mary's fate."

"Peter he was carried to their towns, remained with them some time and than finding his way down the lakes to Montreal with some Frenchmen, than making his way to Philadelphia and there binding himself to the shoe and boot trade and died there. I expect that some of his off-springs are there at this time."

We find the Waggoners being aided by Lewis Bonnett, after this Indian attack, on one of the search parties, on the South Branch (Hardy Co. Va.). As Maj. Lewis Bonnett Jr. gives no dates for this attack one must work slowly to piece together the places and dates as near as possible.

"Cpt. Lewis Bonnett Sr. was a Scout and once a girl was captured and Bonnett and others pursued -- among them a man affianced, who swore he would kill all the Indians, he fired and accidentally killed his intended." A statement found in another letter to Draper.

We know that Wilhelm Waggoner and Anna Elizabeth (Wagnerin) with two children, Mary & John Peter, were on the ship "Patience and Margaret" arriving at the Port of Philadelphia Pa. 25 Oct. 1748. Others arriving on the same ship were Johannes Lantz (30 yr.) and Baltzar Fliesher (20 yrs.). All these people were located in Germantown, Pa., Church & White Marsh near by, some 14 miles to the northwest of the city of Philadelphia.

The Bonnetts and Wetzels came some 15 years earlier and were in Paoli, Chester Co. Pa. for a few years before moving to Frederick Co. Maryland. If the Waggoner's and Bonnetts, meet before the South Branch, I have not found any record of this meeting.

❖❖

The letters from Maj. Lewis Bonnett Jr. to Draper were the best records found, that gave any insight into Wilhelm Waggoner's life on the South Branch.

It must have been very hard for people to survive, once they were away from settlements. So many people were warned out of the larger town near the ports because of overcrowding -- perhaps that is why the Waggoners, Lantzs, Bonnetts and Wetzels went south. Land was offered in many different deals, all demanding hard work.

Around the year 1763-4 on the South Branch of the Potomac, on a farm near Old Field, we find Agnes Waggoner a widow. All in one day she lost her husband Wilhelm, (ca 57 yrs.), killed in an Indian raid, her step-daughter Mary (ca 19 yrs.) was captured and accidentally killed, when a party tried to rescue her from her captives, and she lost a step-son John Peter (ca 16 yrs.) who was captured by the same Indians who had killed her husband, and she not knowing if he was dead or alive.

Agnes was left with her step-daughter Anna Elizabeth (ae 14 yrs.) and her son Johannes (ae 12 years) and daughter Barbara (age 7 years) and a piece of land and no future in sight.

I recently read The Virginia Germans by Klaus Wust, and on page 68 he states "1763 & 1764 were the worst Indian attacks." The Shenandoah settlement attacked in a single day June 1, 1764 -- about 32 inhabitants were killed or carried away. The Mennonite preacher John Rhodes, his wife and six of their children were cruelly slaughtered on the South Fork of the Shenandoah."

Peace made with the Ohio Indians in Nov. 1764 finally brought quite to the valley, but the southwestern frontier continued to be restless for many years.

Johannes Peter Waggoner

I believe the Waggoners were attacked sometime during 1763 or 1764. Based on a statement by Klaus Wust, (on page 67-68), "The fate of those who were carried away remained a concern over many years. Every time a fortunate one made an escape or was ransomed, hopes arose that other loved ones would emerge from the woods. Such as, young Peter Wagner who returned after three years and could not banish the visions of his father's face when he was scalped before his eyes."

Perhaps this is the reason John Peter (step-son) was mentioned in Conrad Lutts will in 1770. He had returned after 3 years, and being unable to live there, had returned to Philadelphia, Pa. This is as good a place to discuss John Peter Waggoner as any. Again I refer to Lewis Bonnett Jr. letter to Draper. "The boy Peter was carried to the lakes and later returned to Philadelphia and became a shoemaker."

I found Peter Waggoner in the 1779 tax records in Philadelphia, Pa. in Mulberry Ward, West part. In 1780 - #286 - (Pennsylvania Archives) Peter Waggoner, Shoemaker- valuation 3,800 - Tax 10.9.0 (Five shilling and six pence in every hundred Pounds) under this tax record we find also the record: For Septimus Coats estimated valuation $16,000. - tax 44.0.0

        Christian Lower, labourer valuation ____tax ____

        Hannah Roberts (widow) valuation   tax ____

The tax records for 1781 had the same names as if it was one house hold.

In the 1790 census of Philadelphia, Pa., I find Peter Waggoner and wife with 5 sons and 4 daughters living at 116 North Third Street between Vine and Race St., occupation cordwaimer or shoemaker.

This being a German family I can imagine some of the children's names; William, Peter, John, Mary, Elizabeth, and Ann and names on the mother's side. The only marriage I find for a Peter Waggoner in Philadelphia or Germantown, Pa. was in 1766 Apr. 17 to a Rosena Roth, but I have no proof of this being our John Peter, and the date is really very early. As he would be an apprentice shoemaker for several years before he would be financially able to afford a family.

The widow Hannah Roberts living in the home in 1780 & 1781 could be a mother-in-law. I found no Peter Waggoner in the 1800 Tax record. In 1802 the area near 116 North Third St. shows a Baltas Waggoner - shoemaker, Bear slickers Court. I've placed John Peter Waggoner here because its the last of the family unit and really all the real proof of him. The reference to his return in three years, seems reasonable that his step-mother Agnes & his step-father Conrad Lutts did see John Peter in 1767-8 and knew of his whereabouts in 1770 as he is mentioned in the Lutts will. Perhaps his sister Anna Elizabeth (Waggoner) Bonnett also knew of his life, for Maj. Lewis Bonnett to have written to Draper about him.

I'm sorry, that on both trips to the Historical Society at 15th. and Locust St. Philadelphia, Pa., I failed to find any record of John Peter's family. When trying to locate 116 North Third St. between Vine & Race Streets' (address of Shoe Shop) they told me it was possible the large Delaware Bridge had changed the area and 116 North Third was no longer there.

Conrad Lutts

The Nuncupatine Will and last testament of Conrad Lutts, of the Parish of County of Hampshire, Va. Deceased, committed to Writing within six days of his death by us. Andrew Young, John Larance, and Philip Mason, who were witnesses to this his last Will and Testamate, made in his own house in his last sickness. 13th day of March 1770-(d-8-9 Mar. 1770)

The Testamentary words were in substance as follows.

"Imprimis,, I give and bequeath to my wife Agnes Lutts during her natural life all that of my claim of land in his Lordships Manor which is now improved, enclosed or in Fence, and the same part with the improvements to descend to my step-son John Waggoner, after her decease on condition, that he the said John Waggoner shall pay to my daughter Barbara Lutts the full sum of eight Pounds in rent money of Virginia at this receiving possession of the said land and Tenements.

Item: I give and bequeath to my said wife, my best feather beds and bed clothes as her own independent property.

Item: I give and bequeath to my said step-son John Waggoner my two year old bay mare colt on condition that he shall well and truly endeavor to promote his mothers interest and behave as becomes a dutiful and obedient son to her, other wise she shall be at Liberty to convert the same to her own property.

Item: My will is that all the rest of my Personal Estate and movables be appraised and divided equally between stepsons John Peter Waggoner and John Waggoner and my son-in-law John Green and my step-daughter Elizabeth Waggoner and Barbara Waggoner and my daughter Barbara Lutts. My wife having her full third of all my personal Estate.

Item: My will is that my said wife and my said legaties shall equally pay each their part of all my just debts.

Item: All the upper part of my said claim of Land I give and bequeath to my afore said son-in-law John Green. The Division of which, between my wifes part (as before mentioned) and the said John Green part is to be according to the Line I formerly mentioned to him, that is to say, along the upper fence toward the timber Ridge, the Course of the road to Col. Hites Mill, being the Line.

These Testamentary words of the said Conrad Lutts, released, we the Subscribers (Witnesses called to hear testimony of the same) do certify were the substance of the said Deceased Numcupative (Verbal) Will and we are ready to prove the same upon Oath wherever we shall be required there to.

In witness where of we have here unto set our Hands and Seals.
The 27th day of January 1770
Andrew Young (seal)
Johannes Lorentz (seal) Lountz
(Lantz)
Philip Masson (seal)

Sealed and Signed
in the Presence of us;
Tho's Barth Bowen
Charles Myers

❖❖

The 13th day of March 1770 this verbal will of Conrad Lutts, deceased was prefected. Allowed by Agnes Lutts and provided by the Oath of Andrew Young and John Laurence.

Compare the two spellings of the witness John Lorentz (Johannes Lountz) this is one and the same person who took an oath on Conrad Lutts verbal will.

The will was excepted and allowed by Agnes (Waggoner) Lutts the 13 day of March 1770. One can assume she lived in her home in Romney with her children -- and as John Waggoner was b 1751, he would have been 19 years old and a great help to his mother.

(Anna) Elizabeth Waggoner b. 27 March 1749, bpt. in St. Michael's Evangelical Lutheran Church in Germantown, Pa. the 24 April 1749 would have been 21 years old and married with in a year or so (1772) to Lewis Bonnett.

We know Lewis Bonnett had only one brother; Samuel Bonnett was in Hampshire Co., Va. in 1777 Aug. 11 (Early Records of Hampshire Co. (W) Va., Sage & Jones, pg 4).

"1777 Aug. 11 Bonnett, Samuel (w Elizabeth) of Hampshire Co. (lease and release) 205 acres on Cedar Swamp to David Myles of Hampshire Co. records 12 Aug. 1777.Wit.: Isaac Parsons & Isaac Means." Samuel Bonnett was not in the (1782) c of Hampshire Co. (W) Va.

"Bonnet, Sam, taken by (Abel Randall) 10 in family".

Virginia's Colonial Soldiers by Lloyd DeWitt Bockstruck. (pg 138 & 145) Rangers.

"1774 Capt. John Harness, John Welton, Lt. John Waggoner enlisted in the army in Hampshire Co., Va. others Stephen Ratcliff, Wm. Ratcliff, John Hyar, Samuel Cartwright, John Simpson, Leonard Bush, Jacob Crites, Jacob Stangley, and others."

This John Waggoner was not our John.

Part Four

Moving West, Dunkard Bottom

Bonnett, Wetzel and Six Families

1769 The Wetzels, Bonnetts and Sixs left the South Branch and came the mouth of Dunkard Creek of Monongahela, (now Monongalia Co.) and settled there.

"In 1772 to Wheeling, in the spring, Lewis Bonnett & John Wetzel staked their claim, made improvements, planted corn, built cabins and fenced the corn, obtained settlement rights for 400 acres, and preemption of 1000 acres."

Maj. Lewis Bonnett Jr. of Marysville, Ohio, described Capt. John Wetzel was of ordinary size, appearance stout and musccular, with black piercing eyes, black hair of German descent."

1774 One must take note of the "Virginia Colonial Soldiers" by Bachstruck (pg 145) under the heading of Dunmores War 1774 - names of soldiers on the payrolls at Pittsburgh under Capt. John Wilson's roll. Sgt. John Witsall (Wetzel), Lewis Bonnett, Martin Westzell (Wetzel), Daniel Ryneheart and others.

Capt. John Wetzel was killed by Indians in 1786 and Mary (Bonnett) Wetzel lived with their son Jacob, and died in 1790-91. In 1774 Capt. John Harness's roll of Rangers, at Romney and Winchester, Va. we find John Waggoner (not on Dunkard bottom with the above). I believe John Waggoner joined the settlement at Dunkard Creek later on around 1780.

Maj. Lewis Bonnett Jr. wrote to Draper in 1849 -- "My Father was a middle sized man, of fair complexion with blue eyes, proverbially honest & of Dutch parentage."

Lewis Bonnett had his family living on Dunkard Creek before Dunmore's War. After the campaign he sold his possessions on

Dunkard and moved back to Wheeling, repurchased his old possession on Wheeling, paying twice what he had sold them for.

The John Sicks (Sixs) always lived on Dunkard and between 1779 and 1780 John Waggoner and wife Margaret (Bonnett) Waggoner arrived at Dunkard Creek.

We have the Wetzel, Bonnett, & Six families meeting in Maryland, but it is conceivabe, they also knew each other in Pennsylvania. All records of the Wetzels, Bonnetts, Sixs, and Waggoners mention the South Branch of the Potomac, Moorefield (now Harly Co. (W.) Va.)

Capt. Lewis Bonnett (1739-1808) and Elizabeth (Waggoner) Bonnett (1749-? 1816) had a family of three daughters and two sons.

1. Elizabeth Bonnett, born 13 Sept. 1773 on Dunkard Creek (d. 11 Mar. 1873 age 99 y. 5 m. 29 d.) m. 26 Mar. 1795 Wheeling Creek. John Lantz Jr. (b. 9 Aug. 1773 Shanandoah Co. Va. d. 1 Sept. 1858. Both buried in Lantz cemetery, (Wayne township) located between Brave and Blacksville, Pa.

   John Lantz Jr. was the son of John Lantz Sr. (17149-1817) and his first wife Clara Fuschon. *The credit for John Lantz Sr.'s first marriage must go to Mrs. Lillian McNutt of Houston, Texas*, she found in Early Records of the Evangelical Lutheran Church of Frederick Co., Maryland (pg. 13 & 43). The following marriage records: "Johannes Lantz eldest first son of George Lantz married 23 June 1772, to Miss Clara Fuschain eldest legitimate daughter of Adam Fuschain, married in church."

   They probably lived on the Shenandoah for several years as some records say John Jr. was born there. They had two other children Andrew Lantz (ca 1775) and Catherine Lantz.

   John Jr. & Elizabeth (Bonnett) Lantz children:
   - Mary Lantz born 22 Feb. 1796, married 12 Nov. 1816 ____Chandler.
   - Margaret 'Peggy' Lantz (b. 9 March 1798, d.1890), married 9 Jan. 1818, Monongalia Co. (W) Va. William Minor (June 1797- 1884) Son of Samuel and Susan (Clegg) Minor.
   - Elizabeth Lantz born 5 June 1800, - marriage bond 20 Oct. 1823 Monongalia Co. (W) Va - Theophylas Minor son of Samuel and Susan (Clegg) Minor.
   - Lewis Lantz (30 Aug. 1802 - d 26 July 1818)
   - John Lantz (3 Apr. 1805 - d 27 Feb. 1816)

- Nancy Lantz (21 Aug. 1807,-8 May 1901) m., 10 Apr. 1828 Monongalia Co. (W) Va. William Johnson ___(11 Dec. 1803-3 Nov. 1857) son of William and Sarah (Van Baskirk) Johnson.
- William Lantz (17 Mar. 1810-24-Jan. 1881) m. - 3 Sept. 1831 - Sarah Thomas (born 1813)
- Sarah Lantz (15 July 1812)- m. 18 Mar. 1836 (Bond 13 Aug. 1836) - Eagon Tygart.
- Jacob Lantz born 22 July 1814 - m. (8 Dec. 1836), Menerva Minor, daughter of Samuel & 2nd wife Permilia (Lancaster) Minor.
- Alexander Lantz born 8 July 1817 - married Nancy Masters

2. Barbara Bonnett (b. ca. 1775 d. 21 Mar 1860), 2nd daughter of Lewis and Elizabeth (Waggoner) Bonnett, married, around 1800, John Rodeffer (ca 1773-28 July 1859).

3. Lewis Bonnett Jr. (11 March 1778 on Drunkard Creek, 10 Jan. 1863) Marysville, Union Co. Ohio, first son of Lewis and Elizabeth (Waggoner) Bonnett married Jane McClain (1780 - 20 Aug. 1839, age 59 yr.)

Around 1800 Lewis Bonnett Jr. studied under William Darby, who taught in Wheeling. Darby wrote under the pen-name of Mark Bancroft and described Lewis Bonnett as a short thick man, as brave as Julias Caesar.

Maj. Lewis Bonnett Jr. is listed as a solider of 1812 and a resident of Union Co., Ohio, he was buried in Mt. Hermon Cemetery, Dover township Union Co. Ohio.

Maj. Lewis Bonnett (1778-1863) and wife Jane McClain(1780-1839) were the parents of:
- Lewis Bonnett(1807-1881)
- John Bonnett(1808-1883)
- Lucenda Bonnett(1810-1888)
- Sarah Bonnett(1811-1891)
- Isabelle Bonnett(1814-1884)
- William Bonnett(1816-1899)
- Samuel Bonnett(1818-1896)
- Elizabeth Bonnett(1819-1853)
- Jane Bonnett(1822-1907)

4. Mary Bonnett (b. ca 1781, third daughter of Lewis Sr. and Elizabeth (Waggoner) Bonnett, married Phillip Rodefer, probably in Wheeling.

5. John Bonnett (2 Aug. 1785 2 Sept. 1816) was the second s/o Lewis Sr. and Elizabeth (Waggoner) Bonnett. He married about 1808 Eva Wolf (1789-1881).

27th Day of November A.D. 1807
Will of Lewis Bonnett (in part)

In the name of God, Amen! I Lewis Bonnett, of the county of Ohio, and State of Virginia, a farmer being very sick and weak in body but of perfect mind and memory. Thanks be given unto God, calling unto the mortality of my body, and knowing that it is appointed for all man once to die, do make and ordain this my last will and testament, and etc.

First: I give and bequeath to my beloved wife Elizabeth one of my horses creatures, whichever one she shall choose and her side saddle and bridle. One milk cow of her own choosing, such choice she may renew yearly out of the stocks which I intend to give to my son John. Also her bed and bedding, table and one chest together with the one-third of all my personal estate, as also her living in the house wherein we now live, and a full third of the part of the land given to my son John, that is the benefits therefrom arising during her natural lifetime or so long as she shall remain my widow and no longer.

Second: I give and devise unto my son Lewis Bonnett all the upper part of the land that was laid off to him as well appear by plot hearing date the 26th of November 1807, to have and to hold to him, after my decease his heirs and assigns forever, free and clear of all manner of encumbrance whatsoever.

Third: I give and devise unto my son John Bonnett all the rest as remainder of my plantation for him to have and to hold to him the said John Bonnett and his heirs and assigns forever, subject still to the third bequeathed to his mother as is herein before mentioned and paying thereunto the sum of $415.00 to be paid in the manner following, that is to say to my daughter, Mary, who is married to Philip Rodeffer, $100.00, to be paid as hereinafter described which with $100.00 already reserved, shall be in full her portion.

So my daughter, Barbara, who is married to John Rodeffer, $100.00, one year after my decease.

So to Elizabeth Lantz $115.00, which to-gether with $85.00 already paid her, shall be her full portion.

To my grandson, Lewis Hooks, I give and bequeath one horse creature with $50.00, to be given him by my son John Bonnett as soon as the said Lewis Hooks shall arrive at the age of 21 years.

Further I will direct that one year after my decease my son John Bonnett shall Pay as follows to Barbara as is directed.

Next I direct he shall pay $15.00 to my daughter Elizabeth Lantz which will make her equal with the rest.

Then I direct that my son John Bonnett shall two years after my decease to pay $100.00 every year so as to pay up the $415.00, and it shall be equally divided among my daughters, Barbara, Elizabeth and Mary, so as their shares shall be equal.

Further, I give and bequeath to my son John Bonnett all the movable property which is not already heretofore mentioned. I further constitutes and appoint my two sons, Lewis Bonnett and John Bonnett my Executors of this, my last will and testament.

Witness my hand and seal this 27th day of November, A.D. 1807
Lewis Bonnett (Seal)

Recorded in Will Book 1 page 13. Ohio County (W) Va. in the County Clark's Office in the Courthouse at Wheeling, W. Va.

Nine years later we find the will of the youngest son John Bonnett age 31 years in Will Book 2 page 8 at the Court House in Wheeling, Ohio Co., (W) Va.-probated 21 June 1816. Naming wife Eva Bonnett - children Benjamin Bonnett, Elizabeth Bonnett, Simon Bonnett and Lewis Bonnett.

The 1810 census shows both Lewis and John Bonnett in Ohio Co. (W) Va., and Philip Rodeffer in Ohio Co. Therefore, Lewis Bonnett must have moved to Ohio just after his father's death in 1807.

John and Barbara (Waggoner) Lantz

This story would not be complete with out the Lantz Family as they are linked with the Waggoners and Bonnetts from date of immigration in Pennsylvania.

In 1748 Philadelphia, Penn., Wilhelm Waggoner and Family were on the same ship with Johannes Lantz (born 1718 Germany) and both are shown on the baptism record of Johannes Waggoner (26th Apr. 1752) in Germantown, Penn. at St. Michael's Evangelical Lutheran Church. The marriage record of Johannes Lantz states he was single & lived with Wilhelm Waggoner in 1752 when he married Maria Margaretha Bender. Perhaps he was a brother of Hans George Lantz (father of John Lantz (1749-1817)).

Many, many Lantz Families immigrated between 1745 - 1750 and settled in Pennsylvania, Maryland and Virginia.

Who was the Johannes Launtz who signed the verbal will of Conrad Lutts in 1770 in Romney, Va. (Hardy Co. Va.)? Could he have been the one who was in Germantown, (Montgomery Co. Pa.) in 1748 & 1752? Was he the Godparent of our Johannes Waggoner? It is not likely it was John Lantz (1749-1817) as he would have only been 21 years old and we do not find him in the Romney area, but in Maryland & the Shenandoah Valley area.

For the Will of (Hans) George Lantz dated 12-7-1792 Probated 3-12-1793 credit Mrs. Lillian McNutt. In part: (copied as written- spelling as written)

I give and bequeath my track of land where on I live now lying in the county of Shanandoah unto my sons George and Jacob Lantz. That is to say I give and bequeath unto my son George and his heirs 100 acres which was sur. by Mr. Jacob Rinker and likewise a piece of meddow on Upper part of the Meddows for the during his natural life.

The rest of the land I give and bequeath unto my Youngest son Jacob and his heirs.

But my son Jacob, he is to give unto my other two sons, John and Andrew and like wise unto the five children of my daughter Margaretha, deceased, the sum of one hundred and fifty pound coesent money of Virginia.

That is to say fifty pounds to my son John, and fifty pounds to my son Andrew and fifty pounds unto the five children of my daughter Margaretha, deceased.

He, my son Jacob is to pay the beforementioned sum of money in the space of nine years. That is to say each year, sixteen pounds, thirteen shillings and four pence after my deceasimy.

The more moveable estate are to be divided equally unto my four sons, John, Andrew, Georg and Jacob Lantz and last unto the five children of my daughter Margaretha, deceased.

Last will and testament, I George Lantz have hereunto set my hand and Seal. this twenty seventh day of December in the year of our Lord, one Thousand Seven Hundredth and Ninety two.

(27 Dec. 1792) George (X)Lountz
His Mark

Jacob Lantz youngest son Executor.

This will establishes Hans George Lantz and Maria Lantz in Shenandoah Co. Va.

"TheVirginia Northern Nick Land Grants", - Vol. II 1742-1775 pg. 198 compiled by Gertrude E. Gray, Book o 1767-1770 - #O-179: George Lantz of Frederick Co. 157 acres on N. R. of Shannondoah in said Co. Robert Rutherford. Adj. Joseph Pugh - Jacob Cohener, George Mowery 19 Aug. 1768.

Frederick Co. was created in 1738 from Augusta Co. Shenandoah Co. was created in 1772 from Frederick Co.

(Hans) George and Maria Lantz had four sons and one daughter:
- <u>George</u> Lantz m. a daughter of Col. Woodford and moved to Barbour Co. (W) Va. and had six children: William Lantz, Henry Lantz, Philip Lantz, George Lantz, Joseph Lantz, and Marian Lantz.
- Johannes (John) Lantz (5 June 1749-27 mar. 1817) (Rev War - Vol. 2 - pg. 126) m. (1st.) Clara Fuschain m (2nd) Barbara Waggoner, lived Greene Co. Pa.
- Andrew Lantz born 15 Nov. 1755 - Monocacy River Md. died 25 Sept. 1824 - Whiteley Creek, Pa. married Barbara Lemley.
- Margaretha Lantz - died before 1793, in will of her father, left her share to her five children.
- Jacob Lantz (b. 4 Jan. 1759 - d. 13 Jan. 1837) m. 5 Aug. 1783 - Shenandoah Co. Va. Maria Miller (1758-1822) Shenandoah Co. Va. Two children; George (1788- 1869), and Mary m. John Bowman Shenandoah Co. Va.

This family immigrated at the Port of Philadelphia, Penn. around 1747. They were in Maryland for a while before the county of Frederick Md. was created in 1748 from Prince George County Maryland.

I believe the family was in the Shenandoah Valley by 1772 June 23rd when John Lantz, eldest son of George Lantz married Clara Fuschain eldest legitimate daughter of Adam Fuschain. (credit Mrs. Lillian McNutt) gives proof of both parent and the fact they were in a church in Maryland.

<u>The Tinmite Country and Its Pioneer Families</u> by Howard L. Leckey. has lots of information on the Lantz Family.

John and Clara (Fuschain) Lantz lived in the Shanandoah Valley for a while and there were three children by the first marriage.
- John Lantz Jr. (b. 9 Aug. 1773, d. 1 Sept. 1853,) m. around 1795, Elizabeth Bonnett (1773-1873) daughter of Lewis & Elizabeth (Waggoner) Bonnett. (see this family with the Bonnett history)
- Andrew Lantz, born around 1775 was left land in Ohio in 1817 in his fathers will. (100 acres of land on Duck Creek, Ohio).
- Catharine Lantz born around 1777 was left $20.00 in her fathers will in 1817.

I believe John Lantz (1749-1817) married Barbara Waggoner at the home of her mother, Agnes (Waggoner) Lutts, in Romney, Va. around 1780. Due to the 1850 mortality Schedule of West Virginia (pg. 18), we now have a date for Barbara (Waggoner) Lantz. "Lantz, Barbara - Wetzel Co. W. Va. 94 years. F. died Feb. 1850 - born Va. cause old age."

Barbara (Waggoner) Lantz was born 1756 on the South Branch, daughter of Wilhelm and Agnes Waggoner. She would have been around twenty four years old when she married John Lantz.

Leckey pg. 636 -"15 Jan. 1785 John Launce (Lantz) was granted a warrant for 250 acres of land, situated on Big Whiteley Creek." (Greene Co. Pa.)

By 1796 he began his land grants on Dunkard Creek, 399 acres on 10 March 1796.

When John Lantz died in 1817 he owned over 1000 adjoining acres laying in Monongalia Co. (W) Va. and Greene Co. Pa. They lived in Greene Co. Pa. so his will was probated there on 5 Apr. 1817. Will Book 1 - pg. 175.

John and Barbara (Waggoner) Lantz Family

1. Anna Maria (Mary) Lantz, daughter of John and Barbara (Waggoner) Lantz, (10 June 1782, Drunkard Creek (W) Va. 4 Sept. 1833) Guernsey Co. Ohio. She was baptized 11 Sept. 1783 by Pastor Weber. Godparents: Ludwig Banet and Elisabetha, (Lewis Bonnett and wife Elizabeth (Waggoner) Bonnett) in the German Reformed Congregations in Westmoreland Co. Pa. (The German Church Records of Westmoreland Co. Pa. - 1772-1791 pg. 88 - Vol. 1 by Paul Miller Ruff)

   Around 1797 Mary Lantz m. Jonathan Stiles (Styles), (18 July 1774, 15 Nov. 1860) son of Stephen and Deborra Styles. Their family of 14 children all born in Greene Co., Pa.:

   - John Styles, b 23 May 1800 - m Betsie Frankbouer.
   - Stephen Styles, (24 Mar. 1802 7 July 1888) m 1st Eliza Linn and 2nd Francena Lanneny.
   - William Styles, b 14 Feb. 1804 - m Mary McCalley (McCullough)
   - Andrew Styles, (18 Mar. 1806 - 25 Sept. 1885) m. 1st Mary Kirkpatrick m. 2nd Amy Henderson.
   - Thomas Styles, (6 Mar 1808 19 Apr. 1890) m. Catharine McCullough
   - Simon Styles, b. 16 June 1810 - m. 1st Phebe Kirkpatrick, 2nd Betsy Donely
   - Mary Styles, b. 88 June 1812 - m. Jesse Gunn.
   - Jacob Styles, (31 July 1814-12 July 1892) m. Mary M. Gunn.
   - George Styles, (6 Aug. 1816-6 Mar. 1904) Martin Co. Indiana m. Sarah Corzinne.

- Margaret Styles, (14 Dec. 1818-1910) Grant Co. Indiana m. Joseph Culbertson.
- Jonathan Styles, (9 Nov. 1820-3 Mar. 1871) Martin Co. Indiana m. Rebecca J Walker.
- Deborra Styles, (6 Oct. 1822-1 Sept. 1890) m. Stout Patterson.
- Lewis Styles, (9 Nov. 1824-15 May 1892) Martin Co. Indiana m. Rosanna Barnes.
- Eliza Styles, (3 Apr. 1827-1909) m. Jacob Barnes.

In 1827 Sept. 14, Jonathan and Mary (Lantz) Styles moved to Guernsey Co. Ohio, most of their family lived there. Jonathan Styles died 15 Nov. 1860, Guernsey Co. Ohio. Mary Styles died 4 Sept. 1833 age 51 years.

2. William Lantz, son of John & Barbara (Waggoner) Lantz, born 29 Oct. 1784, baptized 12 Apr. 1855, by Pastor Johann Wilhelm Weber, Wilhelm Lantz Godparents were Henrick Six and Barbara (Selsor) Six - Ruff. Vol. I (pg. 102) William Lantz was in Guernsey Co. Ohio by 1805, some records say he m. Sarah, he died in 1825 in Ohio.

3. John George Lantz, son of John & Barbara (Waggoner) Lantz born 15 Jan. 1787 baptized 7 Dec. 1787 by Anton Urich Luetge (Rupp - Vol. I pg. 55) never married. 1810 census Monongalia Co., (W) Va. Received $10.00 from his father's will in 1817. John George Lantz died 13 May 1818 age 64 yr. bur Lantz cemetery, Bravo, Pa. (will 17 May 1818 wills estate to slaves he had freed.).

4. Lewis Lantz, son of John & Barbara (Waggoner) Lantz born ca 1789 Green Co. Pa. m. (1st) Barbara _____ m. (2nd) 29 Oct. 1854, Eleanor McCullough (b. 1810 -   ) daughter of William and Rebecca McCullough. Lewis was 65 and Eleanor was 44 when they were married in Tyler Co. (W) Va.

5. Jacob Lantz, son of John & Barbara (Waggoner) Lantz (1 Oct. 1791 14 Apr. 1858) Greene Co. Pa. (1812 War). Married Delilah Coen (1797- 15 Mar. 1866) Wayne, Greene Co. Pa. buried Lantz Cemetery, Bravo, Green Co. Pa.
    - John Lantz, son of Jacob and Delilah (Coen) Lantz, (8 May 1829- 8 Dec. 1911) - m. 19 Sept. 1850, Jollytown, Gilmer township Greene Co., Pa. Sarah Bradford daughter of Jacob and Charlotte Bradford (died 21 Nov. 1888). They had eleven children:
    - Alexander Lantz, son of Jocob and Delilah (Coen) Lantz was born around 1815. In the 1850 census of Wayne township,

Greene Co., Pa, Alexander was listed as age 35, and wife Nancy as age 30 years.

- Simon Lantz, son of Jocob and Delilah (Coen) Lantz married 18 Nov. 1842 to Lucy Thomas.
- William Lantz, son of Jocob and Delilah (Coen) Lantz, (27 Apr. 1835, 18 May 1905) in Greene Co. Pa.; m. 22 May 1856 to Minerva Kent (24 Nov. 1837-20 Sept. 1904). Minerva was the daughter of William and Elizabeth (Odenbaugh) Kent.
- Thomas L. Lantz, son of Jocob and Delilah (Coen) Lantz (1822-1842).
- Elias Lantz, son of Jocob and Delilah (Coen) Lantz, was listed as being 13 years old in the 1850 census.

6. Alexander Lantz, son of John and Barbara (Waggoner) Lantz, (b. 1793, d. 7 Jan. 1873), Jacksonburg, Wetzel Co. W. Va., married 30 Oct. 1817, Monongalia Co. W. Va., Margaret Minor, daughter of Samuel Minor (13 Dec. 1802 - 10 Nov. 1886). Their children:

- Mary Lantz (1818-1863) m. James Cockran.
- Jacob Lantz m. Nemimce Baker.
- John Lantz m. Matilda Clark.
- Samuel Lantz (1824-1920) m. Margaret McCormick.
- Lot Lantz (1842-1881)
- Amassa (Massy) Lantz m. William Ferrell.
- Lewis Lantz
- Susanna Lantz m. Edman Hayes.
- Delilah Lantz m. John Martin.
- Margaret Lantz m. David Lively.

In 1850 Barbara (Waggoner) Lantz was living with her son Alexander Lantz in Wetzel Co. (W) Va.

7. Samuel Lantz, son of John and Barbara (Waggoner) Lantz, (b. ca. 1797, Greene Co. Pa. 1 May 1809, age 12 yr.), buried in Lantz Cemetery, Wayne Township, Greene Co. Pa. (Greene Co. Pa. Cemetery Records - vol. 7-- 1977 Gilmore and Wayne twp, compiled by Dorothy T. Hennen - Waynesburg Pa.)

(*Credit Mrs. Lillian McNutt - Houston TX*)

8. Elizabeth Lantz, daughter of John and Barbara (Waggoner) Lantz, (9 June 1800 23 Nov. 1884). She was born and died within a three mile area of the border of W. Va. and Pa. She married 14 Aug. 1818 to George Fielding Cumberledge, son of George and Rachel (Barker) Cumberledge, born in Maryland on 15 Nov. 1795, and died 17 Nov.

1881, age 86 y 2d. Children of George F. and Elizabeth (Lantz) Cumberledge:

- Barbara Cumberledge born 16 Mar 1819 m. (1st) Francis Coen - d 1843, one son, John Coen b 8 Mar 1844; - m. (2nd) Isaac Stiles.
- John Cumberledge (25 Aug. 1820 15 Feb. 1879) - m. Margaret Weley.
- Rachel Priscilla Cumberledge born 12 Dec. 1821
- Simon Cumberledge (twin) (9 June 1836 22 Dec. 1890) - m. Susan Bradford.
- William Cumberledge (twin) (9 June 1836 31 Oct. 1866) - m. 6 Oct. 1862 Jemina Wise. William served in the Civil War.
- Andrew J. Cumberledge born 24 Aug. 1838 - d 15 Dec. 1915 - m. 14 Aug. 1856 to Martha J. Grim, (30 Sept. 1841-12 Aug. 1911), bur. Pine Bank Cemetery, Gilmore township, Greene Co., Pa.
- Mark Cumberledge (1 May 1840-23 Sept. 1865).
- Nancy Cumberledge born 1858 - m. W. F. Staggers.
- Elizabeth Cumberledge born 28 Mar. 1823
- Alexander Cumberledge born 29 Mar. 1825.
- Mary Cumberledge born 16 Apr. 1827.
- Sara Cumberledge born 17 Nov. 1828
- Margaret Cumberledge born 8 June 1830.
- George Cumberledge born 26 Nov. 1831
- Jacob Cumberledge (30 Aug. 1833 - 1915) m. Milenisa Ann Hoult
- Dililah Cumberledge m. Samuel F. Collins.

Will Book I - pg. 175-176 Greene Co. Pa.
Will of John Lantz - 5 Jan. 1817 - probated 27 Mar 1817 - in part:

2nd <u>Secondly</u> I give and bequeath to my beloved wife Barbara full liberty of the dividing house and her bed & bedding and such household furniture that is sufficient to the full for her and house and furniture. And my son Alexander is to provide her a full and sufficient living of the place I now live on with sufficient appearl during her life and a good cow.

3rd To beloved son John $50.00 to be paid by my son Jacob out of his legacy.

4th To beloved son Andrew - 100 acres of land laying on the waters of Duck Creek, state of Ohio.

5th To my beloved daughter Catherine $20.00 out of my estate.

6th To my beloved daughter Mary Stiles, $50.00 two years after my decease, to be paid by my son Alexander.

7th To my beloved son William, $10.00 three years after my decease, to be paid by my son Alexander.

8th To my beloved son George - the sum of $10.00 to be paid three years after my decease, to be paid by my son Alexander.

9th To my beloved son Lewis the sum of $1.00, to be paid by my son Alexander.

10th To my beloved son Jacob, all the land that is of the North side of Haver's Run, but he is to pay my son John the $50.00 that is afore mentioned of my son John legacy.

11th I give to my beloved son Alexander all the land I possess in the following boundries: from Haver's Run up this creek to where the state line crosses the Creek, to witt, a straight line to his back line, with all the appurtenances thereto belonging, The Widows legacy excepted.

12th To my beloved daughter Elizabeth the whole of the land that I possess above my son Alexander's legacy that lies either in the state of Pennsylvania or in the state of Virginia from Gilliams fork, and a black mare that I now possess and one cow and a bed and bedding.

Exe. sons Alexander and Jacob Lantz

His
5 Apr. 1817 John (L) Lantz
Mark

Signed, Sealed and delivered in the presents of:
Stephen Archer

His
Alexander (X) Clegg
Mark

His
John (O) Lemmons
Mark

There are many descendants in Virginia, West Virginia, and Pennsylvania from this Lantz family. They have spread across the United States, and some of them have corresponded with me, and I thank them.

Part Five

Hacker's Creek Settlement

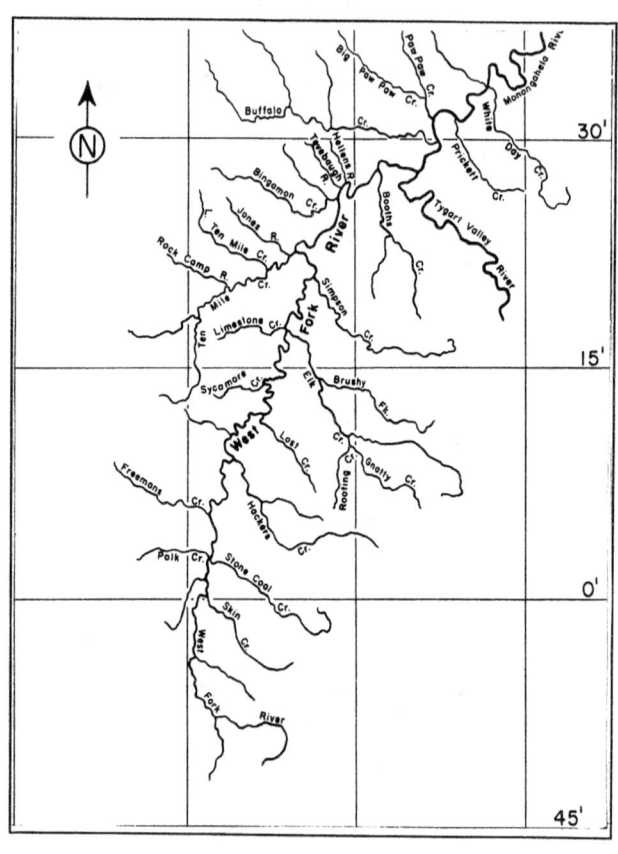

West Fork of the Monongahela River
Monongalia Co. (W) Va. 1776

Samuel Bonnett

I could have just named the Parents of Margaret (Bonnett) Waggoner and her brothers and sisters, but they are a part of this story. I can not tell you what these people thought, or anything about their everyday lives, but I can tell you of their families: where they lived and some of the happenings that made up their lives. You must put yourself in their lives and times to see the picture for yourself of these brave people who left so much for all the people who followed. How their decisions in the 1800 area gave us a foundation for what followed. These people were Parents, Mom and Dad, Grandfather and Grandmother, Aunts, Uncles, cousins, relatives and family.

I have waited until now to record the Hacker's Creek people, in what was then Harrison Co. (W) Va. Harrison County was created in 1784 from the county of Monongalia that had been created in 1776 from the West Augusta district.

As the Bonnett and Waggoner Families were both on the South Branch, and were related through the marriage of Margaret Bonnett and John Waggoner, it seemed fitting to bring these families together now. We have the statement of Maj. Lewis Bonnett Jr. that his father Lewis Bonnett, b 1737, had one only brother who was older and took over the family when the parents died.

Remember the Bonnet's 1744 land survey of "Battle ham", and that they sold the land to John Hoofman in 1753; So nine or ten years later the record says the Bonnetts went to Virginia. There are so many records that prove the relationship between Lewis Bonnett Sr. (1737-1808) and Samuel Bonnett (ca 1733 or 1734 - 1789). Besides Lyman C. Draper's Manuscripts and C. R. Allman's, Lewis Wetzel (Indian Fighter), there are land records of Samuel Bonnett in Frederick Co. Va. and Hampshire Co. and both mention the Cedar Creek. There have been so many researchers on the Bonnett line, I have only copied the records I have references for, because I could not get permission from several people I had corresponded with, either they have moved and their forwarding address have expired, my letters were returned.

Some years ago, when I entered some Waggoner research into the Hacker's Creek Journal, I realized I needed more time and research for these families. After the immigration of the Jacque (Jacob) Bonnett and the mention of John Simon Bonnett age 9 mo. in 1733 there has been no record of him in Maryland or Virginia.

In 1766 Nov. 17, Virginia Northern Neck Land Grants (Vol. I N 318 pg. 185) show a land record for Samuel Bonnett of Hampshire Co. Va., 205 acres on Cedar Swamp, Hampshire Co. Va. This is the same 205 acres. Samuel Bonnett must have been around nineteen years old when he took charge of the family in Maryland and moved the family to Virginia. This would have given his birth year about 1734 and about 32 years old in 1766 on his first land deal in Hampshire Co. Va.

In 1777 when the land in Hampshire Co. Va. was sold, Samuel would have been around 43 years old and in 1784 there were 10 in the families on one tax record. I believe we would have to say they were in Monongalia Co. first, but only because Harrison Co. (W) Va. was not created until 1784, which now the land they lived on would be Lewis Co. (W) Va. after 1816. One must respect the year each county was created, and use the county name that the date indicates. It is very difficult to research County histories when the dates and names of places do not match.

I can not say the exact date Samuel Bonnett came to Hacker's Creek, I'm sure it was before 1781, perhaps a tomahawk claim; but several land records mention the land as adjoining lands claimed by Samuel Bonnett around 1772 and 3. His land adjoined David Sleeth, Jesse Hughes and so on, on Hacker's Creek.

Samuel Bonnett & Mary Elizabeth Bonnett

Samuel Bonnett, (ca 1734 - d. Dec. 1789) was killed by at falling tree in Harrison Co. (W) Va. (Inventory: 17 Dec. 1789), married probably in Maryland or Virginia to Mary Elizabeth and at least eight of their children were born on Cedar Creek or the South Branch of the Potomac; before they came to Hacker's Creek area.

Children of Samuel Bonnett & Mary Elizabeth Bonnett:

John Bonnett born ca 1757 on Cedar Creek, first s/o Samuel & Mary Elizabeth Bonnett, must have been married on the South Branch or the first years they were on Hacker's Creek. John m. Martha Hacker (aunt Martha Bonnett a widow of John Bonnett) Aunt Math Bonnett maiden name Hacker (BS/Nw Va. 307/507). John Bonnett, and his brother-in-law John Waggoner, were with Col. Lowther's party in pursuit of Indians, on the Little Kanawha in 1787, when John Bonnett was shot. He was carried by his comrades on a rude stretcher, but died within four days. His body was placed in a cleft of rock and the entrance securely chinked. (Border Settlers of Northwestern Virginia page 446 -- copied as written. "This trip under Col. Lowther was mentioned by John Waggoner in the court deposition, 7 Aug. 1832 to establish his service record for a pension, he mention the death of his comrade John Bonnett."

The widow Martha Hacker Bonnett resided three or four miles south of Jane Lew. (Lewis Co., (W) Va.).

Margaret 'Peggy' Bonnett, born around 1759 was the first d/o Samuel & Mary Elizabeth Bonnett. She was born on the South Branch (now Hardy Co.) and married there about 1778 to John Waggoner. (This family is found with the Waggoner line).

Henry Bonnett, (8 Oct. 1761-11 Oct. 1799) s/o Samuel & Mary Elizabeth Bonnett. Henry married Elizabeth (Larantz) Lorance born around 1764 Hampshire Co. (W) Va., South Branch (now Hardy Co.), d/o John & Mary Lorance. (see History of Grant and Hardy Co. Va. by E. L. Judy)

pg 315-Will # Bk. 2-274. John Lorence, wife Mary, sons: John, Philip, Andrew, Isaac, Abraham and David, daughters: Mary, Elizabeth Bonnett, Catharine, Catharine's husband John Pancake - 8 July 1817

pg. 316- Will Bk. 2-309 Mary Lorence, sons, John, Philip, Andrew, Abraham, Isaac and Daniel; daughters Catharine, Mary and Elizabeth.

Sage & Jones (pg 44) 1801 Feb. 16, John Pancake (w. Catherine) of Hampshire Co. to John McNeill of Hardy Co. Recorded, 16 Feb. 1801 - Wit. John Pancake

pg 34 1796 Apr. 18 William Linton (w. Mary) of Hampshire Co. sold to John Pancake Jr. of Hampshire Co. (W) Va. 232 acres on South Branch River, recorded, 18 Apr. 1796.

Jacob Bonnett & Lewis Bonnett were twins, born ca 1762 on Cedar Creek, Hampshire Co. (W) Va., s/o Samuel & Mary Elizabeth Bonnett. Both served in The Revolutionary War and have D.A.R. records. Served under Maj. Lowther while living on Hacker's Creek, Monongalia Co. (W) Va.

Jacob Bonnett (ca 1762 - Dec. 1847) Lewis Co. (W) Va. s/o Samual & Mary Elizabeth Bonnett. Jacob m. 6 Mar 1791 in Harrison Co. (Bk. 1- pg 16 - Bond, 21 Feb. 1791), Martha Hughes d/o Jesse & Grace (Tanner) Hughes.

Vol. 1 pg 1, Old Harmony Cemetery Lewis Co. W. Va. Martha (Hughes) Bonnett's stone marker reads; "*This monument erected in memory of Martha (d/o Jesse Hewes) who was born Dec. 1773, made prisoner of the Indians Dec. 1787, returned to captivity 1790- married Jacob Bonnett 1792-Died Dec. 1834 age 61 years.*"

Border Settlers of Northwestern Virginia by McWhorter (page 220) gives a good history of the Hughes family. "Jesse Hughes, born 1750 settled on Hacker's Creek in 1771-2 m Miss Grace Tanner the year of his settlement. He became one of the most famous scouts and Indian fighters of all the west."

Thomas Hughes Sr. settled on Elk Creek (now Harrison Co.) and was killed by Indians on Hacker's Creek in 1778. Little of his life is known or where they came from. Thomas Hughes children were:

- Thomas Hughes Jr. (1754-Oct. 1837).
- Ellis (Elias) Hughes born 1757 (now Hardy Co. W. Va.) died 22 Dec. 1844 near Utica, Ohio, married Miss Jane Sleeth.
- Sudna (Hughes) married Col. Wilham Lowther, who's brother Jonathan Lowther was killed at the same time as Sudnas Father in 1778 on Hacker's Creek, by Indians.
- Job Hughes who m 1791 Mary Hann lived Jackson Co. (W) Va. had a son killed by the Indians, and a daughter who married Joseph Bibbee. (B.S. of Nw. Va. pg 221)

Children of Jacob & Martha (Hughes) Bonnett:

1. Elizabeth Bonnett, (12 Apr. 1792-21 Apr. 1854) d/o Jacob & Martha (Hughes) Bonnett, m. 4 Apr. 1819 Lewis Co. (W) Va. Nicholas Alkire (1792-1852) Both are buried in the Friendship Cemetery, Northeast section of Lewis Co. W. Va. across the road form the Fairview Methodist Church.

Vol. III pg 5 Cemetery Records.

"Alkire, Elizabeth d. 12 Oct. 1852 (w/o Nicholas Alkire, married 4 Apr. 1818 age 55 y. 4 m. Nee Bonnett) Alkire, Nicholas D. 12 Apr. 1854 age 62 y. 7 d."

Their children:

- Martha Alkire, born 29 Nov. 1819, d/o Nicholas & Elizabeth (Bonnett) Alkire, Married 15 Jan. 1846 Lewis Co., Christian F. Holswide, lived Roane Co. (W) Va.
- Elizabeth Alkire, (30 Sept. 1821-21 Mar. 1910) Roane Co. W. Va. d/o Nicholas & Elizabeth (Bonnett) Alkire, married Joseph B. Wolfe (20 Jan. 1819-9 Nov., 1896) Spencer Dist. Roane Co. W. Va. They may have had two daughters, Margaret Alkire and Mary Alkire, but I have no information on them.
- John Alkire (ca 1826-29 May, 1897, ae 72 years) buried in the Friendship Cemetery, Lewis Co. W. Va.
- Nicholas Alkire Jr. (6 May 1828 - 6 Apr. 1902) He married, 14 Mar. 1855 Mary Elizabeth Reger (22 Oct. 1835-23 Dec. 1909), d/o Philip & Elizabeth Reger. Both buried Friendship Cemetery, Lewis Co. W. Va.
- William Harrison Alkire (1833-1920) Lewis Co. m. 24 Oct. 1869, Mary L. Post (1848-1933), d/o John & Sophia S (Cookman) Post; who were married 1 Jan. 1837 Lewis Co. (W) Va.
- Samuel Alkire (Feb. 1835 Lewis Co. died 1914) m 9 Sept. 1862 Lewis Co. Elizabeth Post (1839-1921) d/o John & Sophia A. (Cookman) Post both buried in Friendship Cemetery.
- George Washington Alkire (1839-1883) Lewis Co. m. 24 June 1863 Samantha Post (1843-1927) d/o John & Sophia A. (Cookman) Post.

2. Samuel Bonnett (1 Feb. 1794-11 Nov. 1856) Lewis Co. s/o Jacob & Martha (Hughes) Bonnett. Samuel m. 1st 24 Oct. 1818, Eliza Linger, who died 15 Oct. 1819, a d/o Lewis Linger. Samuel m. (2nd) 5 Dec. 1820, Lucinda Fitzhugh Hove, (Lucy Moore) may be a second marriage for Lucy.

The 1840 Census of Lewis Co. (W) Va. has Samuel Bonnett Jr. with 13 people in his house hold, but not in the 1850 census of Lewis Co. (W) Va.

- Perry Green Bonnett (10 Oct. 1819-21 Feb. 1890) other children
- Mary D. Bonnett 1853.
- Matilda Bonnett 1836.

- Lucinda Bonnett, born 6 Jan. 1839.
- Elmira Bonnett born 25 May 1841.
- Granville N. Bonnett born Oct. 1846.

3. Grace Bonnett (1798-1860) d/o Jacob & Martha (Hughes) Bonnett. m. 14 Sept. 1817 Lewis Co. Moses West (b. ca-1797).

4. Jacob H. Bonnett (28 Dec. 1803-6 July 1881) s/o Jacob & Martha (Hughes) Bonnett, m. Lewis Co. (W) Va. 21 Nov. 1826 Charlotta Hyde (1807) a d/o James Hyde Jr. & Catharine (Hardman) Hyde. James Hyde Jr. died around 1810. Their children were mentioned in his estates settlement of 8 Oct. 1831 with Jacob Hardman administrator for Peter Hardman (dec.). This would have been Catharine's brother and deceased father in 1831 by 4 Nov. 1814. Catharine had married Peter Waggoner.

The estate settlement mentioned children Daniel Hyde, Isaac Hyde, John Hyde and Charlotta (Hyde) Bonnett, her husband Jacob H Bonnett. Commissioner, Thos. L. Hacker received $2.00 for two days work in settling the estate, at one dollar per day.

Jacob H. and Charlotta (Hyde) Bonnett lived in Jackson Co. (W) Va. and their children were:

- Mansfield Bonnett.
- Samuel H. Bonnett born ca 1833. In 1880 census of Jackson Co. he was 47 yr. old living at home, and census indicated "blind".
- Sarah Bonnett, born ca 1834; Jackson Co. m. 24 Dec. 1855, Josiah West.
- Harriet Bonnett born ca 1841, Jackson Co. m. 4 Dec. 1858 in Roane Co. to Laban Shoulders, s/o Joseph & Susan Shoulders.
- William G. Bonnett born ca 1847, Jackson Co. m. 19 Dec. 1869 Roane Co. to Missouri Ellison.
- Nathan Bonnett born 27 June 1849 Jackson Co., m. 14 Sept. 1871, Roane Co. to Minirva S. Hopkins, born 1839 Lewis Co. d/o Robert & Martha Hopkins.
- Elizabeth Bonnett born 1844, Jackson Co. m 8 Apr. 1875 Roane Co. to W. M. Shoulders s/o Joseph & Susan Shoulders.
- Peregrine Bonnett, born ca 1843, was in the Civil War and died at Cloyd's Mountain on 23 May 1863.

5. Delilah Bonnett born ca 1805 d/o Jacob & Martha (Hughes) Bonnett. m. 27 May 1822, Lewis Co. Abraham Hess, born ca May 1800. Some of their children were Clark Hess, Newton Hess, Nancy Hess, Eliza Hess, Javon Hess, Marion Hess, Vinton Hess and Emily Hess. Both

Abraham age 72 y, and Delilah (Bonnett) Hess were in the 1870 C.. of Lewis Co. W. Va.

6. Martha Bonnett (1809- 3 Oct. 1867) Lewis Co. d/o Jacob & Martha (Hughes) Bonnett married 21 Sept. 1825 Lewis Co. Samuel Horner (13 Aug. 1805-18 Feb. 1883, ae 77 y. 6 m. 5 d.). Some of their children were:

- Joseph M. Horner (b 1830-died 13 Jan. 1861) bur Jesse Run Church Cemetery.
- Louisa Horner.
- Monterville Horner.
- Martha J. Horner.
- Amanda Horner.
- Cirina (Sirena) Horner.
- Marinda Horner.
- Lucinda Horner.
- William H. Horner (23 Sept. 1855-14 Mar. 1877 ae 21 y. 5 m. 22 d.).
- Harriet Horner.
- George M. Horner.

7. Eliza Bonnett (ae 63 in 1870 census of Lewis Co.) (b. ca 1807) d/o Jacob & Martha (Hughes) Bonnett, m. 12 May 1842 Lewis Co. Fleming Sprouse. Some of their children; George Sprouse, Lucinda Sprouse, Martha Sprouse, Washington Sprouse (m. Sophia Osborn), Sarah Sprouse, Leonard S. Sprouse, Henry Sprouse, Deborah Sprouse, and Eliza Sprouse.

8. Lucinda A. Bonnett (ca 1817 9 Mar. 1903) d/o Jacob & Martha (Hughes) Bonnett. She married 11 Sept. 1845, Lewis Co. Jesse Butcher (1811-1886) s/o John Anderson & Christiana (Alkire) Butcher Both buried Butcher Cemetery. Some of their children were Virginia Butcher, Elizabeth C. Butcher, William Butcher, Septembeus O. Butcher, John Butcher and Nancy Butcher.

Lewis Bonnett, (twin to Jacob) (1762-7 Jan. 1850) VanBuren Co. Iowa, s/o Samuel & Mary Elizabeth Bonnett. m 5 Apr. 1804, Harrison Co. (W) Va. Mary Linger, d. 1788, d/o Nicholas & Margaret (McNemar) Linger. Around 1835, Lewis and Mary joined Peter Bonnett, (who had just lost his wife Margaret (Linger) Bonnett) with their unmarried children and started for Iowa. Peter Bonnett died in 1835 ae. 71 yr., in Southern Ill. Lewis and family settled in Iowa, where he died in 1850.

After Lewis Bonnett death, his wife Mary (Linger) Bonnett returned to Lewis Co. (W) Va. with her daughter Lucinda (Bonnett) Mathews and two grandchildren, William W. Mathews b. 1846, and Mary Mathews b. 1848. Records show Mrs. Mary Bonnett (ae 66 yr.) d/o Nicholas & Margaret (McNemar) Linger. m. 18 Apr. 1854 Isaac Dix, (ae 65 y) Lewis Co. s/o Stephen & Jemina Dix.

Bk. 7 pg 30, Old Heavner Cem.:

"Isaac Dix d 1860, ae 72 y 1st wife Elizabeth Dix d. 1849 ae 52 y."

Some of Lewis & Mary (Linger) Bonnett's children:

1. Margaret Bonnett (9 Mar. 1805-Sept. 1883) d/o Lewis & Mary (Linger) Bonnett m. 8 Apr. 1824, Lewis Co., John R. Clark (25 Oct. 1798-Sept. 1884, ae 84 y) s/o William & Barbara (Helmick) Clark. Both bur. Mt. Gelead/Georgetown Cem.

   Their children:

   - Marshall Clark (1825-1897) m. 15 Sept. 1845 Matilda West (1826-1905).
   - Gedian Clark, (1833-1900) m. 11 Oct. 1855, Nancy J. Corathers, (1835-1907).
   - Levi Clark, (1831-1890) m. 1854, Upshur Co. Elizabeth Ann Legget (1833-1906).
   - Emily J. Clark, b. 1836, m 4 Mar. 1858, Henry Bevin Witzel (1836) s/o David D. & Margaret (Hardman) Witzel.
   - Lucinda Clark, (1835-1923) m. 2 Sept. 1864 George G Warner (1837-1888) s/o John & Sarah Warner.
   - Lucitta Clark (1828-1907) m. 3 Nov. 1848. David Wetzel Jr. (1822-1896).
   - Margaret Clark (1844-1822) m. 9 Dec. 1863, Nathan N. Marsh, s/o John & Mary (Bonnett) Marsh.
   - Harriet Clark, (1840) m.5 Apr. 1860 Jacob A. Hall.
   - Nathan Clark (1839-1910) m. Mary Margaret Mohler (1849-1936).
   - John J. Clark b. 1844.

2. Nicholas Bonnett (13 Jan. 1808-3 Apr. 1873) Iowa, s/o Lewis & Mary (Linger) Bonnett m. 4 Mar. 1830. Lewis Co. Anna Raines, (1812-1901) Iowa.

3. Catherine Bonnett (1810 2 Oct. 1845) Oregon, d/o Lewis & Mary (Linger) Bonnett, m. 11 Nov. 1834, Lewis Co., John Botts

4. Samuel Jasper Bonnett (8 Apr. 1814- 21 Apr. 1904) s/o Lewis & Mary (Linger) Bonnett, m. 26 Nov. 1840 Annis Parson (1822-1902)

5. Sarah Bonnett (1812-30 Apr. 1874) ae 62y. Vandalia Cem. d/o Lewis & Mary (Lenger) Bonnett, m. 24 Apr. 1834-Lewis Co.-Anthony R. Spaur, (7 Sept. 1813-11 Mar. 1893) (Upshur Co. death record pg 135- age 79 y. 6 m. 4 d.) bur. Vandalia Cem. Anthony R. was the s/o Anthony and Magdalena (Rohrabaugh) Spaur.

Some of their children:
- Gidion D. Spaur (2 June 1835-8 July 1883), m. 17 Mar. 1855, Margaret P. Spaur (29 Apr. 1838-27 Nov. 1880-42 y. 6 m. 28 d.).
- Dafina Spaur (1836 - 10 Nov. 1873), m. 18 Feb. 1858-Lewis Co. John C. Hardman (1 Dec. 1835-22 Sept. 1893) s/o Joshua W. and Susan M. Fultz.
- Abel Spaur, b. Aug. 1839-Lewis Co., m. 5 Apr. 1866 Nancy Butcher.
- David N. Spaur.
- Gilbert Spaur b. June 1842, m.21 Feb. 1871-Mary J. Casto.
- John Spaur.
- Greenbury C. Spaur (9 Dec. 1845-16 Aug. 1908) Lewis Co. m. 7 Aug. 1870-Margaret V. Alkire (22 Jan. 1853-17 Nov. 1902).
- Virginia Spaur born ca. 1848, m. 7 May 1866-Milton Butcher.
- Lafayette Spaur (5 Sept. 1850-14 Nov. 1908) bur. Vandalia Cem.-Lewis Co. W. Va.
- Nancy Spaur b. ca 1855.
- Almirah Spaur b. 10 Oct. 1853.

6. Lucinda Bonnett b. 1819, d/o Lewis & Mary (Linger) Bonnett, m. Mathews in Iowa.

   1860 census, Lewis Co. (W) Va. shows: Mary Dicks (Dix nee (Linger) Bonnett) ae. 72 y. Va., (wid. of Lewis Bonnett.); Lucinda Mathews, ae 40 y. Va. (nee Bonnett), d/o Lewis & Mary (Linger.) Bonnett.); William W. Mathews ae 14 y. Va.; and Mary Mathews ae 12 y. Va.

7. Jacob Wesley Bonnett (22 Apr. 1820-1 Apr. 1853) s/o Lewis & Mary (Linger) Bonnett, m. 2 Jan. 1842 Mary Jane Combs (1827-1900).

8. Lewis Bonnett (12 Jan. 1824-7 Dec. 1890) s/o Lewis & Mary (Linger) Bonnett, m. Evaline Amanda Parsons (1830-1912).

The Linger Cemetery in the Buckhannon district near the Upshur and Lewis Co. Line (Vol. 5 pg 53) This cemetery was read May 1983 by Kenneth and Haroldine Stalnaker. A large monument erected by ancestors of the Linger Family, to the Immigrant:

> In memory of Nicholas D. Linger and Margaret McNemar Linger, immigrant parents of the Linger Family. Nicholas D. Linger b. 1758 in the province of Hesse, Germany. Came to this country at an early age, was a soldier in the Revolutionary War, Married Margaret McNemar in 1785, was a hatter by trade, spent his last years on his farm in the Valley around this Monument and died in the year of 1827.

9. Mary Bonnett (1811-27 June 1887) Smith's Run Lewis Co. d/o Lewis & Mary (Linger) Bonnett m. 25 Feb. 1830, Lewis Co. Jesse Smith s/o Jacob & Catharine (Fench) Smith (D.A.R.)

   Their Children:

   - Marcellus Smith, m. 9 Sept. 1869, Sarah J. Helmick.
   - Granville Smith, m. 4 Nov. 1869, Eliza J. Claypole.
   - Jacob Smith, John Smith, and Jane Smith (d. Sept. 1855).
   - Mary C. Smith, m. 24 Mar. 1867, Christopher C. Yoke.
   - Artenia S. Smith, m. 10 Mar. 1871 John Alkire.
   - Marcelia Smith, m. 21 Mar. 1875 Josiah McVaney.
   - William H. Harrison Smith d. Sept. 1855.

10. Elizabeth Bonnett (22 Feb. 1807-11 June 1880 ae 73 yr..) Smiths Run, d/o Lewis & Mary (Linger) Bonnett. m. 9 Sept. 1826, Lewis Co. George Smith (15 July 1799), Pendleton Co. 23 Aug. 1882) Lewis Co. s/o Mark Smith (24 Oct. 1755-24 June 1840) & Mary Pence Smith. (D.A.R.)

    Their Children:

    - Amanda Smith (1828-1895) m. 11 Mar. 1852, John T. Schiefer, (d before 1870).
    - Rheuhanna Smith (1829) m. 11 Oct. 1855, William T. Patterson (1831).
    - Hanson H. Smith (1834) m. 8 Sept. 1872 Mary J. Kittle.
    - Harriet K. Smith (1835-1913) m. 23 Mar. 1852, m. Elias P. Forinash (1827-1905) s/o Jacob Sr. & Hannah (Paterson) Forinash.
    - Samuel R. Smith (1838-1926) m. 13 Dec. 1865, Ellen T. Stalnaker (1843-1920) d/o William P. & Eleanor (Reeder) Stalnaker.
    - Weeden H. Smith (1840-1908) m. ca. 1869 Mary J. Wade.
    - Adelina L. Smith (1843) m. 27 June 1865, Charles Pritchard b. 1840 Ireland. s/o Benjamin & Amanda Pritchard.

- Edwen Lee Smith (1850) m. 4 Jan. 1874 Cecilia Ann Jackson (1851) daughter George R. & Cecilia (McNulty) Jackson.

Peter Bonnett (1764-1835 age 71 yr..) Southern Illinois, s/o Samuel & Mary Elizabeth Bonnett, m. 4 Mar. 1806 Harrison Co. (W) Va. Margaret Linger (1781-1835) bur. Vandalia Cemetery, d/o Nicholas & Margaret (McNemar) Linger. After Margaret (Linger) Bonnetts death in 1835, Peter loaded up a wagon and started for Iowa territory. About half of his family went, others married stayed in Lewis Co. (W) Va. Others who went were Peter's brother Lewis, Mary Bonnett and part of their family, and Henry Butts. Much credit can be given to The People of the Vandalia Community by Sam Hardman.

Sam Hardman states "Peter and Margaret (Linger) Bonnett had eleven children: Mary (Polly), Sarah, Margaret, Nicholas, Samuel, Elizabeth, Peter, William, Matilda, Catharine, and David."

1. Mary (Polly) Bonnett (17 Nov. 1806 Harrison co. 25 June 1894) bur Vandalia Cemetery. d/o Peter & Margaret (Linger) Bonnett. Mary married 17 Apr. 1831 Lewis Co. John C. Marsh (17 Dec. 1809 Culpepper Co. Va., 23 Aug. 1900) s/o Spencer & Sally (Curtis) Marsh.

   Some of their children:
   - Emily J. Marsh (18 Jan. 1832- 17 Jan. 1835) bur. Vandalia Cem.
   - Margaret Marsh (21 Feb. 1833-17 Dec. 1912) m. 1 Nov. 1855 Lewis Co. Washington E. Bott (ca 1833-1893) s/o Jacob & Jerusia (Rohrbaugh) Bott.
   - Savilla Marsh (10 June 1834-1911) m. 19 Jan. 1854 Lewis Co., John R. Francis (1828-1913) Vandalia Cem.
   - Lucinda Marsh (28 Oct. 1835-1911) m. 23 Oct. 1862 Lewis Co., Nicholas F. Linger (1841-1911) s/o John D. & Lucina (Curtis) Linger.
   - Catharine E. Marsh (4 Mar. 1837-25 Jan. 1840) Vandalia Cem.
   - Sarah L. Marsh (14 Sept. 1839-28 Jan. 1935) Vandalia Cem.
   - Nathan Newton Marsh (4 Oct. 1841-1910) m. 9 Dec. 1863 Lewis Co. Margaret Clark (17 May 1845-13 Sept. 1882) d/o John & Margaret (Bonnett) Clark.

2. Elizabeth Bonnett b.22 Feb. 1808- Harrison Co. (W) Va., d/o Peter & Margaret (Linger) Bonnett.

3. Margaret Bonnett (21 July 1811 d. 7 Jan. 1884) d/o Peter & Margaret (Linger) Bonnett married 19 Dec. 1834 Lewis Co. Rev.

George Irwin Marsh. (9 June 1813-15 May 1874) bur. Vandalia Cem.

Some of their children were:
- Salathiel Marsh born ca 1834.
- Sarah J. Marsh (15 Jan. 1837-27 Jan. 1867-age 30 y.) Lewis Co. m. 7 Dec. 1855-Granville Gibson (10 Mar. 1836-9 Mar. 1913)
- George W. Marsh- (1852-1866).
- Hiram Marsh b. 1839.
- William G. Marsh b.1853.
- Eliza Marsh b. 1840, m. 16 June 1858, John J. Carathers.
- Aramantha Marsh b. 1842, d prior to 1900, m. 3 Sept. 1862, Lear D. Steelman.
- Rheuhana Marsh-(5 Mar. 1843 - 21 Oct. 1875) bur. Vandalia Cem. Lewis Co. m. 1 Mar. 1866-Aaron L. Winemiller (5 Mar. 1847-10 Apr. 1922).
- Albert J. Marsh b. 1846, m. Matilda.
- Gilbert M. Marsh (16 Jan. 1848), m. 18 Mar. 1869- Mary J. Zinn born 1847, Doddridge Co., d/o George W. & Sarah (Gray) Zinn.
- Flanivs A. Marsh (1849-17 June 1884) m. 14 Oct. 1869-Lewis Co. Martha A. Forinash (1852-1918) age 66 y. bur. Machpelah Cem.

4. Sarah Bonnett, d/o Peter & Margaret (Linger).Bonnett.

5. Nicholas L. Bonnett (7 Aug. 1813-18 Jan. 1881) s/o Peter & Margaret (Linger).Bonnett. He did not live in Lewis Co.

6. Samuel L. Bonnett born ca 1817 Lewis Co. (W) Va. s/o Peter & Margaret (Linger) Bonnett, m. 12 July 1840-, Joana Helmick born ca 1812-d/o John H. & Mary Ann (Hacker) Helmick.

Some of their children:
- Mary A. Bonnett.
- William M. Bonnett.
- John T. Bonnett.
- Daniel R. Bonnett (1848- 8 Aug. 1883) Vandalia Cem. 18 Jan. 1877 m. Isabel A. Helmick.
- Margaret E. Bonnett b. 1852, m. 8 Dec. 1875 Benjamin Alkire.

7. Peter Bonnett b. 1824, Lewis Co., s/o Peter & Margaret (Linger) Bonnett m. 26 Aug. 1849 Levina A. Murrow-(Marrow), d/o John Marrow. Some of their children:
- Newton John Bonnett, (Mar. 1850) m. 8 Jan. 1814, Martha A. Ditson.

- Matilda J. Bonnett, (1852) m. 14 Apr. 1872-Noah Flesher.
- Edgar H. Bonnett, (Mar 1855-1916) m. Rosanna Flesher (1870-1943).
- Margaret M. Bonnett, (1857-1869).
- Mary L. Bonnett, b. 1859.
- David S. Bonnett, (1866-1872).

8. William Bonnett, (9 Dec. 1822-19 Mar. 1903) s/o Peter & Margaret (Linger) Bonnett- m. 29 May 1848 Matilda Madara (10 Oct. 1823 - 23 Apr. 1914).

9. Matilda Bonnett. b. 1826, d/o Peter & Margaret (Linger) Bonnett, m. 15 Sept. 1858 (ae 32 y.) Philip W. Dodson (age 46 y.), s/o Joseph & Elizabeth Dodson.

10. Catharine Bonnett b. ca 1828 d/o Peter & Margaret (Linger) Bonnett.

11. David Bonnett b. ca 1830 s/o Peter & Margaret (Linger) Bonnett.

Samuel Bonnett Jr. (4 Apr. 1770-24 Jan. 1840) age 78 y. 9 m. 21 d. bur. Old Harmony Cem. Lewis Co. (W) Va. s/o Samuel and Mary Elizabeth Bonnett. Samuel bought land in 1808 from John and Susannah (Smith) Hacker on Hacker's Creek. Samual m. 9 Apr. 1796- Harrison Co. (W) Va., Martha Radcliff (5 Feb. 1778-12 Sept. 1855 ae 77 y. 7 m. 7 d.). (Death reported by her daughter Elizabeth Allman,) d/o William and Deborah (Hughes) Radcliff. In 1850 Martha (Radcliff) Bonnett was living with her daughter Jane (Mrs. Thomas, Boram).

Some of their children: John, Henry R. Sarah, Lewis Zilla, Susan, Elizabeth (Betsy), Deborah, Katharine, Jane, and Margaret Bonnett.

1. John Bonnett (25 Dec. 1797-2 Sept. 1867 age 70y. 8m. 10d.) Bur. Morrison Cem. (Vol. 1-47), s/o Samuel & Martha (Radcliff) Bonnett, m. (1st) 10 July 1827, Bridget Morrison (27 Feb. 1806-10 July 1837 (ae 29y. 4m. 13d.) m. (2nd), 16 Oct. 1838, Elizabeth A. Yeager (8 June 1816-1 June 1901 ae 84. 11m. 23d.).

Some of their children:

- Martha Bonnett (b. ca 1832), m. 10 Feb. 1853, Marshall Hushman.
- Minerva Bonnett in 1870 living with Minter B. and Harmonetta Kelly -- she was 36 yr. (Minter B. Kelly s/o Helzen & Deborah (Bonnett) Kelly.).
- William Granville Bonnett b. ca 1835, m. 23 July 1836 Lewis Co., Caroline Batton b. ca 1840 d/o Richard Batton.

- Ann Bonnett b. ca 1839.
- Thomas Jefferson Bonnett b. May 1841- m. (1st) 31 Dec. 1865- Olive Malissa Wilson, m. (2nd) ca 1898-9 Margaret E., b. Mar. 1869.
- Joel M. Bonnett b. ca 1847.
- Serina Bonnett b. May 1847, m. 10 Jan. 1867 Eber E. Post.
- Azariah S. Bonnett (July 1849) m. 24 Mar. 1870 Minerva Henzman.
- Henrietta V. Bonnett (b. Oct. 1851-d. 1918) Friendship Cem. m. 10 Nov. 1874 Edward D Bailey (1846-1928).
- Margaret A. Bonnett b. 26 Feb. 1854.
- John C. Bonnett (twin) b. 13 Nov. 1856.
- Harriet A. Bonnett (twin) (13 Nov. 1856-2 May 1932) Woofter Cem., m. 1886 Isaac Hinzman (1860-1946) s/o Robert and Martha J. (Bonnett) Hinzman.
- George W. Bonnett m. 6 Dec. 1865, Nancy A. Woofter.
- Caroline Y. Bonnett m. 28 Jan. 1862, Richard Rinehart.

2. Rev. Henry Radcliff Bonnett (4 Dec. 1798-7 Feb. 1877) age 78 y. 2 m. 3 d. s/o Samuel & Martha (Radcliff) Bonnett. Minister of Methodist Protestant Church, m. (1st) 15 Jan. 1822 Sarah Smith (11 Sept. 1804-16 July 1835) age 30 y. 10 m. 5 d., bur. Old Hacker Cem., (Morrison Cem) d/o David H. & Sarah (Hacker) Smith. m. (2nd) 24 Mar. 1836, Mary Batten (4 Nov. 1808 - 26 Jan. 1873 age 64y. 2m. 22d).

Some of their children:

- Matilda H. Bonnett (7 Jan. 1823-30 Aug. 1900) m. 14 Apr. 1842. Lewis Co., Isaac M. Hinzman (27 June 1818-8 Sept. 1861), Matilda (Bonnett) Hinzman m. (2nd) 22 Apr. 1867 Jacob M. Wolf.
- Elias Hughes Bonnett (21 Sept. 1826-14 Aug. 1904) Lewis Co. m. 25 Sept. 1850 Elizabeth Cookman (16 Sept. 1831-26 Sept. 1885) d/o George & Mary (Mitchell) Cookman.
- Samuel Baxter Bonnett (3 Mar. 1824 - 5 Jan. 1877) age 52 y. 10 m. 2 d. m. 6 June 1858-Margaret Hershman (1 Nov. 1826 19 Feb. 1917) Morrison Cem. d/o Mark & Polly Hershman.
- David S. Bonnett (10 June 1835-19 May 1843).
- Lydia Ann Bonnett, b. 21 July 1828, m. 7 Dec. 1853 Samuel E Cookman, s/o George & Mary Cookman.
- Sarah Jane Bonnett (17 Jan. 1830-24 Dec. 1900) m. 2 Sept. 1852 James Monroe Morrison (17 Sept. 1822 - 10 Mar 1896), s/o Alexander & Elizabeth (Keagle) Morrison.

- Lewis M. Bonnett (18 Jan. 1832-9 Feb. 1903) Kansas. m. 6 Dec. 1853 Harriet Jane Morrison (13 Oct. 1834-6 June 1876) Kansas, d/o Alexander and Margaret (Brake) Morrison.
- Martha Belinda Bonnett (1 Mar. 1837-1 Apr. 1878 age 40 y. 11 m.), bur. Morrison Cem., Lewis Co. W. Va.

3. Sarah Bonnett (10 Feb. 1802-21 Jan. 1882) ae 77 y. 11 m. 11 d. Fairview Cem. Lewis Co., d/o Samuel & Martha (Radcliff) Bonnett. m. 12 mar. 1822 Lewis Co. William Smith (3 Nov. 1799-10 June 1839, ae 39 y. 7 m. 9 d.) Fairview Cem.

In 1850 Sarah (Bonnett) Smith was living in Lewis Co., with these children:

- Samuel B. Smith (6 July 1825-15 Jan. 1904 ae 78 y. 6 m. 9 d.) Fairview Cem., m. 27 Oct. 1853, Lewis Co., Angeline Cookman.
- Henry R. Smith, (22 Mar. 1829-26 July 1914),m. 19 Mar. 1855 Serena A. Duvall (1837-1919).
- Nancy Smith b. ca 1832, Lewis Co. (W) Va. Hardesty's .(vol. 3-pg 115) Braxton Co., m. 15 Dec. 1868, Henderson D. Mitchel, b. 1848, s/o John E. & Prudence (McCully) Mitchel.
- William H. Smith m. 15 Nov. 1860, Mary Welch.
- Gedion G. Smith.
- Sarah J. Smith m.18 Dec. 1855 Oliver G. Forinash.
- David P. Smith (April 1824- June 1837).
- Stephen Smith (Apr. 1834-Aug. 1840).
- Calvin N. Smith (28 Feb. 1830- Nov. 1841).

4. Lewis Barzilla Bonnett (22 Sept. 1803-27 May 1891), Lewis Co., s/o Samuel & Martha (Radcliff) Bonnett m. 7 Feb. 1834, Lewis Co., Margaret Means (1814-4 Feb. 1896) d/o Robert Means. ch.:

- Harriet Bonnett (1835-1882) Walnut Fork Cem. m. (5 Apr. 1869 Lewis Co. Daniel Webster King.
- Otho Bonnett b. ca 1837, (13 y, in 1850).
- Henry Harrison Bonnett b. ca 1840, m. Sarah S. West.
- Samuel Bonnett b. Apr. 1843, m. 22 Aug. 1867 Lewis Co. Martha E. Sprouse b. Mar 1846, d/o Fleming & Eliza (Bonnett) Sprouse.
- John K. Bonnett b. ca 1846, m. 30 Oct. 1870 Lewis Co. Sarah A. King, d/o Elijah & Nancy King.
- William R. Bonnett (15 May 1847-23 Feb. 1936) m. 16 June 1870 Susan E. King d/o William & Sarah King.
- Greenberry C. Bonnett b. Mar. 1849 Lewis Co.

- Zillah Bonnett (1838-20 Mar. 1922 Age 84 y. 6 m. 10 d.) Walnut Fork Cem., m. 3 Jan. 1857, Howard Osburn (13 Oct. 1829-29 Sept. 1896), s/o Philip & Ruth (Ware) Osburn.
- Martha Bonnett b. ca 1851.
- Lewis B. Bonnett b. 20 Oct. 1857.
- Deannah Bonnett (1854-1854).
- Mifflin Bonnett (b. ca 1855).

5. Elizabeth (Betsy) Bonnett (14 May 1809 - 8 Oct. 1872) Harmony Cem., d/o Samuel and Martha (Radcliff) Bonnett, m. 11 Dec. 1828 Lewis co., Madison Allman (12 Jan. 1810 - 17 Nov. 1894) s/o William Allman. See <u>Allman Family</u> by Edward L. Allman).

6. Deborah (Debby) Bonnett (1810-10 Oct. 1893) Lewis Co. W. Va., d/o Samuel & Martha (Radcliff) Bonnett, m. 22 Nov. 1827, Lewis Co., Halzen Kelley (Sept. 1805-16 Apr. 1877), s/o William & Mary Ann Kelley,(Kelly).

    Some of their children:

    - Matilda Kelley.
    - Samuel Kelley b. 7 Apr. 1832, m. 11 Feb. 1856, Pheobe Ellen McKinney.
    - John Kelley m. 17 Aug. 1853 Rulina M Smith.
    - William Henry Kelley (14 Sept. 1832 - 20 Feb. 1912), m. Martha Jane Post (1842- 13 Oct. 1931), Friendship Cem.
    - Elizabeth J. Kelley m. ca. 1873 Lewis Co., Stephen L. Smith.
    - Weeden H. Kelley d. 29 Sept. 1854.
    - Edgar M. Kelley (8 Feb. 1840-29 Apr. 1918).
    - Menter B. Kelley m. Hormonett _____.
    - David S. Kelley b. Feb. 1845 m. Sarah _____ b. Nov 1857.
    - Margaret Kelley b. ca 1849.

7. Jane Bonnett (1820 15 Sept. 1898 age 76 y) Buchannon Run Cem., d/o Samuel & Martha (Radcilff) Bonnett. m. 15 May 1842 Lewis Co. Thomas Boren (1822-1903) Some of their children:

    - Almira Boren, m. 21 Jan. 1861 William Marcellous Hinzman.
    - Angeline Boren m. 6 Apr. 1865 Lewis Co. John Fairlee Staurcher.
    - Mary C. Boren (30 Dec. 1847 - 12 Sept. 1856).
    - Martha E. Boren, m. 17 Nov. 1875, Lewis Co., Philip E. Reger.
    - Margaret J. Boren (1 Dec. 1857 - 4 Apr. 1928), Friendship Cem., m. 28 Nov. 1878, Lewis Co., Marshal Dexter Morrison.
    - Thomas J. Boren (May 1861) m. Leona L. Hodges.

8. Margarit Bonnett (1815-1846), d/o Samuel & Martha (Radcliff) Bonnett, m. 6 Feb. 1837 Lewis Co., John Hinzman, b. 11 July 1813, s/o Henry & Charity Hinzman, they lived in Roane Co. in 1856. Some of their children:
   - Samuel B. Hinzman (b. 20 May 1840)(Civil War) m. 17 Jan. 1861 Roane Co. Lucritia J. Carpenter.
   - Martha M. Hinzman m. 27 Oct. 1868 John Carpenter.
   - James M. Hinzman m. 17 Dec. 1868 Roane Co. Martha J. Reed, d/o Daniel & Susan Reed.

William Bonnett (8 Dec. 1774-10 July 1858 ae 85 y.) s/o Samuel & Mary Elizabeth Bonnett m.5 Mar. 1799 Harrison Co., by Jacob Cozad, Barbara Harpold (Harpole) (5 Feb. 1784-20 Aug. 1867) d/o Adam & Margaret Cunning (Dunkle) Harpole.

They were in Jackson Co. by 1830 and by 1860 Barbara (Harpold) Bonnett was living with her son John A Bonnett. Some of their children: William Jr., John A., Sarah (Sally), Eliza Louise, Matilda, Nicholas H., and Martha Bonnett.

1. William Bonnett Jr. m. 15 Mar. 1835 Jackson Co. (W) Va. s/o William & Barbara (Harpold) Bonnett m. 15 Mar. 1835 Jackson Co. Laura Ann (Lavina) Vandine. Some of their children:
   - Elizabeth W. Bonnett b ca 1836 Jackson Co.
   - Marietta Bonnett m. 11 Apr. 1861 Nelson Stone.
   - Mitilda Bonnett m. 18 Mar. 1858 Charles Campbell.
   - Nancy J. Bonnett m. 29 Jan. 1868 John McIntosh.
   - Samuel Bonnett m. 19 Apr. 1866 Emily C. Goodwin.
   - Louise Bonnett m 23 Aug. 1866 James Buckalew.
   - William T. Bonnett b. ca 1854 Jackson Co.
   - G. H. Bonnett, m.21 Nov. 1901 Annie Stoats.

2. John A. Bonnett b. ca 1825 merchant, s/o William & Barbara (Harpold) Bonnett, m. 20 Jan. 1848 Jackson Co., Mary Margaret Armstrong.

3. Sally (Sarah) Bonnett d/o William & Barbara (Harpold) Bonnett m. 24 Nov. 1831 James Baker.

4. Eliza Louise Bonnett d/o William & Barbara (Harpold) Bonnett, m. 13 Mar. 1834, Jackson Co. William B. McMahan.

5. Matilda Bonnett, d/o William & Barbara (Harpold) Bonnett, m. 16 Nov. 1835 Jackson Co., Christopher W. Craig.

6. Martha Bonnett d/o William & Barbara (Harpold) Bonnett, m. 9 Oct. 1848 Jackson Co. Charles Casto.

7. Nicholas H. Bonnett s/o William & Barbara (Harpold) Bonnett, m. (1st) 24 Mar. 1842, Catharine Staats Jackson Co., m. (2nd) 3 July 1853, Sarah E. Staats, d/o Elijah Staats. Some of their children listed in the 1850 and 1860 census:

- William M. Bonnett, b ca 1836 Jackson Co.
- Sarah Bonnett, b. ca 1837.
- S. A. Bonnett, b. ca 1844, m. 24 Oct. 1861 Charles B. Scott.
- Barbara Bonnett b. ca 1847.
- M. Florence Bonnett, b. ca 1854 m. 16 Jan. 1873, W. M. Casto.
- L. C. Bonnett, b. ca 1856.
- Ida Bonnett, b. ca 1858.

Elizabeth Bonnett (1772-1824 age 52 y.) Old Harmony Cem. d/o Samuel & Mary Elizabeth Bonnett. m. 23 Mar. 1796 Harrison Co. George Straley Sr. (ca 1770-9 Aug. 1846) Lewis Co. s/o Christian Straley (21 Sept. 1742-14 Aug. 1818) and Maria Christina Lentz, b. 23 Mar. 1748 and baptized 15 May 1748, d/o Jacob Lentz and wife Catharina. Sponsors Rudolp Dantzler and Christina Mahnyn at the Williams Township Congregation, Northampton Co. Pa. (Ref. Pa. Birth of Northampton Co. Pa. (1733 -1800) pg 130. Pa. and German Church Records Vol. 2 pg. 49)

Their children:

1. Elizabeth Straley (1799-1864) m. 10 Jan. 1821 Lewis Co. Paul Waggoner (1800-1877) Colfax Indiana s/o John & Susanna (Richards) Waggoner (see Waggoner Family).

2. Mary Straley m. 16 Mar. 1830 (17 Mar. 1831) Lewis Co., Elijah Waggoner, s/o John & Susanna (Richards) Waggoner (see Waggoner Family by Wm. B Waggoner of Grafton W. Va.).

3. Jacob Straley (1816-27 Oct. 1886) m. 15 July 1838 Lewis Co. Katharan Ann Freeman.

4. George Straley Jr. m. 4 Mar. 1826 Lewis Co. Ruth Chapman.

5. Hannah Straley m. 24 Nov. 1836 Lewis Co. John Edmonds.

6. Nancy Straley m. 12 Jan. 1837 Lewis Co. Cornelius King.

7. Christina Straley m. 20 Aug. 1841 Lewis Co. James R. Wolf.

Mary Bonnett (1777-9 Nov. 1845) Lewis Co. (W) Va. d/o Samuel & Mary Elizabeth Bonnett m. 28 June 1793 Harrison Co. Peter Flesher (? 1773 26 Nov. 1814) 1812 War (died below Richmond) s/o Henry & Elizabeth Flesher. Some of their children: Polly, Margaret (Peggy), Nancy, Barbara and Henry Flesher.

1. Polly Flesher m. 8 Mar. 1819-20 - George Smith.
2. Margaret (Peggy) Flesher (11 Feb. 1797-ca 1833) m. 26 June 1818 Lewis Co. Thomas Hanson Lockhart. (19 Sept. 1798-2 Jan. 1881).
3. Nancy Flesher (13 Nov. 1801-27 Dec. 1874) Butchers Cem. m.1 Apr. 1820 Lewis Co. William G. Stringer (31 Nov. 1787-27 Mar. 1866 age 78 y. 3 m. 27 d.) Some of their children: James G., William, John, Charles.
4. Barbara Flesher b. ca 1804, m. 13 Dec. 1823 Lewis Co., Jacob Butcher, b. ca 1796.
5. Henry Flesher (16 Aug. 1808-13 Dec. 1887) Machpelah Cem. m. 17 Dec. 1840 Lewis Co. Mary Baird b. 3 Feb. 1813 in Washington Co. Pa., d. Aug. 1897 Lewis Co., d/o Adam & Barbara (Wilhelm) Baird (died in Iowa). ch.: Jane (1842-1842), William (Henry) (1843-1859), Eliza J. (5 Oct. 1846) m. W. H. Aspenall b. 1841, Jacob (17 May 1849) (Hardestys Vol. 5 pg 212).

Philip Bonnett (1775-26 Mar. 1860-Patterson Creek Jefferson Co. Iowa) s/o Samuel & Mary Elizabeth Bonnett. m. 25 Feb. 1812 Harrison Co. (W) Va. Susan Linger (1795-26 Mar. 1876). They left Lewis Co. (W) Va. around 1835 and settled in Jefferson Co. Iowa Philip Bonnet was a Pvt. in the War of 1812. Some of their children:

1. Elizabeth Bonnett (b. ca 1817) m. 13 Mar. 1839-Henry Penninger Lewis Co. (W) Va.
2. Margaret Bonnett m. Jefferson Co. Iowa.
3. Nicholas M. Bonnett m. Jefferson Co. Iowa.

✣✣✣✣✣✣✣✣✣✣✣✣✣✣✣✣✣✣✣✣✣✣✣✣✣✣✣✣✣✣✣✣✣✣✣✣✣✣✣

Samuel Bonnett was killed by a falling tree in 1789 Harrison Co. (W) Va., the widow Mary Elizabeth Bonnett m. 19 Jan. 1790 Harrison Co. (W) Va., John Mack (Mauck).

Around 1789 Indians had raided the house of John Mack on a branch of Hacker's Creek killing everyone in the house and burning it. One small girl lay in the yard, scalped. The two children who had been sent to the woods for the cattle saw the dead sister and gave the alarm. When John Mack returned home he found most of his family dead and his home burned. Mrs. Mack was found some distance from the house, tomahawked, scalped and stripped naked. Searchers wrapped their hunting shirts about her and carried her to a neighboring house. She lived a few days, gave birth to a child and died. John Mack had two children and a new baby, left of his family. (Ref. *Chronicles of Border Warfare* by Alexander Scott Wilhers pg 382.)

Harrison County (West) Virginia deed Records 1785-1810 by John David Davis on page 74 gives this article. 26 Apr. 1793 - pg 247- Elizabeth Mock, (Mary Elizabeth Bonnett) widow of Samuel Bonnett receives her right to Dower, 400 acres divided into three equal tracts, signed David Sleeth, deputy sheriff.

The 1785 head of familys, as found, Shenandoah Co. on Michael Speagle's list shows John Mauck, 8 white souls in house.

1817 - #476 Land Book -Lewis Co. (W) Va. Land Tax within the district of John Mitchell:

Mary Bonnett - Monongalia 240 acres head of Stoney Run.

Samuel Bonnett - 222 ½ acres on Bonnetts Rum.

Jacob Bonnett - 140 acres on Hacker Creek - 40 acres on Bonnetts Run.

Peter Bonnett 36 ½ acres on Bonnetts Run.

(Mary) Elizabeth Bonnett (Mauck) consort of Samuel Bonnett died 15 Oct. 1819, bur. Old Harmony Cem. Lewis Co. (W) Va.

Some of the stones in Old Harmony Cemetery
near Jane Lew, Lewis Co. W. Va.

Peter Hardman

Both John Hardman and his sister Catharine (Hardman) Hyde married members of John and Margaret (Bonnett) Waggoner family. Both Elizabeth and Peter Waggoner were captured by Indians in 1792 when their mother Margaret (Bonnett) Waggoner was killed along with four young brothers.

Some Hardman history needs to be added here. The Hardman Family has been researched by so many people and for so many years. I hesitate to add dates that I can't give credit for. My recent letter to Mrs. Wilda Kelly was returned, marked "Forwarding Order Expired". She had helped me with her early research into Germany.

Several years ago a Hardman Genealogy was found in the Charleston, W. Va. Library. It had been co-authored by two Great Grandsons of Henry (1780-1870) and Rev. John Hardman (1777-1864). Thanks to J. D. Waggoner for sending the Hardman Genealogy to me.

In 1941 - Paul Hardman of Charleston, W. Va recieved the collection of letters, exchanged between William Edward Hardman, of Del Roy, Ohio and Samuel J. Hardman of Lewis Co. W. Va., on the Hardman Family.

Another Hardman history printed in 1928, The People of Vandalia Community, by Sam Hardman, reprinted in 1973 by The West Virginia Hillbilly, is priceless.

There is a Scrapbook on the Hardman, Bonnett and Waggoner Families for Blanche Maybury Carson, researached by a professional Geneologist in 1910. In 1980, I found this scrapbook at the Historical Society of Philadelphia, Pa. on 1300 Locust St., under file #Me-59-pg 33.

The lineage of Blanche Maybury:

Blanche Maybury, m. Dr. Edwin Carson, d/o (Parents) Herman Maybury m. Josephine Hardman, Gp. Jacob Wolf Hardman (1801-1874) m. Maria Rodman (1806-1874). G.Gp. Rev. John Hardman m. Elizabeth Waggoner. G.G.Gp. John Waggoner m. Margaret Bonnett.

It is sad to realize Jacob Wolf Hardman is not mentioned in <u>The People of Vandalia Community</u> by Sam Hardman, since Jacob was the first living s/o Rev. John and Elizabeth (Waggoner) Hardman who left home early and married Marion (Maria) Rodman, living, and dying in 1874 in Louisville, Ky., ten years after his father died in 1864, and his mother in 1854.

The story of **Peter Hardman** (Hartman) (Hardtmann), s/o Nicholas and Margaret Hartman, of Juliana on-the-Rhine, migrated to America with brothers and sisters. There are other Hardman Familes, in Md., Va. and W. Va. Peter sailed from Rotterdam to the port of New York, and on Saturday 20th Sept. 1764, (ship Richmond) arrived in Philadelphia Pa. (Rapp-30 thousand). I have only seen one other Immigration record.

Peter Hardman married Charlotte Lazier (Leasier) they lived for a time on a tract of land on Patterson's Creek around 1776-Hampshire Co. Va. When the Indian attacks grew worse, they leased the land to two people, Joseph Hanks and George Terry. Then Peter Hardman re-settled his family in Cumberland, Md., on the Big Yochony River (Yoghoney) until the War ended. When he returned to Patterson's Creek, he found the tenants gone and deed of trust given to Peter Putman, they agreed and sold the property to Jacob Doll and Jacob Purgate, thus the mortgage was paid off, and the Hardmans moved on to Monongalia Co. where he secured a grant for 164 acres on Jesse Hughes Run.

Peterman Hardman's will is as follows:

1819 July 2nd. Harrison Co. (W) Va. wife Charlotte Lazier Hardman. "I will and bequeath to my son Jacob Hardman, all that tract of land on which I now live. Laying on Jesse Hughes run containing 164 acres: also I will and bequeath to my son Jacob my other tract of land containing 101 acres adjoining the above tract, to hold to him and his heirs forever: and as to such other estate, real or personal as I shall die possessed of, I also will and bequeath to my son Jacob Hardman and his heirs forever; and it is my will and entention that should my wife survive me, that she is to have and enjoy her equal third part of all the estate above bequeathed to my said son Jacob during her natural life, and to descend at her death to my said son Jacob as above bequeathed."

"I will and bequeath to each of my other sons, Peter, John, Henry and Daniel Hardman, $100.00 each to be paid by my son Jacob with in five years from and after my decease, and to be paid in property at valuation of two men chosen by the parties."

"I will and bequeath to my daughters Elizabeth and Catherine, $50.00 each to be paid by my son Jacob, with in five years from and after my death in property at the valuation of two men chosen by the parties."

"In witness Where of I, Yhe said Peter Hardman, have here unto set my hand and seal this 2nd day of July, in the year of our lord, 1819."

(NOTE: all of his family is named in this will).

Peter Hardman (10 Mar. 1745-13 May 1827) s/o Nicholas and Margaret Hardman, of Juliana-on-the-Rhine Germany. married ca 1769-70 Charlotte Lazier (Leasier) (ca 1748-Nov. 1835 87 yr). (Film #250209 Cem) both Peter and Charlotte Hardman were buried at Harmony Cemetery on Berlin Road, 2 mi. from Jane Lew, Lewis Co. W. Va.

Peter Hardman was a farmer on Jesse Hughes Run, Hacker's Creek, Lewis Co. W. VA. The families of the Rev. John Hardman and Catharine (Hardman) Hyde (Hide) Waggoner will be found under the John and Margaret (Bonnett) Waggoner line.

Catharine Hardman (26 Feb. 1784-2 Apr. 1767), d/o Peter and Charlotte (Lazier) Hardman, m. 20 March 1801 - Harrison Co. (W) Va. James Hide (Hyde) Jr., s/o James Hyde Sr. and Sarah Hyde.

James Hyde Jr. died either in 1810 or 1811 as the Harrison Co. (pg. 119) Estate Settlements gave the S.B. (sale bill) as 23 Dec. 1811 and the estate settlement as 8 Oct. 1831. Catharine (Hardman) Hyde m. (2nd) Peter Waggoner. (see Waggoner for this family)

Children of James Hyde Jr. and Catharine (Hardman) Hyde:

1. Isaac Hyde m. 15 Nov. 1832 Lewis Co. Ermine Smith.
2. Daniel Hyde (b. ca. 1805-d. ca 1875) m. 12 Nov. 1824, Harrison Co. (W) Va. Mary Richards (1805-1880) d/o William & Margaret (Matthews) Richards.
3. John Hyde m. 5 Jan. 1831 Harrison Co. (W) Va. Hannah Swisher.

4. Charlotta Hyde b. ca 1806-7 m. 21 Nov. 1826 Lewis Co. (W) Va. Jacob H. Bonnett (28 Dec. 1803-6 July 1881) Roane Co. W. Va. s/o Jacob & Martha (Hughes) Bonnett.

Their children:
- Mansfield Bonnett-(1829- m. Mary.
- Samuel H. Bonnett b. ca 1834, Jackson Co. (W) Va.
- Sarah Bonnett b. ca 1834 m. 24 Dec. 1855 Jackson Co. Josiah West b. ca 1832 s/o Thomas & Elizabeth West.
- Harriet Bonnett b. ca 1841 m. 4 Dec. 1858, Roane Co. Laban Shouldes b. ca 1837 Lewis Co. s/o Joseph and Susan Shouldes.
- Periguine Bonnett (b. ca 1843 23 May 1863) (a Perry G Bonnett was wounded and left on the field at Cloyds Mountain - Civil War).
- William G. Bonnett b, ca 1847 m. 19 Dec. 1869 Roane Co. Messouri Ellison b. ca 1851 Kanawha Co. d/o Samuel and Sarah Ellison.
- Nathan S. Bonnett b. 1849 Jackson Co. m. 14 Sept. 1871 (ae 22 y.) Roane Co. Menerva S. Hopkins b. 23 Jan. 1854 (ae 17 y.) d/o Robert and Martha A. (Stalnaker) Hopkins.
- Elizabeth Bonnett b. ca 1844-Jackson Co. m. 8 Apr. 1875 (ae 31 yr.) Roane Co. W. M. Shouldes (wid) ae 36 y. s/o Joseph & Susan Shouldes.

Harrison Co. Court House - 8th day of October 1831-
Estate Settlement of James Hyde-deceased.
Jacob Hardman, Adm. of Peter Hardman, deceased, who was Adm. of James Hyde-deceased.

Due to amount of sale bill	$161.08 ½
To note and bonds	78.84
To interest on the above amount	137.58
Total amount	$377.50 ½

Credit the above
1. receipt from Widow (Catharine Hardman Hyde Waggoner)　74.97
2. receipt from Daniel Hyde　66.04
3. receipt from Isaac Hyde　41.00
4. receipt from Jacob H. Bonnett　42.18 ½
5. receipt from Charlathy Bonnett　5.00
6. receipt from John Hyde　83.25
7. to Jonathan Wamsby - alt.　10.00
8. to Thomas Hacker, for two days　2.00
   Setting the estate at $1.00 per day

Here we have proof of the 4 children of James Jr. and Catharine (Hardman) Hyde.

Elizabeth Hardman (ca 1772 -6 Jan. 1861) Warren Co. Ohio d/o Peter and Charlotte (Lazier) Hardman m. 7 May 1792, Harrison Co. (W) Va. Cabel Smith (26 July 1771-13 Aug. 1857) Warren Co. Ohio (some records say 1851) s/o David and Lydia (Ball) Smith (credit Robert B. Smith H. C. J. Jan. 1983 see Vol. -11- #3) also (D.A.R. - Vol. 1 pg. 624- N.J.)

It is interesting to note here The David Smiths originated in New Jersey. In New Jersey Marriage Records (1665-1800), we find many spellings of Lezier (Lashier, Laeser) this is the largest number of people of the family (Lizier), in the Schraellenburgh Reformed (Dutch) Church. in Bergen Co. N.J. I also found Lydia Hacker m. Israel Phillips - 23 Feb. 1773-Christ Church (m. rec. pg 621- N. J. M. Records by Nelson) Cabel Smith was a cainer of chairs, (to day almost a lost art). Some of their children: Elizabeth, Mary, Peter, Catharine, John, David, Caleb, Nancy and Susanna Smith.

Peter Hardman Jr. (23 July 1776 Hardy Co. Va., d 29 July 1859 Landen, Madison Co. Ohio) s/o Peter and Charlotte (Lazier) Hardman. He married (1st) 31 Aug. 1797 Harrison Co. (W) Va.(Bk. 1 -pg 12) Marget (Margaret) Hacker (27 Dec. 1776, Hacker's Creek d. 20 July 1815 Greene Co. Ohio), d/o John and Margaret (Steeth) Hacker.

Harrison Co. Deed Bk. #8 pg 371

18 June 1808-Peter and Margaret Hardman of Harrison Co. Va. to George Arnold of some 240 acres-Hackers Creek -corner to John Davis-Recorded June 1808
Signed Peter Hardman and Margaret (X) Hacker
18 June 1808 Peter and Margaret Hardman of Harrison Co. Va. to John Mitchel, of same for $300.00 119 acres Jesse's Run, a fork of Hackers Creek. Recorded June 1808
Signed Peter and Margaret (X) Hardman.

They must have left for Ohio some time in 1808 or 1809 after they sold the land.. Peter was a blacksmith, a gun smith, as well as a farmer. After Margaret died in 1815 in Ohio he married 26 Oct. 1815- Greene Co. Ohio, Mrs. Sarah (Adams) Edge (28 Aug. 1786-28 Nov. 1875-

ae 89y. 3m. 1d.) buried Mitman Cemetery, Fairborn, Ohio. (Sarah's husband died in the 1812 War in Ohio).

Border warfare - pg. 377-378 - 5 Dec. 1787

"A party of Indians and one white man (Leonard Schoolcraft) came into the Hacker's Creek Settlement meeting a d/o Jesse Hughes, took her prisoner, soon incountered old Edmond West Sr. he was killed. They went to the house of Edmond West Jr. (who had married (9 Feb. 1787, Mary Ann Hacker) where Mrs. West and her sister (Margaret age 11 dau. of John Hacker) and a lad of twelve a brother of West. Forcing open the door Schoolcraft and two of the savages entered killing Mrs. West and the boy. The girl standing behind the door, was struck a blow that knocked her down. She lay as she fell; and they, thinking her dead, took from the press, milk, butter and bread and set down at the table to eat. After eating they prepared to leave, scalping both the women and boy, plundering the house, emptying the feathers to carry off the ticking, and departed dragging the little girl by the hair 40 or 50 yards from the house, then they scalped her and threw her over a fence. Schoolcraft observed her evinced symptoms of life and yelled 'that is not enough' whereby one savage thrust a knife into her side. Fortunately the point of the knife came in contact with a rib, otherwise she would surely have been killed.

Later the little girl (Hacker's daughter) was found in bed at the house of old Mr. West. She related the story and said she had hid in a fallen tree until morning, than walked to Mr. West house. She recovered, and married Peter Hardman in 1797."

Peter Hardman, m. 1797, Margaret Hacker, d/o John Hacker. Peter Hardman & Margaret (Hacker) Hardman, had 10 children. Their children were:

1. Sarah Hardman, (16 Sept. 1798), m. 12 Apr. 1817, Greene Co. Ohio, William Ellensworth.

2. Catherine Hardman, (16 Sept. 1799 ?) m. Manley Richards Pendleton, Ind.

3. Joe (John) Hardman, (20 Jan. 1800), m. Amelia Sleeth.

Please credit Eleanor Womer of Wichita, Ks. with the extended Henry Hardman line.

4. Henry Hardman, (10 Mar. 1801), Harrison Co. (W) Va. s/o Peter & Margaret (Hacker) Hardman m. 29 Nov. 1821, Greene Co. Ohio, Mary Searle. Their children; Cain, Silas, Cynthia, and Cardes.

- Cordis Hardman (29 Apr. 1825-Clark Co. Ohio, 25 Jan. 1876, Cedar Co. Iowa), m. 10 Apr. 1845. Sarah Ann Wise, (10 Mar. 1827, Union Co. Pa. - 6 July 1909, Mallard, Iowa).
  - ♦ Their son Nathaniel Marion Hardman, (5 Feb. 1846, Cedar Co., Iowa-22 Sept. 1882, Downs, Osborne Co. Ks.) m. 1 Jan. 1868, Ellen Willford, (26 Dec. 1851 Beloit, Green Co., Wisc.- 25 Mar. 1917-Rochester, Minn.)bur Downs, Ks.
    - ◊ Their daughter Leslye Hardman, (14 Jan. 1882, Downs, Osborne Co. Ks. 10 Aug. 1974, Phillipsburg, Ks.) m. 31 Mar. 1909 Leonard Edward Womer. (1 Aug. 1882 Smith Co. Ks., 24 Sept. 1971) Phillipsburg, Ks. s/o Sylvester Womer (22 Oct. 1848-9 Center Co. Pa. -8 Feb. 1926) Smith Center, Ks. m. 6 Feb. 1874, Franklin Co. Nebr., Margaret Fender Mithcell, (10 Feb. 1856, Paterson, N.J.- 28 Sept. 1943, Smith Center, Ks.

    This family gave land for the Womer Church and Womer Cemetery at Womer, Smith Co. Ks.

5. Jonathan Hardman (25 Jan. 1803-31 July 1876) Madison Co. Ohio m. Mary Arbogast d/o Peter & Sarah Arbogast.
6. Jacob Hardman (29 Apr. 1804-21 July 1886) South Bend, Indiana m. 26 Apr. 1832 Fairfield, Ohio, Sarah Woodward.
7. Elizabeth Hardman (14 Mar. 1806-28 Dec. 1878) Greene Co. Ohio m. 13 Mar. 1828-John Babcock.
8. Eliza Hardman (25 Feb. 1808-16 Aug. 1849) Greene Co. Ohio m. (1st) James Maxon.
9. Margaret Hardman (20 Mar. 1809-27 July 1847) Ohio m. Obediah Edge.
10. Nelson Hardman (13 Jan. 1813) m. 1836 Clark Co. Ohio Littlie J. Hempleman.

Peter Hardman (1776-1859) m. (2nd) 26 Oct. 1815, Greene Co. Ohio Mrs. Sarah Adams Edge (widow) -(b.28 Aug. 1786, Blountsville Sullivan Co. Tenn. d. 28 Nov. 1875) Greene Co. Ohio (Mr. Edge died in the 1812 War) They had 2 sons: George D. Edge, and Jesse Edge -- Peter Waggoner adopted both of them.

Children of 2nd marriage:

11. Martha Hardman (3 Aug. 1816) m. Owen D. Mills.

12. Stephen Hardman (20 Aug. 1818) Greene Co. Ohio m. 24 Mar. 1843 Margaret Steward.
13. Delilah Hardman (28 Mar. 1820-22 Apr. 1844) Greene Co. Ohio.
14. Charlotte Hardman (13 Feb. 1822) m. 5 Nov. 1845 George W. Looney.
15. Peter Ellis Hardman (1 Apr. 1824) m. (1st) 1 Dec. 1847, Maria Clayton, m. (2nd) Aletha Davis.
16. Nancy Jane Hardman (26 Oct. 1828).
17. William Roper Hardman (20 Apr. 1833-26 Dec. 1906) m. 10 Sept. 1857, Harriet Miller. ch.: W. M. Hardman, Chas. L. Hardman, Hattie Hardman, Lee Adam Hardman, and Della Hardman.

John Hardman (1777-1864) s/o Peter & Charlotte (Lazier) Hardman, m. Elizabeth Waggoner (1779-1854) (see John & Margaret (Bonnett) Waggoner)

Henry Hardman (1 May 1781-Md.-3 Oct. 1870) Lewis Co. W. Va. s/o Peter and Charlotte (Lazier), m. (1st) 27 Sept. 1808, Harrison Co. (W) Va. Elizabeth Hacker (1784-ca. 1813-4), d/o John & Margaret (Sleeth) Hacker. Henry married (2nd) Juliana A. Rhinehart (9 July 1793 July 1880-86 ys.) Lewis Co. W. Va. (b. Preston Co. (W) Va. Children of Henry and Elizabeth (Hacker) Hardman:

1. Charlotte Hardman (b. 3 Nov. 1809) m. 4 May 1829 Lewis Co. (W) Va. John Witzel.
2. John Dexter Hardman (11 Oct. 1811-25 Dec. 1871-age 59) m. 2 Feb. 1838, Lewis Co. (W) Va. by Henry R. Bonnett. m. Mary Life (8 Nov. 1813-28 July 1891-ae 80 y. 8 m. 20 d.) bur. Broad Run Cem. d/o John & Mary (Wimer) Life.
Some of their children:

- Mary Elizabeth Hardman b. 5 Oct. 1838 m. 28 Feb. 1877 John Livingston.
- Alcinda Hardman b. 14 Feb. 1840, m. 25 July 1863 George W. Goldsmith.
- Perry Green Hardman, (3 Mar. 1842-23 Sept. 1904) killed by a horse, m. 15 Jan. 1867 Laura Virginia Brake (6 May 1848-8 Oct. 1911) d/o Granville and Pamilia (Hall) Brake, bur. Mt. Hebron Cemetery.
- Henry Hardman (7 Dec. 1843-14 Sept. 1864) wounded, died from wound.-Civil War Co. P. 10th W. Va.

- George Washington Hardman, b 16 Oct. 1845, m. 21 Sept. 1873 Lewis Co., Matilda S. Lough, b. 1849, d/o George F. & Rachel (Wimer) Lough.
- Margaret Hardman b. 5 Mar. 1848 Lewis Co. m. 26 Dec. 1867 Lewis Co. Robert E. Depriest b 1841, s/o William A. and Louise A. Depriest.
- John Hardman b 9 June 1850.
- Louise Hardman (4 Jan. 1853-13 Oct. 1863).
- Amanda E. Hardman b. 17 May 1855 m. 28 Feb. 1877, John A. Conlin.

3. Margaret Hardman (14 Nov. 1813-15 Sept. 1900) d/o Henry and Elizabeth (Hacker) Hardman, m. 2 Mar. 1835 Lewis Co. (W) Va. David D. Whetsel (Witzel) (2 June 1804-27 Nov. 1882 ae 78 y. 5 m. 25 d.) s/o George & Rebecca Whitsel. Both Bur. Hardman Family Cemetery-Stone Coal, Lewis Co.

Some of their children:

- Henry Bivan Witzel b. 26 Mar. 1836 Stone Coal Lewis Co., m. 11 Mar. 1858 Lewis Co., Emily J. Clark, b. 18 Aug. 1837 d/o John and Margaret (Bonnett) Clark.
- Rheuhana Witzel b. May 1838 Stone Coal Lewis Co., m 5 June 1859 Lewis Co., Zachariah Taylor Tillman (b. 4 Feb. 1833-d. 22 Oct. 1906) s/o Thomas W. and Teresa Tillman.
- Julia A. Witzel, b. Oct. 1841 m. ca 1881 Ephran A. Berry.
- Marietta Witzel (b. ca 1845) m. 15 Aug. 1865-Richard Dean.
- Mariah L. Witzel, (b. Oct. 1846) m. 4 Feb. 1871 Charles T. Cox.
- Alonza A. Witzel, (14 Nov. 1852-d. 29 Dec. 1853) Witzel Cemetery below Stone Coal Dam.

Henry Hardman (1 May 1781 - Md. 3 Oct. 1870), m. (2nd) 14 Apr. 1815 Harrison Co. Juliana Rhinehart

Some of their children:

4. Anna Mabia Hardman (29 May 1816-8 Feb. 1900 ae. 83 y.) (bur. Hardman Family Cemetery) d/o Henry and Juliana (Rinehart) Hardman.

5. Thomas R. Hardman (20 Jan. 1820-19 Dec. 1905) s/o Henry and Juliana (Rhinehart) Hardman m. 17 Apr. 1851 Lewis Co., Susan Elizabeth Sumner (20 June 1828-15 May 1897) d/o George and Elizabeth Sumner. Both Bur. in Hardman Family Cemetery.

Some of their children:

- Alonzo C. b. 4 May 1856-m. Rebecca Stalnaker.
- Diana V. b. 6 Sept. 1858 m. T. S. Taylor.
- Victoria D. b. 26 Sept. 1859,
- Charles G. (4 Sept. 1864-17 Feb. 1867).

6. Sarah Hardman 1821-1829, d/o Henry & Juliana (Rhinehart) Hardman.

7. Jacob Hardman, 1825-1829, s/o Henry & Juliana (Rhinehart) Hardman.

8. Sevilly Hardman, 1827-1828, d/o Henry & Juliana (Rhinehart) Hardman.

9. David Hardman (28 Oct. 1829-28 Sept. 1860 ae 30 Ys) s/o Henry and Juliana (Rhinehart) Hardman m. 27 Dec. 1855 Lewis Co. Harriet Clark (13 Mar. 1837-19 Feb. 1861) d/o Robert H. and Susannah (Rains) Clark.

   Some of their children:
   - Clinton M. b. 22 Oct. 1856.
   - Albert Jenkins b. 23 Aug. 1858 m. Martha F. Law.
   - Martha A. (1860-1861) Mt. Gilead/Georgetown Cem.

10. Louisa Hardman (31 may 1833-3 July 1904) d/o Henry and Juliana A. (Rhinehart) Hardman bur. Hardman Family Cem. Vol. 1 - pg 23.

Daniel Hardman (6 Nov. 1787-19 Jan. 1837 Morrow Co. Ohio) s/o Peter and Charlotte (Lazier) Hardman m. 9 June 1806 Harrison Co. (W) Va., Nancy Fowler (b 29 May 1788, d. 1876). They moved to Ohio around 1833.(*Lucy M. Weaver of Defiance, Ohio researched this line 1980*).

They had a large family, some of their children:

1. Sarah Hardman (1 Dec. 1809-Harrison Co., d. 1889 Van Wirt Co. Ohio) d/o Daniel and Nancy (Fowler) Hardman m. ca 1834 Marion Co., Ohio Job Foust.

2. Hanna Hardman (b. ca 1822 Harrison Co.) d/o Daniel and Nancy (Fowler) Hardman.

3. Abraham Hardman (25 Apr. 1825 Harrison Co.) s/o Daniel and Nancy (Fowler) Hardman m. (1st) Hanna Oliver m. (2nd) Eliza Rogers lived in Canaan twp., Morrow Co. Ohio.

   Gateway to the West by Bowers and Short Vol. 2-pg. 68.

22 July 1837- Will of Daniel Hardman:

Sale of land-subject to dower Nancy (Fowler) Hardman children - Sarah, Henry, John, Eleanor, David, Albert, Naomie, Nancy, Elizabeth & Abraham.

John & Margaret (Bonnett) Waggoner

John (Johannes) Waggoner, born 24 Nov. 1751 White Marsh, (Montgomery Co.) then Philadelphia Co. Pa., he was baptized 26th of Apr. 1752 at St. Michael's Evangelical Lutheran Church in Germantown, Pa. Son of Wilhelm and Agnesa Waggoner

I believe John married Margaret (Peggy) Bonnett on the South Branch, at her parents home on Cedar Creek Swamp, Hampshire Co. Va. in 1778. It had been eight years since Conrad Lutts death in 1770 and John had served some time in the Virginia Militia. They were at Drunkard Bottom on the Cheat River (now Preston Co. W. Va.) when their first child Elizabeth was born 5 Nov. 1779. This settlement is where the Witzels, Sixs, and Bonnetts had lived before they went farther west to the area around the present Wheeling, Va.

John Sicks (Six) always lived on Dunhard Bottom and would have been there in 1778-82 when John and Margaret (Bonnett) Waggoner first came. Their second daughter Mary was born on Dunkard Bottom, 9 Dec. 1780.

By 1782 we find John and Margaret (Bonnett) Waggoner living on Hacker's Creek, not far from her parents, Samuel and Mary Elizabeth Bonnett, and their family (that consisted of twelve children). Margaret had a younger sister Susannah b. in 1779 that would be the same age as her first child Elizabeth b. in the same year.

There are seven years between the birth of Mary, b. 9 Dec. 1780, and Peter Waggoner, who was born 13 Mar. 1787, so there must have been several children born in those years.

Both John and Margaret had known heartache and loss in their young lives. John had lost his father, Wilhelm Waggoner, his sister Mary, and only Brother Peter to an Indian raid on the South Branch.

His mother Agnes Waggoner married Conrad Lutts, who died in 1770. Even though we have record of Peter returning to the family he did not stay.

Perhaps this is why John and Margaret named their children Elizabeth and Mary after his two older sisters and Peter after his only brother. Of course, Margaret's mother Mary Elizabeth Bonnett, could have also influenced the girls names. Peter certainly was named after John's older brother, who was Johannes Peter named in Conrad Lutts Verbal will of 1770.

Margaret lost her older brother, John Bonnett (ca. 1764-1787) who was killed by Indians in Sept. of 1787, Both Border Warfare (pg. 377) and Border Settlers (pg. 42) agree on the year 1787. Two years later, Margaret lost her father Samuel Bonnett (ca. 1734-1789) in Dec. 1789, killed by a fallen tree; leaving her mother a widow with nine children, the youngest ten years old. Her mother married for a second time John Mack-(9 Jan. 1790). Life could not have been easy on Hacker's Creek for the young couple living on Jesses Run. By 1792 they had seven children and Margaret was expecting their eight child. We know the names of three children Elizabeth, Mary and Peter. If I could hazard a guess the other four children could have been named, John, William, Samuel, and Lewis.

Wither's Chronicles of Border Warfare- (pg. 408 to 411) with notes from L. V. McWhorter.

The Waggoner Massacre by Gen. Tecumseh and several of his party of savages, is told in a very factual way.

"About the middle of May (7th) 1792, a party of savages came upon a branch of Hacker's Creek, Jesse's Run, more than two miles above its junction with Hacker's Creek."

John Waggoner, engaged in burning logs in his clearing, he was sitting upon a log, with a handspike laying across his lap.

Tecumseh, having sent the rest of his companions on to the house to make sure of those in the house, placed his gun on the fence and fired deliberately at John. It was thought that Tecumseh mistook his tool for a gun and was nervous. Tecumseh was but thirty paces from Waggoner when he fired, and it is singular that he missed for John was a large man in fair view. Waggoner sprang up and started for his cabin, a short distance only, but when about fifteen yards away saw an Indian chasing one of his children around the cabin, being unarmed, and his gun was in the cabin he feared to enter, so ran for help to the cabin of a neighbor Peter Hardman. But Hardman was out hunting with their guns.

In the mean time, those who had been left to operate against those of the family who were at the cabin, finding a small boy in the yard, killed and scalped him; and then making prisoners of Mrs. Waggoner and six of her children, and departing immediately with them, lest the escape of her husband, should lead to their instant pursuit.

About a mile from the cabin, one of the children was found, badly beaten and scalped. A little farther on lay Mrs. Waggoner and two more of her children, their lifeless bodies mangled in the most barbarous and shocking manner. Having thus freed themselves from the principal impediments to a rapid retreat.

This happened on a Monday evening, the Indians knew the lay of the land well, as once in an earlier time the Indians had camped on Hacker's Creek, and it was said Tecumseh had been born on Hacker's Creek, possibly at a village near the mouth of Jesses run. Years later Tecumseh was said to have visited there and told the whites of his experiences in connection with the Waggoner Massacre. (pg. 411) They killed four small boys and Mrs. Margaret Waggoner who was expecting her eighth child soon. Escaping with Elizabeth age 13 yrs., Mary 12 yrs. and Peter about six years.

Jesse Hughes carried the news into the Fort and a rescue party set out at once. Henry McWhorter helped to carry the bodies to the Fort where they were buried at West Fort near Lane Lew.

A rescue party immediately hastened to the Waggoner place and started in pursuit of the Indians.

The rescue party, under the guidance of West and Hughes pressed the Indians hard. The Whites pursued them to the mouth of Kinchelo Creek, where night coming on, and finding that the Indians were out traveling them, the chase was abandoned.

In later years the children who were taken captive, related after their return, that during the rapid retreat from the scene of blood, both Indians and prisoners had no food of any sort until after they has gained the fastness of the wilderness beyond the Ohio River. Here the Indians killed a deer and roasted venison. Peter declared that even in his famished condition the meat "tasted like rotten wood" (because of the absence of salt) (Border Settlers pg 461)

Tecumseh visited Hacker's Creek after the Treaty of Greenville, and in a conversation with a Miss Mitchell told practically the same story. He also said they had been watching the Waggoner family for some time, waiting until the children were large enough to travel.

John Waggoner not only lost his father, sister and brother due to an Indian massacre on the South Branch, but about 28 years later loses his wife and seven children in a second Indian massacre.

John Waggoner had only his wife's family near him in the next three years, they must have been some very trying years for him not knowing if Elizabeth, Mary or Peter were alive. The eldest girl Elizabeth and another captive Sally Johnson escaped to Detroit, where they found a home with a Mr. Sisney. Some time during 1795 he took Elizabeth to her Uncle Lewis Bonnett in Wheeling, who returned her to her father John Waggoner on Jesses Run.

At a County Court on 19 May 1795 for Harrison County; John Hacker, Jacob Cozad and John Waggoner came into ask the court to lend their aid to assist them in the application to apply for certain persons captured by the Indians at the Greenville Treaty held by Gen. Wayne June 1795.

The Peace Treaty was finally signed on Aug. 7-1795 and the various tribes were directed to bring in and surrender all white captive in their possession to Gen. Wayne ((pg. 121) H/o Harrison Co. by Haymond). Some of the Cozad and Waggoner children were recovered. This is how John Waggoner got his second daughter Mary back, after three years.

Peter Waggoner was not heard from until the war of 1812, some twenty years later, when he was seen and bearing a strong resemblance of features to his father, was recognized as Waggoner's captive son and a Mr. Baker sent word to John Waggoner.

John Waggoner and his son-in-law John Hardman went to visit Peter on Paint Creek, a tributary of the Scioto River. Peter was married to an Indian woman and had two small daughters. "Finally he was enticed to return home if only for a visit, and when it was time for Peter to return to his Indian family, his relatives kept him under guard and then he feared returning as he had broken his word".

The 1910 printing of <u>The History of Harrison Co., (W) Va.</u>, by Henry Haymond, (pg. 120-126), gives a clear picture of the problems in Harrison Co. in 1792 May 5,-- A letter to Henry Lee, Governor from George Jackson asking for Scouts for Harrison Co. for protection against Indian raids.

"Col. Wm. Lowther writes to the Governor from Clarksburg, dated 5 May 1792 accepting the Military Commission forwarded to him and stated that he had organized his Company, but is afraid that on account of the low rate of pay allowed them and the difficulty of procuring provisions, he will have to discharge them." He further says: "We have every reason to expect a very troublesome summer. There has been frequent discoveries already made of the approach of the enemy and much mischief done in the neighboring counties."

Of all the Books that mention the Waggoner Massacre; <u>Chronicles of Border Warfare</u> by Alexander Scott Withers, first published in 1895 by The Robert Clark Company of Cincinnati.; gives a fairly accurate description of the massacre and in agreement with other references. L. V. McWhorter added his version to the local tradition of the affair, "Henry McWhorter helped to carry the bodies to the Fort. (West's Fort in Jane Lew).

<u>Border Settlers of Northwestern Virginia</u> by Lucullus Virgil McWhorter in 1915 Published in Hamilton, Ohio has a similar report agreeing on some things, and disagreeing on others.

In comparing the three references, one has to collect these facts. The Waggoner family, John and Margaret (Bonnett) Waggoner, Margaret was expecting her eighth child, Elizabeth-the oldest was over 12 yrs by a 6 months, born 5 Nov. 1779 captured 7 May 1792. From the <u>Hardman Scrapbook at the Historical Society of Philadelphia, Pa.-Me 59</u> pg. 33-Re Elizabeth (Waggoner) Hardman. states, "Elizabeth was carried to an Indian town on the Maumie River, put up for sale and bought by a Squaw, who treated her cruelly. Tecumseh threatened the Squaw for her cruelty and was always kind to the prisoner."

In 1793 Gen. Wayne began a war against the Indians. The latter (Indians) left their camp where Elizabeth was held and she and Sallie Johnson, another captive girl, escaped to Detroit, where they found a home with a Mr. Sisney, until after the treaty in 1795, when he took Elizabeth to her Uncle, Lewis Bonnett in Wheeling who returned her to her father.

It is difficult to extract the data from the Scrapbook on these families, Hardman, Bonnett and Waggoner, that Blanche Maybury Carson submitted to the Researcher she had hired in Philadelphia, Pa. to research her line. From the material added on the Waggoner line by the researcher around Oct. 1910, lacked proof and referances.

The line for Blanche Maybury m. Dr. Edwin Carson d/o Hiram Maybury and Josephine Hardman Gd/o Jacob Wolf Hardman and Maria Rodman, GGd/o Rev. John Hardman and Elizabeth Waggoner, GGGd/o John Waggoner and Mary Bonnett.

Perhaps because Elizabeth wasn't returned to her Father, John Waggoner, until after the signing of the Greenville Treaty in 1795, they mixed her up with her sister Mary who was returned at the Treaty signing, in 1795 when her father and others appeared to claim children. Mary was 11 years and 4 months old when she came home. It would seem that none of the children were together after capture.

The Scrapbook listed the family of John and Margaret (Bonnett) Waggoner naming only 3 children. Remember this history must have been related by Elizabeth (Waggoner) Hardman (the Captive) first son. John Wolf Hardman, to his children and they to their children, because Blanche Maybury Carson was a 3rd Great, Grandchild of Rev. John and Elizabeth(Waggoner) Hardman. Peter Waggoner b. 1787 was just over 5 years. Some of the other children killed were surely older than Peter.

This Scrapbook contained letters to Mrs. Carson and copies of information sent, plus receipts for time spent in researching; very little of the researched was correct.

Once the birth and death dates were found, many of the above facts came out. But each and every article written about their lives, held some truths and help complete what picture we have of their times and lives.

There are several versions of Peter Waggoner's story and they can be found in <u>Border Settlers of Northwestern Virginia</u> by McWharter (pg 197 to 204). <u>Border Warfare</u> by Alexander Scott Withers (pg. 408 to 411) <u>History of Harrison Co. W. Va.</u> by Henry Haymond (pg. 121 - 122).

There are so many stories of Peter Waggoner and his return that I hesitate to chose any one of them. One has to remember life was very different then and this would have been a horrid experience for anyone to have lived through. There is little doubt all these people suffered greatly and this part of their life certainly had a great effect on their life. So many stories, told by so many people down through each generation and here again some two hundred years later, it is being retold again.

John Waggoner deeded each daughter, Elizabeth and Mary acres (pieces) of land upon their marriage.

Mary Waggoner, (b 9 Dec. 1780 on Dunkard Bottom, Monongalia Co. (W) Va., d. 7 June 1871 age 90 y. 5 m. 28), bur. Polk Cem. W. Va.) second d/o John and Margaret (Bonnett) Waggoner. Mary was returned to her father, John Waggoner at the Greenville Treaty signing 3 Aug. 1795. She returned home to her sister Elizabeth (who had recently been returned by her Uncle Lewis Bonnett), and her father, a home with out her mother and five small brothers (Peter did not return until 1812). Elizabeth married some three years later, her father married some four years later, his second marriage to Susannah Richards in 1799. Mary married the 15 Apr. 1800, Jacob Wolf Jr. (1778-ca. 1840), s/o Jacob Wolf Sr. (1755-1823 and Anna Straley. (no issue) Book I.(pg. 14) Mary Wolf, b. 9 Dec. 1780, d. 7 June 1871-age 90y. 5m. 28d. of old age, Parents John and Peggy Waggoner; Husband Jacob Wolf death reported by brother Henry Waggoner (half brother).

The first Old Harmony Church on Old Berlin Road, Lewis Co. W. Va.

Elizabeth (Waggoner) Hardman

Elizabeth Waggoner (5 Nov. 1779-1 Feb. 1854 ae 74 y.) d/o John and Margaret (Bonnett) Waggoner. (captured 7 May 1792, returned 1795). She married the 21st of Nov. 1798 Harrison Co. (W) Va. John Hardman (7 Oct. 1777-9 May 1864) (who we will refer to as Rev. John Hardman in the future), s/o Peter and Charlotta Larsier (Lazier) Hardman. (See The Hardman Family records..)

The Marriage Bond-Book I page 310.

> Know all men by these present: That we, John Hardman and Elijah Runyon, both of the County of Harrison, and the state of Virginia, are held and firmly bound to James Wood, Chief Magistrate of this commission in the first and full sum of $150.00 to the payment and truely to the _____ and _____.
>
> We have our _____ one _____ execution and administration firmly by those present. _____ our hand and sealed this 10th day of Nov. 1798 of 22 years of the Commonwealth.
>
> The condition of the above obligation is such that should there be no lawful cause to obstain said John Hardman marriage with Elizabeth Waggoner, d/o John Waggoner of the said county.
>
> The above obligation to be void otherwise to remain in full force and value.
>
> 26 Nov. 1798
> John (X) Hardman
> Elijah (O) Runyon
>
> Sir: There are to request you to grant unto John Hardman, Licence to get married, as therefor certified that I am fully satisfied and compliance will oblige, Your Hum(ble) Ser(t) First-Peter Hardman
>
> John (X) Waggoner

> Elijah Runyon affirmed he saw John Wagoner set his ;mark to this Certificate.   Benj. Wilson

John would have been 21 yr. old and Elizabeth 18 yr.

Rev. John and Elizabeth (Waggoner) Hardman lived at the mouth of Curtis Run on Little Skin Creek, Lewis Co. (W) Va. all their lives and had a family of 13 children, two died in infancy, the first and fourth child.

Harrison Co. (W) Va. Deed Book (1785-1810) pg. 269, 17 Oct. 1803 (pg. 338) "Maxwill and Catharine Armstrong of Harrison Co. Va., to John Hardman of same for $10.00 - 100 acres, left hand fork of Skin Creek. Signed, Maxwill Armstrong and Catharine Armstrong. Recorded, Oct. 1803."

1. Jacob Wolf Hardman, (7 June 1801 - 25 Apr. 1874 or 1876 Louisville, Ky., s/o Rev. John and Elizabeth (Waggoner) Hardman, m. Marion Rodman (6 July 1806-20 Oct. 1874 in Louisville Ky.) There are Rodmans in Rockingham Co. in 1810 -- Alexander Rodman.

   Some of their children:

   Credit: The Hardman Genealogy by Paul Hardman, of Charleston W. Va., who compiled the works of Samuel J. Hardman and Wm. Edward Hardman, his cousin, through years of correspondence.

   Sarah, Laura H., Marian, and Josephine Hartman who m. Hiram Mayberry and their daughter Blanche Mayberry, m. Dr. Edwin Carson; thus the research in the Pa. Historical Soc. Me-59 - pg. 33- Hardman Scrapbook.

2. Henry (Dexter) Hardman (19 Feb. 1803-24 Dec. 1886 ae 83 y. 10 m. 5 d.) Vandalia Cem. s/o Rev. John and Elizabeth (Waggoner) Hardman m. 30 Mar. 1826 Lewis Co. Mary West (26 Dec. 1807-22 May 1871, ae 63 y. 4 m. 26 d.) Skin Creek, d/o Charles West and May McLaughton (People of Vandalia, by Sam W. Hardman 1928). This record, found in Harrison Co. m. (probably is the correct m. date) "16 Mar. 1807-Charley West m. Jane McGloughlin d/o James & Mary McGlaughlin m. by John Davis."

   No matter how hard one tries, mistakes happen -- they call it a human error. I found a James McLaughlin in Harrison Co., in 1810 Census. The 1850 Census shows Charles West ae 64 yr. living with his family (but no wife in the home) on a farm next door, Henry D. Hardman, and Mary (West) Hardman.

Their children:

- Matilda J. Hardman (2 Apr. 1827-31 Mar. 1883 ae 55 yr.) Vandalia Cem. Lewis Co. d/o Henry D. & Mary (West) Hardman, m. 4 Jan. 1854 Martin Hyre (1832-1864 ae 54 y. 11 m. 29 d.) s/o Noah and Catharine (Kesting) Hyre.
- Marcellus L. Hardman (28 Aug. 1829-16 July 1894) Vandalia Cem. (Bk. 2 pg. 140) s/o Henry D. & Mary (West) Hardman m. 19 Jan. 1854, Upsher Co. Mahala A. Hyre (Sept. 1835-d. 1920) Vandalia Cem.
- Mary Elizabeth Hardman (1832-17 Oct. 1895) ae. 63 yr. Harrison Co. d/o Henry D. and Mary (West) Hardman m. Cornelius Gribble, lived Lost Creek. (People of Vandalia).

3. Samuel Baxter Hardman (1805-1891) Tazewell Co. Ill, s/o Rev. John and Elizabeth (Waggoner) Hardman m. Margt (Margaret) Bonnett, d/o Peter & Margaret (Linger) Bonnett. Samuel B. m/2 Mrs. Mary Shurtoff in Tazewell Co. Ill.

Child of 1st m.:

- Salathiel B. Hardman (6 Apr. 1834-17 May 1908) Lewis Co. s/o Samuel Baxter and Margaret (Bonnett) Hardman m. 21 Apr. 1859 Lewis Co. (Bk. 7-pg. 263) Rebecca A. McNeamer (4 Mar. 1836-15 Jan. 1917) d/o William and Elizabeth (Liloy) McNeamer.

    Their children:

    - Edgar Bruce Hardman b.24 Feb. 1858, m. Sarah Butcher.
    - Cora Adaline Hardman b. 17 Feb. 1860, m. David B. Casto.
    - Samuel W. Hardman b. 2 Apr. 1866, n.m.
    - Margaret Lilly Hardman, Aug. 1870, m. James West.

4. Thomas M. Hardman b. ca 1807-s/o Rev. John and Elizabeth (Waggoner) Hardman, m. 30 Sept. 1831 Lewis Co. Rebecca Clark d/o William Clark. They moved to Marion Co. Ohio.

5. William Hardman, (1809-1840) s/o Rev. John and Elizabeth (Waggoner) Hardman. I believe he moved to Dayton, Ohio, was a dentist.; some records say he died in an accident with a runaway horse and buggy in Lexington, Ky.

6. Joshua W. Hardman (1811-1893 ae 82 yr.) Big Skin Creek, Lewis Co. s/o Rev. John & Elizabeth (Waggoner) Hardman, m. 15 July

1834, Shenandoah Co. Va. (m. pg. 110) Susan Foltz (1816-1885 ae 69 y.) b. Shenandoah Co. Va., d/o Joshua Foltz (half-sister to Reganah Foltz who m. 5 Dec. 1812 David Witsel of Shenandoah Co.) (Foltz or Fultz).

Some of their children:

- Elizabeth Hardman (3 Apr. 1835-18 Nov. 1856-ae. 21y.) d/o Joshua W. & Susan (Foltz) Hardman.
- John Columbus Hardman, (1 Dec. 1835(?)-22 Sept. 1893) Vandalia Cem. Lewis Co. s/o Joshua W. & Susan (Foltz) Hardman, m.(1st) 18 Feb. 1858 Lewis Co. Dafina Spaur (12 Aug. 1839-19 Nov. 1875-ae. 36 y. 7 m. 7 d.) d/o Anthony R. & Sarah (Bonnett) Spaur, m.(2nd) Nancy Spaur (sister of Dafina) (4 children).

Children:

- ◆ Sarah Matelda Hardman (4 July 1859-16 June 1892 ae 32 y.) Bk. 2nd.-147.
- ◆ Jacob Hardman (1860-1936 ae. 76 y.) Illinois.
- ◆ Joseph Hardman b 29 Apr. 1861-m. 1st Eva Corathers, m. 2nd Dora Winemiller, Weston, Lewis Co. W. Va.
- ◆ Virginia Hardman (1 Sept. 1863) Illinois.
- ◆ Nathan Hardman (1864) m. Mattie Corathers.
- ◆ Mary (Molly) Hardman (1866) Wisconsin.
- ◆ John Hardman (1867) Mamie Malia, Colorado.
- ◆ Nancy Hardman (1868).
- ◆ Anthony Hardman (27 Sept. 1869-12 June 1941) Lewis Co., m. (1st) Francis Winemiller, (2nd) m Bertie Snyder.
- ◆ Marshall Hardman -(ca 1871) Bloomington, Ill.
- ◆ Able Hardman (29 May 1872-1937) m. Matilda Linger.

- Mary Hardman, b. 1840, d/o Joshua W. & Susan (Foltz) Hardman m. _____ Stalnaker. She is mentioned in Me 59-pg. 31 "Mary H. (d/o Joshua H.) Stalnaker confirms. John Waggoner was a private in the Rev. War, married 1st Mary Bonnett, 2nd Richards."
- Ann Hardman (1838-6 Sept. 1880) ae 42 yr., d/o Joshua W. and Susan (Foltz) Hardman, m. 8 June 1865 Lewis Co. Edward H. Ballard.
- Samuel Hardman, s/o Joshua W. and Susan (Foltz) Hardman went west.
- David Hardman, s/o Joshua W. and Susan (Foltz) Hardman went west.

- Rebecca Hardman b ca 1846- d/o Joshua W. & Susan (Foltz) Hardman.
- Melvenia Hardman (1849-8 Apr. 1855 ae 8 y.) Lewis Co.
- Joshua A. Hardman Jr b 6 Mar. 1853, s/o Joshua W. and Susan (Folts) Hardman.
- Valentine E. Hardman, b. 24 Apr. 1856 Lewis Co., s/o Joshua W. and Susan (Folts) Hardman.
- Ida Hardman 20 Jan. 1855 d/o Joshua W. and Susan (Foltz) Hardman.
- Imogene H. Hardman b. 1860-1939 Mt. Gilead, d/o Joshua W. & Susan (Foltz) Hardman, m. Minter L. Stalnaker (1852-1939) s/o Bailey and Mary (Peterson) Stalnaker.

7. Elizabeth Hardman (24 June 1813-4 Sept. 1855 ae 42) Mt. Gilead or Georgetown Cem only d/o Rev. John and Elizabeth (Waggoner) Hardman m. 10 Oct. 1833 Lewis Co. Jacob W. Hudson (6 Dec. 1811-Shenandoah Co. Va. d. 9 Dec. 1901 ae 90 y.) Mt. Gilead Cem. only s/o Jacob Hudson (dec) and Mrs. Regina (Foltz) Hudson Wetzel. Mrs. Reginia (Foltz) Hudson (8 Sept. 1790-8 Aug. 1850) Lewis Co. m. 5 Dec. 1812-Shenandoah Co. Va. David Wetzel Sr.

Jacob W. Hudson was sheriff of Lewis Co. (W) Va. and a Union sympathizer, and later in life a minister he m. (2nd) Pernillia (Watson) Jackson, 21 June 1860.

Children of Jacob W. & Elizabeth (Hardman) Hudson:

- Parthena Hudson (28 Aug. 1834-19 Apr. 1891 ae 56 y. 7 m. 12 d.) McCue Town Cem. m. 20 Dec. 1855 Lewis Co. Charles Franklin McCue (1832-6 June 1892 ae 61 y. 5 m.8 d.) s/o William B. and Frances McCue (nee. Winebarger) Their children: Elizabeth F., Mary A., Martha J., William H. m. Arthela Waggoner, John F. m. Fidella Gould, Arminta A., George W., and Alice McCue.
- Almina (Elmira) Hudson (27 Oct. 1839-21 July 1919-ae 79 y.), m. 5 Nov. 1867 Lewis Co., Andrew Lunsford, b. May 1847. Almina (Hudson) Lunsford-died in a Baltimore hospital where she had gone for treatment, bur. Machpelah Cem. Their children: Dora B., William O., Andrew Jackson and Commodore Perry Lunsford.
- Matilda Hudson (8 Aug. 1844-15 Aug. 1910) Mt. Gilead, m. 1 Aug. 1865 Lewis Co., Ellis Lee Smith (1843-1924) s/o Martin J. and Margaret (Talbott) Smith. Some of their children: Clarence,

Flavilla F., Margaret, Jacob, Ellis Lee Jr., Myrtle, Hugh, Grace, and Esta Smith.
- Commodore Perry Hudson (21 June 1837-1879) ae. 42 y. 2 m. 10 d. accident in Florida, m. Hellen C._____.
- William Worth Hudson (twin) born (22 Oct. 1848-25 Oct. 1872 ae 24 y. 3 d.) Mt. Gilead.
- George Washington Hudson (twin) born (22 Oct. 1848-25 Oct. 1872 ae 24 y. 3 d.) Mt. Gilead.
- Marion Hudson (14 Apr. 1842-27 Nov. 1848 ae 6 yr. 6 m. 7 d.).

Children of the (2nd) m. of Jacob W. Hardman to Parmalia (Watson) Jackson:

- Regina Victoria Hudson (9 Aug. 1861-1886) m. David A. Rohrbough.
- Ilasca Hudson b Jan. 1866- m. Floyd O. Smith.
- Thomas J. Hudson.
- Hosea M. Hudson.

The 1870 c. of Lewis Co. also shows the following children (perhaps they were the children of Parmalia's first m. 21 Oct 1850 to Jacob J. Jackson) ch.:

- Margaret D. Jackson ae 17 y.
- George W. Jackson ae 19 y.
- Cecilice B. Jackson ae 15 y.

8. Peter Jamison Hardman (1819-ca 1891) s/o Rev. John and Elizabeth (Waggoner) Hardman m. in Indiana, Hannah C. Finley. (Served Civil War).

9. John G. Hardman (2 May 1817-10 Nov. 1897) bur. Fall Run, Braxton Co. W. Va. (Green Hill Cem.) s/o Rev. John & Elizabeth (Waggoner) Hardman m. 23 Dec. 1838 Lewis Co. Malinda Forenash (15 Mar. 1822-8 Apr. 1884) d/o Jacob Sr. & Catharine (Kritz) Forenash. Around 1866 to Braxton Co. (W) Va.

Some of their children:

- Jacob M. Hardman (12 July 1840-23 Aug. 1887).
- William Henry Hardman (20 Mar. 1842-ca. 1864) Civil War-31 Va. Infantry under "Stonewall" Jackson, taken prisoner, died in Federal Prison at Point Lookout, (served in Confederate Army 1st as Imobdeno's Command).
- Martha Ann Hardman (29 Aug. 1844-20 Aug. 1883) m. 24 Dec. 1863 Lewis Co. James M. Morrison.

- Mary Elizabeth Hardman (12 July 1846-21 May 1882 ae 36 y. 10 m. 9 d.) Alkire Braggs Cem. Braxton Co. W. Va. (Vol. 1 pg. 128-Lewis Co. Cem.) m. 3 Oct. 1867 Lewis Co. William S. Heck.
- Cynthia J. Hardman (26 Mar. 1848)   ) m. 11 Mar. 1868 Braxton Co. W. Va.(pg. 22) William D. Forenash b. 25 Nov. 1848 s/o Isaac and Millie Ann (Plant) Forenash.
- Perry Worthington Hardman b. 27 June 1850 Lewis Co. m. 16 Mar. 1870 Braxton Co. W. Va. (pg. 55) Mary Melessa Berry b. 16 Nov. 1853-Upsher Co. d/o William D. and Hannah Loverna (McCray) Berry.
- Samuel M. Hardman MD. b 9 Nov. 1852 Lewis Co. m. 14 Sept. 1871 Lewis Co. Mary E. Cummings (divorced) m. 2nd Dora Propst.
- Margaret M. Hardman (27 May 1855-13 Sept. 1906) m. 6 Mar. 1873 Lewis Co. H. R. Morrison.
- Hanna Matilda Hardman (20 Oct. 1857-18 May 1886).
- Catharine V. Hardman (17 Apr. 1861-14 Mar. 1882).
- Sarah Ella Hardman b. 18 Sept. 1863.
- John C. Hardman b 28 June 1866- d. 1866).

10. Daniel Hardman b. 1822 and 11. David Hardman b. 1826 both died the same day, of diphtheria in middle childhood and are buried on a hillside near Georgetown Schoolhouse.

Peter Waggoner (1787-1879)
son of John and Margaret (Bonnett) Waggoner

Peter Waggoner

Peter Waggoner (15 Mar. 1787 - 26 Mar. 1879) s/o John and Margaret (Bonnett) Waggoner.

From all the histories, stories and family stories told over the past 200 years, here I am adding another version. Peter was one of seven children when the massacre occurred. He was just over six years old, saw four of his brothers, and his mother killed. Even though children matured earlier in pioneer days, he was still a very young child to experience this horror. The escape from Hacker's Creek to Ohio must have been a long hard trip for the three children, especially for one as small as Peter. I can only imagine the horrid scene these young children had to undergo and the effect it had on them. The children were separated, and Peter was adopted by a squaw who had lost her own child. Forced into a totally new and foreign mode of living, he grew to young manhood living with the Indians.

Peter eventually married to an Indian woman and it is said he had two children by her. They were living in an Indian Village on Paint Creek, a tributary of the Scioto River in Ross Co. Ohio, where a Mr. Baker, from the Hacker's Creek Region, saw Peter and recognized him from his resemblance to John Waggoner, his father. Once the news reached John Waggoner, he and his son-in-law John Hardman, traveled to the Indian Village to get Peter to come home. After much talking Peter agreed to make a visit home to Hacker's Creek -- his Indian wife sensed that she would never see him again. When the time came to return to the Indian camp, Peter was held captive by his family, until much time had passed. An Indian woman came to the Hacker's Creek area, in search of her husband (Peter). She never contacted Peter and passed out of the area, to the east, never to be seen again.

Peter missed his Indian family and was a lonely person. He had lived some 20 years with the Indians and tried hard to take up the white man's way of life. Peter was given land on Millstone Run, a branch of Hacker's Creek, and married on 4 Nov. 1814, Catharine (Hardman) Hyde (the widow of James Hyde Jr.), and she had four children. The families were close, and there is little doubt they wanted something to tie Peter to them again. Peter's sister Elizabeth was married to John Hardman.

I have visited the site of Peter and Catharine's home on Millstone Run, the only evidence of the cabin built in 1814 was a corner of local field stones, used for the foundation and topped by huge rotting hewn logs. I could still see the size of the logs. Four or Five Cedar trees framed the area where the log cabin originally stood. A small stream, below, and to the east of, the cabin, would have furnished water in the early years. There is little doubt the ways of the Indian's life remained with Peter through his life, the love of nature, hunting and the forest life. We have record of two children born to Peter and Catharine (H. H.) Waggoner: William and Perry Green.

<u>Records of the Berlin Church</u> by Mrs. Fred D. Law in the Weston Democrat, 18 Apr. 1973.

The Berlin Church was formed in the Spring of 1830 by Rev. Cornelius Springer and Rev. John Mitchell.

Rev. John Smith was elected leader of the class, some of the members were:

- John Starcher and wife (Jenny Radcliff).
- Peter Waggoner and wife (Catharine Hardman Hyde) m. 1814.
- Catharine Allman (1825 wid/o Peter Allman) nee Sims).
- George Straley and wife (Elizabeth Bonnett).
- Jane Bonnett Boran (m. Thomas Boran-1842).
- Matilda Heinzman (w/o Isaac M.-nee Bonnett).
- Catharine Law (probably nee Swisher-Thomas Law).
- Annie Waggoner.
- J. B. Hatcher and wife.
- Rev. John T. Hacker and wife (Sarah Howkins).
- Rev. John Hersman.
- Ora Batten (nee Menas-w/o Richard.
- Samuel Horner and wife (Martha Bonnett).
- Elias Bonnett and wife Elizabeth Cookman (m. 1850).
- Lewis Bonnett and wife Mary Linger.
- James R. Moore and wife (Matilda).

- James W. Watson and wife (Margaret Morrison).

I have found no record of Annie Waggoner and she was certainly not one of Peter's Indian children, as some have suggested. But I find references of William Waggoner's wife as Ann and Annie (Nancy Ann Ball). The above list would have been after 1843 because several couples were married in 1842 and 1843. Lewis Co.

Note added to church list; *A s/o Rev. Henry Radcliff Bonnett, Elias H. Bonnett, was very active and influential and joined the church in 1840, age 16, in 1870 was "licensed to exhort". m. 1850 Elizabeth Cookman.*

There is a list of members in the Book, <u>The M. P. Church in W. Va.</u> (Lewis Co. W. Va.) pg. 20. (See picture of Old Harmony Church.)

1819. Charter members of Harmony Church. Rev. John Mitchell and Family, Martha Alkire, Elizabeth Alkire, Mary Straley, Christina Wimer, Jamie Belt and wife and their colored woman Emaline. Thomas Sims and wife, George Bent and Wife, Thomas S. Straley and wife, David H. Smith a wife, Otho and Isaac Means and their wives. George Waggoner, Greenberry Duvall, Peter Waggoner and wife.

Some of the above moved to the Berlin Church in 1830 when it was organized.

This gives us an idea of the neighbors of Peter and Catharine (H. H.) Waggoner on Millstone Run.

Peter Waggoner (13 Mar. 1787-Harrison Co. 26 May 1879, ae 93 y.) Millstone Run, Lewis Co. s/o John and Margaret (Bonnett) Waggoner, m. 4 Nov. 18 by William Hacker, Harrison Co., Catharine (Hardman) Hyde (wid. of James Hyde Jr.), (26 Feb. 1784 2 Apr. 1867-ae. 83 y. 1 m. 24 d), Lewis Co., d/o Peter and Charlotte (Lazier) Hardman. Both are buried in Harmony Cemetery on the hill above the Old Harmony Church. (Vol.-1-pg. 8-9) (see Catharine (Hardman) Hyde 1st m. in Hardman line). Some years ago a new stone was erected by their descendants and friends, for Peter and Catharine.

The Stone erected by their descendants and Friends reads:

Peter Waggoner March 13, 1787 - March 26, 1879
Catharine Waggoner Feb. 26, 1784 - April 2, 1867

He was abducted by Shawnee Indians when five years of age and lived with them for 20 years. Mark the perfect man and Behold the Upright, for the end, of that man is peace. Great loves live on.

Harmony Cemetery - on Old Berlin Road, Lewis Co. W. Va.

I believe it was John Waggoner and Goodloe Sutton who had the monument placed on Peter and Catherine (Hardman Hyde) Waggoner's grave in Harmony Cem.

Hewn logs - corner of log cabin built around 1816 on Millstone Run. the Home of Peter and Catharine (Hardman) Waggoner.

William Waggoner
(1816-1903)

William Waggoner (11 Mar. 1816 - 19 Mar. 1903, Bible records), Lewis Co. W. Va., s/o Peter and Catharine (Hardman) Hyde Waggoner, m. 21 October 1837 Lewis Co., Nancy Ann Ball (8 Nov. 1818- 19 June 1881, ae. 62 y. 7 m. 11 d.), d/o Jas. & M. Ball. In both the marriage and death records Nancy Ann, was Ann Ball. She could have been the Annie Waggoner that was a member of the Berlin Church ca. 1850. Note: after years of searching for William Waggoner's death record, 19 Mar. 1903 -- *Thanks to Wm. Burl Waggoner of Grafton W. Va. and Mrs. Curry*, who was kind enough to share her Bible records.

Their children Rheulina L., Martin Green, Virginia, Tacy Catharine (Tacey C.), Fernando, Peter and Harriet Lucinda. Waggoner, (Bible rec. gives Rhulina S. Waggoner b. Dec. 13, 1832).

Please credit this line to Elizabeth (de Gruyter) Turner of Glenville W. Va.

1. Rhuelina L. Waggoner (21 Dec. 1839-17 Oct. 1914) Roane Co. W. Va. d/o William & Nancy Ann (Ball) Waggoner, m. 23 Dec. 1861 Lewis Co. Walter (Watt) Stalnaker (11 Sept. 1837 Harrison Co. d. 1 Oct. 1903 Roane Co. W. Va.) s/o Samuel Stalnaker and Elizabeth McWhorter d/o Walter Fields McWhorter and Margaret (Hurst) McWhorter.

   Some of their children:
   - Elizabeth Ann Stalnaker (22 Oct. 1862-17 Aug. 1895), Hebron, Cem., Roane Co. W. Va. m. 25 Dec. 1879-Roane Co., Alexander Morrison Hersman, (22 Aug. 1855-2 June 1940) s/o Rev. Mark Jr. and Margaret Ann (Morrison) Hersman.

Their children:
- Harvey Harrison Hersman(26 Oct. 1880-9 May 1882).
- Romie Dale Hersman (10 May 1882-9 Aug. 1936) m. 6 Jan. 1910- Nettie Taylor (19 Oct. 1889-31 July 1976)

    Children: Lillian Ruth Hersman (1910-1973) and Walter Taylor Hersman (1916-1936)
- Bruce Ireland Hersman (4 Feb. 1884-3 Jan. 1964) Ohio m. 6 Dec. 1908-Oma Gray Lowrentz (2 Nov. 1888-4 Apr. 1955) Yorkstown, Ohio.

    Children are:
    ◊ Ralph Hersman, (1909-1977; Roy b. 1911 Ohio.
    ◊ Alexander Madison Hersman, b. 1914 Ohio.
    ◊ Eula Margaret Hersman, b. 1917 Craig, Colorado m. 25 June 1936 Leland Frederick Knoedler, Ohio.
    ◊ Beatrice Elizabeth Hersman, b. 1921, m. 1942 Harold Irwin Fitzsimmons.
    ◊ Mary Lou Hersman, b. 1929, El Segundo, Ca.
- Maude Margaret Hersman (14 Jan. 1886-30 Mar. 1969) m. 7 Sept. 1913 Roane Co., Olin Ferdinand deGruyter (8 Jan. 1888-31 May 1973) s/o Otto deGruyter b. Prussia, and Rhoda Jane (Hill) de Gruyter (m. 4 Oct. 1885 Roane Co.)

    Children are:
    ◊ Elizabeth Eileen deGruyter m. 7 Sept. 1949, Spencer, Byron Jarvis Turner (8 July 1912-16 Mar. 1978). Son. John Mark Turner, m. 1981, Natalie McClendon.
    ◊ Etha Doris deGruyter m. 22 July 1937, Maurice S. Giersch.
    ◊ Ferdinand deGruyter (1917-1982 m. 19 June 1948), Anna Mary McVaney (1920-1982) bur. Spencer W. Va.
    ◊ Roberta Gail deGruyter m. 1 Mar. 1941, Howard Davis Conley.
    ◊ Paul Arnold deGruyter (1922-1982) m. 26 Dec. 1952 Tampa, Fl. Bernice Marie Bradley.
    ◊ Margaret Louise deGruyter m. 20 Sept. 1945 Wash. DC., John Russell (Russos) b. Athens, Greece.
    ◊ Noel Kent deGruyter (8 Oct. 1924-10 Sept. 1939).
    ◊ Charles Conrad deGruyter m. 15 Dec. 1950 Betty Jean White.
- Bertha Hattie Hersman (12 May 1888 6 Dec. 1903)

- Elizabeth (Lizzie) Gertrude Hersman (2 Aug. 1890-5 Apr. 1957) m. 25 Dec. 1913 Roane Co. Arthur Waitman Lowe (16 Feb. 1889-6 Feb. 1976.
- Alma Kate Hersman (13 Aug. 1892-1 Jan. 1887) m. 6 Apr. 1913 Roane Co. Hartford Clyde Morris.Children:. Cecil, Donald, Ernest, Lyndall and Daniel Alexander Morris.
- Alice Faye Hersman (25 Oct. 1893-26 Nov. 1951) m. 5 Mar. 1916 Roane Co. James Smith Taylor,(17 Mar. 1891-1 Nov. 1954).

• Alexander Morrison Hersman m. (2nd) 12 Apr. 1903 Roane Co. Allie Rowe (5 Aug. 1876-29 Jan. 1966).

Their children:

- Mark Kenneth Hersman, (b. 13 June 1904-28) m. 11 Aug. 1928 Pauline V. Mullins.
- Thelma Inez Hersman m. 18 Dec. 1950, Ira Lee Hanshaw
- Elmer Earl Hersman (1907-1908).

• Eunice Virginia Stalnaker b. 2 Apr. 1864 d/o Walter and Rhuelina L. (Waggoner) Stalnaker m.2 Nov. 1884 Roane Co. William E. Critchfield b. 13 Aug. 1863 s/o William E. Critchfield and Melinda A. Watson.

• George Whitman Stalnaker (8 Aug. 1866-1945) Roane Co. s/o Walter & Rhuelina L. (Waggoner) Stalnaker m. 23 Feb. 1887 Priscilla Victoria Morford (4 Oct. 1867 Greene Co. Pa. 31 Jan. 1942) d/o John and Hanna (Taylor) Morford.

Children:

- Guy Stalnaker b. 18 Oct. 1888 Roane Co. m. Ruth Henry, ch. Ruth Ann Stalnaker, Pomeroy, Ohio.
- Maude Stalnaker (3 Apr. 1891-1970) m. 6 Mar. 1913 Webster Mace (1876-1948). Ch.: Edna Mace (1913-1963) Jacksonville, FL. and John Mace (1916-1977).

• Mary Oliva Stalnaker, b. 16 Nov. 1867 Harrison Co. m. 13 Sept. 1885 Roane Co. Marcellus Davis.
• Elwood (Bud) A. Stalnaker, (16 July 1869-20 Feb. 1941) m. 23 Dec. 1891 Roane Co., Sarah Nichols.
• Spencer Cleber Stalnaker, m. 1 Oct. 1893 Amanda B. Marks.
• Dessi Julia Stalnaker, m. 27 Dec. 1893 Jonah L. Westfall.
• Walter Everett Stalnaker, m. 1897 Victoria S. Parsons.
• Ida Mae Stalnaker (22 Sept. 1878-19 Nov. 1959) m. 13 Feb. 1896 Thomas P. Skeens.

- Robert Hughes Stalnaker, (22 Jan. 1881-25 Apr. 1967) m. 26 Jan. 1899 Lenora E. Coon (22 Aug. 1887-22 Mar. 1949) Fairplain Cem. Roane Co. W. Va.

2. Martin Green Waggoner (3 July 1842-20 Aug. 1914 ae. 72 y.1 m. 17 d.) Old Harmony Cem. s/o William and Nancy Ann (Ball) Waggoner m. 12 Oct. 1865 Lewis Co. Sarah Jane Ball (b. 24 May 1849).

Children:

- Sherman Waggoner (28 Oct. 1866-29 Aug. 1878).
- Laura 'Lewey' Waggoner (31 May 1871-25 Aug. 1878).
- Sarah Waggoner (31 May 1871-before. 1880).
- Nancy N. Waggoner (12 Oct. 1879-1920) Harmony Cem.
- Gertrude D. Waggoner (20 Apr. 1883-4 Feb. 1949) m. 24 Oct. 1900, Lewis Co., C. Romeo Bargerhuff, (13 Oct. 1872-14 Apr. 1947) s/o Abner and Margaret (Reger) Bargerhuff.

3. Virginia Waggoner (15 June 1846-28 Oct. 1912) d/o William and Nancy Ann (Ball) Waggoner, m. 5 Sept. 1867 Lewis Co., George Washington Stalnaker (22 May 1841-14 June 1918), s/o Samuel and Elizabeth (McWhorter) Stalnaker.

Children:

- Emma Louisetta Stalnaker m. 1 Aug. 1886 Roane Co. John L. Santee: Ch.: Osty 1887, Lycla 1890 and Sella 1898.
- Claude Festus Stalnaker (1871-1915)

4. Casey (Tacy) Catharine Waggoner (6 Sept. 1848-4 Feb. 1920), d/o William & Nancy Ann (Ball) Waggoner, m. 15 Oct. 1868 Lewis Co., Noah H. Rinehart, (5 Feb. 1845 Harrison Co. - 18 Jan. 1879 ae 34 y. 11 m. 13 d.), Jesse Run Church Cem., s/o Abraham Rinehart, (27 Dec. 1803-22 Jan. 1881) and Elizabeth Humphery, (7 Mar. 11807-4 July 1887), d/o William Pelham Humphery.

Children:

- Orlando Rinehart [twin of Fernando] (6 June 1869-17 June 1939) m. Icie Kelly (1876-1958).
- Fernando Rinehart [twin of Orlando] born one day later (7 June 1869-2 Dec. 1941), m. 8 Nov. 1893, Emma O. Marple, (16 Nov. 1866-12 June 1948).

children:

♦ Reta B. Rinehart m. 16 Apr. 1921-Milo Arol MacIntyre (1893-1973).

- ♦ Gladstone Addison Rinehart m. 25 June 1932 Hazel Reger d/o Romulus S. and Ida (Lewis) Reger. lived on Hacker's Creek.
- ♦ Elizabeth A. Rinehart (10 Mar. 1870-21 Apr. 1924) Jesse Run Church Cem. m. 15 June 1893 John Rinehart (1871-1951).
- ♦ Alice C. Rinehart(7 May 1872-5 Feb. 1912) m. 17 Oct. 1894 Lewis Co. Sida H. Luzader. Children; Muriel, Noah, and Rosilla Luzader.

5. Fernando Waggoner (21 Aug. 1852-26 May 1926) s/o William and Nancy Ann (Ball) Waggoner, m.(1st) 26 Jan. 1871 Lewis Co. Barbara E. Westfall (6 Apr. 1854-after 1900) d/o George, and Mary Ann Westfall. Fernando m. 2nd 20 Aug. 1907 Ella Bird (wid.) d/o Gidion and Elizabeth Frances (Simmons) Morrison.

Children:

- Henry Wilks Waggoner m. 19 Apr. 1898 Harrison Co., Rose Rhealina Golden.
- Mary Columbus Waggoner m. 10 Jan. 1895 Lewis Co. Burtie Rinehart s/o Abraham & Sarah (Eckard) Rinehart. Ch.: Goldie Barbara, Ernest, and Brenice Rinehart.
- Ida Dirah Waggoner m. 24 Oct. 1902 Lewis Co. George A. Morrison s/o Gidion and Fannie Morrison.
- Samuel Waggoner (b. ca 1872) Lewis Co.

6. Peter Waggoner (27 Aug. 1854-22 June 1935) s/o William and Nancy Ann (Ball) Waggoner m. 29 Mar. 1885 Lewis Co. Louisa Jane Wilson b. Apr. 1859) d/o George T. & Maria (Rinehart) Wilson. *In the 1900 census Peter's father William was living with them.*

Children:

- Leora Waggoner (24 Feb. 1886 - 20 Sept. 1927) m. 16 Feb. 1912 Lewis Co. Richard H. Beeghley (wid.) (Aug. 1874 - 21 June 1924), s/o John Beeghley (b. Pa.) and Caroline Norris Hall Beeghley.

  Children:
  - ♦ Ethel Beeghley (7 Nov. 1912-7 Oct. 1980).
  - ♦ Barl Beeghley b. (9 Dec. 1916-.
  - ♦ Wirt Beeghley m. 7 Feb. 1942 Elizabeth Swisher.
  - ♦ Evelyn Beeghley m. June 1959 Frank McDonald.

- George Waggoner (26 Dec. 1887 - 29 Mar. 1888)

- Luther Everett Waggoner (4 June 1890-11 Apr. 1966) m. 17 Nov. 1912 Lewis Co. Ethel May Strader d/o Willis I. & Julia A. Strader.

    Children:
    - Everett Waggoner m. 6 Oct. 1934, Macel Johnston.
    - Lucille Winifred Waggoner m. 31 Jan. 1937, Merna Queen.
    - Verona Alda Waggoner (7 Jan. 1917-4 Oct. 1969)
    - Geraldine Waggoner m. 11 July 1942 Adiain Gay.

- Alda M. Waggoner (4 Aug. 1891-31 July 1969) m. 31 May 1926, Lewis Co. Grover Curry.

    Child:
    - Harold Curry m. 25 Dec. 1957, Mary L. Paugh.

- Harvey P. Waggoner b. 14 Nov. 1892, Hacker's Creek, m. 15 Feb. 1920 Lewis Co. Erma Augusta Taylor d/o J. O. and Sadie V. Taylor.

    Children:
    - Oliver Eugene Waggoner b. 15 Aug. 1924.
    - Sadie Jo Ann Waggoner b. 20 June 1926.

- Edward Burl Waggoner b. 8 Aug. 1895, Buckhannon Run m. 18 Apr. 1920, Lewis Co. Mary Phyliss Stalnaker d/o T. E. and Julia V. (Hall) Stalnaker.

    Children:
    - Eugene Waggoner m. Apr. 1946 Genevine Hannigan.
    - Joann Waggoner b. 20 June 1926.

- Iris Waggoner b. 10 Dec. 1897 m. 21 Nov. 1925 Arden Norman s/o Shumate & Victoria Norman.

Please credit Ina Hersman & Mildred (Gould) Pringle

7. Harriet Lucinda Waggoner (11 Mar. 1861-13 Oct. 1926) Friendship Cem. Lewis Co. d/o William and Nancy Ann (Ball) Waggoner m. 26 Nov. 1883 Lewis Co. Millard Fillmore Pringle (8 Oct. 1859-11 Apr. 1945) b. Upsher Co. s/o John Pringle who m. 3 Dec. 1857 Rachel Cartwell d/o Christopher and Sinai Cartwell.

    Children:

- Clarence Wm. Pringle (27 Oct. 1885-17 Apr. 1962) m. 4 Apr. 1907 Lewis Co. Ola Lena Bush (1891-1951) (1900 living with Grandparents Nathaniel & Martha E. (Jackson) Bush).
- Millard A. Earl Pringle (1890-1935) Ritchie Co. (W) Va. m. (1st) 22 Nov. 1919, Lewis Co. Etta Mae Boran (1889-1929) m. (2nd) 3 June 1933, Rulena Pearl Lawson (1888-1935) Fairview Cem. Lewis Co. W. Va.
- Cecil Pringle b 24 July 1896 lived San Diego, CA.
- Reta Ariella Pringle (1 Apr. 1898-19-) m. (5 June 1918 Lewis Co. Daniel Monroe Eagle (1886-1971) both Bur. Friendship Cem. (Bk. 3-pg. 16)
- Ella May Pringle m. 20 July 1918 Lewis Co. Frank W. Regester, s/o Arthur R. & Nettie M. Regester.
- Moss Monroe Pringle m. Amy Elizabeth Wilson.

William Waggoner (1816-1903)
son of Peter and Catharine (Hardman) Waggoner

John Starcher (1767-1825)
Lived on Jesse's Run

The Virginia Stalnakers

The Virginia Germans - by Klaus Wust
(pg. 41)

"The Stalnaker family were among the early New River settlers. Samuel Stalnaker carried on an extensive trade with the Cherokees, at the same time contracting the hatred of others Indians in the area.

Samuel Stalnaker left the New River community and moved his family westward in order to be closer to his trading partners.

1748 Stalnaker was between Reedy Creek and Holston River when he met Dr. Thomas Walker and is credited with having indicated to Walker where the Cumberland Gap was located. (See Old Virginia Map.)

In 1750 Samuel and Adam Stalnaker moved to the North side of the Holston. Stalnaker renoun as a frontiersman spread throughout the colony and soon Governor Dinwiddie would have reasons to avail himself of the services of this man, "well acquainted with the woods, and a good Pilot or Guide upon occasion".

"The road workers at new River in 1746, not only included the well-known Samuel Stalnaker but also all the Dunkers that are able to work." (pg.51)

"October 1754 when the first massacre occurred on Holston River. The Shawnees struck again on Holston, on 18 June 1755 singling out the Samuel Stalnaker home, where they murdered his wife and his son Adam, while carrying the well-known trader away with them as a prize captive. News of Stalnaker's capture traveled rapidly along the entire southern frontier. It was believed he would be cruelly tortured since the Indians hated him.

Many settlers were killed, families fled east, only to be meet by Indian raiding parties. Broddoch's defeat on July 9, 1755 shattered all hopes of security.

In the late summer, German neighborhoods on Greenbrier and South Branch were raided. One bright moment in this dreadful summer, was in the middle of June 1756, Samuel Stalnaker appeared in Williamsburg. After one year of captivity, during which he was subjected to much suffering and torture, he had made his escape. Stalnaker in July 1756 attended the council of war held at Augusta Court House. The Governor ordered that Captain Stalnaker be given 100 pounds to raise his company and build a stockade fort at Draper's Meadows. After the war years Stalnaker returned to his old home on the Holston where he inspired courage and hope in his fellow settlers." (pg. 59-61)

Virginia Colonial Solders by Lloyd DeWitt Bockstruck (pg. 165)

3 June 1757-

"The account of Capt. Samuel Stalnaker for pay for himself, officers, and soldiers in his company of militia from Augusta County and for horse hire for use of said company amounting to 208.0.4 is just. He had received 100.0.0 and is due 108.0.4."

Augusta County Court Records-Order, Book No IV (pg. 61)

14 Aug. 1753-

"Road ordered from Samuel Stalnaker's, on Holston River, to James Davis'. Samuel Stalnaker to be overseer, with these workers: James Davis and his sons, Frederick Starn, Jacob and Adam Stalnaker, Hamphry Baker and son, George Stalnaker and others."

The Journals of The House of Burgess of Virginia, (vol. 9, pg. 274) Mentions the location of Samuel's house. "Monday, 30 March 1761, Stalnaker (Stahllnacker) was located on the Fry and Jefferson map of 1751, on the Middle Fork of the Halston, a few miles above its junction with the South Fork. -- 1750 Dr. Thomas Walker & his fellow travelers meet with Stalnaker and helped him build his house." (on Patton's land)

The Halston is located in present day Smyth Co. c.-1832, and was then in Washington Co. c. 1776-7. So this early 1755, it would probably have been Augusta Co.

Also see Draper Mss. for about the same information on Stalnaker.

1743 -The New River, settlement of Germans had reached the farthest frontier of Virginia, at that time, they were called the Harman Group. These Germans were from Eastern Pennsylvania and the Shenandoah Valley, and were in Virginia long before the Waggoners.

The Swen index of Virginia: shows records from, The Virginia Magazine of History and Biography, The William & Mary College Quarterly, and Tyler's Quarterly on Samuel Stalnaker life and times.

History of Randolph County by Dr. A. S. Basworth (pg. 293) "Stalnaker derived from the German word 'Stahal' or 'Stahl' meaning steel, and 'Negel' meaning a sharp point or spear. The original word was Stahlnegel, meaning sharp pointed steel spear. So the name was perhaps, first applied to a worrier who was armed with such a weapon. Samuel Stalnaker surely lived up to his name.

The Compendium of American Genealogy, Vol. 4 pg. 574, Vol. 6 pg. 602, Vol. 1 pg. 96, gives the following information:

"Capt. Samuel Stalnaker d. 1775, Holston, Va., 1746 explorer and discoverer of Cumberland Gap. Capt. in French and Indian Wars, mediator between Indians and early Virginia Government, built a stockade Fort at Draper's Meadows."

We know his wife and son Adam Stalnaker were killed on 18 June 1755 when he was captured by the Indians. He escaped one year later in 1756. I find no record of the rest of Samuel's family. We know Jacob Stalnaker was his son and was Granted 194 acres on the east side of Tygerts Valley river in 1780- (more later on about this family)

Some other records found:

Capt. James Booth (b. 1709 d. 17 June 1778) m. Nancy Stalnaker. Some of their children: William, John, James C., Daniel, Sarah, Bersheba and two others daughters. Vol. 2 pg. 26 of The Monongalia Story by Earl L. Core.

Harrison Co. Land Records pg. 103:

Valentine Stalnaker on 19 Oct. 1795 (pg. 53) (Dito to Dito for 5 shillings, 2000 acres on File Creek)

1782 Magongalia Co. shows 5 people in the home.

D.A.R. records show, Valentine Stalnaker b. 1758, d. 28 Nov. 1833, m. (1st) Catharine _____ m. (2nd) 1806 Lucretia (Lucy) Jenkins, Patriotic Service,Va.

H/o Randolph Co. (m. (62) Va. by Dr. A. S. Bosworth.

Jacob Stalnaker m. 1802,Nancy Channel d/o Joseph Channel.

J. W. Stalnaker m. 1803 Mary Chenowith d/o John Chenowith.

Rebecca Stalnaker m. 1803, Jacob Larentz d/o Val Stalnaker.

John Stalnaker m. 1804, Elizabeth Hadden.

Andrew Stalnaker m. 1812, Clarissa Danbury.

Bosworth (373) "The Stalnaker's came to America from Holland. They were pioneers of Greenbrier, Augusta, (Smyth Co. now) "and Rockingham Co's before coming to Randolph Co. Va."

Augusta Co. was created from Orange Co. in 1738-45, Rockingham Co. from Augusta Co. in 1778, and Greenbrier Co. from Montgomery Co. in 1777. This would place them in the Southern part of Virginia. Randolph Co. was created in 1787 from Harrison Co.

The Jacob Stalnaker line by *Elizabeth (de Gruyter) Turner. of Glenville, W. Va. She gives credit to Stalnaker Genealogy, Ina Hersman and Mildred Pringle and others.*

2nd Gen.: Jacob Stalnaker will probated 1792 Randolph Co. W. Va. m. Elizabeth Truby, who d. ca 1816, d/o John Truby.

3rd Gen.: Samuel Stalnaker (1763-1835) m. 26 Feb. 1788 Susannah Radcliff (1765-1840) d/o William and Debra (Hughes) Radcliff.

4th Gen.: Samuel Stalnaker (20 Aug. 1800-28 March 1845) m. 2 Oct. 1827 Elizabeth McWhorter (15 Jan. 1804-21 Nov. 1886) d/o Walter Fields McWhorter & Margaret (Hurst) McWhorter.

5th Gen.: Walter Stalnaker (1837-1903

George Washington Stalnaker (1841-1914)

Susan (Cosner) Waggoner (1824-1910)
wife of Perry Green Waggoner

Perry Green Waggoner

Perry Green Waggoner, b. 15 June 1822 Millstone Run Hacker's Creek, d. 15 Apr. 1861, s/o Peter and Catharine (Hardman Hyde) Waggoner m. 27 Mar. 1843 Lewis Co. (Bk. 5 pg. 200) Susanna Cosner (27 Apr. 1824-7 Oct. 1910) d/o Margaret Cosner. They lived with Peter and Catharine on Millstone Run and are both buried in Old Hacker or Morrisons Cem. Lewis Co., (m. 27 Mar. 1843 by Henry R. Bonnett - ref. Lewis Co. m. pg. 25).

In searching for Susanna Cosner's parents, the only record I could find was on the marriage record, 15 Mar. 1843. "Cosner, Susanna & Perry Green Waggoner, Parents, Margaret Cosner, Bondsman: Isaac Wamsley and Perry Green Waggoner m. by Henry R. Bonnett" (Bk. 5 pg. 200). There is a I.G.I. m. record for Adam Cosner and Margaret Michael, 11 Dec. 1823 Hardy Co. (W) Va. But I have no proof Adam was her father only that Margaret is her mother.

Children:

1. First child was (b. 1843-d. 1843)
2. Anderson Erwin Waggoner, b. 4 July 1845 - Lewis Co., s/o Perry Green Waggoner and Susanna (Cosner) Waggoner, m. 8 Aug. 1867 - Lewis Co. Virginia, L. Borem, b. ca. 1844, d/o George W and Mary (Hinzman) Borem - m. 27 Aug. 1843 - Lewis Co. (W)Va.

    Children:

    - Herbert E. Waggoner (26 Apr. 1869-22 Jan. 1870).
    - Samuel L. Waggoner b. 2 Oct. 1871 Hacker's Creek.
    - Clements P. Waggoner b. 22 Mar. 1875 Gilmer Co.
    - Howard W. Waggoner b. 4 Jan. 1879 Gilmer Co.
    - Charles G. Waggoner, b. 18 Sept. 1888 Gilmer Co.

3. George Columbus Waggoner (26 Aug. 1847-28 July 1849) ae. 1 y. 11 m. 2 d. Morrison Cem., Lewis Co., s/o Perry Green and Susanna (Cosner) Waggoner.

   Credit: Sue (Sutton) Darnall of Buckhannon W. Va. for the Sutton lines and other helpful information. Sue has Peter Waggoner's (1787-1879) clock, made by E. Terry and Son, listing the data from 1818-to 1836. Sue is now the proud owner of the Sutton Bible, that belonged to John A. and Luverna Catharine (Waggoner) Sutton, by the New York: American Bible Society 1860.

4. Luverna Catharine Waggoner (31 May 1850-23 Aug. 1888) Friendship Cem., Hacker's Creek dist., Lewis Co. W. VA. d/o Perry Green and Susanna (Cosner) Waggoner, m. 30 Nov. 1871 Lewis Co. by Henry R. Bonnett, John Abernathy Sutton (25 Sept. 1843-1920, ae. 77 yr.) s/o Jacob and Dinah Sutton. John Sutton m. (2nd) 21 Nov. 1889, Virginia A. Reger (Aug. 1856-1941) Upsher Co. d/o Anthony and Mary (Lynch) Reger (m. 4 Mar. 1836) Lewis Co.

   Children:

   - George Ralph Sutton b. 28 Sept. 1872 Lewis Co., lived in California.
   - William E. Sutton (16 May 1875-1954) Lewis Co., m. Eva Grace Reger (1873-1957) Lewis Co.,

     Children:

     - John Hayward, Ruth and Edwin Sutton.
     - John Hayward Sutton (22 Nov. 1901 Upshur Co. - 1 June 1958 Upsher Co.) m. Lucy Eugenia Summers (11 May 1901- 21 Aug. 1981 Upsher Co.).

       Children:

       ◊ Dorothy Lee Sutton m. Ralph Pockrus.
       ◊ Mary Sue Sutton m. Thomas A. Darnall Jr.
       ◊ Jo Ann Sutton m. James F. Remley.

   - Goodlow (John G.) Sutton b.18 Mar. 1879, Lewis Co. m. Dorothy Heavner.
   - Roy C. Sutton b. 12 Jan. 1883 Lewis Co. moved to El Darado, California.

   Thanks to Mr. John Hersman of Buckhannon W. Va.

   - Maude Florance Sutton, (b. 20 Dec. 1885, Lewis Co. d. 18 Nov. 1986) (after her mother, Luverna Catharine (Waggoner) Sutton died, Maude was raised by her aunt Alcinda Margaret (Waggoner) Sutton), m. 19 Sept. 1909, Lewis Co., Stanley B. Hersman (17 June 1888 - 8 Jan. 1949) Grass Valley, Ca. bur. Fairview Cem. Lewis Co. W. Va., s/o Mark Hersman (1 Mar. 1845-9 Dec. 1916) m. 14 Apr. 1872 Upshur Co. Olive Rebecca Hinzman (22 Aug. 1844-9 Apr. 1922), d/o Isaac M. Heizman & Matilda (Bonnett) Heinzman. Mark Hersman was the s/o George Hersman (2 Jan. 1812-1 May 1865) who m. 17 June 1834 Lewis Co. Sarah Starcher.

Stanley B. Hersman & Maude Florance (Sutton) Hersman children:

- Harry B. Hersman
- Harold (Bill) Sutton Hersman.
- John Clark Hersman (30 July 1917-19 Aug. 1987) m. 22 Aug. 1943 Ina Beatrice Tenney.
- Ethel Grace Hersman.

- Audrey R. Sutton, (29 Aug. 1890-20 Feb. 1980) s/o John A. & Virginia A. (Reger) Sutton.

5. Alcinda Margaret Waggoner (26 June 1852-7 Dec. 1929) d/o Perry Green and Susanna (Cosner) Waggoner, m. 29 Nov. 1874 Lewis Co. Samuel C. Sutton (21 June 1848-12 June 1921) both bur. Friendship Cemetery, s/o Jacob and Dinah Sutton.

Samuel and Alcinda had one son:

- Andrew Elias Sutton (25 Nov. 1876-25 June 1988 ae 82 y.) Lewis Co. m. Stilla Hinzman (Feb. 1884-3 Apr. 1970 ae 86 y.) d/o William C. and Columbia A. (Moore) Hinzman.

From the Sutton Bible:

Jacob G. Sutton (16 Dec. 1808-29 Nov. 1865) m. Dinah (5 April 1812-17 Nov. 1857)

There children were:

- Synthia J. or G. Sutton b. 1 Sept. 1836.
- Rachel A. Sutton b. 8 May 1841.
- Mary V. Sutton b. 31 May 1842.
- John A. Sutton b 29 Sept. 1843.
- Andrew N. Sutton b. 8 Feb. 1845.
- Margaret C. Sutton b. 20 Oct. 1846.
- Samuel C. Sutton b. 21 June 1848.

- James W. Sutton b. 25 Sept. 1849.
- Henry A. Sutton b. 27 Nov. 1851.
- Amanda A. Sutton b. 27 Aug. 1853.

6. Elias Marion Waggoner, (2 June 1856, Lewis Co. (W) Va.-4 July 1945, Rogers, Benton, Co., Ar.) (home of his son Lee Elias Wagoner) bur. Mt. Hope Cem. Ellis Co., Ks. s/o Perry Green & Susanna (Cosner) Waggoner. His father, Perry Green Waggoner (d. 1861) when Elias Marion was 5 years old, his mother and siblings continued to live with his Grandparents, Peter and Catharine (H.H.) Waggoner. In 1876, age 20 years, Elias M. caught a train west to California, and dropped one "g" from Waggoner. After several years he returned to the state of Kansas in 1878. He homesteaded 12 miles southwest of Ellis, Ks. in 1883 in Trego Co., KS.

Elias Marion Wagoner m. 16 Apr. 1884 Hays City, Ellis Co. Ks. Margarita Christiana Pohlmann (4 June 1863, in Kleinschrvarzenbach, state of Bayern, Germany, she d. 13 Feb. 1943 Rogers, Benton Co. Ark.) bur. Mt. Hope Cem., Ellis, Ellis Co. Ks. d/o Johann Konrad and Margareta Johanna Pohlmann (see The Pohlmann Family).

In Aug. 1881, Nicholas Pohlmann accompanied his cousin Margareta Christina Pohlmann on this trip to America, arriving Ellis Island, NY. and traveling to Paradise, Ks. the same month. Margaret came to visit her sister, Mrs. John Smith, who passed away 3 days before she arrived.

She stayed with the Smith family seven months and in March of 1882 went to Victoria, Ks., to stay with the Joe Grant family. In 1884 she m. Elias M. Wagoner and they lived on the farm in Trego Co. Ks for 56 years. They joined the Congregational Church in Ellis, Ks., in 1928 and moved to the home of their son, Lee E. Wagoner in 1940 near Rogers, Ark.

Their children were:
- Henry Grant Wagoner (29 Sept. 1885, Trego Co. Ks. 7 Mar. 1963) m. 10 Sept. 1913, Leda Ziegler, who died in 1926. Two sons; Preston Berne, and Warren Grant.
- Ida Mable Wagoner (11 May 1887-11 June 1976) m. (1st) 3 Sept. 1913, Louis Hearting m. (2nd) Harvy Richardson lived Bronwell, Rush Co. Ks.
- Alcinda May Wagoner (25 July 1896-11 Mar. 1991) Maple Park Cem. Aurora, Mo., m. 27 Mar. 1918 Vance Kirby.

- Lee Elias Wagoner (5 Mar. 1899, Trego Co. Ks.-13 May 1988 ae. 87 y. 3 m. 5 d.) Rogers, Benton Co. Ark. m. 17 Sept. 1921 Wakeeney, Trego Co. Ks. Inez Lucille Solomon (b. 17 June 1903 Ellis Co. Ks.) d/o Elmer Christian Solomon-(1867-1940) and Florance Laura (Burnham) Solomon (1875-1959).
  (see Solomon-Selbitz (Selwitz) lines).

  (see Burnham-Fry lines)

  In Jan. 1940 Lee and Lucille (Solomon) Wagoner moved to a farm just north of Rogers, Arkansas. They had lived there 49 years when Lee E. Wagoner died in 1988.

  Their children, Elvena Blanche, Marvin Lee, Annalee, Robert Dale, Norman Leroy, and Darrell Eugene Wagoner.

  - Elvena Blanche Wagoner, b. Hays, Ellis Co. Ks., m. Robert Roy Walter, b. Kress, Swisher Co., Texas. s/o Clyde Lyman Walter, b 26 Dec. 1885. Crab Orchard, Johnson Co. Ne. d. 26 May 1961, and Augusta Dorthea Brener, b. 28 July 1893, Hamburg, Germany d. 5 Apr. 1973.

    The name Augusta Dorthea Brener Walter is on the Ellis Island Wall of Immigrants, put there by Mr. & Mrs. Robert R. Walter.

    Children:
    - ◊ David Roy Walter, m. Marsha Winkle, d/o Allen & Ruth (Tarbox) Winkle.
    - ◊ Lynda Deane Walter m. John T. Slover.
    - ◊ James Stuart Walter m. Sherrie Lynn Meridith.
    - ◊ Daniel Robert Walter, m. Janie Sisemore, d/o Arlis & Mildred Sisemore.
    - ◊ Steven Michael Walter m. Peggy Jo Lawless, d/o J. C. & Dorothy (Roper) Lawless.
    - ◊ Mark Lyman Walter, m. Brenda Darlene Campbell, d/o Edgar Cleulin & Wilma Beatrice (Nicholson) Campbell.

- Marvin Lee Wagoner m. Crystal V. Jones, d/o Clarence Homer & Ettie (Watson) Jones. (see Jones & Watson Families)

    Children:
    - William Lynn Wagoner m. Nancy Kay Budd, d/o Kenneth Robert Budd (29 Mar. 1916-17 Jan. 1994), & Margaret Roberta (Moore) Budd (3 Jan. 1919 - 19 Feb. 1980) Dallas, Tx., d/o Alexis Evanda & Roberta Benedict (Surbaugh) Moore. (See Moore & Hughes lines, Budd and Surbaugh lines.)
    - Charles Dean Wagoner
    - Cynthia Lucille Wagoner m. Gordon Ross Smith Jr.

- Annalee Wagoner m. Neal H. Runge.
    - Robert Neal Runge Jr. m. Pam Richardson d/o William & Virginia (Kraft) Richardson
    - Mary Leone Runge m. Erik Michael Olson s/o Gordon Harold & Helen Kathryn (McKuskie) Olson.

- Robert Dale Wagoner m. Patricia Ann Howland, d/o William McKenley & June Jane (Cowan) Howland.
    - Terry Ann Wagoner m. Jonathan Craig Deans, s/o Leroy Ray & Betty Love (Darlington) Deans.
    - Tony Dale Wagoner m. Stephanie Maria Merrill, d/o Phillip H. Merrill.
    - Ginger Lea Wagoner m. Gregory Gene Treece, s/o Eugene Treece.

- Norman Leroy Wagoner m. Martha Haskett.
    - Ramona Danette Wagoner m. Richard Allen Mays, s/o Ronald F. Mays.
    - Norman Wagoner Jr.

- Darrell Eugene Wagoner m. (1st) Norma Shapiro.

    Children:
    - Darrell Ann Wagoner.
    - Lee Charles Wagoner.

    Darrell Eugene Wagoner m. (2nd) Mary Lore Stephens, d/o Alfred William Stephens b. 23 Dec. 1918 London, Ontario,

Canada d. 27 July 1978, Glendora, Ca., and Dollie Lee Moore b. 10 June 1923 Gatesville, Texas.

Children:

◊ Jodi Maria Wagoner.
◊ Juli Rene Wagoner

Aaron Budd Family Line

Credit Nancy Ann (Budd) Wagoner

1-Gen: Aaron Budd (N. Y.- 1847 Pike Co. Illinois) m. Phoebe Ogden (20 June 1795 NY.-11 Feb. 1888), Marion Co. Oregon.

children:

2-Gen: Daniel Budd (1818-1890) m. 20 Aug. 1846, Pike Co. Ill., Ruth Jane Potter (1830-1895).

3-Gen: William Budd m. 15 Jan. 1873, Mt. Sterling, Pike Co. Ill, Josephine Murphy (27 Oct. 1857, Ark-17 May 1933), Houston, Harris Co., Tx., d/o James & Anna (Dempsey) Murphy (Civil War).

4-Gen: Henry Marvin Budd (23 July 1883, Honey Grove, Lamar Co. Tx - 29 Dec. 1946, Dallas, Dallas Co. Tx.) m. 18 Dec. 1910, Margaret Lucille Hughes (18 Apr. 1889 Richmond, Henrico Co. Va. - 7 Dec. 1979), Dallas, Dallas Co. Tx.

3-Gen: d/o Richard Adolphus Hughes (2 Sept. 1862 Richmond Hervieco Co. Va. 15 July 1983, Dallas, Tx,

2-Gen: s/o John Cargyle Hughes (29 June 1822-4 Feb. 1899) m. 15 Nov. 1843 Lucy Ann Duke (17 Mar. 1823-14 Aug. 1903).

3-Gen: Richard Adolphus Hughes m. 6 May 1885 Florence Hedley Dammeron (24 Aug. 1868-9 Apr. 1952) Dallas, Dallas Co. Tx.

2-Gen: d/o Zechariah Dammeron (22 Feb. 1826-26 Mar. 1892) m. 8 Dec. 1849 Margaret Willis Rucker (22 Feb. 1834-16 Nov. 1915).

5-Gen: Kenneth Robert Budd (29 Mar. 1916 Dallas, Tx-17 Jan. 1994, Dallas, Tx), s/o Henry Marvin & Margaret Lucille (Hughes) Budd. m. 3 Mar. 1939, Dallas, Tx. Margaret Roberta Moore (3 Jan. 1919 Dallas, Tx-19 Feb. 1980), d/o Alexis Evanda & Roberta Benedict (Surbaugh) Moore.

Children:

- Nancy Kay Budd m. William Lynn Wagoner.

- Sandra Lee Budd m. Willis LePori.
- Kennith Robert Budd Jr.

Moore Line with Surbaugh Line.

1-Gen: Indemion Benjamin Moore (1807-10 Dec. 1859) m. Nancy Templeton (15 Sept. 1810-12 Oct. 1854)

    2-Gen: Edward Gleason Moore (31 Aug. 1836 Sparta, White Co., Tenn. 19 Aug. 1873 Sparta, Tenn.) m. Permelia Hill (21 Sept. 1835-Sparta Tenn.-27 Feb. 1905), Dallas, Dallas Co. Tx.

    3-Gen:Alexis Evanda Moore (13 July 1859 Sparta, Tenn. 4 Nov. 1929 Dallas, Tx.) m. 3 Oct. 1897, Roberta Benedict Surbaugh, (4 Aug. 1873, Saline Co., Mo. 18 Feb. 1930) Dallas, Tx.

    2-Gen: d/o Henry Clay Surbaugh, (13 Apr. 1844 Golden City, Mo. 15 Dec. 1909 Mo.)

    1-Gen: s/o William Surbaugh (12 Nov. 1804-18 Sept. 1878) m. 25 May 1862, Hannah Hisey (22 Sept. 1806-11 Nov. 1864), Greenbrier Co. Va.

    2-Gen: Henry Clay Surbaugh m. 24 Nov. 1870 Susan Frances Doke, (10 Mar. 1849 Boyle, Mercer Co. Ky.-15 Nov. 1914) Dallas, Tx.

    1-Gen: d/o Thomas Jefferson Doke (b. 10 Sept. 1825) m. 14 Sept. 1845. Susan Harrison Gains, b. 1 Apr. 1826 Mercer Co. Ky.

The Pohlmann Family credited Mrs. Irene Pohlman of Russell, Ks.

In Aug. 1881 Nicholas Pohlmann accompanied his cousin Margarita Christiana Pohlmann on their trip to America, landing at Ellis Island off New York City, N. Y. and traveled to Paradise, Ks. in the same month. Margarita came to visit her sister, Mrs. John Smith, who passed away three days before she arrived. She stayed 7 months with the family, and in March of 1882 went to Victoria, Ks. to stay with the Joe Grant family.

Margarita Christiana Pohlmann Wagoner's name can be found on the Wall of Immigrants on Ellis Island (1992) on Panel # 439. (Credit Robert & Elvena (Wagoner) Walter, who registered this name for the Wall)

I believe Margarita Christiana Pohlmann's parents were Johann Konrad Pohlmann (17 Nov. 1819-1898) and Margaritha Johanna Pohlmann (17 Nov. 1826-1896) They had 9 children, 3 came to America. A daughter who married John Smith and d. Aug. 1881 Paradise Valley near Natoma, she came to this country in 1873. In Aug. 1881 a daughter Margaritha Christiana Pohlmann immigrated, accompanied by Nicholas Pohlman, a cousin, who operated a saloon in Natoma.

Johann Konrad Pohlmann
(17 Nov. 1819 - 1898)

Margaretha Johann Geiben
(17 No. 1826 - 1896)

Kleinschurarzenback, State of Bayern, at Helmbrechts, Germany

Kleinschrvarzenbach

Adam Henry Pohlman s/o Johann Konrad & Margaretha Johanna Pohlmann was born 18 Feb. 1869 at Kleinschrvarzenbach, in the state of Boyern, at Helmbrechts, Germany, where he grew up and served his time, of three years, in the German Army.

Adam left Germany in Oct. 1893 and came to America to make his home with a sister, Mrs. E. M. Wagoner, who lived on a ranch south of Ellis, Ks.

Mr. Adam Henry Pohlman homesteaded in the same community and resided there until the winter of 1895, when he moved to the Paradise Valley, near Natoma and worked for his brother-in-law John Smith. In 1899 he started the furniture and undertaking business at Natoma -- he helped build the Presbyterian Church.

Adam Henry Pohlmann m. 1 July 1900, Miss Emma Taubald at Osborne, Ks., they had corresponded since he left Germany. Emma Margaret (Maggie) Taubald (8 June 1872, Bavaria, Germany, d. 16 June 1912 in Natoma, Ks.).

Children:

- Alma Emma Pohlman, 9 Aug. 1901 m. Edwin Meyer.
- Adam Frederick Pohlman, 19 Apr. 1903 m. Irene Gladys Kaiser 3 Sept. 1927, Council Bluffs, Iowa. children: A. Fred Jr., A. Henry II, and A. George.
- Bertha Plasman, b. 13 Feb. 1905, (nee Pohlman).
- Ellen Herl, b. 11 Aug. 1907, (nee Pohlman).
- Alice Jackson b. 26 Mar. 1910, (nee Pohlman).

Adam Henry m. (2nd) Cora Kaser Harres who d. 23 Jan. 1961 and Adam Henry d. 4 Mar, 1932 Salina, Ks.

Pohlmann in Kleinschrvarzenback, Germany, State of Bayern, at Helmbrechts

Johann Konrad Pohlmann, of Germany, wife Margaretha Johanna Geiben (Goisser) from Wendischingrun (Lutheran) listed children all born Kleinschrvarzenbach:

- Anna Margaretha Pohlmann b. 26 Feb. 1849 d. 26 Jan. 1869.
- Katharina Margaretha Pohlmann b. 20 Feb. 1850 m. 18 Apr. 1869 Johann Christian Flechtner
- Johann Georg Pohlmann, (26 Dec. 1852-15 Mar. 1855)

- Elizabetha Margaretha Pohlmann (2 Dec. 1855-14 Mar. 1880) m. Johann Hoffman.
- Johann Adam Pohlmann (18 Mar. 1858-27 May ?1910)
- Katharina Christiana Pohlmann b. 4 June 1860 m. Jakob Nikol Grabner
- Margaretha (Maggie) Christinna Pohlmann. (4 June 1863 Germany, 13 Feb. 1948) Rogers, Benton Co. Ark m. 16 Apr. 1884 Victoria, Ellis Co. Ks. Elias M. Wagoner.
- Katharina Margaretha Pohlmann, b. 4 June 1866.
- Adam Hunrich Pohlmann b. 18 Feb. 1869.

I'm sorry I do not know the person to credit this research.

The names of child 2 and 8 are the same, perhaps a mistake in copy, I enter this because two of the children were acknowledged.

Margaretha Christian Polhmann (1863-1943) - upper left corner
with her sister before she left for America

Part Six

John and Susannah (Richards) Waggoner

Around 1795, the year both of John Waggoner's captured daughters (Elizabeth and Mary) came home, John built onto his cabin- and before 1799, he had another cabin, near by with a water well in between the two cabins.

John Waggoner (24 Nov. 1751, White Marsh, Pa. d. ca. 1842 when his will was probated) Lewis Co. (W) Va. s/o Wilhelm and Agnesa Waggoner, m. 19 Feb. 1799 (Bond, 16 Feb. 1798) Harrison Co. Susannah Richards, ward of John Runyon. I have always felt Susannah was a daughter of Paul Richards, as she named her first son Paul. I can only estimate her age as b. ca 1782, as she needed a guardian's concent to marry and she was not mentioned in John's will in 1840. (Probated in 1842)

Border Settlers of Northwestern Virginia by McWhorter (pg. 245) "Richard's Fort" was undoubtedly located near the mouth of Sycamore, although it is claimed that it was two miles further up the river. (pg. 480) Arnold Richards owned 300 acres on the West Fork adj. lands of William Lowther (1773). Paul Richards 400 acres adj. Arnold Richards (1774).

"In August 1782, as Arnold and Paul Richards were returning to Richard's Fort, they were shot by some Indians, who were lying behind a fence in a cornfield, adjoining the fort and both fell from their horses. The Indians leaped over the fence and immediately tomahawked and scalped them. Thus the necessity for a guardian for Susannah Richards when she married John Waggoner."

Susannah (Richards) Waggoner, mother of 12 children, is certainly deserving of more credit than I am able to give her, but I can only find one other mention of her presence as follows:

Harrison Co., (W) Va. Deed Records, 1785-1810 by John David Davis (pg. 254).

> July 1800 (pg. 211) John and Susannah Waggoner, of Virginia to George Bush, of Harrison Co., Va. for 95 pounds, 103 acres West Fork River adj. Peter Shall and John Runyon.
>
> Signed, John Waggoner and Susannah Waggoner Recorded Oct. 1802.

Could this be land left to Susannah, from her father? She was a ward of John Runyon and wife Susannah Runyon.

One of the quickest ways to establish the children of John & Susannah (Richards) Waggoner is John's Will (P. 36 Book B Lewis Co.) Probated 1842.

From Mary K. Holt, Clerk of the County Court Weston, W. Va. April 8, 1970.

> I, John Waggoner, of Lewis County, State of Virginia, do hereby make this my last will and testament.
>
> 1st, I desire that the land on which I now live being one hundred and 78 and 1/2 acres to be equally divided between my two sons (to wit) George and Samuel Waggoner to be enjoyed by them and their heirs forever.
>
> 2nd, That the said George and Samuel Waggoner pay to my other children (to wit) Peter Waggoner, John Waggoner, Paul Waggoner, Jacob Waggoner, Wm. Waggoner, Catherine Dobson, last Catherine Waggoner, Susanna Sims late Susanna Waggoner, Mariah Cottrill, late Mariah Waggoner, and Margaret Waggoner the sum of sixty dollars each within the period of five years after my decease.
>
> In witness whereof I have hereunto set my hand and affixed my seal for his last will and testament and in his presence have subscribed our names as witnesses.
>
> His
John (X) Waggoner
Mark
>
> Wm. Powers
> Parker B. Cookman
> Recorded in Will Book B, page 36 -- Also recorded in Early Records of Vital Records #464954 - Lewis Co. Va. (W)

Susannah (Richards) Waggoner was not mentioned in the will, so I am assuming she died before 1840.

Peter Waggoner, mentioned in the will, we know to be the only remaining son of the first family of Margaret (Bonnett) Waggoner. Land records show both Mary and Elizabeth were deeded 60 acres, on Hacker Creek when they married. Henry and Elijah Waggoner, 2nd & 3rd sons, were not mentioned in the will.

I have found no mention of the Margaret Waggoner who was named in John's will; no marriage and no death record. There was a Margaret Waggoner who m. 17 Nov. 1819, Peter Heckart of Preston Co., d/o Jacob & Catharine Waggoner in the Aurora Documents by Karl L. Gower and she did have a Brother Henry Waggoner who was a witness. This could not have been the son of John & Susannah (Richards) Waggoner who were named as her parents. John's son Jacob, b. ca. 1810, who married Catharine Bonnett in 1831, would have only been 9 years old in 1819.

Revolutionary War Pension Application of John Waggoner
Pension   S7824
John Waggoner

State of Virginia)
Lewis County   )SS

On this 7th day of August A.D. 1832 personally appeared in open Court before the Justice of Lewis County Court now sitting, John Waggoner aged 80 years, a resident of Lewis County in the State of Virginia, who being first duly sworn according to law, does on his oath make the following declaration in order to obtain the benefit of the act of Congress passed 7th of June 1832-

That he entered into the army of the United States under the following named officers and served as he states herein. He was born 14 miles from Philadelphia at a place called White Marsh in the year 1752; his parents moved to Virginia in what is now Hardy County, was drafted to go a tour in the Virginia militia under Captain John Harness, Major Corroll Van Meter, Col. Riddle or Ruddle, marched to Big Beaver in the now State of Ohio, passed through a part of Pennsylvania, went to McIntosh's Fort, from thence to Tuscaraws and built a Fort there which was called Fort Lawrens. He was permitted to return home at the end of tour 6 months and 15 days. He was discharged by the orderly Seargant named Joseph Mall at a place called McIntosh's Fort. There were in this expedition about 2200 men. This was in the 1778, as he now thinks. He then removed to a place now in Preston County Va. called Dunkard Bottom on Cheat River. He was then called into the service by a draft or some such requisition and marched to Prickett's Fort on the Mogongalia or Mongahala river; there he was kept for six months as an Indian spie, his Captain's name was Owen Davey, his Col. was Col. Charles Martin; returned home having been discharged by his Captain Owen Davy. He was then in the Spring of 1781 drafted to go a tour of duty as a Militia man. He marched to Richmond, then retreated up the country before the British, then returned, went to Williamsburg, thence to Yorktown in Va. where he was in the battled and at the capture of Lord Cornwallis. His officers were Capt. John or Thomas Neal, Col. Lewis, Genl. Stephens or Stevens (he thinks Edward Stevens). He went from Yorktown to a place 4 miles from Wichester in Va. with the prisoners taken at Yorktown, he guarded them three months and received his discharge from Capt. Neal, having been in the service this tour not less than nine months, returned home. Then removed to the place where he now lives, this was in the Fall of 1782 as he now recollects he reenlisted as an Indian Spie under Edward Freeman and served three months, the term for which he enlisted, received his discharge. Then was ordered out under order of Col. William Lowther to guard frontier, was stationed at West's Fort for a while, then went out as a Spie, was gone eleven days. The Indians killed his comrade John Bonnett. He continue as a Spie or ranging and searching parties until about the middle of May 1792. The celebrated Tecumseh with a party of Indians, came to his house on a branch of Hacker Creek where he yet lives. Tecumseh sent the other Indians to the house and fired at John Waggoner himself, this affiant, the ball passed through his sleeve without injuring him. Tecumseh dropped his gun and ran after him, Waggoner, but could not catch him, they killed his small son in the yard and scalped him, took his wife and six other children prisoners, started and about a mile from the house one of the children was found with its brains beaten out and scalped. A short distance further on was found Mrs. Waggoner and two other children were found dreadfully mangled and scalped and dead. One of his captive sons (Peter) was recognized in 1812 among the savages by an acquaintance of John Waggoner and brought in and still stays here, is now married, although he had a wife and several children amongst the Indians; one of his daughters soon escaped by way of Detroit, the other continued in captivity till the treaty with the Indians when she was given up by them.

  His discharges were all destroyed in the general destruction of his property by the Indians. He has therefor no documentary evidence of his services during the Revolutionary war nor of his subsequent services. It may be that he can prove his services under Captain Freeman by Alexander West and David M. Sleeth. He hereby relinquishes every claim whatever to a pension or annuity except the present and declares that his name is not on the pension roll of the Agency of any State.

Sworn to and subscribed the day and year aforesaid.

His
John (X) Waggoner
Mark

The said John Waggoner being interrogated by the Court in the manner prescribed by the War Department, answered the several interrogatories propounded by that Department as follows:

1st I was born in the year 1752 at a place called White Marsh about 14 miles from Philadelphia in the State of Pennsylvania according to accounts of my parents.

2nd I have no record of my age.

3rd I lived when first called into service in that part of Virginia called Hardy County, I think it was then Hampshire County.

4th I was drafted each campaign until the one under Captain Freeman, I then enlisted as a Spie. I served in all not less then twenty five months during the war.

5th I can remember General McIntosh, his first name I never knew. I knew Col. Gibson too, this was in my first campaign. We left Col. Gibson at Fort Lawrens which we built on the bank of Tuscarawa river. In my second campaign I knew my own Col. and Col. David Morgan. He killed two Indians in this year and skinned and tanned their hides. The Indians were trying to capture two of Col. Morgan's children, viz., Stephen, about 16 years old and his daughter Sarah, about 14 years old, Col. Morgan upwards of 60 years old. This was done in April 1779, as well as I can now recollect, in the immediate neighborhood of Prickett's Fort about 12 or 14 miles above Morgantown. In my third campaign I knew, or rather saw, Genl. LaFayette, Genl. MacKlinberg. Genl. Stevens, Genl. A. Wayne, Genl. Lincoln and Genl. George Washington. General Lincoln marched the British Troops out to stack their arms. I saw and then heard the names of many other Field officers, whose names I have forgotten.

6th I rec'd four discharges, all of them as I have already mentioned and were lost in the way I have stated when the Indians destroyed my family and property in 1792.

7th I know in my neighborhood John Mitchell, a Methodist preacher, an old man; Henry McWhorter, and Alexander West, old men; William Powers, too an old man. They can all testify as to my veracity and their belief of my services as a soldier of the Revolution.

His
John (X) Waggoner
Mark

We, John Mitchell, a Clergyman residing in the County of Lewis and Mark Smith residing in said County of Lewis, and Alexander West residing the said County of Lewis certify that we are well acquainted with John Waggoner who has subscribed and sworn to the above declaration, that we believe him to be 80 years of age and that he is reputed and believed in the neighborhood where he resides to have been a soldier of the Revolution.

---

30 of Oct. 1846 Henry Butcher, Wm. J. Baily, Adam Fisher, and Luie Maxwell, adm. The Lewis County Court, September term 1848 the appraisment bill of the personal estate of John Waggoner deceased, was this day returned to the Court of Levi Maxwell Administrator of said estate and ordered to be recorded.

Inventory of personal property of John Waggoner deceased, sold on the 25th of June 1846. Some of the items, readable & of interest:

Item	Buyer	Price
2 planes and Augur	to Adam Bush	.50
1 pick axe	Luie Maxwell	.50
1 half inch agger and chisel	John Waggoner	.40
1 ogger	Presley McIntire	.85
1 ogger & chisel	Henry Waggoner	.76
1 Drawernife	Martin Sims	.27
1 Saddle	Samuel Bonnett	10.13
1 Grindstone	Martin Sims	.88
1 Sieve	David Smith	.18
1 Clock & Case	John Edmonds	4.64
1 Bedsted	Susan Sims	1.37
1 Beehive	George Waggoner	1.65
1 Bull Calf	G. W. Dobson	2.06¼
1 Cow	Abram Henzman	9.25
1 Colt	William Kelly	11.40
1 Gray Mare	Martin Fox	46.50
1 Red Cow	G. W. Dobson	9.50
6 head of sheep	George Waggoner	5.12½
1 loom	Samuel Waggoner	1.25
1350 ft. ½ inch and inch plank - 50 cts per hundred		6.75

1 Old Waggon		10.00
1 Eight day brass clock		25.00
5 Chairs		2.50

Sold separately to different individuals
30 head of cattle were sold separately - 48 pigs - 50 sheep - 13 horses & 3 colts - household goods, furniture, bedding.

31 Wool at 25 cents per lb.		7.75
2 Hay Stacks		9.50
1 lot of Wool	William Watson	1.42
15 bushels of buckwheat		5.56¼
1 Cupboard	Francis Waggoner	4.12½
1 Teakittle	Christopher Stasel	.37
25 Bushels of Corn	Wm. Alexander	9.56¼
1 lot of dishes	Amos Waggoner	1.12½
1 set of Tablespoons	Francis Waggoner	2.06½
1 Great Coat		1.50
2 pair Sheep Shears		.25
1 Foot ____ (can't read)	Peter Waggoner	1.31

Everything was sold and they called in all notes:

1 note of hand on Jacob Waggoner owed 1 Jan. 1833	30.00
1 note of hand on George Waggoner	11.75
1 note of hand on Samual Waggoner	23.28
1 note - due Sept. 1842 - Elijah Waggoner	11.00
1 note on John Waggoner - due Oct. 11th - 1842 -	24.00
to account on Jacob Wolf	18.12½
to account on John Flescher, Borrowed money	2.00
to account on Leonard D. Sims - Borrowed money	5.00

29 Sept. 1842

❖❖❖❖❖❖❖❖❖❖❖❖❖❖❖❖❖❖❖❖❖❖❖❖❖❖❖❖❖❖❖❖❖❖❖❖❖❖

After reading the 10 page inventory of all the sale items, many of which I had never seen, or even heard of; I felt it was truly the end of 91 years of John Waggoner's life. Think of what those 91 years held -- born in Pennsylvania -- lived on South Branch, Cheat River, Jesse's Run, and Hacker Creek, John led a long and useful life, - almost a century of history.

To help with the second family of John Waggoner we need to look at land records in Lewis Co. W. Va.

John & Susannah (Richards) Waggoner sold 103 acres in Oct. 1802, on the West Fork River. I believe this could have been part of Susannah's dowry, as it was adjacent to John Runyon.

1817 John Waggoner paid tax on (160 acres) on G. Lick Run.

1819 John Waggoner has (300 acres) on Jesse Hughes Run & added (28 1/2 A.) purchased from Weeden Huffman on Jesse Hughes Run.

1819 Paul Waggoner has (150 A.) on left Hand fork of Hacker's Cr.

1819 Peter Waggoner from Tobias Miller (54 A.) Hacker's Creek.

1823 John Waggoner from Joseph Johnson (90 A.) Hacker's Creek.

1831 Henry Waggoner from John & Susanna Waggoner (103 A.) Jesse Hughes Run.

1831 Elijah Waggoner from John & Susanna Waggoner (97 A.) Jesse Hughes Run.

1831 Henry W. Sleeth from Jacob & Catharine Waggoner (100 A.) Finks Fork of Leading Creek.

1834 Wm. Waggoner from Joseph Waggoner (150 A.) Buckhannon Run.

1838 Peter Waggoner from Isaac Morris (300 A.) Hacker's Creek.

1839 Jacob Waggoner from Samuel Bonnett Jr. (100 A.) Laural Lick of H. Cr.

1839 Peter Waggoner from Elijah Arnold (12 A.) Millstone Run.

In 1985 Robert B. Smith, was kind enough to send me:

1791 July 1, 200 Acres was surveyed for John Waggoner, assignor of Jesse Hughes Run of Hacker's Creek. (Survey Book 3-pg. 360)

1801 Oct. 31-(Bk. 4 pg. 342) another 160 acres were surveyed for John Waggoner and adjoining piece of land. Mr. Smith was also kind enough to send pictures of some grave stones he found.

John Waggoner ae 90 (Pens.) living with Samuel Waggoner in the 1840 census of Lewis Co. (W) Va.

John and Susannah (Richards) Waggoner had these children: 1. Paul, 2. Henry, 3. Elijah, 4. John, 5. Jacob, 6. Catherine, 7. George, 8. William, 9. Susanna, 10. Meriah, 11. Samuel, 12. Margaret ?.

Paul Waggoner
(1800-1877)

Several years ago I meet Mrs. Arva Stine, Osark, Mo. Through letters, about this Waggoner line, she has been kind enough to share her research on Paul Waggoner and Elizabeth (Straley) Waggoner. Mr. & Mrs. Charles Stine visited the Hacker Creek area some years ago and have shared pictures with me. (Charles Stine passed away on 8 Nov. 1993.)

Paul Waggoner, born 1800-Jesse Run, Hacker Creek, Harrison Co. (W) Va., died 1877 Colfax, Clinton Co. Indiana, s/o John and Susannah (Richards) Waggoner. The name *Paul* has not been used before in the Waggoner line, perhaps it was the name of his mother's father, a Paul Richards was killed in 1782 in an Indian attack at Richard's Fort, Harrison Co. (W) Va., and I believe that this Paul Richards was Susannah's father.

Paul, m. 10 Jan. 1821, Lewis Co. (W) Va. by John Mitchell, Elizabeth Straley (ca. 1799 Harrison Co. (W) Va. d. 1864 Colfax Clinton Co. Indiana.), d/o George and Elizabeth (Bonnett) Straley. It is believed that Paul moved his family to Ohio around 1828, and then later on to Indiana.

Their children were; John Straley, Elizabeth, Mary, George, Stephen, Susannah, Peter, William Melton, Virginia Catharine, Oliver H.P. and James M. Waggoner.

1. John Straley Waggoner, b. ca. 1822 Lewis Co. (W) Va., s/o Paul and Elizabeth (Straley) Waggoner, m. 1 Jan. 1846, Clinton Co., Ind. Amelia Jane Mitchell. Their children:
   - Peter M. Waggoner, 1847 Boone Co. Ind.
   - Jefferson Waggoner, 1849.
   - Amelia Jane Waggoner, 1853.
   - America C. Waggoner, 1857.

Paul Waggoner (1800 - 1877)

- Paul Waggoner, 1848.
- Joanna Pifer Waggoner, 1851.
- Frank M. Waggoner 1855.
- John C.B. Waggoner 1859.

2. Elizabeth Waggoner, b. 1823 Lewis Co. (W) Va. m. William Thorp.
3. Mary Waggoner b. 1825 Lewis Co. (1860 census, ae. 35 y. Boone Co. Ind.) both d/o Paul and Elizabeth (Straley) Waggoner.
4. George Waggoner b. 1826 Lewis Co. (W) Va. s/o Paul & Elizabeth (Straley) Waggoner. (ch.: Stephen, Edward, Florance & Libby)

Mrs. Stine credits Oliver Ray Waggoner of Oklahoma with the children of Paul & Elizabeth (Straley) Waggoner & the line of Stephen Waggoner.

5. Stephen Waggoner (1828-Colfax, Clinton Co. Ind.-d. 1897, Ashton, Kansas.), s/o Paul and Elizabeth (Straley) Waggoner, m. (1st) 1855 Margaret E. Moore, (1838-1856, ae. 18 yr.) (had one son.) m. (2nd) 1861-Margaret E. Goodnight (1841-1879).

Children:(1st m.):
- Oliver M. Waggoner (1856-1882 ae. 25 yr.).

Children (2nd m.):
- James R. Waggoner (1862 Colfax, Ind. d. 1940) lived Mulhall, Okla. and Gueda Sp. Ks., m. May McClaskey (1867-1956) ch.: Edith (1888-1935), Elsie, Aluina & Louisa.
- Virginia Elizabeth Waggoner b. 1864 Colfax, Ind. m. Al Tibbetts, lived Cresent, Okla., ch.: Oliver, Roy and Lucille.
- McClellen Waggoner, b. 1866 Colfax, Ind. m. Cordelia Olive Tibbetts lived Billing, Okla. ch.: Alta Ruth, 1892, George Edward, 1894, Calvin Roy, 1897 and Chester 1900.
- Daniel Voorhees Waggoner b. 1869 Colfax Ind. d. 1937 Ashton, Ks. m. Mary Ellen Cooperbarger(1873-1935) d/o Joe & Elizabeth Cooperbarger. ch.: Warren, Floyd, Margret, Oliver, Bertha & Beatrice.

The 1850 & 1860 Census of Indiana show Paul Waggoner in Boone Co., 7th Dist. Colfax is located in the south west corner of Clinton, Co. and very near the border of Boone Co. Perhaps their land was in both counties.

Bess-Paul- Wesley- Maybelle and Junetta.
Peter Waggoner- Elmer -Minerva (Climer) Waggoner.

Peter Waggoner & Family

6. Susannah Waggoner b. 4 Oct. 1829 d/o Paul & Elizabeth (Straley) Waggoner, m. 8 July 1847 Boone Co. Ind. Wm. Albert McCay. ch.: Hamilton, Perry, Paul, Peter, Fielden, & Jim. Jim McCay lived at Coldwater, Ks.

7. Peter Waggoner, (born 1831 Clinton Co. Ind. 1895,) Ozark, Christian Co. Mo., s/o Paul and Elizabeth (Straley) Waggoner, m. (1st) Barbary (___) Waggoner b. 1833 Va.

They had 2 children:
- Emily E. (Amy) Waggoner b. 25 Dec. 1859.
- Seymour Waggoner, b. 4 Jan. 1860.

Peter Waggoner, m. (2nd) Minerva Climer. They came to Missouri in a covered wagon in 1871, and their first child Junetta was b. 3 June 1871 in Clinton, Mo. in route to Ozark, Christian Co. Mo. Peter and Minerva (Climer) Waggoner had six children: Junetta, Wesley, Paul, Maybelle, Bess & Elmer Waggoner.

- Junetta Waggoner (3 June 1871-3 Feb. 1946) m. Frank Biers (26 Oct. 1866-6 Mar. 1929) from Columbia City, Ind. ch.: Bessie and Maxie.
  - Bessie Biers (6 July 1892-4 Sept. 1970) m. Jess Graham (4 Mar. 1891-17 Nov. 1993).
  - Maxie Biers (17 June 1897-28 Dec. 1975) m. Ralph Thomas (21 Aug. 1896-9 Sept. 1977). Their children; Arva, Lois, Junetta and Frank Thomas.
    - ◊ Arva Thomas (13 Feb. 1915- Ozark, Mo. m. Charles W. Stine (10 Apr. 1914-8 Nov. 1993). Two sons Tom Stine and Terry Stine.
    - ◊ Lois Thomas (15 Oct. 1918-3 Nov. 1989) m. Frank Estes. Ch; Ronnie Estes, Jerry Estes, and Gary Estes.
    - ◊ Junetta Thomas (4 Sept. 1923-Ozark Mo. m. Glen Mooney (18 June 1919); ch; Carol , June , David and Nancy Mooney.
    - ◊ Frank Thomas (30 Dec. 1925. Ozark, Mo. m. Lalia Fitzpatrick (29 Oct. 1929). ch.: Max and Donald Thomas Fitzpatrick.
- Wesley Waggoner (17 Aug. 1873-21 Feb. 1934) s/o Peter & Minerva (Climer) Waggoner m. Flossie Wills (11 Feb. 1876-11 Nov. 1959) ch.: Jessie and Ermgne Waggoner.

- Jessie Waggoner, (30 Aug. 1896-8 Nov. 1991) m. Clarence Shelton (3 Mar. 1894-14 Feb. 1953)
  ◊ Annabell Shelton b. 17 June 1919 Ozark, Mo. m. Earnest Stevens b. 28 Sept. 1916.
  ◊ Dorothy Shelton Z., b. 29 July 1925 Ozarka Mo. m. Bill McCurdy, b. 5 June 1924. ch; Lynn, Lana, and Scott.
- Ermyne Waggoner (30 Oct. 1902-17 Oct. 1981) m. Albert Thomas (1 Mar. 1902-9 July 1987) Ch; Irene Thomas, Ray Wesley Thomas, Earl Thomas, Verl Thomas, Ruth Thomas, Junetta Thomas and Carol Sue Thomas.
  ◊ Irene Thomas b. 19 May 1925, m. Larry Roth b. 1 Aug. 1912.
  ◊ Ray Wesley Thomas b. 2 May 1927-m. Jorene Robinson b. 5 Feb. 1930. ch: Janet and Cindy Thomas.
  ◊ Verl Thomas b. 9 Dec. 1930 m. Verba Cane, b. 5 Aug. 1939. ch; Douglas, Danny, Dorthea, Dwane, Dana & David Thomas.
  ◊ Earl Thomas, b. 9 Dec. 1930. m. Carol Dean Robinson, b. 22 Dec. 1934. ch: Greg, Curt & John Thomas.
  ◊ Ruth Thomas b. 7 Apr. 1937 m. Bill Jardine (18 Mar. 1926-2 Dec. 1985). m. (2nd) James Brooks.
  ◊ Juanita Thomas. (15 Dec. 1938-8 Oct. 1985) m. Kieth Bowden, b. 23 Mar. 1936, ch; Beth & Scott Bowden.
  ◊ Carol Sue Thomas, m. Tom Cobb, ch; Lisa and Sara Cobb.

• Bess Waggoner (23 Feb. 1875-13 Oct. 1927) Ozark, Mo. s/o Peter and Minerva (Climer) Waggoner. m. Della Mae Wills (18 Aug. 1874-14 Sept. 1963). ch; Lydia, Pete, Lola and Max Waggoner.
- Lydia Waggoner (20 July 1897-13 Jan. 1983 m. Ben Marley, (17 Mar. 1897-17 Oct. 1937) ae. 40 yrs. m. 2nd Dan Robinson (18 Jan. 1913-29 Dec. 1970) ch.: Mary Lee.
- Pete Waggoner (23 May 1901-31 Oct. 1981) m. Ramah Brazeal b. 15 Sept. 1905).
- Lola Waggoner, (31 July 1905-18 Feb. 1994) m. Layman Payne b. 17 Nov. 1901, ch: Lynn, Ella Mae & Janet Payne.
  ◊ Lynn Payne b. 31 Aug. 1926 m. Mattie Wallace, ch: Lynette, Cindy, Lana, & Dixie Payne.
  ◊ Ella Mae Payne, b. 12 July 1928 m. Clifford Bishop.

- ◊ Janet Payne, b. 4 Aug. 1940 m. Ronnie Johns. ch.: Payree & Aaron Johns.
- Paul Waggoner (10 Feb. 1880-29 Jan. 1927) s/o Peter and Minerva (Climer) Waggoner.
- Maybelle Waggoner (16 Oct. 1881-12 Aug. 1976) m. Stanton Spivey. ch.: Ward and Joe Spivey.
    - ♦ Ward Spivey (17 July 1905-28 Oct. 1972) m. Jessie (12 Mar. 1907-19 June 1969).
    - ♦ Joe Glenn Spivey (27 June 1914-15 June 1991) m. Betty, ch.: Peggy & Mary Francis Spirey.
- Elmer Waggoner (16 Apr. 1886-31 May 1945) s/o Peter and Minerva (Climer) Waggoner Ozark, Mo. m. Della Park (26 Oct. 1894-11 Jan. 1982). ch.: Georgia, Joseph, James Franklin, Thelma & Robert Bess Waggoner.
    - ♦ Georgia Waggoner b. 15 Feb. 1918. m. Robert Harvey ch.: Ronnie and Donnie Harvey.
    - ♦ Joseph Waggoner, b. 9 June 1920. m. Irene, ch.: Donna, Larry, Karen, Della & Ruth Waggoner.
    - ♦ James Franklin Wagoner b. 28 Oct. 1922 m. Ada, ch.: Linda Waggoner.
    - ♦ Thelma Waggoner, b. 17 May 1925 m. Marvin Hall ch.: Jenny Hall.
    - ♦ Robert Bess Waggoner, b. 29 Sept. 1929. m. Betty, ch.: Karen, John, Steve, Gary, Jeffrey & Barbara Waggoner.

8. William Milton Waggoner b. ca. 1832 Colfax, Clinton Co. Ind. s/o Paul & Elizabeth (Straley) Waggoner m. Martha Climer. (1860 census lived Boone Co. Ind.) ch.: Malissa, May, Belle, Lena, Stella & Joseph Waggoner.

- Malissa Waggoner, (1886-1909) m. Martin Crose, ch.: Clarence Crose.
- May Waggoner m. Robert Wyant. ch.: Floyd & Willard Wyant.
- Belle Waggoner m. Aden Evans.
- Lina Waggoner m. George Coulter.
- Stella Waggoner m. Stephen Laymons m. (2nd) Howard Ruse.
- Joseph Waggoner m. Pearl Boyd.

9. Virginia Catharine Waggoner b. ca. 1835, d/o Paul and Elizabeth (Straley) Waggoner.

10. Oliver H. P. Waggoner (1837-1880) s/o Paul & Elizabeth (Straley) Waggoner, m. 1862, Colfax, Ind. (1st) Rhoda Jane Cory (d. 1876) m.

(2nd) 1878 Mary Lanam. ch.: Voarhees, Elias Straley, Willard & Florence Waggoner.

- Voarhees Waggoner (1863-1864)
- Elias Straley Waggoner (1865-1942) m. 1892 Colfax, Ind. Margaret Harbaugh, ch.: Florence Constance, Maurice Walton, Mary Elizabeth & Dorothy Ann Waggoner.
- Willard Waggoner (1867-1889) Colfax, Ind.
- Florence Waggoner (1870-1915) m. Arkansas City, Ks. Alfred H. Constant. ch.: Harold Waggoner Constant, m. Dora (Ada, Ok.); and Edith Constant.

11 James M. Waggoner, b. ca. 1840 s/o Paul & Elizabeth (Straley) Waggoner. m. Mary A. Climer, ch: Ira S., Ida A., Carrie M., and Raliegh Benton Waggoner.

- Ira S. Waggoner m. Laura Rickey (d. 1897) m. (2nd) Grace Caldwell d. 1933). ch.: (1st m.) Russel & Adah; (2nd) Paul R., James M. and Gertrude Merle Waggoner.
- Ida A. Waggoner m. Albert R. Hickerson, ch.: Amy M. Porter Daves of Thorntown, Walter Heckerson.
- Carrie M. Waggoner m. Roy Bartholmew. ch: Nova, Neome, Ralph & George A. Bartholmew.
- Raleigh Benton Waggoner (1877-1956) Colfax, Ind. m. Clemma Mae Rutan (1878-1949). ch.: Helen, Charles, Leo Waggoner.

Henry Waggoner
(1802-1886)

Henry Waggoner, b.1 Mar. 1802, Jesse Run. Harrison Co., d. 8 Dec. 1886, ae. 84y. 8m. 26d., bur. on John Waggoners farm, (John & Susannah (Richards) Waggoner may be buried in this family cemetery.)

In 1985, Aug. 11 Robert B. Smith sent me pictures of four stones located on the old farm of Henry Waggoner, then belonging to John Kolb of Jane Lew, Lewis Co. W. Va. Located on the original 200 Acre track of land owned by John Waggoner (1751-1842 will probated). Once two log cabins stood on this property, some forty feet apart, with a well in between the two cabins. The second track of 160 acres of land, adjoining up Clay Lick, could have been the home of Henry Waggoner -- several other houses were on this property.

I do not believe our Henry Wggoner was m. twice. In 1819 Nov. 17 a Henry Waggoner was bondsman for Peggy Waggoner, d/o Jacob & Caty Waggoner who m. Peter Heckart of Preston Co. (The Aurora Documents by Karl K. Gower Bk. 1 & 2 of the Oregional Records of St. Paul's Lutheran Church). Right away one thinks of our Henry, who was b. 1802 & would have been 17 yrs. of age, then the parents of Peggy brings to mind the Margaret Waggoner (in John's will 1840) and if Jacob & Caty were the parents-in 1819-our Jacob would have been around 10 years old, and not yet have married Catharine Bonnett in 1831. But the parents Jacob and Caty Waggoner do fit the Jacob Waggoner and Catharine (Troxel) Waggoner parents of Johan Georg Waggoner-12 May 1793- (Aurora Doc. pg. 21). Most of the Aurora Waggoners went west.

8th Nov. 1827-Henry Waggoner m. Susan Bonnett (30 May 1806- Harrison Co. d. 11 Apr. 1899 ae. 92 y. 10 m. 11 d.), d/o Samuel and Martha (Radcliff) Bonnett.

Tombstones of Henry and Susan Waggoner

Henry Waggoner b. 1 Mar. 1802 d. 8 Dec. 1886 ae 84 y. 8 m. 26 d. Lewis Co. Farmer, P. John & Susannah Waggoner, Rpt by wife.

❖❖❖❖❖❖❖❖❖❖❖❖❖❖❖❖❖❖❖❖❖❖❖❖❖❖❖❖❖❖❖❖❖❖❖❖

Susan (Bonnett) Waggoner b. 21 Mar. 1806 d. 11 Apr. 1899-Rpt by son Henry E. Waggoner.

Children of Henry & Susan (Bonnett) Waggoner were, Samuel B., Margaret R., Henry E. and Olive Malissa Waggoner.

1. Samuel B. Waggoner (20 July 1828-4 May 1911) Old Harmony Cem. Lewis Co. m. 14 June 1852, Lewis Co. by H. R. Bonnett, Francis C. McAvoy (4 Sept. 1832-2 Apr. 1895 ae. 63 y.) d/o John McAvoy and Jane McAvoy.

Their children:

- Lloyd Bascom Waggoner (30 March 1854-22 Aug. 1871 ae. 18 y. 4 m. 22 d.) James Miflin, Alice Columbia, Alvin L., John H., Susan Jane, Samuel C., Sarah E. and Francis Ruie Waggoner.
- James Miflin Waggoner, b. 30 May 1856 Jepes Run. m. 21 May 1885. Sarah Elizabeth McWhorter, b. Aug. 1855 Lewis Co. (W) Va. Their children; Whitman H. (b. Dec. 1890), Anna F. (b. May 1892), Lela A. (b. Mar. 1896 and Bessie J. (b. Mar. 1886).

1931 Obituary from newspapter of Northern West Virginia.

> Mrs. Miflin Wagner, Jane Lew April 1-Word has been recieved here by John Waggoner (s/o Samuel B.) of the death of Mrs. Miflin Wagner, a sister-in-law of Ohio. Mrs. Wagner was a former resident of Jane Lew.

- Columbia A. Waggoner (7 Mar. 1859-1939) Harmony Cem. m. Bender.
- Alvin L. Waggoner (Apr. 1862-1935) Old Harmony Cem.
- John H. Wggoner (Oct. 1864-1950) old Harmony Cem.
- Susan Jane Waggoner (24 May 1867-1933) Harmony Cem.
- Samuel C. Waggoner (28 Feb. 1869-1940) Harmony Cem.
- Sarah E. Waggoner (twin) (6 Dec. 1872-1949).
- Frances Ruie Waggoner (twin) (6 Dec. 1872).

2. Margaret Ruhana Waggoner (1834-12 Feb. 1916, ae. 82 y. 2 m. 14 d.) d/o Henry & Susan (Bonnett) Waggoner, m. 9 Oct. John S. Reger. s/o Henry Reger (19 Dec. 1793-3 Dec. 1856 and Barbara (2nd wife) (7 Jan. 1804-2 Nov. 1882) Philip Reger Cem. Buckhannon dist.

Upshur Co. (W) Va. (John (S. or L.) Reger was m. (1st) to Mary L. McWhorter 1 Jan. 1851) Lewis Co. she was (b. 18 Apr. 1830 d. 30 Jan. 1852). There is a note along the name John S. Reger (buried in Ohio). I found Margaret Reger and a John S. Reger in the Upshur Co. Death Records (pg. 117).

- Margaret E. Reger (1852-1931) Harmony Cem. m. 26 Sept 1870, Upshur Co. W. Va. Abner Bargerhuff s/.o James & Letisia Bargerhuff.
- Linda E. Reger, (Mar. 1857-Lewis Co. m. 1 Apr. 1879 Upshur Co. George W. West (June 1853-1933) Lorentz Cem. Upshur Co. W. Va. (Vol. 6 pg. 116) s/o John & Elizabeth West. There were other children listed in The Philip Reger Cem. Buckhannon. Infant Reger d. 30 Nov. 1855, s/o J. S. & M. R., Henry Reger d. 21 July 1859, Birdie Reger d. 14 Oct. 1862.

3. Henry E. Waggoner (18 Apr. 1838-31 Dec. 19__) s/o Henry and Susan (Bonnett) Waggoner.

4. Olive Malissa Waggoner (17 Feb. 1850-25 Aug. 1851 ae. 1 y. 6 m. 8 d.) buried Old Waggoner Cem. on John Waggoner's Farm. (see Cemetery Stones Picture)

Kansas Sod House "Sodie"

Elijah Waggoner
(1804 - 1899)

Elijah Waggoner
(1804-1899)

Please Credit William Burl Waggoner of Grafton, W. Va. for this line, Elijah & Mary (Straley) Waggoner.

Elijah Waggoner (10 Jan. 1804, Jesse Run, Harrison Co., 31 May 1899, ae 95 y.) Hacker Creek, Lewis Co. W. Va., s/o John and Susannah (Richards) Waggoner m. 16 Mar. 1830, Lewis Co. by John Mitchell, Mary Straley (27 Dec. 1804-30 Aug. 1882) d/o George and Elizabeth (Bonnett) Straley. Both are bur. at Harmony Cem. Lewis Co.

Elijah was not mentioned in his father John Waggoner's will. However, Elijah's death record states that his Parents were John & Susannah Waggoner.

12 Aug. 1831, John Waggoner sold 97 acres on Clay Lick, to Elijah Waggoner where Elijah built his first cabin.

On 14 June 1852 Elijah Waggoner bought the track called "The George Straley Farm" on Hacker Creek, adj. lands of Joseph Straley, containing the shares of Samuel B. Straley; Susan Allen; Elias Straley; James Straley; Elizabeth Shanet; Jacob Straley; Joseph Straley; Geo. Presley Straley; Caroline Straley; Simmons Straley; Mary Straley; Eliza Jackson, Heirs and representatives of Joseph Straley (deceased). Elijah paid about $10.00 per acre for the 300 acre tract.

Children of Elijah & Mary (Straley) Waggoner:
- Elias W. Waggoner (8 Feb. 1831-28 Sept. 1917 ae 86 y. 7 m. 20 d.), s/o Elijah & Mary (Straley) Waggoner m. 20 June 1861, Lewis Co., Harriet Cookman (21 Mar. 1836-17 Dec. 1903, ae. 77 y. 8 m. 0 d.) d/o Jeremiah & Elizabeth (Betsy) (Tracey) Cookman. Both bur. Freemans Creek united Methodist Cem.

- George Washington Waggoner (29 Oct. 1863-19 July 1938) s/o Elias W. & Harriet (Cookman) Waggoner, m. 29 Oct. 1884 Rose May Kemper (5 Nov. 1863-23 Apr. 1930) d/o Rev. Reuben & Rosamond Kemper
  - ◊ Ella Blanch Waggoner, (18 Aug. 1885 - 27 Oct. 1972), m. 26 Oct. 1904 James A. Burnside (30 July 1881-17 Mar. 1961) children:
    - * Ethel Blanch Burnside (1905-1987) m. 1 Apr. 1925 Garley Sprouse (d. 26 Feb. 1986). ch.: Arnette Wayne Sprouse and Ruth Ann Sprouse.
    - * John Lee Burnside (7 Oct. 1906-10 June 1986), m. 19 May 1928 Orpha Grace Freeman, b. 25 Dec. 1910. ch.: Wade Eugene Lee Burnside, Stella Blanch Burnside, John Kent Burnside, and James Lynn Burnside.
    - * Joseph E. Burnside, d. 17 June 1968 m. (1st) Margaret Brown.
    - * James William Burnside (29 Dec. 1819 - 8 Jan. 1977), m. Pauline Putman.
  - ◊ Stella (Estella) Waggoner (twin) (2 Mar. 1887-21 Mar. 1931) m. Sept. 1919 Otterbein Gum. (10 July 1886-23 Aug. 1965) ch.: Mary Kathleen Gum m. (1) John Roberts m. 2nd Windell Byerley, Leslie Jennings Gum m. Carol Weekley.
  - ◊ Marella Waggoner (twin) (2 Mar. 1887-17 June 1956) m. 3 June 1913 John Harley Hull, ch.:
    - * Ishmael Hull, m. Jesse Calvert.
    - * Robert Hull m. (1st) Eula Dean White, m. (2nd) Mary K. Barr.
    - * Rose Mary Hull m. ___ Williams.
    - * Betty Dell Hull m. Edward Joe Craft.
  - ◊ Grace Waggoner (29 Jan. 1890-1 Jan. 1891)
  - ◊ Harriet Rose Waggoner (30 July 1891-16 Mar. 1953) m Clarence Halterman.
  - ◊ Emma Pearl Waggoner (10 May 1893-23 Aug. 1979) m. John W. Chew (12 May 1888-10 Jan. 1980) ch.: Beth Ann Chew (b. 6 Feb. 1927) m. 27 Sept. 1952 Junior Hamrick b. 31 Aug. 1925.
  - ◊ Willa Ruth Waggoner (12 Aug. 1895-5 June 1989) m. 3 June 1917 Emmett Hull, (5 Jan. 1884-30 Oct. 1958) ch.:

* Ruth Ann Bette Hull b. 8 July 1919 m. 1943 Nicholas Murin.
* Carolyn Hull (1927-1982) m. Robert Arnold.
* Mary Kemper Hull, b. 35 Nov. 1939 m. 17 June 1963 Anthony Gum.

◊ George Kemper Waggoner (25 Sept. 1898-7 Dec. 1966) m. 11 Sept. 1920, Margaret Ellen Williams (4 Feb. 1902-1 Apr. 1981).

* George Wilson Waggoner-(b. 17 Jan. 1922) m. 3 Dec. 1945, Mildred H. Wilson b. 16 Jan. 1926. ch.: George Jr., Raymond Carus, Margaret Jane and Delores Waggoner.
* Carus Jennings Waggoner (2 May 1923-1930)
* Kathryn Ann Waggoner b. 5 Aug. 1925. m. 23 Aug. 1941, Harvey K. Small (16 Oct. 1918-11 Aug. 1975) ch.: Mary K., Bea Ann, Michael Lynn and Sharon Lee Small)
* Alice Ruth Waggoner b. 24 Oct., 1930,m. 23 Aug. 1946 Dorsey Frazier Hamrick Sr. b. 30 Sept. 1923.
  + Janet Rose Hamrick m. Glenn Smith Dawson.
  + Alice Faye Hamrick m. William Wooden Kolbaugh.
  + Elizabeth Carol Hamrick m. Robert David Brown.
  + Dorsey Frazier Hamrick Jr. m. Eunice Ritchier.
  + Barbara Jean Hamrick m. Willard Evans.
  + Vickie Lynne Hamrick m. (1st) Harold E. Butcher m. 2nd Ronald Ray Erickson.
  + William Everett Hamrick m. Lisa White.
  + Tina Louise Hamrick.
* Jack Elias Waggoner b. 14 July 1933 m. 30 Sept. 1953 Cerilda MacLemasters, ch.: Perry Robert, m. Grace A. Lipscomb, Jenny Lou, Shiela Marie, Donna Lynn, & Daniel Lee Waggoner.
* Joseph Clinton Waggoner b. 14 Aug. 1934 m. 20 Jan. 1954, Janet Louise West, (ch.: Joseph C. Jr., Judith Ellen, Jeffery Allen, & Jack Douglas).
* James Edwin Waggoner b. 7 May 1939- m. 13 June 1959, Linda Lou Wheatley, (ch.: James E. Jr., Catherine Lynn, David Wayne, and Gary Adam.)

- ◊ William Carus Waggoner (29 Oct. 1900-14 Dept. 1955) m. 19 July 1930 Orpha Snyder b. 23 May 1910, (ch.: Marjorie Joan m. Bernard Hyatt.
- ◊ R. E. Bland Waggoner (6 Nov. 1906-15 Nov. 1972) m. 7 Oct. 1928, Lewis Co. Florance B. Bailey. d. 9 Oct. 1970) (W.W. 2 - U.S. Army) Both buried Freemansburg Cem. V. F. W. 1976.
- ♦ Ishmael (Eddie) Waggoner (5 Feb. 1866-1956) Lewis Co. s/o Elias W. & Harriet (Cookman) Waggoner m. ca. 1890 Lewis Co. Minnie B. Riffee b. Apr. 1866. Both bur. Freemans Creek Cem.
  - ◊ Earnest Gale Waggoner (1890-1962) m. Myra Cumpston.
  - ◊ Edna D. Waggoner (1992-1969) m. Willis Cumpston.
  - ◊ Nellie Mae Waggoner (4 Feb. 1894-June 1991) m. Lloyd Burnside.
- ♦ Harriet Ella Waggoner (9 Oct. 1874-30 Mar. 1916 ae 41 y. 7 m. 18 d.), d/o Elias W. & Harriet (Cookman) Waggoner, m. ca 1896 Lewis Co., Willard R. Burnside, (29 June 1873-24 Oct. 1907 ae 34 y. 3 m. 25 d.) Freemansburg U.B. Church Cem. Lewis Co. W. Va. ch.: Edward Brent Burnside (6 Jan. 1897-5 Dec. 1978) m. Estelle Brohard.

Children:
- ◊ William Burnside.
- ◊ Charles Richard Burnside m. Dorris Lowther.
- ◊ Elizabeth Burnside m. Beecher Rhodes.
- ◊ Robert Bland Burnside m. Janet Curtis.

Elias W. Waggoner, in 1863 bought from Adam Peck, 140 acres on the Right Hand Fork of Freeman's Creek.

In 1878 John Kemper sold 40 acres on the right Hand Fork of Freeman's Creek, to Elias W. Waggoner.

- • Peter G. Waggoner b 21 Aug. 1833 died young s/o Elijah & Mary (Straley) Waggoner.
- • Christina Waggoner (6 Nov. 1835- Dec. 1914 Seymour Cem.) Lewis Co., d/o Elijah & Mary (Straley) Waggoner m. 20 Sept. 1860 Lewis Co. Sobisca Stalnaker (8 Jan. 1839-15 Jan. 1923) Skin Creek, Lewis Co. W. Va. s/o Samuel Stalnaker (13 Nov. 1800-25 Mar. 1845) and Elizabeth McWhorter, b. 15 Jan. 1811- d/o Walter Fields & Margaret (Hurst) McWhorter.

Samuel Stalnaker m. 25 Sept. 1827 Elizabeth McWhorter.

Children of Samuel and Elizabeth (McWhorter) Stalnaker:
- Andrew Stalnaker m. 25 Nov. 1852 Lewis Co. Eunice Brown.
- John Stalnaker, b ca 1829 Lewis Co.
- Charles Stalnaker, b. ca. 1830 m. Julia M.
- Julia Ann Stalnaker (1832-26 Aug. 1869) m. McWhorter.
- Levi Stalnaker, b. ca. 1835.
- Samuel Stalnaker, b. ca. 1837.
- Walter Stalnaker m. 23 Dec. 1861 Lewis Co. Rhuelina L. Waggoner d/o William & Nancy Ann (Ball) Waggoner.
- Sabisco Stalnaker m. 20 Sept. 1860 Lewis Co., Christina Waggoner d/o Elijah & Mary (Straley) Waggoner.
- George Stalnaker b. ca. 1841.
- Elizabeth Stalnaker, b. ca. 1845.

Sabisco & Christina (Waggoner) Stalnaker are buried Horner Cem. (Rt.-33) they had 11 children, 9 living. (see Stalnaker line):

- Marcellus Elias Stalnaker, (4 July 1861-1947) Lewis Co., m. 13 Oct. 1891, Emma McWhorter, b. 18 Oct. 1866.
- Mary Olive Stalnaker (5 Jan. 1863-28 July 1865).
- Elizabeth Rebecca Stalnaker (13 Mar. 1864-14 Feb. 1937) Lewis Co., m. 20 June 1882 Lewis Co., Alonzo C. Hardman (4 May 1856-May 1940), s/o Thomas R. & Susan Elizabeth (Summers) Hardman. ch.:
  ◊ Ada May Hardman, b. 2 June 1883 Lewis Co., m. 7 Aug. 1904 Alvin Summers (7 Apr. 1882-21 Jan. 1946).
  ◊ Porter Hardman, b. 13 May 1886 m. Eleanor Brock.
  ◊ Ira S. Hardman, b. 26 Jan. 1888 m. Elizabeth Davisson.
  ◊ Foster Hardman, b. 15 Nov. 1894, m. Virginia Kidd.
- Samuel Elijah Stalnaker, (28 Jan. 1865-3 July 1917) m. 18 Nov. 1893, Rose Summers. ch.:
  ◊ Eula Stalnaker, b. 8 Jan. 1895 m Kurts Wood.
  ◊ Hobert Stalnaker m. Meryl Stalnaker.
  ◊ Bassel Stalnaker.
  ◊ Kenneth Stalnaker.
  ◊ Harold Stalnaker.

- Thomas Edward Stalnaker, b. 2 May 1867 m. 5 Sept. 1888, Julea V. Hall, b. Sept. 1870. ch.:
  - Roy S. Stalnaker, b. 7 Jan. 1890, m. Margaret McMullen.
  - Thomas Curl Stalnaker, b. 3 Nov. 1891, m. (1) Alta Hinzman, m. (2) Edna Garten.
  - Anna G. Stalnaker, b. 29 Dec. 1893, m. 2 Apr. 1914, Jacob J. Jackson.
  - Freda Stalnaker, b. 14 Jan. 1896, m. 2 June 1917, Ray J. Jennings.
  - Ethel Stalnaker, b. 15 June 1898 m. July 1920, Stokes Swisher.
  - Mary P. Stalnaker, b. 2 Sept. 1900, m. Edward Burl Waggoner.
  - Walter Stalnaker, b. 28 May 1903 m. Inez Linger.
- George William Stalnaker, b. 28 Sept. 1868, m. 25 Dec. 1895, Matilda Shafer, Braxton Co. W. Va.
- Christina Victoria Stalnaker (17 Apr., 1870-19 Feb. 1922) m. 5 Sept. 1889 Asa Warren Hall, (1868-1907) s/o William D. & Nancy S. (Law) Hall. ch.:
  - Madge V. Hall b. 25 Sept. 1890 m. Thomas E. Miles.
  - Pearl Hall, b. 7 July 1892, m. Hustus Taylor.
  - William D. Hall, (17 Mar. 1894-11 Sept. 1911).
  - Christine Hall, b. 5 Oct. 1897 m. 22 June 1916, A. Ross Miles.
  - Sobisca Stalnaker Hall, b. 18 June 1899, m. Martha A. Thompson.
  - Robert Hall, b. 14 July 1901 m. June 1925 Ruth Lunsford.
  - Juanita Hall, b. 3 Nov. 1905, m. Apr. 1927 Thomas Ferguson.
  - Warren Hall, b. 1 Oct. 1907, m. 8 Oct. 1926 Auagistine Sutton.
- Thaddeus Stalnaker, (5 Sept. 1871 5 Apr. 1944) m. 1900 Lelia Gaston. ch.:
  - Vesta Stalnaker, b. 17 Feb. 1901 m. 15 May 1920, Paul T. Butcher.
  - Thomas Brooks Stalnaker, b. 20 Dec. 1902.
  - Clyde E. Stalnaker b. 4 June 1906.
  - Laura H. Stalnaker, b. 19 Apr. 1908 m. Frank Hadneck.

- ◊ Albert V. Stalnaker, b. 14 May 1910.
- ◊ Matthew C. Stalnaker, b. 16 Nov. 1912.
- ◊ Mary E. Stalnaker, b. 17 Aug. 1917 m. Burl A. Fortney.
- ♦ Ira Alonzo Stalnaker b. 16 Aug. 1873 m. 22 Sept. 1895 Elizabeth Heffner. ch.:
  - ◊ Edna Mable Stalnaker, b. 9 Aug. 1896 m. Ruskin Ward.
  - ◊ Ernest Ross Stalnaker, b. 22 Jan. 1898 m. Geneviena Houston.
  - ◊ Emma Merly Stalnaker, b. 3 Sept. 1899, m. Hobart C. Stalnaker.
  - ◊ Lelia R. Stalnaker, (20 Dec. 1902-25 July 1917).
  - ◊ William Paul Stalnaker, b. 25 Sept. 1904.
  - ◊ Torcia Stalnaker (d. 12 Jan. 1912.
- ♦ Charles Burton Stalnaker, b. 10 Aug. 1875 m. 19 Aug. 1891, Agnes Lee Hefner. ch.:
  - ◊ Rita Stalnaker b. 18 June 1893 m. Clark Smith.
  - ◊ Leda Verona Stalnaker, b. 13 June 1904 m. (1) Boyd Queen, m. (2) John Beech.
- ♦ Henry W. Stalnaker (27 Dec. 1877-3 Oct. 1880).
- Amazith Waggoner b. 20 Nov. 1837-d. young s/o Elijah & Mary (Straley) Waggoner.
- George S. Waggoner (24 Feb. 1840-7 Sept. 1917) m. 16 Dec. 1866, Eliza Smith (30 Mar. 1844-1926) both Friendship Cem. lewis Co. W. Va.
  - ♦ Alonzo Waggoner (1867-1912) m. Emma A. McWhorter (1873-1956). ch.:
    - ◊ Waifferd A. Waggoner (1894-1963) m. Mennie B.
    - ◊ George Waggoner m. Virginia Halterman.
  - ♦ Harvey W. Waggoner (1869-1944) m. Laura B. Life, (1879-1942) Friendship Cem. ch.:
    - ◊ Auagustine Waggoner m. Lyle Smith.
    - ◊ Irene Waggoner m. Thomas Eiseman.
    - ◊ Fred Waggoner.
  - ♦ George Burl Waggoner (9 Nov. 1881-10 June 1953) m. 29 June 1910- Vida Goodwin (30 June 1887-11 July 1980) Harrison Co. (Sutton, History of Braxton Co. W. Va.).

◊ Sarah Burline Waggoner b. 29 Nov. 1911 m. 28 Dec. 1935, Okey B. Spangler. ch.:
  * Sarah Kathleen Spangler m. John C. Stokes,(Jonda Kay, Cynthia, & Brian Stokes).
  * Jane Ellen Spangler m. William Clinger, (Todd & Amy Clinger).
  * Robert Burl Spangle m. Toni McIntyre, (Ryan Spangley).
◊ Eliza Kathleen Waggoner, b. 19 Dec. 1913.
◊ Olive Majorie Waggoner, b. 13 Sept. 1917- m. Chas. B. Brinkley. ch.:
  * Chas. Brooks Brinkley II m. Margaret Mary King, (Chas. Brooks III, Catherine Mary & Robert Brooks Brinkley).
  * Majorie Anne Brinkley m. Chas. Stuber (Charles & Thomas Stuber).
  * Katherine Jane Brinkley b. 25 Jan. 1954 m. Robert Walls, (Amanda, Holly & Robert Walls IV).
  * Janet Louise Brinkley b. 22 May 1959.

• John Calhoun Waggoner (5 Jan. 1843-5 Mar. 1936) Lewis Co. s/o Elijah & Mary (Straley) Waggoner m. 1 May 1881 Lewis Co., Emma Cornelia Starcher, (Oct. 1855 - 1924) Harmony Cem. Lewis Co. d/o John T. & Mary Ann (Ferrell) Starcher, d/o Lewis William Ferrell (1796-1875).

In 1882 John Calhoun Waggoner bought 41½ acres on Strait Run of Finks Creek from G. W. West. In 1883 J. C. Waggoner Bought an additional 40 acres on Strait Run., lived there for about 19 years, than moved to the Old Egan Farm, just below Glenville, W. Va. (see Starcher Line)

John Calhoun Waggoner's Cabin (See picture of), on Strait Run of Finks Creek, is now a part of Fort New Salem, at Salem W. Va. ch.:

♦ Edwin Waggoner, (Twin) (11 Feb. 1882-17 Sept. 1946) s/o John Calhoun & Emma C. (Starcher) Waggoner m. 15 Jan. 1905, Madge Wolfe d. 15 Apr. 1958. Both buried at Cedarville Cem. ch.:
  ◊ Adran Waggoner, (3 Nov. 1905-29 Jan. 1910).
  ◊ Ava Waggoner b. 20 May 1909 m. ____ Ackerman.

- ◊ Pauline Waggoner, b. 16 Mar. 1912, (ch.: Eddy, Maryln, Carol & Rudy).
- ◊ Paul Waggoner (29 Mar. 1913-7 May 1982).
- ◊ Glen Waggoner, (30 July 1915-26 Apr. 1952) (ch.: Patricia & Karen).
- ◊ Geneva Waggoner (17 Sept. 1917-1 Sept. 1977) (ch.: Marion Kay).
- ♦ Alvin Waggoner, (Twin) (11 Feb. 1882-1945) s/o John Calhoun & Emma C. (Starcher) Waggoner. m. (1) Bessie Harper d. 10 Dec. 1912. ch.:
  - ◊ Mildrid Waggoner, b. 6 Dec. 1912), m. (1st) Harmick. m. (2) 7 Oct. 1917 Carrie L. Dougherty (1891-1941).
  - ◊ Mary Elizabeth Waggoner, (13 Feb. 1918- Mar. 1920).
  - ◊ John Andrew Waggoner, b. 11 May 1920- m. Ruth Lee, (ch.: John & Rebecca).
- ♦ Charles Garland Waggoner (4 Mar. 1884-3 Dec. 1971) s/o John Calhoun & Emma C (Starcher) Waggoner m. 13 July 1909, Grace Dell Kittle, (21 June 1884-17 Aug. 1963), d/o Chas. Kittle. ch.:
  - ◊ William Burl Waggoner b. 30 Apr. 1910 m. 29 Nov. 1934, Zelda L. Grant (25 Aug. 1912-19 Jan. 1973) d/o George W. Grant.
  - ◊ Thelma May Waggoner (twin) (26 May 1913-15 Oct. 1937).
  - ◊ Selma Gay Waggoner (twin) b. 26 May 1913, m. 27 May 1934, Bailey B. Curtis (1 Oct. 1912-22 Feb. 1990). ch.:
    - * Robert Lee Curtis b. 30 May 1935 (div.) (Chas. Neil, Cecelia, Patricia, Wm. Bradley & Sherri Lynn).
    - * Sandra Laverne Curtis, b. 20 Dec. 1936- m. 7 Apr. 1956, Ralph E. Louk (23 July 1926-15 Nov. 1991) (Paul E., James, Debra Lynn, Paula Sue & Leslie Ann Louk).
    - * Mary Helen Curtis (31 Aug. 1937-d. y.).
    - * Charlotte Ann Curtis, b. 20 Oct. 1944 m. 30 Apr. 1966, Brad Rainey (div.) (Lee Ann & Jay Rainey).
- ♦ John C. Waggoner (b. Oct. 1888) Lewis Co. W. Va. s/o John Calhoun & Emma C. (Starcher) Waggoner. (1900 census).

John Calhoun Waggoner's cabin

- Orville Clarence Waggoner (29 Oct. 1890-14 Feb. 1975) s/o John Calhoun & Emma C. (Starcher) Waggoner m. (1) Edna (Dutch) Workman m. (2) Lorina Hinkle.
  ◊ Eleanor Waggoner b. 31 Jan. 1914, m. John Porter.
  ◊ Jackson Waggoner b. 2 Jan. 1918 m ____.
    * Jackson Lee b. 5 Dec. 1947 (went to Japan after college, m. there).
    * Lynn Ruth b. 3 Aug. 1949.
- Gladys Dorothy Waggoner (21 Jan. 1891-23 Dec. 1966) d/o John Calhoun & Emma C. (Starcher) Waggoner m. 1908, Rev. Orie Eugene Wilson Thorne, (2 Aug. 1885-1 Oct. 1963). ch.:
  ◊ Myrdith Evelyn Thorne, b. 3 Aug. 1910 m. Winifred Cline Sheppard, b. 20 Nov. 1910.
    * Jonathon Clive b. 20 Aug. 1934, m. 2- Feb. 1956 Donna Jean Eckart. ch.: (Lynn Ann m. Gary Dean Reed. Candace Sue, m. Clinton Keith Cooper, Jill Annette).
    * Hugh Prater b. 28 Apr. 1940 m. Carol Ann Coe b.27 Aug. 1942. (Gwendolyn Leigh m. Thomas Alexander McManus).
    * Jesse Eugenus b. 9 Feb. 1942 m. Margaret Grace Armel. (Angela Marie m. Bryan Patrick Hunt. Rebecca Lynn & Matthew Clive).
  ◊ Frederick Wilhelm Thorne (7 Oct. 1912-16 Feb. 1991), m. (1) Edith Gerwig, b. 20 May 1913 (div.). m. (2) Violet Butcher b. 14 May 1929. ch.:
    * Ronald Lee b. 9 Aug. 1939 m. Lois Belcher b. 26 Aug. 1944, (Rhonda Kay, & Ro Ann Lee).
    * Frederick, b. 30 June 1954 m. Donna Jo Harris b. 9 Apr. 1955 (Andrew Phillip).
    * Beverly, b. 11 Apr. 1947 m. Howard N. Keener, (Stephen Michael & Robert Allen).
  ◊ Paul Eugene Thorne, (16 Apr. 1915-1 May 1988) m. 4 Aug. 1944 Faiery V. Slacum Porter b. 23 Mar. 1915, ch.:
    * Mary Elizabeth Porter, b. 3 Oct. 1936- m. Theodore Russell, (Janet, Teddy, Linda, Dale & Mark).

John Calhoun and Emma Cornelia (Starcher) Waggoner

- * Jean Thorne, b. 9 May 1946 m. Timothy Dineen (Shelly, Katie & Heather).
- * Paul Jr. b. 30 Sept. 1947, m. (1) Grace Francis Benner (div.) m. (2) Shirley Mae Schlag.
- ◊ Adrian Upton Thorne, (1923-1948).
- ♦ Georgia Waggoner (9 Feb. 1901 ca. 1925) d/o John Calhoun & Emma C. (Starcher) Waggoner m. 1916 Lewis Co. Ray Taylor, ch.: Howard Taylor, (30 Aug. 1918-14 Nov. 1972) m. (1) Mary Belle Reed (div.) m. (2) Virginia Lucas. (Mary Emma & John)

Lewis W. Ferrell
War of 1812 Memorial

John Waggoner
(1805-1879)

John Waggoner b. 29 Oct. 1805, Lewis Co., s/o John & Susannah (Richards) Waggoner, m. ca. 1833 home of Wm. Kelly, Mary Ann Kelly (24 Sept. 1809-29 Jan. 1874) bur., Morrison Cem. d/o William Kelly (1776 Va. 30 July 1854 ae. 76 yr.) and Mary A. Kelly (1778-Md.-July 1859 ae 81 Lewis Co.). ch.: Mary, Purdy, Oliver, Rebecca & John E. Waggoner.

May or Mary Waggoner b. 7 Nov. 1833 Lewis Co., d/o John & Mary Ann (Kelly) Waggoner, m. ca. 1861, William R. Starcher, b. ca. 1811-Harrison Co. (W) Va. s/o John Starcher (1767, Monongalia Co.-8 Nov. 1825, Lewis Co.) m. 25 Aug. 1800 Harrison Co. Jane (Jenny) Radcliff, b. 1783, d/o of William & Deborah (Hughes) Radcliff.

Harrison Co. Deed-pg. 271

On 30 Mar. 1803, John & Jean Starcher of Harrison Co. Va. to Samuel Nickols of same, 80 pounds for 90 acres on Jesse Hughes Run-Patented by Jacob Starcher in 1783. Corner to John Bouher, Clay Lick Run. Signed John Starcher & Jean Starcher rec. Oct. 1803.

Harrison Co. Deed pg. 296

4 Dec. 1805: Anna Starcher, wife of Jacob Starcher, of Mason Co. Ky. releases her right of dower in sale to John Starcher. signed Wm. Owens & John McCollough.

William R. & Mary (Waggoner) Starcher-(2nd m.) Children:
- Two sons died young.
- Purdy F. Starcher (2 Apr. 1862-16 Jan. 1865).
- Rebecca A. Starcher b. 1863, m. 14 Sept. 1882 Lewis Co. Jefferson Leo Rinehart.

- William Elmore Starcher (b. 24 Aug. 1865-Lewis Co.) m. 31 July 1884 Rose Barton.
- Quincy Oliver Starcher b. 27 Jan. 1867, Lewis Co. m. 17 Nov. 1886 Lewis Co. Lurana Burton.

William R. Starcher (1st) m. 25 July 1829 Lewis Co. by Jacob Cozad (Bk. 3-46) Martha Frances Rains, (d. 25 May 1860) d/o John & Frances (McDonald) Rains, d/o Alexander & Elizabeth McDonald. ch.:

- Elizabeth Starcher m. 20 Mar. 1851 Jacob Hinzman.
- Jane Starcher m. 13 Aug. 1857 Philip Rogers.
- John T. Starcher m. (1st) Mary Ferrell, m. (2nd) 6 Feb. 1865 Rebecca A. Teter.
- Mary Starcher m. (2nd) 23 Dec. 1885 John Brake Morrison.
- Mifflin Starcher m. 28 Nov. 1861 Louisa Hinzman.
- George W. Starcher m. 22 Mar. 1868 Margaret (Mary) Batton.
- Martha Ann Starcher m. 17 Aug. 1865, Benjamin Franklin Bailey.
- Amanda C. Starcher m. 13 Feb. 1881 Whiston H. Hurst.
- Jacob Jasper Starcher m. 4 Jan. 1916 Florence Woodward.
- Francis Starcher (May 1860 before 1870) Lewis Co.

Starcher Family.

Ref. W. Va. Heritage Encyclopedia vol. 21-pg. 4491

Starchers in West Virginia; Five Starchers, believed to have been brothers, settled in Central W. Va. early in 1800's. They probably came from Hampshire Co., since one of the five, Phillip W., listed his place of birth as Hampshire Co. Va. Four of the five, Phillip W., Daniel, Abraham, and Jesse, settled in Calhoun Co. near the Roane-Calhoun Co., line. The fifth, Jacob, settled in what is present day Jackson Co. The town of Ripley is said to be located on what was a portion of the Starcher farm.

If the five were brothers, as generally believed, the name of their father may have been Jacob. A marriage record found in Harrison Co. dated, 5 Dec. 1801 - Phillip Statur (sic) gives his fathers name as Jacob.

Jacob Starcher, settled in what is now present day Jackson Co. Jacob Statzer (sic) (not a mistake, to be read as stands) m. Ann Staats on 28 Nov. 1795 in Harrison Co. Va. she was the d/o Abraham Staats. They were the parents of, William Starcher, Jacob Starcher, John Starcher, and Manuel Starcher.

If Jacob was the father of Abraham, Daniel, Phillip W., and Jesse, then Ann Staats would have been a 2nd wife. I believe there was a son Jacob Jr., as shown in these land records of Harrison Co. (W) Va.:

This is not research, it has been copied as is and hopefully will throw some light on the early family.

Harrison Co. (W) Va. - Deed Records 1785-1810 by Davis

Pg. 194: Apr. 1801-Richard & Martha Bennett of Harrison Co. Va. to Jacob Starcher, of same, for 40 pounds, 100 acres Jesse Hughes Run- between Jacob Bennett & Elijah Runyon. Signed Richard Bennett & Martha (X) Bennett. Wit: Francia Leggett, Jacob (X) Statzer and John Leggett - Rec. April 1801

Pg. 97 Nov. 1796- Richard & Martha Bennett of Harrison Co. Va. to Elijah Runyon, of same, for 25 pounds, 100 acres, Hacker Creek, adj. land of Jacob Starcher Jr., Signed Richard & Martha Bennett. rec., Nov. 1796

20 April 1801 - Ditto to Jacob Bennett Jr. of Harrison Co. Va. for 30 pounds, 20 acres, Hacker Creek between Jacob Starcher Sr. & Jacob Starcher Jr. rec. Apr. 1801

Pg. 293. 21 Sept. 1805 Jacob & Anna Starcher, of Mason Co. Va. to John Starcher of Harrison Co. Va. for $333.33 - 100 acres, Jesse Hughes Run, between Jacob Bamett (Bonnett ?) & Elijah Runyon.

Signed; John Starcher, Wit.: Samuel Starcher, Philip Cox, William Powers, & Philip Bonnett. Rec. Oct. 1805

Pg. 296 4 Dec. 1805 - Anna Starcher, wife of Jacob Starcher, of Mason Co. Kentucky (yes there was a Mason Co. Ky. -c. 1789) releases her right of Dower in sale to John Starcher. Signed William Owens & John McCallough.

Pg. 271 - 30 Mar. 1803 - John & Jean Starcher, of Harrison Co. Va. to Samuel Nichols, of same, for 80 pounds, 90 acres on Jesse Hughes Run, patented by Jacob Starcher 1783 - corner to John Bouher, Clay Lick Run, Signed John & Jean Starcher Rec. Oct. 1803

Pg. 308 17 Feb. 1806 - Jacob & Anna Bennett, of Harrison Co. Va. to John Starcher, of same, for $200.00 - 200 acres, Hacker Creek - between Jacob Starcher & Jacob Starcher Jr. crossing Jesse Hughes Run. Signed Jacob & Anna Bennett Rec. Feb. 1806

Abraham Starcher b. ca. 1790- 60 y. in 1850 Gilmer Co. wife Elizabeth Nutter, b. ca. 1805, d/o John Nutter. ch.: Mary, Sarah, Daniel ca. 1829, Andrew ca. 1834, Henry ca. 1837, Barsheba b. ca. 1840 m. 3 Apr. 1861 George P. Blankenship, b. ca. 1838 s/o Millie Blankenship.

Phillip Starcher, b. ca. 1780, states, b. Hampshire Co. Va. in 1860 census of Calhoun Co. (Phillip Statur (sic) gives his fathers name as Jacob.) m. (1) 5 Dec. 1801, Harrison Co. to Mary Bush, d/o Adam Bush.

- One Son, Adam Starcher, b. ca. 1802 Kanawka, Co. he m. Phoebe Coger d/o Peter Coger.
- The 1850 c. of Gilmer Co. P. Starcher ae 71 b. Va. wife Rebecca ae. 61 Va.

After Mary Bush Starcher death, Phillip m. (2nd) Rebecca Mace, d/o Isaac Mace.

- Henry Starcher 1807.
- Jacob Starcher 1812.
- Abraham Starcher 1815.
- William (Billy Bluehead) Starcher b. 30 Sept. 1822.
- Isaac Starcher 1824.
- Arnold Starcher 1826.
- Mary Starcher 1816.
- Sarah Starcher. (see Vol. 21 pg. 4493 - W. Va. Heritage Enc.)

Daniel Starcher m. Nancy Brannan b. ca. 1800 d/o William Brannan.

- William B. Starcher 1818, m. (1st) Nancy Tanner d/o Jesse Tanner.
- Joseph P. Starcher 1832 m. Nancy Jane Nichols.
- Hannah Staracher m. Daniel Coger.
- Elizabeth Starcher m. Reese Ross.
- Barbara Starcher m. Henderson Coff.

Jesse Starcher b. ca. 1782 in 1850 living at the home of William Truman, Gilmer Co. (W) Va.

Credit William J. Morrison for this line of Starchers.

If John Starcher was related to this family, he was older (b. ca. 1767- Monongolia Co. d. 8 Nov. 1825) Lewis Co. m. 25 Aug. 1800 Harrison Co., Jane (Jenny) Radcliff (1783 Monongalia Co. Va. - 7 Feb. 1865, Upsher Co.), d/o William Radcliff (1744-1827 Wood Co.) and Deborah Hughes (1746-1813), d/o Thomas Hughes & Mary Baker Hughes.

Children of John and Jane (Jenny) (Radcliff) Starcher:
- Mary Starcher (ca, 1805-18 Jan. 1870) m. 29 Aug. 1822 Lewis Co. Henry Hinzman (b. 20 Mar. 1803.
- Deborah Starcher (13 June 1806 Harrison Co. 25 Nov. 1879) Lewis Co. m. 6 Apr. 1820 Lewis Co. Thomas Columbus Hinzman (2 Mar. 1797-23 Nov. 1880).
- Martha Starcher (28 Nov. 1807-2 Aug. 1855 ae. 47 y. 9 m. 4 d.) Lewis Co. m. 8 Sept. 1825 Lewis Co. James Jeffries.
- Anna Starcher (b. ca. 1807) m. 13 Apr. 1826 Hezekeah Dennison.
- Jacob Starcher (26 Aug. 1808 11 May 1891 ae. 82 y. 9 m. 15 d.) bur. Old Heavner Cem. Lewis Co. m. 29 Nov. 1831 Lewis Co. Jane Wolf (1812-7 Feb. 1865 ae. 53 y.) d/o Thomas Wolf.
- Catherine Starcher (b. ca. 1809) Harrison Co. m. 13 Dec. 1821 Lewis Co., Otho Means (b. ca. 1803) Harrison Co..
- Nancy Starcher, (b. ca. 1810) m. 10 Sept. 1840 Armstead Queen.
- William R. Starcher (b. ca. 1811) m. (1st) 25 Jan. 1829 Frances (Fanny) Raines (b. ca. 1808 Pendleton Co. Va.-25 May 1860 Lewis Co. d/o John Raines & Frances (McDonald) Raines (d/o Alexander & Elizabeth McDonald), m. (2nd) (ca. 1860-61) Mary Waggoner (b. 7 Nov. 1833) d/o John & Mary L. (Kelley) Waggoner. (see Waggoner line)
- Jane Starcher m. 16 Dec. 1841 Levi White.
- John Starcher (6 Jan. 1812-4 Nov. 1888) m. 17 Oct. 1834 Lewis Co. Juliana Swisher (11 Jan. 1816-2 Dec. 1865 ae. 49 y. 10 m. 22 d.) d/o Peter Swisher & Susanna Swisher.
- Sarah Starcher m. 17 July 1834 William George Hushman.
- Stephen Starcher (27 May 1817-12 Aug. 1890) Roane Co. W. Va. m. 12 Oct. 1837 Lewis Co. Charity (Hinzman) (some records Charity Bennett) (m. by Henry R. Bonnett).
- Susanna Starcher m. 23 Oct. 1834 Wilson Osburn.

✧✧✧✧✧✧✧✧✧✧✧✧✧✧✧✧✧✧✧✧✧✧✧✧✧✧✧✧✧✧✧✧✧✧✧✧✧✧✧

Purdy Waggoner (10 July 1839-27 May 1919, Friendship Cem.) d/o John & Mary A. (Kelly) Waggoner m. 4 Oct. 1860 Lewis Co. by Henry R. Bonnett, Francis Taylor (15 Dec. 1836 Queens County, Ireland-30 Jan. 1922 Lewis Co.) s/o Thomas & Margaret Taylor. ch.:

Please credit, Mildred Pringle for giving this information to Elizabeth Turner in 1982.

- Mary Margaret Taylor (10 Oct. 1861-26 Apr. 1946 Friendship Cem.) m. 10 Apr. 1901 Lewis Co., Waldo G. Gould (12 May 1874-26 May 1954, 80 yr.)
  ch.: Mildred Gould (6 Sept. 1903-1985) m. Ronald Pringle (1897-1967) Both bur. Fairview Cemetery Lewis Co. W. Va..
- Edward Oliver Taylor (6 Sept. 1865-1957, Friendship Cem.) m. ca. 1898, Ardelia Maud Swisher (1876-1973) d/o George & Mary (Boram) Swisher.
  ch.: Francis Edward Taylor b. 7 Mar. 1906 m. Floe Swisher.

Oliver Waggoner (8 Nat 1843-14 Mar. 1919) Lewis Co. s/o John & Mary Ann (Kelly) Waggoner m. 4 July 1867 Lewis Co. Pronetta Boram (19 Feb. 1848-11 Feb. 1918) Otterbine Cem., near Glenville W. Va. d/o William & Elizabeth A. (Hinzman) Boram. ch.:

- Arthelia G. Waggoner (6 Apr. 1868- 1931), McCue Town Cem. Lewis Co. m. 14 Mar. 1888 William Henry McCue, (Apr. 1863-1926) s/o Charles F. & Parthinia McCue. ch.:
  - Ora McCue m. John Linger.
  - Dorothy McCue m. Goff Lemons.
  - Thelma McCue.
  - Firth McCue.
  - French McCue (30 Sept. 1891-21 May 1953).
- Columbia D. Waggoner b. 28 Mar. 1871 Lewis Co. m. 14 Dec. 1891 Davies Allen Morris s/o Allen J. & Hannah (Lawson) Morris. ch.:
  - Adra Morris.
  - Gratice Morris.
  - Ottis Morris.
  - Aubra Morris.
- Infant Child born and died in 1877.

Rebecca Waggoner (11 or 13 Oct. 1846-23 Dec. 1869 ae. 22 y. 2 m. 11 d.) Morrison Cem. d/o John & Mary A. (Kelly) Waggoner.

John E. Waggoner (27 July 1851-28 Dec. 1928) Morrison Cem., s/o John & Mary A. (Kelly) Waggoner (1900 c. living with sister Purdy (Waggoner) Taylor.)

Jacob Waggoner
(1810-1847)

Jacob Waggoner (1810-ca. 1847) Harrison Co. s/o John & Susannah (Richards) Waggoner m., 27 Jan. 1831 Lewis Co., Catherine Bonnett (5 Apr. 1811-7 Dec. 1869, Rpt by Jasper Peterson) d/o Samuel & Martha (Radcliff) Bonnett.

Jacob Waggoner owned the farm where Laurel Lick Run Cem. is located, he buried infant children there & later on neighbors were also buried there. This cemetery is located on Laurel Lick Run, a branch of Hacker Creek, in the Northeast section of Lewis Co. W. Va. It is 1.9 miles upstream from the Village of Berlin.

On Nov. 23, 1906, Francis & Purdy (Waggoner) Taylor deeded the cemetery to the trustees of the Laurel Lick Church, also deeding more ground than what was in use. Frances Taylor bought the farm in 1906, of the Jacob Waggoner heirs. Purdy (Waggoner) Taylor would have been Jacob Waggoner's niece. (Lewis Co. Cem. Bk. III- pg. 57)

Several years ago, when researching this family, I wrote Howard G. Peterson, and he was kind enough to take the time to set me in the right direction with this family. Howard G. Peterson, d. May 1990. Mrs. Gertrude (Peterson) Hill, Howard's sister, gave me permission to the data he had sent me. Howard's research is as follows:

In 1840 census Jacob Waggoner had 5 people in his household. After Jacob's death, in 1850 c. of Lewis Co. we find Catherine (Bonnett) Waggoner m. 7 Aug. 1849 to Richard N. Atkins, blacksmith Lewis Co. W. Va.

Martha O. Waggoner (17 Feb. 1838-1 Mar. 1914) only living child of Jacob & Catherine (Bonnett) Waggoner m. 19 Dec. 1860 Lewis Co. Jasper N. Peterson (13 Dec. 1839-15 Apr. 1903) Stone Cool, Lewis Co. W. Va. s/o John P. Peterson (17 Oct. 1815-14 Jan. 1890, ae. 74 y. 2 m. 27

d.) Peterson Cem., m. 27 Jan. 1839 Lewis Co. Nancy Alkire (3 Oct. 1815-4 May 1890).

Children of Jasper N. and Martha O. (Waggoner) Peterson; Laura, Blanche, Gertrude, Clara, Maggie, John Peterson, Jacob Waggoner Peterson. (Two babies d. in 1860 & 1875 bur. Peterson Cem.)

- Laura Peterson m. George Smith.
- Blanche Peterson m. Grant Peterson.
- Gretrude Peterson m. _____ Shaver.
- Clara Peterson m. A. J. Lunsford.
- Maggie Peterson m. Oscar Lunsford.
- John Peterson Peterson m. Minnie Gaston.
- John Waggoner Peterson (29 July 1868-7 Feb. 1954) m. June 1893 Martha Ann Eckers (25 May 1873-12 July 1959).

Children of John P. and Nancy (Atkire) Peterson:

1. Jasper N. Peterson (was a twin to Newton Peterson served Capt. Union Army Co. D. 15th W. Va. Inf.) s/o John P. & Nancy (Alkire) Peterson.

2. Newton Peterson (twin) (13 Dec. 1839-28 July 1909) m. 20 May 1861 Lewis Co. Mary A. Bush, d. 22 Sept. 1886, d/o Jacob & Helen E. (Langford) Bush.

3. Samantha Peterson (10 Aug. 1842-13 Jan. 1899 Gaston W. Va.) m. 24 Sept. 1861 John W. Divers.

4. Lenura Peterson b. Feb. 1843 m. 30 Aug. 1864 Lewis Co. Thomas E. Swisher.

5. Joseph Peterson m. 24 Dec. 1848, Lewis Co.

6. Hannibal Peterson m. 22 June 1873 Zina Bush.

7. Kate Peterson m. 27 May 1875 Thomas Batten.

8. Eliza Peterson b. ca. 1853 Lewis Co..

9. Lewis Peterson (1855 - 8 May 1898 Lewis Co.)

✧✧✧✧✧✧✧✧✧✧✧✧✧✧✧✧✧✧✧✧✧✧✧✧✧✧✧✧✧✧✧✧✧✧

Richard N. Atkins (1818-13 Aug. 1866) s/o John & Louisa Atkins was a widower in 1849 with two sons. m. (2nd) 9 Aug. 1849 Mrs. Catharine (Bonnett) Waggoner (wid of Jacob Waggoner).

In 1860 we find: Richard N. & Catharine (B.W.) Atkins with Martha O. Waggoner (1838-1914), William H. Atkins (1842-3 Aug. 1884)

Harrison Co. m. 10 May 1866. Alice Flanigan, d/o James & Mary Flanigan.

John G. Atkins (b. 1845 Lewis Co. m. 16 Mar. 1869 Caroline Ramsbury d/o (probably) John W. & Sarah A. Ramsbury, both b. Md., s/o Richard N. & Catharine (B. W.) Atkins.

Samuel M. Atkins, (1855-1930) Lewis Co. bur Butchers/Butcherville, (Court House Dist.) m. 1881 Elizabeth L. Butcher (July 1858-1933) d/o Thomas L. & Mary L. Butcher. (1870 Samuel was living with his sister Martha O. (Waggoner) Peterson.

Catharine Waggoner
(1809-ca 1879)

Catherine Waggoner (ca. 1809-before 1879 Wirt Co.) d/o John & Susannah (Richards) Waggoner, m. 28 Jan. 1831 Lewis Co. by Jacob Bennett, George Wallace Dobson (ca. 1811 b. Culpeper Co. Va. d. before 1860 Wirt Co.) s/o George Dobson (25 Jan. 1769-15 July 1828, ae. 59 y. 5 m. 20 d. Harmony Cem.) Lewis Co. (Bk. 1-pg. 4) and Mary Dobson (1772-15 Nov. 1841 ae. 69) Lewis Co.

George W. & Catharine (Waggoner) Dobson lived in Lewis Co. until 1842 then moved to West Co. (W) Va. by 1848. George W. Dobson died before 1860.

Wirt Co. m. records, pg. 11.

Bryant Utter (ae. 55) b. Harrison Co. s/o William & Elizabeth Utter m. 6 Dec. 1861 Catharine Dobson (ae. 52) b. Lewis Co. (wid of George W.) d/o John & Mary Waggoner (John & Susannah (Richards) Waggoner). On page 34 of Wirt Co. W. Va. m. records, we find Briant Utter (ae 72 yr.) m. 31 Dec. 1879 Polly McDade (ae. 62 yr.). Catharine (Waggoner, Dobson) Utter died before 1879 Wirt Co.

George W. & Catharine (Waggoner) Dobson's children; John, Mary A., Susan, Mariah, Sarah, Nancy Rebecca, William and Oliver Dobson.

- John Dobson b. 1832 Lewis Co. m. 24 July 1855, Wirt Co. Mary Rebecca Williams (b. 1838 Wood Co.) d/o Joel & Mary Williams.
- Mary A. Dobson b. 1834 Lewis Co., m. 19 Apr. 1857 Wirt Co., Wm. J. Vandle (Vandale) b. 1833 Fayette Co. s/o John & Rachel Vandle.
- Susan Dobson b. 1836 Lewis Co. m. 2 Oct. 1856 Wirt Co., Henry George, b. 1834 Pendleton co. s/o Henry & Elizabeth George.
- Mariah (Maria) Dobson, b. 1 Apr. 1838, Lewis Co., m. 3 Apr. 1859 Wirt Co., John Wesley Shaver (Shafer) 17 Oct. 1837

Kanawha Co. (now Roane Co.), s/o John Shafer b. Ohio & Mary (Cox) Shafer b. Lewis Co. (W) Va. John Wesley Shafer served in the Civil War 1862. <u>Hardestys</u> Vol. 5 - pg 299 - Roane Co. W. Va.

John Wesley & Maria (Dobson) Shafer's children:
- Viola V. Shafer b. 9 Dec. 1859 Roane Co. (W) Va. m. 29 Nov. 1877 Roane Co. W. L. Hackney.
- George B. Shafer b. 1 Jan. 1862 Roane Co.
- David Lee Shafer b. 1 Apr. 1864 m. 26 Mar. 1884 Roane Co., Mary Comer.
- Sarah C. Shafer, b. 11 Apr. 1872 Roane Co. m. 27 Jan. 1889, Roane Co. Whetzel B. Casto.
- Mary A. Shafer, b. 27 Aug. 1876 Roane Co. m. 25 Feb. 1894 Raone Co., Hannibal Paxton.
- Charles S. Shafer b. 30 Oct. 1878 Roane Co.
- Ezra Shafer b. 8 Sept. 1881 Roane Co. W. Va.

- Sarah Dobson, b. 1842, Lewis Co. m. 19 Mar. 1858 Wirt Co. Abraham Williams b. 1836 Wood Co. s/o Joel & Mary A. Williams.
- Nancy Rebecca Dobson, b. 1848 Wirt Co. m. 5 Mar. 1868, Jackson Co. Squire Staats, b. 1850 Jackson Co. s/o Isaac & Ann E. Staats.
- William S. Dobson, b. 1854 Wirt Co. m. 28 Apr. 1875, Wirt Co. Mary Ellen Goff b. 27 Mar. 1858 Ritchie Co. (W) Va. d/o Thomas R. & Susannah (George) Goff; children: Elliott Dobson, Harmon Dobson, Wirt Dobson, Charley Dobson, Marjorie Dobson, Onie Dobson, Anna Dobson, Ida Dobson, & Minnie Dobson.
- Oliver Dobson (13 Oct. 1843-16 Aug. 1843) Lewis Co. (W) Va. bur. Mt. Harmony Cem.

George Waggoner
(1812-1877)

George Waggoner (4 Apr. 1812 Harrison Co. d. 17 Apr. 1877, ae. 65 y. 0 m. 14 d.) Roane Co. W. Va., s/o John & Susannah (Richards) Waggoner. m. ca. 1833 Lewis Co. Melinda Cottrell, b. 16 Nov. 1813. Both Bur. Hersman Cemetery 5 miles south of Spencer, Roane Co. W. Va. By 1800 they lived in Jackson Co. (W) Va. Their children; Elijah, John, Rachel, Samuel, William, Susanna, George W. & Malinda Waggoner.

- Elijah Waggoner (10 Nov. 1834-24 Dec. 1903) Lewis Co. m. 18 Aug. 1859 Roane Co. Mary O. Mitchell (28 May 1835-16 Jan. 1881 d/o Thomas & Peggy (Snider) Mitchell. Elijah served in the Federal Army 1862-65 Civil War. m. (2nd) 23 July 1882 Margaret E. Mitchell d/.o Thomas & Peggy (Snider) Mitchell, (sister of Mary O. Mitchell), children of Elijah & Mary O. (Mitchell) Waggoner.
  - Rasabell Waggoner b. 1860 Roane Co. (W) Va. m. 25 Sept. 1892, Roane Co. John W. Stanley b. 1866 Wood Co.
  - George T. Waggoner b. 10 Apr. 1861 Jackson Co. m. 29 Dec. 1886 Roane Co. Elizabeth Upton.
  - Margaret M. Waggoner b. 20 Sept. 1864 Jackson Co. m. 23 Aug. 1883, Roane Co. F. L. Bowen b. 1861 N.C.
  - Susan M. Waggoner (21 June 1868-6 Oct. 1878).
  - Charles O. Waggoner b. 12 Mar. 1870 Roane Co. m. 8 Mar. 1899 Roane Co. Virginia Waggoner b. 1876.
  - Robert M. Waggoner b. 29 Oct. 1871 Roane Co. m. 22 Apr. 1897 Roane Co. Emma Bowen.
  - Mary E. Waggoner (20 Oct. 1873-6 Oct. 1878).
  - Elijah H. Waggoner (9 July 1875-4 Oct. 1878),
  - Eliza J. Waggoner (6 Oct. 1878-2 Sept. 1879).

- John Waggoner b. 1837 m. Mary A. s/o George & Melinda (Cottrell) Waggoner.
- Rachel Waggoner b. 1836 Harrison Co. (W) Va. d/o George & Melinda (Cottrell) Waggoner m. 1 Nov. 1863 Wirt Co., Reuben Reynolds b. 1834, Jackson Co. s/o William & Nancy Reynolds.
- Samuel Waggoner b. 1841 Lewis Co. s/o George & Melinda (Cottrell) Waggoner m. 21 Feb. 1867 Roane Co. Angelina Westfall b. 1851 Lewis Co. d/o John C. & Elizabeth Westfall.
- William Waggoner b. 1843 Lewis Co. s/o George & Melinda (Cottrell) Waggoner m. Roane Co. Teletha.
- Susanna Waggoner b. 1847, d/o George & Melinda (Cottrell) Waggoner.
- Malinda Waggoner b. Aug. 1852 Jackson Co. d/o George & Melinda (Cottrell) Waggoner.
- George W. Waggoner b. Aug. 1849 Jackson Co. s/o George & Melinda (Cottrell) Waggoner. m. 15 Jan. 1873 Roane Co. Julina E. Harris, b. ca. 1949 North Carolina, d/o Charles & Nancy Harris; ch.: John H. Waggoner, James E. Waggoner, and Nervy J. Waggoner.

William Waggoner
(1813-1895)

William Waggoner (9 July 1813 Jesses Run Harrison Co. (W) Va.) s/o John & Susannah (Richards) Waggoner. I have never been able to prove this line, one m. that might be considered Harrison Co. pg 175. William Wagner-m. 16 Feb. 1832-Elizabeth Rhyner, by Joseph Morris; one record has his wife Malinda, but no proof.

Susannah Waggoner
(b. 1814)

Susannah Waggoner b. 16 Mar. 1814, Harrison Co. d/o John & Susannah (Richards) Waggoner. m. 16 Mar. 1837 Lewis Co. by Henry R. Bonnett. Martin Sims (12 June 1815-15 Feb. 1882) Reedy, Roane Co. W. Va. s/o John W. & Mary (West) Sims.

Martin Sims was a carpenter, and by 1845 they were in Jackson Co., actually the part of the country that became Wirt Co. in 1848. Martin and Susannah (Waggoner) Sims' children: Granville, John Wesley, Edward J., Henry M., Perry Green (Perigrine), Oliver M., Mary Louisa, Susanna Elizabeth, Minton B., & Martin Luther Sims.

- Granville Sims b. 1838 Lewis Co., m. 25 Mar. 1857, Wirt Co. Sarah K. Sheppard b. 1835, Jackson Co. d/o Henry & Diana Sheppard.
- John Wesley Sims, b. 20 Oct. 1839, Lewis Co. served in Civil War, Confederate, June 1861 Co. G. 10th Va., was a farmer and shoemaker, Reedy W. Va. m. (1st) 18 Dec. 1867, Roane Co. Ann E. Pickrill, b. 11 Mar. 1849, Jackson Co. d/o Levi Pickrill, b. 10 Dec. 1802 Fauquier Co. Va. and Mariah Rader (15 Oct. 1815-5 Oct. 1875, Roane Co.

  John Wesley Sims m. (2nd) 25 Sept. 1888, Wirt Co. Sarah C. Price. ch.: Okey J. Sims b. 15 Sept. 1868, Susan B. Sims (1870-1883) Lucy C. Sims, (1872-1883) Olive M. Sims (1875-1877), Ida M. Sims b. 2 Dec. 1877, m. 15 July 1893, Roane Co. James McCroskey and Claudius W. Sims (1881-1882).

- Edward J. Sims b. 1842 Lewis Co.
- Henry M. Sims b. 1844, Lewis Co. m. 27 Apr. 1864 Wirt Co., Roseline Walker, b. 1844 Greenbrier Co., d/o Marire Walker.

- Perry G. (Perigrine) Sims, b. 1846, Lewis Co. m. 21 Oct. 1869 Wirt Co., Nancy George.
- Olive M. Sims, b. 1847 Jackson Co., m. 13 Aug. 1868, Lewis Full, b. 1843, Wirt Co. s/o Ruben & Elizabeth Full.
- Mary Louisa Sims, b. 1849 Wirt Co., m. 12 Dec. 1872, Roane Co., William P. Price s/o William & Susan Price.
- Susanna Elizabeth Sims, b. 1853, Wirt Co. m. 9 Mar. 1873 Roane Co. A. J. Pickerill, b. 1851, s/o Levi & Mariah Pickerill (Pickrell).
- Minton B. Sims b. 1852. Wirt Co.,
- Martin Luther Sims, b. 1856 West Co. m. 26 July 1874 Wirt Co. Elizabeth C. Sleath.

Mariah Waggoner
(1818-1905)

Mariah Waggoner (21 Nov. 1818-13 July 1905, ae. 87 y., Broad Run Cem. #39 Lewis Co. W. Va.), d/o John & Susannah (Richards) Waggoner m. 29 May 1840 Lewis Co., (by Henry R. Bonnett) Andrew Cottrill b. 1815 Harrison Co. moved to Jackson Co. around 1841.

1850 c of Jackson Co. shows a Rachel Cottrill ae. 74 yr. Va. living with Andrew and Mariah (Maria) Cottrill. Their Children; Elizabeth, Gilbert, William, Sylvester, Lucetta, Susan, Nancy, Manerva, and Malinda Cottrill.

- Elizabeth Cottrill, b. 1841 Jackson Co. m. 14 Mar. 1871 Roane Co., Ashbury Westfall, b. 1831, s/o Jacob & Elizabeth (Smith) Westfall who were m. 8 Aug. 1878 Lewis Co.
- Gilbert Cottrill, b. 1843, Jackson Co. served Civil War Co. G. 60th Va. (Confederate) Vol. Inf. Roane Co., m. 1 Jan. 1868 Roane Co., Nancy E. Peters, b. 1848 Mercer Co. d/o Christian S. & Mary S. Peters.
- William Cottrill, b. 1844, Jackson Co. not in 1860 census.
- Sylvester Cottrill (5 Dec. 1845, Jackson Co., 6 Feb. 1916, Hersman Cem., Roane Co.) m. 10 Jan. 1867, Roane Co. Sarah J. Jack (1 Nov. 1846, Lewis Co., 11 Dec. 1912, Roane Co. d/o John & Catharine Jack.
- Lucetta Cottrill, b. 1848 Jackson Co., m. 13 Jan. 1875, Roane Co. J. H. Harris b. 1856, N. Carolina, s/o Charles & Nancy Harris.
- Malinda J. Cottrill, b. 1849 Jackson Co.
- Susan Cottrill, b. 1850, Jackson Co.
- Nancy Cottrill, b. 1851 Jackson Co. m. 5 Aug. 1869 Roane Co. Martin Hammack, b. 1851 Kanawah Co. s/o St. Clair & Catharine Hammack.

- Manerva J. Cottrill, b. 1857 Jackson Co. m. 17 Dec. 1873 Roane Co., James N. Nickles b. 1853, Lewis Co., s/o John & Nancy Nickles.

Samuel Waggoner
(b. 1821)

Samuel Waggoner b. 1821 Lewis Co. s/o John and Susannah (Richards) Waggoner, m. 5 May 1840 (by Henry R. Bonnett) Nancy Garrison b. ca. 1820 d. between 1957-1860. Children; Susanna A., Mary, Olive C., John W., George, Dempsey F., & G. L. Waggoner.

- Susanna A. Waggoner b. 1841 Wirt Co.
- Olive C. Waggoner b. 1848 Wirt Co.
- Mary Waggoner b. 10 Sept. 1846, Wirt Co. d. 4 Sept. 1907. Laural Lick Cem. (Vol. 3 pg 57) m 7 May 1874 Lewis Co. W. Va. William D. Warner, (31 Aug. 1837-23 June 1916) served Grand Army of the Republic. s/o Oren & Elizabeth (Davis) Warner. ch.:
    - Delia Warner b. Feb. 1875 Lewis Co.
    - Nettie J. Warner (1878-1929) Lewis Co.
    - John W. Warner b. July 1876, Lewis Co. m. Annie Maria Flaherty b. 18 Nov. 1874, Harrison Co. d/o John P. Flaherty (1842-1924) and Synthia A. Flaherty, (1844-1908) Lewis Co.
    - Anna M. Warner, b. Mar. 1881 Lewis Co.
    - James F. Warner, b. Mar. 1883 Lewis Co.
    - Thomas A. Warner, b. July 1886, Lewis Co.
    - Ova E. Warner, b. Sept. 1889, Lewis Co.
- John W. Waggoner b. 1849, Wirt Co. m. (1st) 1 Dec. 1871 Jackson Co., Lelita Vannoy, b. 1853, Jackson Co. d/o John & Susan Vannoy m. (2nd) 9 Mar. 1873 Jackson Co. Caroline Thorn, b. 1855, Wirt Co. d/o J. H. & E. Moore. (d/o Jehu & Elizabeth Thorn).
- George Waggoner, b. 1853, Wirt Co.
- G. L. Waggoner, b. 1857, Wirt Co.
- Dempsey F. Waggoner, b. 1855 Wirt Co., m. 12 July 1874, Roane Co. Nancy Rader b. 1854, Jackson d/o Jackson & Saphronia Rader.

Part Seven

The Allman Family in West Virginia

by *Edward Lee Allman, Clarksburg, West Virginia*

From some known and some unknown researchers we have learned the origin of our name ALLMAN.

Research by John L. Allman, R. F. D. #1, Clio, Michigan in the 1930's- '40's states: "The name ALLMAN is derived or descended from the ALEMANNI NATION of ancient renown whose territories were in southwest Germany and in east-central France including Alsace-Lorain and the Dauphine. The family had its rise or came into prominence in A.D. 211. Magdeberg on the Elbe River 88 miles southwest of Berlin became the principal seat of the German Allmans."

In the year A.D. 990-5 this rich valley of the Dauphine was being pillaged by a horde of Saracens. One Baron Allman gathered the Allman Clans to assist the Bishop of Grenoble in driving out the invaders. For this service he received the "Grant and Investure of the Lands of Uraige." They built the "Castle of Uraige" on a dominant hill of the Belledonne range of the Dauphine Alps (now Vosgee Mts.). This castle is owned in 1989 by Mrs. Templeton who lives on the premises. During the war years 1940 to 1945 and until 1978, it was used by the French Army as a school and headquarters. This last information was furnished to Emit K. Ward, Portland, Oregon, through a letter to him from the LeMaire (the mayor) de Saint-Martin - D'Uriage dated January 17, 1989.

An extensive research of the family in England during the centuries 1300 through 1600 was published in 1984 by Roots Research Bureau, Ltd. as Manuscript number 29. Ships' passenger lists indicate early Allman immigrants settled in Massachusetts, Rhode Island, Pennsylvania and Virginia. Virginia has to be the originating settlement of the Allman family of West Virginia. The first record of a land holding in Virginia was Samuel Allman with 200 acres in 1637 and

600 acres in Henrico County March 16, 1639.

The National Archives, Washington, D. C. Microcopy, number T-498, roll 3, for Virginia shows the Census of 1780 for Hampshire County, (West) Virginia, Romney county seat. This lists John Alman with 9 whites, 0 blacks. Since we know our immediate ancestor in central West Virginia was William Allman, this John could possibly be a brother.

Sims Index to West Virginia Land Grants, copyright 1952 by State of West Virginia lists William Allman in Hardy County, Book 1, page 292 and William Allman in Harrison County, Book 5, page 161.

The Hardy County (West) Virginia Tax List for 1786 lists William Allman, 1 poll, white male 18 yrs. and older (b. ca. 1760).

The Norman Family History, published in 1988 by Forest A. Norman, on page 75 states - "Jacob and Hendrix Allman (presumed to be brothers) came to Gloucester, Virginia in 1740. Jacob and wife were parents of a large family. Some of their children were William (our ancestor), John, Alice, Jenny, Bailey, Jacob, Thomas, Edward. In 1773 William Allman left Gloucester County, crossed the mountains and patented 200 acres of land on Fink's Run in what is now Upshur County. His neighbors on Fink's Run were Jacob Brake, Henry Jackson, Edward Jackson, Jacob Lorentz, John Bozarth and Phillip Reger." Fink's Run is a tributary of the Buckhannon River just 3 miles west of the town of Buckhannon, Upshur County.

Hacker's Creek Pioneers Journal, Volume III, page 38, October 24, 1984 from the Hardman article- "Peterman (Peter) Hardman came to America on the ship Richmond, October 20, 1764 arriving at the port of Philadelphia. Peter settled at Oldsfields (now Moorefield, West Virginia). On the same ship was John Allman and Henrich Allman. Our William may have been a brother or son to one or either or both."

Upshur County History, 1907, by W. B. Cutright, page 186 says 1772 witnessed considerable accessations to the Buckhannon and Hacker's Creek settlement with Samuel Oliver, Thomas Carney, Zachariah Westfall, George Casto, Joel Westfall, Abraham Carper, Jacob Brake, Henry Jackson, Edward Jackson making claims along the Buckhannon River and tributaries. On Fink's Run was Jacob Hyre, Henry Fink, William Allman, Jacob Lorentz and John Bozarth. Many others are listed for other areas in the immediate vicinity. This history book gives a wealth of information about the early settlements in what is now Harrison, Lewis, Upshur and Randolph Counties.

Other important sources of information are ---
1. History of Lorentz Community, 1923, by A. J. Marple.
2. West Virginia Blue Book, page 602, about Jackson Fort on William Allman's farm.
3. All the published census', birth, marriage, death records for said four counties. Most are in the library of Hacker's Creek Pioneer Descendants, Center Street, Weston, West Virginia.

The wealth of research shown here does not positively prove the lineage of our immediate ancestor, William Allman, but his arrival at the Buckhannon settlement to the present is proven by existing vital statistics.

WILLIAM ALLMAN b. ca. 1760, d. 1828, bur. on hillside behind his home on Fink's Run, Upshur Co., W. Va. Married to a Miss Elizabeth or Jane Weatherholt, per Upshur History Book, 1907 by W. B. Cutright and Weatherholt family research by Gary Weatherholt, Indianapolis, Indiana. He has the will of Nicholas Weatherhold and a Deed of 1818 gives Peter Weatherhold, Christian Weatherhold and WILLIAM ALMAN as the bodily heirs of Nicholas Weatherhold. This would mean that William Allman was the survivor of his wife, a d/o Nicholas and possibly named Elizabeth, with her death date PRIOR to 1818. Research by Mrs. Gay Allman Ellis, a granddaughter of David S. Allman says William Allman married an Elizabeth Martin. Could William have had 2 wives? His wife or wives are buried with their husband.

William's homestead on Fink's Run was acquired by Land Patent April 24, 1805 issued by Governor Page for 200 acres on a land office warrant dated Dec. 24, 1783. Later surveys to prove ownership are found in Randolph Land Record Book 1, page 219 and Book 1, page 248 and Harrison Survey Volume 4, page 387.

William Allman also owned 128 acres in Hardy County on the Shenandoah River per Land Office Treasury Warrant number 14, page 733, dated Oct. 25, 1790 adjoining a line with John Allman (maybe a brother).

William acquired farms other than the homestead on Rooting Creek, Stone Coal Creek and Stony Run. These farms were given to his sons -

Jacob per Harrison Deed Book II, page 75 and Lewis Deeds C-267 for 107 acres on Stone Coal Creek; Peter per Harrison Deed Book II, page 564 and Lewis Deeds C-243 for 110 acres on Stony Run.

WILLIAM ALLMAN and wife Elizabeth are documented in his well-written will dated May 27, 1827 (the will is witnessed by Jacob Lorentz, James Barnes and Cornelius Clark because he is BLIND).

The children of William (1) Allman are ---

Peter David b. March 24, 1789 / Catherine b. 1789/ John b. 1791 / Mary b. 1793 / Jacob b. 1794 or '99 / George b. 1800 / Isaac b. 1802 / Abraham b. March 31, 1805 / Martha b. 1807 per Norman Book, page 76 but not mentioned in father's will Elizabeth b. 1809, wife of John Westfall / Nicholas b. 1810.

Hereinafter all reference to our pioneer ancestor William Allman (1760-1828) will be referred to as William (1).

LEGEND OF ABBREVIATIONS

County Birth Records	)BR
County Marriage Bonds	)MB
County Marriage Records	)MR
County Death Records -	)DR

The counties involved are H, Harrison/ L, Lewis/ U, Upshur/ G, Gilmer/ R, Randolph/ V, Vinton-County, Ohio.

PETER DAVID ALLMAN, s/o William (1) Allman, b. March 24, 1789 in Hardy County, Brock Gap, d. October 13, 1825, bur. Old Harmony Cemetery on Hacker's Creek (stone), killed by tree fall on Stony Run Farm. He marr. Dec. 20, 1813, HMR by Morris by Rev. John Mitchell & HMB 2-420 and his bible to Catherine Sims, b. 1785 or '94, d. June 6, 1856, LDR 1-19, she is bur. Old Harmony Cemetery (no stone). She was d/o William Sims of Cheat River and 1st marr. Susanna Sims (1760-); 2nd marr. Margaret Dever (1798-) in 1824. Peter was in the War of 1812.

The children of Peter David Allman are ---

James Madison b. January 12, 1810 (either adopted or an early arrival) / Susannah L. b. October 12, 1814 / Elizabeth b. January 18, 1817 / Eliza

b. September 6, 1818 / William b. November 11, 1821 / Sarah b. July 15, 1824 / David S. (Stanton) b. May 25, 1825.

From Border Settlers of Northwestern Virginia by McWhorter, page 35 - "Mrs. Catherine Simms-Allman remembered that when she was a little girl, Jesse Hughes came to her father's house on Hacker's Creek, one mile below West's Fort, early one morning, and ordered them to run to the fort. Upon that occasion his dress consisted of the hunting shirt and moccasins only. He was riding a pony without a saddle, and mounted her mother behind him, and with one of the children in his arms, galloped to the fort. This incident occurred while Hughes lived at the mouth of Jesse's Run. At the end of his cabin, Hughes erected a "lean-to" where at all times he kept his pony ready for instant use in case of an Indian alarm."

Peter Allman's progeny ---

James Madison Allman (known only as Madison) b. January 12, 1810 on Stony Run from Peter Allman bible, d. Nov. 14, 1894, LDR 2-152 84y.10m.5d., bur. Old Harmony Cemetery (stone). He marr. Dec. 11, 1828, LMB 1-47, to Elizabeth Bonnett, b. June 6, 1810 or ' 13, d. October 8, 1873, LDR 1-79 63 yr., (stone is 60 yr.), bur. Old Harmony Cemetery. She is d/o Samuel Bonnett (1770-1849) and his 2nd. wife Martha Radcliff (1778-1855), both bur. in Old Harmony Cemetery.

Madison Allman and Elizabeth Bonnett children ---

Peter T. b. October 10, 1826(9), d. March 27, 1913, HDR 5-1, bur. Rockford Cemetery, marr. December 27, 1860, LMR 5-17, to Mary (Post) Swisher. Peter T's children are --- Martin Post (1864-1924) marr. (1) Mary Bond (1867-1899), marr. (2) May 12, 1904 Beatrice Miles (1883-1964) / James Madison (1868-1944) not marr. / Orion Francis (1874-1943) marr. June 30, 1909 to Annie M. Irey (1882-1934) / Christopher C. (1860-1862). All members of this family are bur. in Rockford Cemetery near Lost Creek, Harrison County.

The families of Peter T's children as recorded by me covers Martin Post with 11 children, 15 grandchildren, 4 great-grandchildren, 1 great-great-grandchild; Orion Francis with 2 children, 2 grandchildren, 2 great-grandchildren.

Madison Allman and Elizabeth Bonnett children ---

Samuel B. b. 1831 (stone 1835), d. 1889 (stone), bur. Arlington

Cemetery, marr. March 13, 1853 to Nancy E. McCoy or McAvoy (1837-1897). Records are so incomplete the true name of McCoy or McAvoy cannot be ascertained. Nancy is bur. Arlington Cemetery. Samuel B's. children are --- Martha E. (1854-) marr. December 28, 1876 to John F. Andrew (1853-) UMR 1853-37-86. / Phillip Madison (1856-1917) bur. Kincaid Cemetery, Bablin, W. Va., marr. April 24, 1884, UMR 1-105 to Mary E. Corinna Waugh (1867-1961). /Elizabeth Jane (1858-1916) bur. Rock Cave Cemetery, marr. November 4, 1878 to Enoch W. Andrews (1854-1895) UMR 1853-37-86. / Sarah Margaret C. (1860-) UBR-1-35-219, marr. July 26, 1888, UMR 2-140 to John W. Lane (1868-) / Ernestine Ann (1862-1905) UBR 1-41-9, bur. Cow Run Cemetery, marr. September 3, 1885, UMR-1-229, to Spenser S. Lane (1864-1923), bur. Cow Run Cemetery. / John E. (1865-1930) HBR 1-102, bur. Arlington Cemetery, marr. April 19, 1900, RMR-4-244 to Minerva Lewis (1875-1955), UDR 4-6 / Harvey Ugena (1867-1944) HBR 1-123, bur. Cow Run Cemetery, UDR 4-4, marr. January 9, 1890, UMR 2-232 to Roxie A. Lane (1873-1941) UDR 4-3. / Mariam or Marion (1871-) Upshur Census 1880, 9 yr., no other record. / Lloyd Samuel (1875-1951) UBR 1-106, bur. Rock Cave Cemetery, UDR 4-5, m. January 29, 1921, UMR 14-105 to Ellen F. Lewis Snyder (1885-1957). / May (1879-) Upshur Census 1880, 1 yr., marr. December 24, 1913, LMR-13-440 to B. T. Bailey, for his 2nd wife. / Ella M. (1879-) UBR 1-130, marr. June 6, 1917, UMR 12-288, to C. H. Williams (1857-) a 60 yr. old widower. / Nevada (ca 1883-) marr. August 21, 1889, UMR 2-242, to Burton Roby (1860-).

The families of Samuel B's children as recorded by me covers approximately 128 persons in four generations.

Madison Allman and Elizabeth Bonnett children ---

Margaret b. 1833, marr. September 25, 1855, LMR-4-85 and 5-5, to Marshall Hershman (1831-). Margaret's children are --- Margaret L. (1863-) / William Bruce (1868-1938) UBR-1-61, not marr. / Isaac B. (1867-) UBR-1-56 / George P. W. (1872- UBR-1-86 / C. L. and M. S. ???. No further information on this family.

Madison Allman & Elizabeth Bonnett children ---

Isaac Newton b. December, 1834, d. April 4, 1891, LDR 2-68, bur. Morrison Cemetery, Hacker's Creek, marr. October 2, 1857, LMR 5-10, to Nancy C. Swisher b. Nov. 29, 1835, d. October 22, 1912, LDR 3-310 by son L. M. Allman, bur. Morrison Cemetery, she a d/o Lewis D. Swisher and Martha Margaret Smith. Lewis D. (1809-1896), Martha M. (1813-1899) bur. Morrison Cemetery. Isaac Newton's children are --- Fernando

Wood (1 858-1942) bur. Fairview Cemetery, Berlin, W. Va., marr. Sept. 10, 1884, LMR 5-113, to Sarah Olive Post (1858-1956), bur. with husband, a d/o John and Sophia Post. / Davisson Gaston (1862(3)-1949), bur. Fairview Cemetery, marr. September 13, 1888, LMR 5-146, to Verdie M. Post (1872-1911), bur. with husband, a d/o Eber E. and C. C. Post. / Sarah Ann (1865(3)-1937) LDR 5-3, bur. Fairview Cemetery, not married. / Alice M. (1860-1936) LDR 5-3, bur. Fairview Cemetery, not married. / Margaret E. (1867-1869) LBR 1-124, on bead stone in Morrison Cemetery. / Lewis (Louis) Madison (1870-1946) LBR 1-147, LDR 6-3, bur. Fairview Cemetery, marr. August 11, 1898, LMR 8-334, to Stella M. Swisher (1878-1976), a d/o Edwin C. Swisher and Cecelia Lawson. / James David (1872-1961) LBR 1-162, LDR 8-11, bur. Fairview Cemetery, marr. October 15, 1900, LMR 9-245, to Minnie R. Morrison (1876-1969) a d/o Albert N. Morrison and Mary Hinzman. / Sylvanius Columbus (1875-) LBR 1-189, marr. October 19, 1916 to Verta Layola Morrison, LMR 14-370, a d/o Lewis C. and Ida E. Morrison / a child R. C. b. 1857 / Lewis County Will F-442 probated March 22, 1937 for Sarah A. Allman leaves her estate to brother Sylvanius Columbus. The families of Isaac Newton's children as recorded by me covers approximately 58 persons in four generations.

Madison Allman & Elizabeth Bonnett children ---

Lydia Elizabeth b. 1839(7), marr. September 11, 1856, LMR 4-103 and 5-7 by Rev. H. R. Bonnett says m. October 8, 1857 but several of his entries in court house do not agree with other records. She marr. Perry Green Cunningham, b. 1836, Lewis Census 1850, 14 yrs. old. He is a s/o George H. Cunningham b. 1800, and Catherine Smith b. 1805, marr. March 7, 1822. This 1850 census lists George and Catherine with children Temperance, Perry, Julia, Francis M. and George P. No further record of the Perry Green Cunningham family has been found.

Madison Allman & Elizabeth Bonnett children ---

John Columbus b. June 15, 1850, d. August 27, 1921, HDR 6-6, bur. Fairview Cemetery, marr. 1872, LMR 5-56, to Olive D. Gordon, b. 1851, d. 1925, bur. with husband, HDR 7-6, she a d/o Joseph F. Gorden and Matilda C. (Martha C.) Smith. John Columbus' children are --- Sarah E. (1876(5)-1878(7)), LBR 1-199, bur. Fairview Cemetery. / Eber P. (1873-1911), LBR 1-171, LDR 3-246, bur. Fairview Cemetery, marr. December 12, 1901, LMR 9-420, to Bertha A. Swisher (1874), a d/o John B. Swisher and Ailsy V. Lawson. / Emery V. (1879-1950), LBR 2-11, bur. Fairview Cemetery, marr. to Laura (Cunningham) Jones. No further information on her has been found. / Evert F. (Everett) (1881-1953), doctor of Veterinary Medicine in Clarksburg, bur. New Bethel Cemetery, Good Hope, W. Va., marr. June 29, 1911, HMR 21-204, to Ethel J. (Thrash) Foster, a d/o Benjamin F. Thrash and Martha E. Bell. / Matilda Fay (1886-1972), LBR 2-74, bur. Fairview Cemetery, marr. March 7, 1912 to Rev. Otto Reeder (1889-1961), bur. Fairview Cemetery, a s/o Thomas A. Reeder and Willie Moore. The families of John Columbus' children have not been recorded.

Madison Allman & Elizabeth Bonnett children ---

James Madison b. April 16, 1844, d. June 12, 1929, LDR 4-3, in Gilmer County, bur. Newberne Cemetery, marr. April 20, 1865, LMR 5-27, to (1) Virginia Louisa Wilson b. June 4, 1844, d. February 19, 1899, bur. Newberne Cemetery, a d/o Archie Wilson and Emily B. His 2nd marr. Nov. 12, 1899, GMR 1-63 to (2) Sophia Powell b. 1854, d. 1930, bur. not known. James Madison's children are --- Mary Catherine (1866-1929), LBR 1-117, bur. M.P. Church, Alum Bridge, marr. October 21, 1886, GMR-1-37, to Scott Fisher of Wood County. / Desky Virginia (1868-1886) LBR 1-131, bur. Newberne Cemetery, marr. October 26, 1884, GMR 1-34, to Newton Law (1862-) of Ritchie County. / Lenora May (Mary) (1870), LBR 1-147, marr. October 11, 1888, GMR 1-40, to M. Scott Bush (1868- no place of bur. for either. / Isaac Upton (1878-1948), GBR 1-4, LDR 6-5, bur. Weston Masonic Cemetery, marr. September 16, 1900, GMR 1-65, to Maude Bush (1884-1954), bur. with her husband. / Bertie Cleveland (1884-1884) male, no name in GBR, bur. Newberne Cemetery. / Joseph B. (1875-), GBR 1-4, no further record found. / Henry Irvin (1873-1944) LBR 1-171, bur. Horn Creek Cemetery, Cox's Mills, W. Va., marr. June 21, 1896 to Tensey Fay Zinn (1873-1958), LDR 8-5, bur. Horn Creek Cemetery, a d/o Marion Bukey Zinn (1846-1927) and Alice Bush, (1851-1927). / Jasper Sylvester (1875-1915), bur. Horn Creek Cemetery, marr. July 21, 1895. GMR 1-53, to Martha Della Zinn (1878-1950) LDR 7-3, bur. with husband, a d/o Marion Bukey Zinn and Alice Bush. The families of James Madison's children as recorded by me covers approximately 29 persons.

Madison Allman & Elizabeth Bonnett children ---

Martha Catherine b. September 13, 1846, d. September 6, 1929, bur. Fairview Cemetery, Berlin, W. Va., marr. March 16, 1865, LMR 5-26 by Rev. Henry R. Bonnett, to David Rinehart Swisher, b. July 6, 1840, d. January 27, 1918, bur. Fairview Cemetery, a s/o Lewis D. Swisher (1809-1896) and Margaret Smith (1813-1899) both bur. Morrison Cemetery. Martha Catherine's children are --- Isaac M. (1866-) / Zora or Dora (1867-) marr. a Brake. / Sara A. (1867) / Samantha M. (1870-

1949), bur. Fairview Cemetery, not married. / Emma E. (1872-1960), bur. Fairview Cemetery, not married. / Willard D. (1874-1943), bur. Fairview Cemetery, no other information. / Lydia E. (1876-1954) bur. Fairview Cemetery, not married./ Meade, no dates, information from obituary for his mother./ Per. H.C.P.D. Cemetery Book III, page 60 is Dora Swisher b. April 12, 1867, d. March 20, 1893, bur. Laurel Lick Cemetery, d/o David and Martha Swisher, marr. Charles E. Hersman. / Lewis Census 1900 lists David Rinehart Swisher residence with Winfield Snodgrass, son-in-law, 39 yrs. old, b. Dec. 1860, widower; Nola Snodgrass, granddaughter, 3 yr. old and Esta M. Hersman, granddaughter, 8 yr. old. Lewis D. Swisher was a s/o Peter Swisher, Jr. and Susannah Rinehart. I have not recorded any of the descendants of these children.

Madison Allman and Elizabeth Bonnett children ---

Sarah Jane b. December 31, 1840, d. March 13, 1906, marr. December 24, 1863, LMR 5-23, to William Dexter Morrison, b. 1839, a s/o William Morrison and Mary. This information was supplied by Mary Morrison. No further records have been found.

Madison Allman and Elizabeth Bonnett children ---

George W. b. January or June 1839, d. April 3, 1905, bur. Swecker Cemetery, right fork of Canoe Run, marr. December 6, 1860 to Virginia L. Batten b. Nov. 18, 1839 or 1840 on gravestone, d. January 11, 1913, LDR 3-310, bur. with her husband, a d/o Richard L. Batten (1812-1903) and Nancy Ann Smith (1817-1889). George W. 's children are --- Mary Ellen (Ann) (1861-1902) LBR 1-103, bur. Stout's Mills, marr. April 8, 1880, LMR 5-89, to George Lewis Smith, a s/o Henry R. Smith. / Ida M. (1865-1956) LBR 1-114, bur. Swecker Cemetery, marr. Nov. 14, 1905, LMR 11-125, to Eddy M. Swecker a s/o Samuel Swecker and Minerva J. / Nancy Elizabeth (18681918), bur. near Roanoke, maybe Swecker Cemetery, marr. July 25, 1889, LMR 6-4, to William Lowther Post, widower, a s/o Charles and Jane Post. / Vada Columbia (1870-) LBR 1-151, marr. May 14, 1891, LMR 6-20, to Thaddeus Waldo Brinkley, a s/o Fleming K. Brinkley and Margaret A. / Eddy C. (female) b. July 5, 1871, LBR 1-159, no other information / Catherine A. b. May 12, 1874, LBR 1-184, no other information / Nettie C. (Nellie) b. May 12, 1874, d. 1937, bur. Swecker Cemetery, marr. October 31, 1893, LMR 7-207, to John E. Swecker. Her father gave the marr. information; could she be a twin to Catherine or the same person? / Wade Hampton (1877-1941 LDR 6-1, bur. Canoe Run Cemetery, marr. July 27, 1898, LMR 8-331, to Ida Rachel Post, a d/o Charles and Julia Ann Post. / George A. (1885-1954)

LDR 7-9, bur. Swecker Cemetery, not married. / James J. (1893-1893) LDR says 20 da., s/o Geo. W. and Lon V. Allman (maybe Virginia). / Unnamed Allman, LDR says Nov. 1 - Nov. 22, 1862, age 21 days, s/o or d/o G. W. and Virg. Allman. / Lewis Census 1900 at residence of George W. Allman is Adam H. Minere (adopted) born 1885. Virginia L. Batten's sister, Lydia, marr. Albert Morgan Allman, a s/o William Allman (1821); Virginia L.'s brother, Rev. David Batten, marr. Sarah Catherine Allman, a d/o David S. Allman. The families of George W's. children as recorded by me covers approximately 31 persons.

Peter Allman's progeny --

Susannah L. Allman b. October 12, 1814 per Peter Allman's bible, marr. April 8, 1836, LMR 2-14, to Joseph Shoulders or Shouldis, b. 1810. Her marr. bond was approved by her brother Madison. This is my proof that Madison was a s/o Peter Allman and Catherine Sims. The Shoulders' children were Laben 1837/ William 1839/ Catharine 1840/ Edward 1843/ and David 1848.

Elizabeth Allman b. January 18, 1817 per Peter Allman's bible, marr. March 27, 1838, (LMB-Madison Allman, her brother gave oath that she was over 21 years old), to Noah Lawrence b. 1817. The Lawrence children were Alexander 1838 / Rebecca 1840 / Peter 1844 / and Daniel 1847.

Eliza Allman b. September 6, 1818 per Harrison Census 1850, marr. March 19, 1841, LMR 2-59, (bondsman was Madison her brother) to William Edgar Davisson b. 1808. The Davisson children were George 1842/ Sarah 1844/ Mary 1846 who marr. November 28, 1872 to John M. McWhorter (1845-1928) a s/o Levi McWhorter and Eliza Alkire/ Edgar 1847/ and Jonathan 1849.

Peter Allman's progeny ---

Sarah Allman b. July 15, 1824 per Peter Allman's bible, marr. October 22, 1841, LMR 2-61, (bondsmen were George Hersman and her brother, William Allman). Authority for her marriage was given by her guardian, Thomas Wolf, she was under 21 years of age. She marr. George Davisson (b. 1813) and their children were

Caroline b. 1845/ Granville W. (1847-1898) marr. January 16, 1870 to Caroline B. Hawkins./ and John 1850. Sarah d. February, 1853 per Peter Allman's bible.

Peter Allman's progeny ---

William Allman b. November 11, 1821 per stone and bible, d. October 18, 1897, LDR 1-227, bur. Old Harmony Cemetery, marr. first December 22, 1846, LMR 2-124, to (1) Margaret Jane Echard b. 1825 per stone, d. January 22, 1853 per stone, a d/o Jacob Echard and Sarah, both bur. in Broad Run Cemetery. William (1821) Allman's second marr. December 15, 1859 was to (2) Kitturah (Batten) Dean (1829-1911), bur. Fairview Cemetery, a d/o Thomas Batten and Hannah Telitha Jones.

The children of William (1821) and (1) Margaret Jane Echard are ---

John William b. September 13, 1847 per father's bible./ Albert Morgan (Absolom) b. August 16, 1849 per bible, d. August 11, 1929, LDR 4-3, bur. Alum Bridge Cemetery, marr. September 27, 1876, LMR 5-71, to Lydia Batten (1854-1928), a d/o Richard L. Batten and Nancy A. Smith. / Jacob L. b. February 27, 1852 per bible. / Peter Elihu b. March 24, 1854, LBR 1-19, d. December 28, 1934, bur. Fairview Cemetery, marr. March 24, 1886, LMR 5-124, to Mary Marcelia Swisher (1862-1952). / Elias Ervin b. April 11, 1856 per bible, d. December 8, 1862 per stone in Harmony Cemetery. / George W. b. September 30, 1858, LBR 1-65, d. October 10, 1878, LDR 1-103, bur. Old Harmony Cemetery, not married. / Mary Catherine b. 1850 per Bailey Book by Guy Bailey but not listed in Peter Allman's bible, marr. Isaac Columbus Swisher.

William (1821) Allman and (1) Margaret Jane Echard children ---

Peter Elihu (1854-1934) and Mary Marcelia Swisher (1862-1952) had a child Aubra Roscoe, b. June 6, 1890, LBR 2-111, d. May 30, 1943, LDR 6-2, bur. Fairview Cemetery, marr. Dec. 22, 1914, LMR 14-111, to Carrie Woofter (1893-1984), d/o Oliver Woofter and Mary Zobrist.

Albert Morgan (1849-1927) and Lydia Batten (1854-1928) had the following children---

Daisy Florence (1878-) marr. November 21, 1900, LMR 9-270, to H. E. Hartley (1868-), s/o Jacob K. Hartley and Mary A. Bolton. / Kasper Kimball (1880), LBR 2-21, marr. (1) February 20, 1907, LMR 11-327, to Retta Pratt and marr. (2) October 22, 1917 to Lillie Nestor. / Harold (1887-1887) bur. Woofter Burying Ground. / Wade E. (1882-1882) LDR-1-133, bur. Woofter Burying Ground. / Alma B. (1892-1902) LDR 1-265, bur. Woofter Burying Ground. / Anna B. or Amy B. (1892-1902), b. 1891 on stone in Woofter Burying Ground, LBR 2-120, this is probably same person,. / Clyde Dale (1888-1925) LBR IA-42 and LBR 2-921, bur.

Woofter Burying Ground, LDR 4-2, his death record says divorced and 50 days fasting, died of starvation.

The children of William (1821) and (2) Kitturah (Batten) Dean are ---

Mary Catherine (1860-1920) / Talitha Jane (1861-1911) / Eliza Irene (1864-1936) / David Thomas (1865-1945) / William Francis (1867-1942) / Ambrose (Amrose) Kitturiah (1872-1946) / Novel Evans (1876-1936) / Albert and Alice, these names from Mayrie Lou Brissey but are not named in family bible: Kitturah Batten b. July 19, 1829, d. June 2, 1911, LDR 3-246, bur. Fairview Cemetery, a d/o Thomas Batten and Hannah Jones. Kitturah Batten marr. (1) Thomas Dean, March 11, 1854 and had 2 children-Alice Virginia Dean (1855-1899) and Adalade Victoria Dean (1857-1936). Thomas Dean (1819-1857), a s/o James and Leanoh Dean.

William (1821) Allman and (2) Kitturah Batten children ---

Mary Catherine Allman b. December 10, 1860, d. April 26, 1920, bur. Fairview Cemetery, marr. March 8, 1883, LMR 5-104, to Isaac Columbus Swisher b. September 6, 1861, d. March 3, 1953, bur. Fairview Cemetery, a s/o James Lee Swisher (1832-1908) and Mary Hinzman (1835-1908). The Swisher children were James Blain (1884-1964) / Rella May (1889-1970) / Dora Ethel (1892-1936) per information from "Rocky" Swisher.

Talitha Jane Allman b. June 10, 1861, LBR 1-99, d. November 15, 1911, LDR 3-246, not married. AKA Selitha and Falitha in various records. Mary Morrison, Salem, Virginia lists two persons b. June 10, 1861 and March 7, 1862, with names Talitha Jane and Tabitha.

Eliza Irene Allman b. February 12, 1862, d. December 5, 1936, bur. Newbern Cemetery, Gilmer County, marr. March 25, 1886, LMR 5-124, to (1) Alfred Washington Swisher b. April 4, 1863, d. May 7, 1898, a s/o James Lee Swisher and Mary Hinzman. The Swisher children are Mrs. Gertie Law and Mrs. E. I. Singleton. No stone is found for Alfred Washington Swisher but in 1898 A. W. Swisher surveyed the Fairview Friendship Cemetery. Eliza Irene later marr. (2) George A. Conley of Newberne, Cox's Mills.

David Thomas Allman b. March 20, 1865, LBR 1-108, d. February 13, 1945, LDR 6-2, bur. Fairview Cemetery, marr. October 24, 1894, LMR 7-342, to (1) Anne Sarah Hinzman b. September 28, 1867 (stone), d. August 1, 1911, LDR 3-246, bur. Fairview Cemetery, a d/o P. G.

Hinzman and Sarah J. Swisher. Their children are Darrell (1895-1918) / Nellie F. (1897-1980) / Clarence Dalton (1903-1987). David Thomas marr. (2) Sophia L. Hinzman July 2, 1915 LMR 14-177, she a sister to (1) Anne Sarah.

William Francis Allman b. October 15, 1867, LBR 1-124, d. April 12, 1942, LDR 61, bur. Fairview Cemetery, probably not married.

Amrose Kittorah Allman b. December 30, 1872, LBR 1-162, d. 1946 (stone), bur. Fairview Cemetery, marr. September 30, 1891, LMR 6-22, to Ira Erwin Swisher (1867-1906), bur. Fairview Cemetery, a s/o Isaac R. Swisher and Eda A. The Swisher children are Harland A. (1892) / Arden H. (1896) / and Odbert (1898),/ Eugenia per Barbara McCarty / and in Laurel Lick Cemetery is stone for infant son of Ira and Antirose (Allman) Swisher, per HCPD Journal, Vol. 1, 148.

Novel Evans Allman b. March 8, 1876, LBR 1-199, d. February 1, 1936, LDR 5-3, bur. Fairview Cemetery, marr. March 27, 1902 to (1) Viola Victoria Vincent b. August 13, 1881, d. January 18, 1911, LDR 3-246, bur. Fairview Cemetery, a d/o Joseph Israel Vincent and Florence Hartley. Their children are William Vincent (1903-1965) / Joseph W. with same birth date as William Vincent, LBR 2-230 and LBR 3A-136 / Alice D. (1906-1985) who marr. Arthur J. Rinehart.--Novel Evans marr. October 29, 1912, LMR 13-258 to (2) Odd or Addy Maude Bonnett (1881-1969), a d/o Eli M. Bonnett and (1) Sarah Jane DeBarr. They had a daughter Virginia Maude (1913-) who marr. William Brooks Probst.

Peter Allman's progeny --

David S. (Stanton) Allman b. May 25, 1825 per bible on Stony Run, Hacker's Creek, d. October 23, 1893, LDR 1-199, bur. Broad Run Cemetery, marr. September 1, 1847, LMR 2-138 to (1) Janetta Echard b. October 1829 in Rockbridge, Va. d. February 9, 1873, LDR 1-79, bur. Broad Run Cemetery, a d/o Jacob Echard and Sarah. There were 11 children by this marriage--namely---

Jacob Presley a s/o David S., b. August 30, 1848, d. January 14, 1879, LDR 1-111, bur. Broad Run Cemetery, marr. Amanda Cookman; one child Flores J. (male) (1877-1930).

Theodore Sylvester a s/o David S. b. November 4, 1850, d. August 27, 1925, LDR 4-2, bur. Broad Run Cemetery, marr. December 12, 1878, HMR 5-125 to (1) Mary Christine Thrash (1858-1916), a d/o Michael Thrash. Their children - Guy (1879-1973) marr. Mary B. Musser / Zelma

(1880-) marr. Howard R. Hammer / Lora aka Dora, Sona (1882-) marr. Bryon Pitt Bailey / Loomis Clyde (1886-) marr. Florence Will / Florence (1887-) marr. Hugh Ramsburg / Arziel C. (1890-), marr. Ora B. Maxon / Russell (1893-1958) marr. Ruth M. Hitt / Gerald aka Gus and Gur (1896-1897) / Hazel (1898-1899) / Raymond (1901-) marr. Lea Hoover.

Sarah Catherine a d/o David S. b. November 29, 1852, d. September 1, 1926, bur. Fairview Cemetery, marr. October 19, 1870, LMR 5-51, to Reverend David Batten b. March 1, 1847, d. February 5, 1897, bur. Fairview Cemetery, a s/o Richard Batten and Nancy Smith. The Batten children - David Richard (1873-1936) marr. Loretta McKeever / Alder Virginia (1874-) marr. William D. Hitt / Vada C. (1871-) marr. a Morrisett / Ida May (1876-) single / Henry B. (1878-) / Rosa C. (1883-1966) marr. a Halterman / Bertha D. (1886-1972) marr. a Collins.

Peter Cecil, a s/o David S. b. March 13, 1855, d. January 9, 1936, LDR 5-3, bur. Broad Run Cemetery, marr. December 20, 1883, LMR 5-109, to Sarah Ellen Barb, b. February 17, 1864, d. April 20, 1932, bur. Broad Run Cemetery, LDR 5-1, a d/o Philip E. Barb and Joanne Fernandez. Their children are - Nola Gay (1884-) marr. E. J. Thrash / Ova Jannetta (1887-) marr. Albonus Trustin / Ernice Carl (1890-) marr. Mary Ellen Lortow / Laura Grace (1891-1976) marr. (1) John W. Garton, marr. (2) Reed, marr. (3) Byron P. Bailey / Bertha Audra (1896-1919) marr. G. W. Burch / David Bryan (1898-1967) marr. Dora Vi Law / Cecil Paul (1906) marr. Billie Eldridge / Rubert Howe (1901-) and possibly Peter C., Jr. and Paul McPherson Allman.

Virginia Olive, a d/o David S. b. March 19, 1857, LBR 1-51, d. June 15, 1934, marr. December 21, 1880, LMR 5-87, to Morgan Minor Hall, b. June 4, 1846, d. March 30, 1915 in Greensboro, N. C., a s/o J. S. and C. I. Hall, bur. Piney Grove Cemetery, Guilford County, N. C. The Hall children are - Esse (1880-1881) / Lulu (1881-1904) / Richard B. (1883-1952) marr. Nora Snyder / James (1885-1902) / Florris (1889-1941) / Dora Ann (1891-) marr. J. C. Crutchfield / May or Mary (1893-) marr. Clay Swisher / Minor Hall (1896-1945) / Ollie (1899-) marr. a McLear.

Lloyd Manor, a s/o David S. b. August 13, 1859, LBR 1-79, d. August 30, 1927, LDR 4-3, bur. Broad Run Cemetery, marr. November 12, 1884, LMR 5-114, to Nancy Louella Hall b. September 3, 1868, d. February 19, 1927, LDR 4-3, bur. Broad Run Cemetery, a d/o James M. Hall and Catherine E. Lovett. Their children are -- Chloe Maud (1885-) marr. Reverend Earl Wimer / Samuel McClellan (1887-1973) marr. Cora Beeghley / Bertha A. (1889-1899) / Worthy Dale (1890-1953) marr. Mary E. Hitt / Catherine Eulalia (1893-1926) marr. Waitman E. Smith / Rella

Vieva (1896-1899) / Mayme Oeeta (1899-1963) marr. John William Smith / Zella Zueleta (1901-1972) marr. Truman Brown / James Hall (1905-1949) marr. Katherine Cunningham.

Alice May or Mildred, a d/o David S. b. September 27, 1859 (61), d. May 6, 1922, bur. Machpelah Cemetery, Weston, marr. December 28, 1879, LMR 5-87, to Eli Alexander Chittum, b. July 1857 at Rockbridge County, Va., d. June 22, 1942. The Chittum children are -- George David 1880 / Floris Cecil 1882 / Thomas C. 1882/ Ora Sherman 1884(5) / Loa Veda 1887 / Rose Jane 1889 Cromer D. 1891 / William Avara 1894 / Lewis Stanton / Russell Alexander 1900 maybe Lois S. 1897.

George McClellum or McClelland, a s/o David S. b. June 10, 1863(4), d. September 5, 1941, LDR 6-1, bur. Fairview Cemetery, marr. ca. 1900, LMR 9-137?? to Weese Hardman, b. November 23, 1875, d. October 22, 1969, LDR 10-2, bur. Fairview Cemetery a d/o Perry G. Hardman and Laura V. Brake. Their children are -- Daphne Virginia (1904-) marr. Forrest A. White / Dwight L. (1903-1988) marr. Virginia Cottrill / Olive changed to Bernadine (1905-) LBR 3-9 says Olive (changed to Bernadine 8/12/1941), marr. William H. Miller / Willis or William Perry (1908-) marr. Catherine Timms / Wilma Mary (1908-) marr. Oscar Hillies or Hiller / Laura J. (1911-) marr. Charles E. Slabaugh / Eleanor Louise (1919-) marr. Daniel Albert Knicely.

David Alonso, a s/o David S. b. September 19, 1867(8), d. May 20, 1947, LDR 6-4, bur. Broad Run Cemetery, marr. August 3, 1891, LMR 6-21, to Margaret Esther Barb, b. April 11, 1873, d. June 18, 1944, LDR 6-2, bur. Broad Run Cemetery, a d/o Philip E. Barb and Juan Fernandez or Joan Pritt. Their children are -- David Claude (1892-1896) / Bertha Burl (1894-1964) marr. Ray R. Lough / Grace, LBR 1A338 gives March 2, 1894 same date for Bertha Burl, they may have been twins / Junie William (1896-1964) marr. Marie B. Clark / Ernie R. (1897-1943) single / Eula Gay (1899-1976) marr. Fred Ellis, Sr. ; she made an extensive listing of the families of David S. Allman and shows William(l) as married to Elizabeth Martin. / Blonda (1901-1911) single / Hazel May (1903-1926) marr. Joseph R. Throckmorton / Ethel Jeanette (1905-1913) single Slater David (1908-1978) marr. Cora Lillian Butcher / Thelma Pauline (1911-) marr. Charles Rich.

Flora Aldine, a d/o David S. b. July 20, 1870, LBR 1-147, d. 1952, marr. February 23, 1892, LMR 7-13, to John Henry Funk (1862-1899). The Funk children are --

Gernie J. (female) (1892-1985) single / Rella Jane (1894-1972) marr.

Minter E. Bailey / Rose D. (1899-) marr. Hobert Beeghley.

William Columbus, a s/o David S. b. January 8, 1873, LBR 1-171, d. January 4, 1954, LDR 7-8, bur. Machpelah Cemetery, marr. November 15, 1898, LMR 8-378, to Gertrude Melvina Hall, b. September 23, 1875, d. February 8, 1959, HDR 2l-7A, bur. Machpelah Cemetery, a d/o Peyton R. Hall and Sarah E. Brown. Their children are -- David Randall (1899-1982) marr. M. Adean Lockhart / George Rudolph (1901-1983) marr. Ruth Vassar / William Hall (1906-1968) marr. Gladys Bailey / Dorothea Virginia (1909-) marr. Bernard Bailey.

Peter Allman's progeny ---

David S. (Stanton) Allman (1825-1893) - Second Marriage - marr. January 15, 1874, LMR 5-61 by Reverend P.L.T. Queen was to (2) Virginia Bertie Butcher, b. January 29, 1846, d. September 13, 1924 (stone) bur. McCann's Run Cemetery, a d/o Jesse Ray Butcher and Lucinda Bonnett. Their children are --

John K., a s/o David S. b. August 22, 1874(6), d. March 29, 1932, LDR 5-1, bur. McCann's Run Cemetery, marr. January 22, 1895, LMR-7-370, to Lillie Mae Barb, b. April 4, 1879, LBR 180, d. February 2, 1972, LDR 10-6, bur. McCann's Run Cemetery, a d/o Abraham Barb and Melissa Carolyn McClain. Their children are ---Rosa Grace (1895-) marr. 1934 to E. F. Carder / Infant son (1897-1897) / Glen Argil (1898-) marr. 1923 to Beatrice Hayes / Edna Gay (1900-1978) marr. 1923 to Harry L. Hinton / Elsie Euena (1902-1903) LDR 1-273, says Mary, 10 mo. old / Infant sons (1904-1904) twins / Archie E. (1905-1911) Lottie Edith (1908-1911) / Infant son (1910-1910) / Robert Wayne (1911-1962) Thurman Elza (1914-) marr. 1937 to Agnes Reed (1903-1978) / Gladys Ernestine (1916-), marr. 1937 to Dorsey Stanton Snyder / Virgil Harvey (1925- I am uncertain of source of this name.

Jesse Lee, a s/o David S. b. August 12, 1876, LBR 1-199, d. May 25, 1959, UDR 5-1, bur. McCann's Run Cemetery, marr. November 19, 1893, LMR 7-352, to Jessie Mae Barb b. February 1880, LBR 1-199, d. January 3, 1945, LDR 6-2, a d/o Philip E. Barb and Joanne Fernandez Pritt (1843-1921). Their children are -- Harvey Ebert (1895-1969) marr. 1920 to Retta Ramsburg / Peter Elza (1896-1952) marr. Ina Tutwiler / Pearl Lulu (1899-) marr. 1914 to (1) H. J. Postlethwait and marr. 1928 to (2) Roy McKinney / Roscoe Doil (Doyle) (1902-1952) marr. 1940 to Gertrude Hough / Laco David (1904-1950) marr. 1925 to (1) Freda Campbell and marr. 1926 to (2) Sylvia Fink / Claude Barb (1908-) marr. Evelyn Lough / Rupert Clarence (1910-) marr. Louise Mann / Basil

Edward (1911-) marr. Mildred O. Wyant (1910-1981) / Lena Murl (1915) marr. Ross Lauden King, Jr. (1905-1993) / Lee Burner (1917-1919) stone McCann's Run Cemetery.

Jannattah May, a d/o David S. b. January 26, 1878, d. May 29, 1931, marr. December 14, 1913, LMR 13-440, to Blackwell Taylor Bailey, b. 1871, a s/o Alstopius Bailey and Cordelia. Jannattah was the second wife of Blackwell Bailey. Mr. Bailey had three children by his first wife, Effie E. Funk. I have no record of children by Jannattah May.

Ida N., a d/o David S. b. October 13, 1879(81), LBR 2-11, d. unknown, marr. July 26, 1902, LMR 10-61, to Albert Lewis Radcliffe, b. 1882, a s/o Henry Radcliffe and (1) Anna. The Radcliffe children are -- Ada / Eldee / Robert / Rubert Quiner / William.

Reason, aka Resa and Jake, a s/o David S. b. November 8, 1882, LBR 2-39, d. February 13, 1955, LDR 7-10, bur. McCann's Run Cemetery, marr. July 16, 1908, LMR 12-85, to Reta Elizabeth Smith, b. August 8, 1893, d. June 23, 1966, LDR 9-10, a d/o Willis Smith and Mary Ellen (Radcliff) Hinkle. Their children are -- Homer (1910-1989) marr. 1937 to Lucy Webb Wetzel / Willis David (1912-1969) marr. 1942 to Flora Ellen Webb / Nella Grace (1914-) marr. 1933 to C. M. Bonnett / Pauline (1915-) marr. 1930 to F. Skinner Beatrice (1919-) marr. 1946 to Ray K. Webb / Virginia Ellen (1922-) marr. 1946 to Joaquin F. Martin / Annabelle (1923-) marr. 1946 to C. H. Davisson / Archie Lee (1926-) marr. 1950 to Betty Freeman / Mary Katherine (1928-) marr. 1948 to Murl Perkins / Bayward (1933-) marr. to P. J. Lough.

Ola, a s/o David S. b. April 14, 1885, LBR 2-67, d. January 15, 1960, LDR 8-7, bur. McCann's Run Cemetery, marr. October 13, 1913, LMR 13-405, to Nancy Cordelia Bailey b. April 8, 1895, d. October 8, 1975, UDR 5-5, bur. McCann's Run Cemetery, a d/o Blackwell T. Bailey and Florence E. Funk. Their children are -- Everett Dale (1914-1930) single / Vencil Forest (1917-) marr. 1941 to Lillian Gautchia or Goucher / Merrill (Mervill) Howard (1922-) marr. 1949 to Anna Jean Keith / Agnes Virginia (1924-) marr. 1946 to Kenneth Adair, Sr.

Myrtle Belle, a d/o David S. b. August 4, 1887, LBR 2-83, d. July 12, 1952 (stone), bur. McCann's Run Cemetery, marr. August 18, 1908, LMR 12-103, to Ison Duane Butcher, aka Doane and Dome, b. December 23, 1874, d. April 19, 1953 (stone) bur. McCann's Run Cemetery, a s/o Michael E. Butcher and Euphemia Bankhead. The Butcher children are -- Clete Duane marr. Reva Merle Bailey Lester, single / Mabel Virginia marr. Harry Yates / Paul Edward, single.

The extensive family of David S. Allman as I have recorded includes ---

First wife, Jannetta Echard with eleven children; 74 grandchildren; 89 great-grandchildren; 49 great-great-grandchildren; 11 great-great-great-grandchildren. --Second wife, Virginia Bertie Butcher with seven children; 48 grandchildren; 90 great-grandchildren; 17 great-great-grandchildren; 4 great-great-great-grand-children. Plus many more I have not been able to research and record. This totals over 400 descendants of David S. Allman.

This concludes the progeny of Peter David Allman (1789-1825), the s/o William (1) Allman.

CATHERINE ALLMAN, d/o William (1), was b. 1789, d. prior to 1834 in Morrow County, Ohio, marr. April 17, 1809, HMR by Morris, to Samuel Oliver, Jr., b. 1787(8), d. prior to 1834 in Morrow County, Ohio, he a s/o Samuel Oliver, Sr. and Lydia. Further details of this family will be found elsewhere in this book.

JOHN ALLMAN, s/o William (1), was b. 1791, d. unknown, marr. September 7, 1811, HMB 2-383, to Clara Heir/Clorah Hier (Hyer); she was b. 179(5) a d/o John Hier (1754-1829) and Patience, John being her bondsman on the marr. bond. John and Patience Hyer are bur. in Hyre Cemetery on Brushy Fork. John was a s/o Leonard II and Mary (House) Hier. In Lewis County Deed Book, G-373, March 12, 1838, Augustine J. Smith sells to John Allman 18 acres of land on Big Sand Run for $18.00. No further record of this family has been found.

MARY ALLMAN, d/o William (1), was b. ca. 1793, d. unknown, marr. December or July, 1813, HMR 2-14, and Reverend John Mitchell list (Bondsman was William Allman, Harrison Co.), to John Oliver b. ca. 1795, Harrison Census 1810. He was a s/o Samuel Oliver, Sr. and Lydia; Samuel Sr. was a s/o Reuben Oliver and Elizabeth. Further details of this family will be found elsewhere in this book.

JACOB ALLMAN, s/o William (1) Allman was born 1791 (94) (99) per various records, d. September 21, 1873 in Vinton County, Ohio, VDR 1-44, 83 years old, bur. Mingo, Vinton County, Ohio. Jacob marr. March 14, 1814, HMB 2-442, (bondsman was William Marks) to (1) Elizabeth (maybe Marks). Elizabeth b. 1792 in Maryland per Vinton Census 1850, d. after 1836 per Deed when they sold the farm in West Virginia per Lewis Co. Deed Book, F-525, November 4, 1836. Jacob's second marr.

was May 16, 1867, VMR-2-311, to (2) Elizabeth Mace, per Vinton Census 1850. She was born 1793, d. March 24, 1876, VDR 1-25, 83 yrs. old. The Allman children per Vinton Census 1850 were --- Nicholas b. 1824 / Barbara b. 1826, marr. Mr. Riffle / Eleanor (Cleanor) b. 1836 /. The Vinton Census 1850 also lists Lyons and Riffle children at same residence but no relationship is shown. Further research must be made in Athens and Vinton Counties to resolve this family line.

GEORGE ALLMAN, s/o William (1) Allman was born ca. 1800 per Lewis Census 1850, 49 yrs. old, d. August 7, 1877, UDR 1853-39-1, 75 yrs. old, bur. on family farm with his parents. George received 100 acres of the original homestead which included all the improvements in his father's will. George marr. December 12 (21), 1820 LMB 3-1 by Reverend John Mitchell, to (1) Barbara Westfall, b. 1802, d. September 4, 1854, UDR 1853-3-136, 52 yrs. old, bur. on family farm with husband. She was a d/o Cornelius Westfall and Elizabeth Helmick; Cornelius b. 1768, marr. 1796. Barbara Westfall was a sister to John H. Westfall who marr. Elizabeth Allman, a sister to George. George Allman (1800-1877) second marr. March 27, 1855, UMR 1853-2-64, to Mildred C. Brown, b. 1818 in Orange County, Virginia, d. January 31, 1903, UDR-85 yrs. old, bur. on family farm with her husband. No children by this second marriage.

Lewis County Deed Book, G-878, July 21, 1840, John Haye (deceased) and wife Mary sell 448 acres bounded by John Bozarth and John B. Armstead's line and the ridge between Bell's Run and head of Hickory Cabin Run to George Allman for $896.00. Why was this deed delivered to Peter Cutright? Peter was the father of Barbara Cutright, the second wife of Abraham Allman, a brother of George. Abraham and Barbara were not married until 1851.

Progeny of George (1800) and Barbara Westfall ---

Mary Elizabeth b. 1833, d. 1850, bur. on Fink's Run farm with parents per grave stone.

Progeny of George (1800) and Barbara Westfall ---

George William b. 1838, d. 1924, on Saul's Run, bur. at Lorentz Methodist Cemetery, marr. April 8, 1869 by Reverend Joseph Flint, UMR 1853-24-24, to Columbia Laverne Marion Fury, b. 1853, d. 1925, bur. with her husband, she a d/o Harrison H. Fury (1823) and Mary Jane Brown. The children of George William (1838) and Columbia Fury are ---Mary Elizabeth (1876-1965) m. 1893, UMR 3-295, to Washington Summers (1857-1946), bur. Lorentz Cemetery / Lucy Lee (1886-1973) m. 1917, UMR 12-330, to John Ostrowske (1882-1950), bur. Lorentz Cemetery / Mildred Lenora (1881-1980) UDR 56, 99 yrs. old, bur. Lorentz Cemetery, single / Burton Ray (1892-1981) UDR 5-6, bur. Lorentz Cemetery, single, Pvt. U.S. Army, WWI /Henry Clay 1894-1979), bur. Lorentz Cemetery, m. 1920 to Mary Elizabeth Parker (1903-1984) John Beauregard (1896-1972), bur. Lorentz Cemetery, marr. 1924 to Oleta Dean (1905-1973) / Fredric(k) Arthur (1878-1960), bur. Heavner Cemetery, m. 1910 to Bertha Rohrbough, no children / Charles Emerson (1871-1910), bur. Lorentz Cemetery, marr. 1899, UMR 5-400, to Mary C. West / Edgar A. or Edward Austin (1873-1946), LDR 6-3, bur. Lorentz Cemetery, marr. 1898 to Grace McWhorter (1881-1976), LMR 8-388 / Earle Cleveland (1883-1924), LDR 4-2, bur. Lorentz Cemetery, marr. 1910 to Mattie Jane Shoulders, LMR 12-413 / Herbert Hamilton (1889-1961), UBR 1-190 and LDR 8-9, marr. 1911 to Rosa E. Shoulders, (1892-1982), both bur. Lorentz Cemetery, no children.--- Private G. W. Allman, Upshur County 133rd. Militia, W. Va. State Troops, in Capt. Nimrod Mundy's Company "D", also with 1st Lt. Wm. M. Clark, J. M. Allman, Nathan Allman, William Allman and J. W. Lorentz. I also have a commission certificate for George Allman, 2nd Lt. in L. W. Ward's Company of 192nd. Regiment, July 6, 1863 (This is possibly the above George William).

Progeny of George (1800) and Barbara Westfall ---

Jacob Marion b. July 31, 1843, d. January 2, 1923, UDR 3-84, bur. Lorentz Cemetery, marr. July 30, 1884, UMR 1-26, to Eva Casto b. September 26, 1864, d. August 24, 1945, UDR 4-4, bur. Lorentz Cemetery, she a d/o Paris Casto and Martha R. Hays. Paris Casto b. 1835, marr. 1860, was a shoemaker, farmer and was a captain in the Civil War. The children of Jacob Marion and Eva Casto are --Edward Kane (1889-1977) UBR 1-190 and UDR 5-5, bur. Lorentz Cemetery, marr. Eva Fitzgerald / George Karl (1885-d. maybe prior to father's obit. in 1923) marr. 1913, HMR 23-399, to Nellie Clayton Pletcher (1888-1954) / Ada or Addie V. (1897-1987), bur. Lorentz Cemetery, marr. to J. O. Marks.

An item of interest - In 1989 Clyde Ballard Grose who lives on Bridge Run, near Lorentz, Upshur County told me this story about Jacob "Jake" Marion Allman. Jake lived on the original farm left to his father George (1800) Allman by George's father William (1). This was 100 acres of the original 200 acre land patent of 1783. Jake always wore decrepit clothes and his appearance was much like a tramp. His barn was across the wide bottom in front of the house and one day when he was returning to the house after tending the cattle, he encountered a true tramp or beggar standing in the road. Since it was obvious that Jake was going on up the bank to the large white house - the tramp remarked, "No use going up there, the old bitch won't give you anything to eat." He, of course, was referring to Jake's wife, Eva Casto Allman.

The grandchildren and great-grandchildren of George and Barbara Allman constitute the majority of the Allman families in the Upshur County communities.

ISAAC ALLMAN, s/o William (1) Allman, was b. ca. 1802 per Lewis Census 1820, d. unknown, marr. January 20, 1820, LMB by Reverend John Mitchell, John Malcom, bondsman. Isaac may have resided in Marion County, Ohio per Census 1830. He marr. Dorothy Malcom, b. ca 180?, a d/o Alexander Malcom. No further information has been found on the family. John L. Allman, Clio, Michigan, in his 1939 era "Allman Geneology" lists an Isaac Allman (1780-) living in Pennsylvania who married in 1808(10) to Dorothy Malcom (1790-) Strange two husbands and wives of the same name.

ABRAHAM ALLMAN, aka. ABRAM, s/o William (1) Allman, was born March 31, 1805, d. April 25, 1885, IJDR 1853-53-12, bur. on family farm on Fink's Run with his father and brother George. Abraham received 100 acres of the original homestead by will from his father. He kept this from 1828 until 1847 at which time he sold to Jacob Lorentz and bought 107 acres of virgin forest at the head of Bridge Run also from Jacob Lorentz. My grandfather, Isaac Marion, told of spending his early years helping to clear this land.

Abraham's first marriage was to Winifred Crites, b. 1807(5), d. 1846(9) on Bridge Run. She is bur. with her husband on the Fink's Run farm. Winifred was a d/o Michael Crites and Catherine Hyer. The Crites and Hyers settled in Upshur County prior to 1800 per Upshur History, page 420. Abraham and Winifred marr. May 27, 1827, LMB by Reverend James Shurtliff. Their children are --Nathan b. December 14, 1829 / Aurilla b. October 25, 1830 / George b. 1831 Barbara b. 1833 / Michael b. 1834 / Catherine b. 1838 / William b. April 3, 1838 / Mary Elizabeth b. 1840 / Valentine b. May 1843(5) Abraham b. 1846(8).

Progeny of Abraham and Winifred are ---

Nathan b. December 14, 1829, d. October 11, 1918, UDR 3-21, bur.

Lorentz Cemetery, marr. February 11, 1850, LMR 3-25, to Elizabeth Bligh (Bleigh), b. March 25, 1830, d. January 1, 1928, UDR 3-135, bur. Lorentz Cemetery, she a d/o James Bligh, b. 1800 in Rockingham Co., Virginia and Mary Burkholder. Nathan and Elizabeth's children are ---

Alexander Simpson (1851-1930) marr. 1881 to Nancy A. Abbott / George C. (1853-) a doctor of medicine in Hoquiam, Washington State / Lurana (1855-1930) marr. 1895 to Mallory T. Clark / Jacob Marion (1857-1862), UDR 1853-15-1 / William Jefferson (1859-1940) marr. 1890 to (1) Rachel Lavernia Rinehart and marr. 1904 to (2) Roberta M. Grose / Thomas M. (1862-), marr. 1896 to Evva E. Rinehart, they lived and died in the lumber business in Hoquiam, Washington / Nathan L. b. April 17, 1865, UBR 1-48, and Nathan E. b. October 1, 1866, UBR 1-48, both s/o Nathan and Eliz.; no further records have been found / Martha E. (1866-1949) marr. 1885 to Charles M. Betts John M. b. 1868, UBR 1-60 operated 2 boats on Hoquiam River, Washington State Harrison Theodore (1871-1958) marr. 1895 to Cora Virginia Rinehart / Albert William per UBR 1-106 December 25, 1875 or Alfred Wesley on 1944 gravestone, marr. 1904, UMR 7-238, to Connie G. Berry / source unknown for Lee Allman, timber worker, killed in woods at Hoquiam, Washington. He had 2 daughters.

Nathan Allman and Elizabeth Bligh children --

Alexander Simpson b. July 25, 1851, d. March 19, 1930, UDR 4-1, bur. Lorentz Cemetery, marr. September 22, 1881, UMR 1853-47-63, to Nancy A. Abbott b. April 8, 1854, UBR 1-05, d. March 12, 1936, UDR 4-2, bur. Lorentz Cemetery, a d/o Biven Abbott and Martha Steward. Their children are -- Alpha (female) (1884-1942) LDR 6-1, single, bur. Lorentz Cemetery / Mason (male) (1882-1955) UBR 1-148 and UDR 4-6, single, bur. Lorentz Cemetery.

Nathan Allman and Elizabeth Bligh children --

William Jefferson b. December 16, 1859, UBR 1-26, d. June 24, 1940, UDR 4-3, bur. Lorentz Cemetery, marr. July 5, 1890, UMR 2-336, to (1) Rachel Lavernia Rinehart, b. October 27, 1863, d. November 9, 1902, UDR 1862 Incomplete, bur. Lorentz Cemetery, a d/o Isaac C. Rinehart and Amanda Hartley, no children to this marriage.

William Jefferson second marr. was October 16, 1904, UMR 7-343, to (2) Roberta May Grose, b. April 7, 1881, d. May 31, 1962 in Huntington, W. Va., bur. Lorentz Cemetery, a d/o George Washington Grose and Phoebe Allman. Their children are: Isaac Denver (1905-1973), marr. 1925 to

(1)Mary Bowen and marr. 1963 to (2)Tina Hamilton / Thelma Alpha (1911-) marr. 1935 to (1) Adrian B. May (1902-1941) and marr. 1948 to (2)John J. West / Phoebe Elizabeth (1918-) marr. 1940 to (1)Paul Parsons and marr. (2) to Ralph J. McConnell.

Nathan Allman and Elizabeth Bligh children --

Harrison Theodore b. January 3, 1871, UBR 1-78, d. February 25, 1958, UDR 5-1, bur. Lorentz Cemetery, mair. April 25, 1895, UMR 4-197, to Cora Virginia Rinehart b. April 5, 1872, d. February 11, 1957, UDR 5-1, bur. Lorentz Cemetery, a d/o Isaac C. Rinehart and Amanda Hartley. Their children are--

Mabel Gertrude (1902-1976) marr. 1922 to (1) Roy W. Linger and marr. (2) a Mayo Elva Vetra (1895-1980) marr. 1916 to G. A. Berry (1890-1957) / Grace V. (1897) marr. 1917 to Cletus R. Kidd / Jessie (1898-) marr. to Frank Reger.

Isaac C. Rinehart and Amanda Hartley had three daughters who married Allmans: Rachel L. marr. William Jefferson Allman / Evva E. marr. Thomas M. Allman / Cora Virginia marr. Harrison Theodore Allman.

Nathan Allman and Elizabeth Bligh children --

Lurana Allman (4 spellings have been found) b. August 1, 1855, UBR 1-11, d. 1930 per grave stone, bur. Lorentz Cemetery, marr. May 29, 1875, UMR 1853-34-33, to Mallory T. Clark b. March 27, 1854, UBR 1-05, d. 1936 per gravestone, bur. Lorentz Cemetery, a s/o Jacob Clark (1812) and Susanna M. Crites (1822). The Clark children are-- John Mifflin (1887- 1891) / Viola (1888-1888) UBR 1-176 / Lura or Laura (1876-) / Isa or Iza (1878-1966) marr. Kent Lorentz (1874-1948) / Roy McCtellen (1879 or February 12, 1880) per UBR 1-137 / Jacob W. (1882-) / C. E. b. August 14, 1884 per UBR 1-162.

Nathan Allman and Elizabeth Bligh children --

Alfred Wesley b. December 25, 1875, UBR 1-106, d. January 12, 1944, UDR 4-4, bur. Lorentz Cemetery, marr. February 24, 1904, UMR 7-238, to Connie Golden Berry b. March 3, 1881, d. November 11, 1943, UDR 4-4, bur. Lorentz Cemetery, a d/o Andrew Jackson Berry (1858-1934) and Arminta T. Dormer (1856-1930). Alfred Wesley lived in Akron, Ohio and had three sons - the first is unnamed in UBR 1905-214 on July 28, 1905.

Andrew Jackson Berry had a son Gillette Andrew (1890-1957) who marr. Elva Vetra Allman, a d/o Harrison T. Allman.

Progeny of Abraham and Winifred are ---

Aurilla (4 spellings have been found) b. October 25, 1829, d. unknown, bur. unknown, marr. January 5, 1850, LMB 3-25, to James W. Kelley b. 1831 a s/o possibly William W. Kelley and Sarah. Aurilla's brother Michael marr. Mascena Kelly, a d/o William W. and Sarah Kelley. Upshur History 1907, page 489 says James W. Kelley was a red-haired Irishman in the Union Army. The Kelley children are -- Charles Clinton (1851) / Sarah Jane (1853) / Rose Anna (1856) marr. a Davis / Abram C. (1861) marr. Rosa Lee Tenney / Janice Virginia (1859) marr. Abe Black / Elizabeth A. (1860) marr. William Coon; Elizabeth may be a d/o Sarah thus a sister to James W. / Ellen (after 1860 Lewis Census) marr. Gilbert Coon, a brother to William Coon / No Name (1866),UBR 1-52 / Maria E. (1869),UBR 1-64. James W. Kelley not listed in any local census after 1860.

Progeny of Abraham and Winifred are ---

George b. 1831, d. prior to a Quit Claim Deed of 1883, marr. March 10, 1853 per Vinton County, Ohio H.R.-1-36, (Jacob Allman gave consent) to Eleanor or maybe Permelia.

I have the commission certificate as follows --

THE COMMONWEALTH OF VIRGINIA
To GEORGE ALLMAN greeting:

Know You, that from the special trust and confidence reposed in your fidelity, courage, activity and good conduct, our Governor, in pursuance of the authority vested in him for that purpose by the Constitution and Laws of the Commonwealth, doth commission you the said GEORGE ALLMAN as FIRST LIEUTENANT in the Hundred & thirty third Regiment of INFANTRY OF THE LINE, in the 20th. Brigade and 3rd. Division of the VIRGINIA MILITIA, to rank as such from the 5th. day of July,1849. In testimony whereof, these our Letters are sealed with the Lesser Seal of the Commonwealth, and made patent. Witness, John B. Floyd, our Governor, at Richmond, this 13th. day of July, 1849. signed- John B. Floyd.

I have been unable to determine if this commission was to GEORGE ALLMAN, b. 1801, s/o William (1) Allman and Elizabeth Martin or

George Allman, b. 1831, s/o Abraham (1805) Allman and (1) Winifred Crites.

The children of George (1831) Allman are --

John (ca. 1850) marr. Louisa E. Caldwell / Amanda / Catherine marr. a McCarty / Manerva marr. a Kelley / Mary Jane marr. a Douglas / Margaret marr. a Gates Martha / Nancy Ann / William.

Progeny of Abraham and Winifred are ---

Michael b. 1834(2), d. ca. 1857, marr. December 10, 1853, Taylor H.R.-pg. 9 H.C.P.D. record to Mascena or Marcenia Kelley, b. 1834, a d/o William W. or S. Kelley and Sarah. The only child of Michael is Sarah E. Allman b. October 7, 1854, UBR 1-5, who marr. January 15, 1873, UMR 30-5, to A. W. C. Lemmons (1829-1907), for his second wife. A.W.C. Lemmons' first wife was Margaret E., with children Minor b. 1848 / Elsey A. b. 1851 / Warwick b. 1853. Harrison County marr. record 5-11 says M. (Mascena) Allman (widow) marr. J. J. Hooper, age 19 yrs. on July 11, 1858. J. J. Hooper (ca. 1839) a s/o H. R. Hooper.

Progeny of Abraham and Winifred are ---

William Franklin b. April 3, 1838 stone, d. March 13, 1911, stone, bur. Waterloo Cemetery near French Creek, Upshur Co., marr. September 22, 1856, LMR 5-7 and 496, to (1) Joan Rogers b. 1838(6) in Paquire County, Virginia, d. prior to 1871, bur. unknown, a d/o William Rogers b. 1780 and Mary A. b. 1788. Their children are -- Josephus (1857-prior to Upshur Census 1880) / Mary Alice (1859-prior to father's will 8/13/1910) marr. October 27, 1887, UMR 2-66, to Andrew Howes / William Alexander (1861), UBR 1-36 / Martha Elizabeth (1862-) marr. July 25, 1879, UMR 1853-42-33, to John D. Crites, b. 1856, a s/o Abram Crites and Wealthy Pringle / John C. (1865-1924), UDR 3-93, marr. January 1, 1907, UMR 8-303, to Libbie Neely (1876-1939), a d/o Joseph Allen Neely / Andrew Jackson (1868-1939) UBR 1-60, marr. November 21, 1899, LMR 9-116 to Edith M. Miller (1872-1966) a d/o James W. Miller.

William Franklin's second marriage was April 13, 1871, LMR 5-52, to (2) Armissa (Massa) Dixon b. May 10, 1836 in Marion County, d. September 10, 1877, UDR 1853-39-2, bur. Waterloo Cemetery, a d/o Asa P. Dixon and Mary. The children of this second marriage are - Verlonia May (1872),UBR 1-82-no death date on stone in Waterloo Cemetery, marr. 1908 to A. M. Hartman, UHR 9-180 / Cora M. (1874marr. 1898,

UNR 5-223, to Enoch E. Martin (1872-1904); Upshur Census 1880 lists Cora Alman (adopted) b. 1874 as a child of John Killingsworth b. 1818 with wife Jane b. 1816 and with four of their own children. This Cora could be the true d/o William (1838) Allman and his second wife Armissa Dixon. Armissa died from childbirth September 10, 1877 along with her child Bessie J. (September 1, 1877September 28, 1877). Possibly Cora was adopted by the Killingsworths after Armissa died. / Bessie (1877-1877) UBR 1-119 and UDR 39-3, stone in Waterloo Cemetery.

William Franklin's third marriage was February 16, 1879, UMR 1853-52-5, to Mary Jane Bean (widow) b. May 10, 1844 in Mineral County, d. February 13, 1901, bur. Indian Camp Cemetery, a d/o Henry I. Bean (1814-1882) and Julia A. Bosley b. 1813. The children of this third marriage are -- Bessie Jane (1879-no death date on stone in Waterloo Cemetery) marr. 1905, UMR 8-53, to Teter Neely (1850-1936) / Gaver Hamilton (1882-1961) UBR 1-148, bur. Orlando Cemetery, marr. Artie Mishie Mills (1883-1970) bur. Orlando Cemetery. The Upshur Census of 1880 lists in household of William Allman and Mary J. (Bean) the children Arminda Bean b. 1866 and Andrew Bean b. 1868. I do not know why these children carry the maiden name of their mother, Mary Jane, nor do I know the name of their father. Mary Jane's father Henry I. Bean was a millwright and miller from Hampshire County who came to Upshur County in 1852, built his mill at Bean's Mill, Upshur County (Upshur History, pg. 191,2).

The descendants of William Franklin and his three marriages produced a sizable group of families, some with multiple marriages, which has been difficult in documenting.

Progeny of Abraham and Winifred are ---

Sarah Catherine b. 1838(6), d. July 30, 1927, UDR 3-132, bur. Mt. Union Cemetery on Sand Run, Upshur County, marr. 1856, UMR 1851-1860, to E. Howard Rowan (Roan) b. 1834, d. February 12, 1905, UDR 1A-104. The Rowan children are --- Mary Elizabeth b. 1863, UBR 1-46 / Abram b. 1857, UBR 1-18 / Joseph b. 1871, UBR 1-76 / Granville b. 1877, UBR 1-118 / George W. b. 1880, UBR 1-135 / James b. 1868 / Robert T. b. 1866 / Sarah J. b. 1869 / John b. 1874 / Nancy V. b. 1869, d. August 15, 1876, UDR 1-37. This Rowan family needs further research.

Progeny of Abraham and Winifred are ---

Mary Elizabeth b. March 9, 1837, d. unknown, bur. unknown, marr. July 18, 1850, LMR 3-25, to (1) Robert Stewart (this has not been proven to be the above Elizabeth); marr. November 22, 1857, UMR 1853-5-48, to (2) John S. Tenney, b. ca. 1837, a Civil War soldier 1861-65, a s/o Peter Tinney and Lavina (Lebany). The Tenney children are -- Anna D. b. November 10, 1860, UBR 1-35, d. unknown, marr. to Jonathan Milroy Tenney, (1863-), UBR 1-46, a s/o Jonathan Tenney and Ann Cutright / George W. b. October 8, 1858, UBR 1-23 / Thomas G. b. June 4, 1875, UBR 1-109 / Homer b. September 2, 1884, UBR 1-159 / Rebecca b. December 17, 1881, UBR 1-142 / Frederick b. February 22, 1886, UBR 1-181. The UMR 1853-5-48 is clear and complete showing John S. Tinney w/parents listed and Elizabeth Allman w/parents listed. An original marriage list in Lewis County files submitted by Reverend J. L. Simpson shows these marriages - James W. Kelly and Arrilius Allman, January 5, 1850 / Nathan Allman and Elizabeth Bleigh, February 11, 1850 / Robert Stewart and Elizabeth Allman, July 18, 1850.

Progeny of Abraham and Winifred are ---

Abraham (Abram) Junior b. 1846(8), d. January 4, 1879, UDR 1853-42-1 (record information by father Abram), bur. unknown, marr. ca. 1868 to Lucinda Grose b. ca. 1850, d. ca. 1880. Only records found are Lewis Census 1850, Upshur Census 1860 and Lucinda Allman is listed as 30 yr. old widow in Upshur Census 1880. Their children are -- George Washington b. November 5, 1868, UBR 1-60, d. March 31, 1948, LDR 6-2, bur. Glady Fork (Reeder Cemetery), Lewis County, marr. April 14, 1892, LMR 7-24, to Louvernia C. Sims (1874-1955) a d/o William Sims and Joanna Samantha Curtis. / No name, stillborn, (1871-1871) UBR 1853-1-78 / Leonard L. b. June 28, 1872, UBR 1-85 / Abram C. b. January 28, 1875, UBR 1-106, d. March 31, 1875, UDR 1853-36-2 (info by Barbara Cutright Allman, grandmother).

ABRAHAM ALLMAN, aka ABRAM, s/o William (1) Allman, (1805-1885). His second marriage was February 23, 1851, LMR 3-38, to (2) Barbara Cutright b. October 10, 1817, d. December 3, 1906, bur. Lorentz Cemetery, she a d/o Peter Cutright and Mary Helmick (maybe Nancy Westfall).

Harrison Marriages by Earle H. Morris lists Peter Cutright marr. Nancy Westfall (d/o Cornelius Westfall) on December 11, 1816 by Reverend John Mitchell. This marriage was 10 months prior to the birth of Barbara Cutright above and she named a son Cornelius.

Further notes of interest - Upshur History, pg. 598 says Samuel

Westfall b. 1832 was a s/o John H. Westfall and Elizabeth Allman and a grandson of Cornelius Westfall. - Lewis County Census 1840 lists Peter Cutright with 12 people, possibly this is the father of Barbara. - Harrison County Marriage Records show John Cutright married Christina Wetherholt in 1817.

Abraham Allman's will left his farm at the head of Bridge Run to his daughter Phoebe Allman Grose and his son Isaac Marion Allman provided they care for their mother Barbara until her death. I have the Quit Claim Deeds from several of their half-brothers and sisters relinquishing any claim to said property.

The children of Abraham Allman and Barbara Cutright are --- Nancy Jane (18511936) marr. John Grose / Phoebe (1853-1928) marr. George Grose / Peter (1855-1865) / Isaac Marion (1858-1939) marr. Emma Jane Lawman / Cornelius J. D. (18611890).

Progeny of Abraham and Barbara are ---

Nancy Jane b. 1851, d. 1936 at Sago, Upshur County, bur. Sago Cemetery, marr. December 17, 1876, UMR 1853-37, to John Andrew Grose, b. 1828, d. 1911 at Sago, a s/o Samuel Grose and Polly (Mary) Hoover. The Grose children are -- Edward Rutherford (1878-1964) marr. Lulu Floyd / Silvester Carson (1879-1960) marr. Mell Fowler / Arthur Garfield (1881-1977) marr. 1957 to Almira Ours / Willie Wilbur (1884-) marr. 1916 to Iva Ours / Annie Maude (1891-) marr. Charlie Cutright.

Progeny of Abraham and Barbara are ---

Phoebe b. 1853, d. 1928 at Bridge Run, bur. Lorentz Methodist Cemetery, marr. July 4, 1880 to George Washington Grose, b. February 14, 1857, d. January 6, 1941 at Bridge Run, bur. Lorentz Cemetery, a s/o Samuel Grose and Polly (Mary) Hoover. The Grose children are -- Roberta Mary (Bird) (1881-1962) marr. William Jefferson Allman / Charles Columbus (1883-1962), marr. Alice Vertenice Allman.

Progeny of Abraham and Barbara are ---

Peter b. December 25, 1855, UBR 1-11, d. September 1865, UDR M&D 20-1, bur. probably on original family farm on Fink's Run.

Progeny of Abraham and Barbara are ---

Cornelius J. D. b. May 22, 1861, UBR 1-36, d. July 27, 1890, LDR 2-62, bur. at Weston State Hospital Cemetery. Per his birth record he died at 29 yrs. of age but on his death record he is 35 yrs. old per T. M. Hood, physician. The death record says "M" for married, but no marriage record has been found. The cause of death was "Insanity from abscess on brain from Typhoid Fever."

Progeny of Abraham and Barbara are ---

Isaac Marion b. September 28, 1858, UBR 1-22, d. July 24, 1939, HDR 12-7A, bur. Sunset Memorial Cemetery, Clarksburg, marr. December 27, 1894, UMR 4-153, to Emma Jane Lawman, b. August 12, 1869 on Rover's Run, a tributary of Hacker's Creek in Upshur County, d. January 1, 1939, HDR 12-7A, bur. Sunset Cemetery. She was a d/o William Henry Lawman and Olive Malissa Curtis. William Henry was a s/o Barnard Lawman and Pemelia Campbell; Olive Malissa was a d/o Henry L. Curtis and Catherine Perry. The children of Isaac Marion are ---

Virgil Henry, b. August 18, 1895, UBR 1A-109, d. June 29, 1976 in Bradenton, Florida, bur. in Manasota Memorial Park, marr. September 5, 1914, UMR 11-246, to Ethel Addie Tenney, b. February 19, 1896, UBR 1A-117, d. March 24, 1960 at Otterbein Home, Lebanon, Ohio, bur. St. Mary's, Ohio. Ethel was a d/o Rufus Tenney, a s/o Peter Tenney. The children of Virgil Henry are -- Ketha Emma (1916-1988) marr. 1936 to John Raymond Keller / Virgilene Hattie (1920-1991) marr. 1941 to Clayton D. Bucher / Maxine Genevieve (1923-) single / Nadine Anna (1927-) marr. 1947 to Mahlon Wenger / Glendalene May (1915-1915) / Norma Bell (1929-1929). Virgil Henry was a minister in the United Brethren Church. He preached in West Virginia but moved to Ohio about 1923 and served various churches; then became the Conference Superintendent of Sandusky Conference for over 25 years. He retired to Florida and marr. January 1, 1961 to (2) Elnora Wells, the widow of a minister. All of Virgil's children grew up and lived in Ohio.

Roscoe C., b. October 25, 1896, UBR IA-126, d. APril 10, 1971, HDR 71-146, bur. Sunset Memorial Cemetery, marr. December 25, 1919, HMR 32-33, to Catherine Ruth Waters, b. January 20, 1895, HBR 6-24, d. August 3, 1982 in Frederick, Md., bur. Sunset Memorial Cemetery, she a d/o Ulysses Elsworth Waters and Lyda Jane Jenkins. The children of Roscoe are Martha Jane (1924-) marr. 1950 to Lacy Andrew Mann / Anna Lea (1927-) marr. 1947 to (1) Galvin Larry Bucklew, Jr. and marr. 1950 to (2) Arthur Weihrer, Jr.

Orval Lee, b. April 23, 1900, UBR 1900-165, d. October 13, 1966, HDR

24-7B, bur. Sunset Memorial Cemetery, marr. March 23, 1922, HMR 35-221, to Freda Mae Day, b. January 23, 1901, HBR N2 delayed, d. April 9, 1982, HDR 82-145, bur. Sunset Memorial Cemetery. Freda was the only d/o Festus Ithameur Day (1873-1941), a s/o John Wesley Day and Elvina Hinkle, and Amanda Belle Fultz (1876-1949), a d/o William Scott Fultz and Elizabeth McGlothan. The children of Orval Lee are -- Mary Kathleen (1923-) marr. 1943 to Carl Edwin Hornor / Edward Lee b. 1924 marr. 1951 to Jeanne Marie Sayler / Betty Jean (1926-) marr. 1946 to Thomas Fred Flint / James Robert (1930-) marr. 1949 to Sue Ann Coffman / David Dav (1934-) marr. 1956 to Wilma Jo Costlow.

Mary Kathleen Hornor has 6 children -- Edward Greig, Charles Allman, John Randolph, Mark Richard, Stephen David, Kathleen.

Edward Lee has no children.

Betty Jean Flint has 3 children -- Deborah Jean, Thomas Patrick, Tamarah Lynn.

James Robert has 3 children -- Glenna Sue, Paula Deanne, Katrina Kay

David Day has 3 children -- Nancy Ann, Diane Kay, Pamela Sue.

Isaac Marion and Emma Jane Allman lived on the farm at the head of Bridge Run which he inherited from his father, Abraham, until 1924 when their sons, Roscoe and Orval, got a five-acre farm on Davisson Run near Clarksburg with a comfortable home and modern facilities. They were able to be independent but near their family - so spent the remainder of their lives enhancing the childhood of their grandchildren. Their sons, Roscoe and Orval, came to Clarksburg in 1917 and spent the next 50 years as partners in the grocery business, operating Allman Brothers Grocery and five A. & L. Stores. These brothers did everything in partnership always with a most congenial relationship. In their last several years each acquired productive farms and enjoyed their lifelong dream of raising purebred polled hereford cattle. We children were fortunate to have experienced the wholesome examples shown us by our parents and grandparents. One of the few stories I remember was my grandfather, Isaac, telling that when he was a child they got whooping cough. His father, Abraham, rode many miles to find a Grey mare with foal so he could get her milk to treat the illness.

ELIZABETH ALLMAN, a d/o William (1), was b. 1809, d. October 15, 1850, bur. unknown, marr. October 4, 1825, Lewis County Marriage

Bond, to John H. or W. Westfall, b. 1806 in Harrison Co., d. May 1, 1870, UDR, bur. unknown, he a s/o Cornelius Westfall (1768) and Elizabeth Helmick, who marr. January 13, 1796 in Randolph Co. The Westfall children are --- Mary b. 1828 / Barbara b. November 22, 1829 / Samuel b. February 18, 1832 / Lorenzo Dow b. April 6, 1834 / George W. b. May 23, 1836 / Ruhama b. August 2, 1837 / Peter b. December 6, 1840 Harrison b. 1842 / Albert S. or L. b. April 16, 1844(6) / Virginia b. 1849.

After Elizabeth died, John H. Westfall marr. April 19, 1851 (2) Lydia Smith, b. 1820, (widow of Solomon Smith) and they had a son Nathaniel b. 1852, d. 1915, bur. Harrison Grove Cemetery, Lewis County.

NICHOLAS ALLMAN, s/o William (1) was b. ca. 1810, d. unknown, bur. unknown, marr. May 24, 1825, LMR 1-35 by Reverend Jacob Cogar to Margaret (Peggy) Clark Roan, b. ca 1800(10), d. unknown. Peggy was a d/o William Clark and Barbara Helmick. Her first husband was Thomas C. H. Roan (Rowan), marr. April 12, 1819, LMR (William Clark was bondsman). Cris Wagoner of Katy, Texas has found the Ohio Census of 1840, Vol. 3 listing Nicholas Allman #108 with males - I under 5 yr., 2-10/15 yr., 1-15/20 yr., 1-20/30 yr., 1-30/40 yr., and females- 1 under 5 yr., 1-5/10 yr., 1-10/15 yr., 1-20/30 yr. This means Nicholas (b. 1810) with 1 son b. 1820 and 1 daughter b. 1820. This does not agree with Nicholas' age so Peggy Clark Roan had to have 2 or more children by her first marr. to T. C. H. Roan making her birth ca. 1800. The Lewis County Marriage Bond shows William Allman gave consent for his son Nicholas to marry Peggy Roan, the widow of T.C.H. Roan. Nicholas would have been about 15 years old at his marriage. No further information on this family has been found.

How interesting it would be if our ancestors had put in writing their experiences in the trying times from 1775 to this century. Since they were mostly of German heritage, probably few could write or even speak English. William Allman, our ancestor, must have been a remarkable man to have come across the Alleghany Mountains, established a homestead in the wilderness at Buckhannon Fort and acquired enough property to provide for his seven sons and four daughters. What a different life they had compared to what we enjoy today.

Samuel Oliver
(1752-1819)

Ref. Vital Records of Kent & Sussex Co. 1686 - 1800 by F. Edward Wright (pg. 25-30

Milford-Sussex Co. Delaware.

On 25 Nov. 1769-Duck Creek Monthly Meeting.

"Levi Reuben & Reuben Oliver, requested for themselves, wives & children to come under the care and notice of Friends"

Both families of Levi & Jane, and Reuben & Elizabeth are in the records of Duck Creek (one hundred) monthly meetings.

Levi Oliver, will probated 20 Nov. 1797, Ceder Creek (hundred) Milford, Sussex Co. Delaware, wife Jane (Jenny) Oliver, ch.: Benjamin Oliver, b. 16 Sept. 1762, Mary Oliver b. 10 Jan. 1766, m Nathaniel Bowman, Anna Oliver b. 13 Apr. 1768, m. Parker Morgan, Rachel Oliver, b. 6 May 1770, Aaron Oliver, b. 27 Feb. 1772, m. Abegail Oliver, Joseph Oliver, b. 6 June 1774, Jane Oliver, b. 18 Aug. 1776, m. Elijah Reed, Levi Oliver, b. 8 Sept. 1778, Reuben Oliver,b. 22 Feb. 1781.

On pg. 31 "Murtherkill (Murderkill hundred) preparative (sic) M.g.t. - brought a complaint agns't Samuel Oliver for bearing arms in Millatary service and Inlisting himself as a soldier in one of their companies."

Thus Samuel Oliver, s/o Reuben & Elizabeth Oliver, breaks from the Friends (Quaker Church) in Milford, Sussex Co. De.

Samuel Oliver Sr.

Samuel Oliver, (15 Sept. 1757-3 June 1819) Pvt. Deleware m. Lydia. (D.A.R. record Vol. 1 pg. 503).

The D.A.R. record, Private Delaware lead to a search in Delaware, Sussex Co. Delaware became the first state in the Union, ratified the Constitution of the United States, 7 Dec. 1787.

One record has Samuel Oliver, b. 15 Sept. 1757 New Rochelle, N. Y. (could have been before Delaware became a state in 1787).)

We Find Reuben Oliver & Elizabeth, his wife, in Delaware records.

Samuel Oliver b. 3 June 1757, Sussex Co. Delaware

(Rev. War-Pension (W) Va.-Will Ohio)

Gallaudett Oliver, b. 5 Oct. 1759 Sussex Co. De. (1810-census of Va. Gulidath Oliver, Harrison Co. Va.)

Elesha Oliver, b. 13 Sept. 1762 Sussex Co. De.,

Mary Oliver, b. 2 Mar. 1765 Sussex Co. De.,

Deborah Oliver, b. 15 Nov. 1767 Sussex Co. De.,

Thomas Oliver b. 23 May 1770, Sussex Co. De.

Monongalia Co., (created 1776, from Dist of West Augusta) Harrison Co. -c- 1784, from Monongalia Co.

Lewis Co. -c- 1816 from Harrison Co.,

Upshur Co. -c- 1851 from Lewis, Co.

The history of Upshur Co. (W) Va. by Cutright gives these little bits of news about Samuel Oliver.

(pg. 186) Samuel Oliver, planted his clearing on Cutright's run, on the John Burr, now D.D.T. Farnsworth heir's land. Mr. Oliver had the first negro slave in Buckhannon Valley, in 1771-2.

(District of West Augusta pg. 355) Samuel Oliver made wool hats for people after he came here from New England.

(pg. 251) First settlers were Samuel , John & William Pringle, John Cutright & Samuel Oliver.

(pg. 329) (Sept. 1818, for the sum of $700.00, Samuel Oliver & Lydia, his wife, granted by deed to Abraham Carper, 135 acres of land on Cutrights run, bounded by lands of William Clark, Gillaudott Oliver & Abraham Cutright.

On the same date, Gillaudott Oliver & Mary his wife, conveyed to Abraham Carper 67 acres on Lick run. (Could this be a son of Samuel & Lydia Oliver, named after his brother Gallaudett Oliver b. 5 Oct. 1759?)

Randolph Co. Va. m. records:

1803 Gaudaudat Oliver m. Mary Ann Bogart d/o Cornellius Bogard.

West Virginians in the Revolution, complied by Ross B. Johnston.

(pg. 214) Samuel Oliver --Service Virginia-- No-S-38270- Enlisted, Frederica, Delaware, 12 Feb. 1776, and served as a private, six years. Served under Capt. Adams in Continental Regiment commanded by Col. Hazlett & Lord Sterling, and fought at Long Island, White Plains, Trenton & Princeton. Reference is made to the Delaware blues, with which he may have served.

Pension applicated was made in Lewis Co., Va., which was granted in 1819. The widow, Lydia died in 1839, before the pensioner.

William Oliver, an heir, died in 1852.

D.A.R. records show Lydia Oliver d. 18 Aug. 1839 Licking Co., Ohio, (m. in Delaware). Samuel Oliver made his will and it was found in Licking Co. Ohio.

23 Aug. 1819-will of Samuel Oliver proved on oath of Charles Marstella, and Jonathan Daniels, Witnesses; Executor, Lydia Oliver.

(Ref. Vol 1 pg 181-Gateway to the West Coup. by Bowers & Short.

If the above Revolutionary War record is right that Lydia Oliver, d. before Samuel Oliver he would have d. some time after 1839 in Licking Co. Ohio, no probate date was given.

Samuel & Lydia Oliver must have left (Upshur Co.) Lewis Co. (W) Va. after they sold their land in 1818, as the will in Licking Co. Ohio is dated 1819. I do not have a complete list of their children, some records picked up in Harrison Co. (W) Va. (Harrison Co. m. records), pg. 63 Samuel Oliver Jr. m. 17 Apr. 1809, Catherine Allman (d/o William & Elizabreth (Weatherholt) Allman).

pg. 81 John Oliver m. 30 Dec. 1813, Mary Allman (d/o William & Elizabeth(Weatherholt) Allman) by John Mitchell.

pg. 93 William Oliver (s/o Samuel) m. 15 Jan. 1816 Sally d/o Phillip Reger (1766-1846) & maybe Mary Jane Fornash). May have gone to Ohio then settled in Indiana. (see Allman Family)

We know The Olivers went to Ohio about 1819 Samuel and Lydia Oliver Sr. settled in Licking Co., Samuel Jr. & Catharine (Allman) Oliver show up in the 1830 c. of Marion Co. Samuel Jr. must of d. around 1829 as Catharine is shown as head of the household and has six children; 5 sons, 1 under 10 yrs, 2 under 15 yrs, 1 under 20 yrs, and 1 under 30. (I believe this son b. in (Lewis) Harrison Co.) and 1 daughter under 15 yrs. (which would have been Elizabeth Oliver who m. 25 Feb. 1836 Jonathan Boyles Marion Co. Ohio.)

Several of the Allman Families were in Ohio by 1830.

Both Isaac Allman & Nicholas Allman were in Marion Co. Ohio.

In 1860, Vinton Co. Ohio, Venton twp.: Jacob Allman, 68 yrs. Farmer b. Va.; Elizabeth ae. 67 yrs. b. Md.; Nicholas 37 yrs.; Catharine Lyons, 48 yrs; John 21 yrs. Ohio; Barbara Riffle 34 yrs. Va.; and Sarah 33 yrs. Va.

(Catharine Almon m. 13 Apr. 1833 Philip Lyons Athens Co. Ohio).

There are many Allmans in Ohio, and I can not collect the families of Samuel & Catharine (Allman) Oliver.

Jonathan Boyles

From the History of De Kalb Co. Indiana (pg. 515-517)

"**Jonathan Boyles**, one of the first settlers of Concord Township, was born in Knox County, Ohio, Feb 13, 1815, a son of John and Nancy (Merritt) Boyles, the former a native of West Virginia, son of Jonathan Boyles, of English and Irish descent, and the latter a daughter of Moses Merritt, of Irish and Welsh descent. In 1825 his parents moved to Morrow County, Ohio, where he grew to manhood. His father being in feeble health, he was obliged to take charge of the family, and before he was twenty-one years old had cleared and fenced sixty acres of land and built a good house. He was married Feb. 25, 1836, to Elizabeth Oliver, daughter of Samuel and Catherine (Alman) Oliver. In the fall of 1836 his house and all its contents were destroyed by fire. Soon after he left home and came to De Kalb County, Ind. and entered eighty acres of land on section 17 Concord Township, and again began to make a home. He returned to Ohio, and in August, 1837, moved his family to their new home. In company with Henry Brown and family, Isaac Brown and family, his father and mother, grandmother Knight, James Herrod and son James, in all, sixteen in the company, with two wagons, with three horses to each, they were eleven days on the way, camping out nights and cutting their roads through the unbroken forest. On arriving in the vicinity of Brunersburg the company stopped at the cabin of a pioneer to water their teams. There was no door to the cabin, a quilt serving its purpose. His father and James Herrod went to the door and pulling aside the quilt found no one at home, but discovered a quantity of meat hanging from the walls. They concluded it to be venison and thought they could not go on without a supply. Securing what they thought sufficient for their purpose, they deposited money to pay for it on the table. After traveling a few miles they met a man and his wife, who upon inquiry, they learned were the owners of the cabin, who informed them that it was part of an ox that had broken his neck by turning the yoke. Pursuing their journey, they arrived at their destination on Saturday, the first day of September, 1837. Having no house, they stopped at the cabins of David and Michael Knight, who had preceded them with their families. Within one week after they arrived twelve out of the sixteen were down sick from the ague, including the entire family of Mr. Boyles. He had a chill each day for sixty-three days. He had but $10, and sold forty acres of his land, and had built a cabin about twelve feet square. His wife and her small brother sawed timber and split it in shape, laid the floor, chinking and daubing the best they could; they then carried him to it, he being now afflicted with dropsy. Their only window was a log sawed out with sticks crossed in it and greased paper pasted over them. The door was made the same way, with a quilt hung over it. During the winter his wife cleared five acres of ground up to trees of one foot, the tender twigs serving as the only feed by which he wintered two cows and one horse. By the month of April, 1838, their scanty supplies were exhausted, and he, in company with three others, secured a pirogue and started for Fort Wayne down the St. Joe River, without a cent of money, in quest of food for their starving families, leaving them to subsist for four days upon one meal of thickened milk and a few dried pumpkins. They applied to Thomas Swaney for corn, who, upon finding they had no money, refused to supply their wants. They then applied to Col. Spencer, who after inquiring their names, and where they were from, and the amount of their probable wants, directed them to "go down the Maumee River six miles, shell what they wanted, and pay me seventy-five cents a bushel when you can. And if any of your neighbors are in need, they shall not starve while I have anything to supply them with." They lived upon parched corn while away from their families. During his absence on this expedition, the wolves surrounded his house at night, fighting his dog. Mrs. Boyles sallied forth armed with a fire shovel, and with the assistance of the dog drove them away. He has undergone all the hardships and privations of pioneer life, but by presistent effort has accumulated a good property, having a pleasant home where he has now lived forty-eight years. His wife died Feb. 16, 1849. They had a family of seven children, four of whom are living; Nancy C. Boyle, Martha J. Boyle Newton Boyle, and Emma Boyle. The three eldest are deceased, John Boyle and William Boyle (twins) died in infancy, and Artemus Boyle, while a soldier in the war of the Rebellion. June 30, 1850, Mr. Boyles was married to Susan Rummel, and to them have been born three children: Maggie M., Anna Eliza, and Elaora M. Mrs. Boyles died Feb. 10, 1870. In politics Mr. Boyles was formerly a Democrat, but since the war has affiliatd with the Republician party. he has been an active member of the Methodist Episcopal church for nearly half a century, and assisted in the organization of the first Methodist church in the township."

Jonathan Boyle

Gateway to the West, Comp. by Bowers & Short (pg. 697)

Knox County, Ohio - Will abstracts 1808-1828. (Bk. A-1)

Jonathan Boyle of Clinton twp. dated 24 Nov. 1807; recorded, 3 May 1808. Wife Elizabeth Boyle, sons; John Boyle, James Boyle, & Thomas Boyle. Daughters: Christiana Boyle, Hannah Boyle, Sarah Boyle & Mary Boyle, all not of age.

Executors: Mathew Merrit & John Mills.

Signed Jonathan (his -X- mark) Boyle.

Witnesses: Jonathan Hunt, Zeba Leonard & Daniel Dommick.

John Boyle (21 Jan. 1789-11 July 1882 ae. 95 y. 5 m. 20 d.) De Kalb Co. Indiana bur. Coburn Cem. m. Nancy Merritt (28 Aug. 1796, Pa. 13 May 1864 ae. 68 y. 8 m. 15 d.) d/o Moses Merritt (of Welsh & Irish decent) ch.: Jonathan Boyle, Moses Boyle, Rhoda Boyle, John Boyle Jr. & Ephriam Boyle.

1. Moses Boyle b. ca. 1819 Ohio m. Effana b. Ohio, ch.: Nancy, Sarah & John Edward Boyle.

2. Rhoda Boyle b. ca. 1830 Ohio m. 20 Mar. 1851 by J. T. Bliss, De Kalb Co. Ind., Alfred Scott, b. ca. 1822 s/o Henry (1795) & Eliazabeth (1800) Scott.

3. John Boyle Jr. b. ca. 1831 Ohio m. 19 Mar. 1851 by J. T. Bliss De Kalb, Co. Ind. Ellen (Eleanor) Lowhead, b. ca. 1835, Pa. ch.: James Boyle, William Boyle, and Jefferson Boyle.

4. Ephriam J. Boyle b. ca. 1833 Ohio m. 16 Apr. 1856 De Kalb Co. Ind. Mary E. Johnson b. ca. 1835 Ohio, ch.: Sarah L. Boyle, Merranda Boyle, Frank Boyle and Ida Boyle.

5. Jonathan Boyle (12 Feb. 1815 Knox Co., Ohio-11 Oct. 1908, De Kalb Co. Ind. m. (1st) 25 Feb. 1836, Marion Co,. Ohio, Elizabeth Oliver (21 Nov. 1820 Ohio-16 Feb. 1849 De Kalb Co. Ind. (d. 8 Feb. 1850 cemetery records Coburn Cem. by Harter.) d/o Samuel Jr. & Catharine (Allman) Oliver. ch.: Twins John Boyle & William Boyle

(b. 1837-1838), Artenas Boyle, Nancy Catharine, Martha Jane, Newton & Emma Boyle.
- Artenas Boyle, b. 1839 De Kalb Co. Ind. m. 12 Aug. 1858 DeKalb Co. Barbara A. Beaty, b. ca. 1841.
- Nancy Catharine Boyle, b. 1843 DeKalb Co. m. 5 Jan. 1862 DeKalb Co. Owen William Remmell.
- Newton Boyle, b. 1847 DeKalb Co. m. 23 July 1875 De Kalb Co. Arena J. Hay.
- Emma Boyle b. 1849 DeKalb Co. m. 13 Feb. 1868, DeKalb Co. Vencen Bowers.
- Martha Jane Boyles (21 Apr. 1845 Concord twp DeKalb Co. 7 May 1899 Cora, Smith Co. Ks. m. 5 Feb. 1865, Spencerville, DeKalb Co. Ind. Hulbert Jones (7 Apr. 1841 Allen Co. Ohio-26 Oct 1900) Cora, Smith Co.Ks. (See Jones Family)
- Jonathan Boyle (1815-1908) m. (2nd) Susanna Rummell (12 Feb. 1820 10 Feb. 1870) KeKalb Co. Ind. ch.: Amarinza Boyle, Margaret (Maggie) Boyle, m. 5 June 1873 Philitus A. Shurts, Anna Boyle, Elizabeth Boyle, and Elnora Boyle, m. Will B. Lucus.

Nicholas Jones
(1789-1878)

Nicholas Jones (15 Nov. 1789 Pa. 5 Aug. 1878 ae. 88 y. 8 m. 21 d.) DeKalb Co. Ind.

I feel there were several marriages, due to the age of the children. In 1850 the wife was Catharine age 51 y. b. Penn.

ch.: Oliver Jones b. 1818 Pa. (1st) wife Rachael Jones b. 1818 Ohio (2nd) wife Rose Jones, ch.: Nicholas Jones (1837) Limuel Jones (1843) Thomas Jones (1846).

Calvin Jones b. ca 1833, Ohio m. 17 June 1858, DeKalb Co. Martha Hannah (b. 1839) Ohio, ch.: Nancy Jones & Veala R. Jones.

Luther Jones b. 1836 Ohio d. 18 Apr. 1912, DeKalb Co. Ind. m. 23 Apr. 1857, Auburn, DeKalb Co. Polly (Mary) Beanas, b. 1838, Ohio or Pa. 1870 Luther Jones was a shoemaker.

Catherine Jones, b. 1845, Ohio m. 14 Dec. 1862, DeKalb Co., William Stofer.

Hulbert Jones (7 Apr. 1841, Spencerville, Ohio. 26 Oct. 1900) Smith Co. Ks. m. 5 Feb. 1865 DeKalb Co. by Rev. Henry Hill. Martha Jane Boyle (21 Apr. 1845-7 May 1899) Bellaire, Pawnee twp. Smith Co. Ks. Both bur. Cora Cemetery d/o Jonathan Boyle (1815-1908) and Elizabeth Oliver, (1820-1849) DeKalb Co. Indiana.

Hulbert & Martha Jane (Boyle) Jones homesteaded in Pawnee twp., Smith Co. Ks. around 1895 with their family.

- Elizabeth Catherine Jones (28 Apr. 1866-DeKalb Co. 29 May 1956 (ae. 90 yrs.) Manitue Springs, Colo m. 19 Mar. 1891, Smith Center, Smith Co. Ks. Harry A. Coulson (1868, Oil City, Pa.-19 Sept. 1952, Colorado Springs, Colo. (ae. 84 y.), ch.: Keith

Coulson, b. 14 June 1892, Dale Coulson b. 1 Aug. 1904, Smith Co. Ks. & Eunice Coulson (4 Jan. 1893 Smith Co. 11 Feb. 1973 Colorado Springs, Colo.) m. Steve Campbell. ch.: Steve and Warren Campbell.

- John Clarence Jones (24 May 1871, Kirkville, Wapello Co. Iowa 23 Feb. 1959, Smith Center, Ks. m. 24 Dec. 1891, Monmouth, Warren Co. Illinois. Dora Esmerilda Scott (20 May 1875, Monmouth, Warren Co. Ill. 3 Mar. 1965, Smith Center, Ks. Both bur. Fairview Cem. Smith Center Ks. d/o Simpkin Riely & Catharine Ann (Fairburn) Scott. ch.: Earnest Orlando, George Lee, Homer Clarence, Harry Hector & Mary Elizabeth Jones. (See Scotts Family)

  ♦ Earnest Orlando Jones (3 Feb. 1893, Cora, Smith Co. Ks. 27 July 1968, Valley Center, Sedgwick Co. Ks. ae 71 y. 3 m. 13 d.) m. 15 Nov. 1911 Smith Center, Ks. Lois Mary Ritter (15 Mar. 1891 Macksburg, Iowa, 28 May 1962.) Valley Center. Ks., d/o E. W. & Diantha (Wheeler) Ritter, ch.: Ernest Laurel, John Edward (Ted), Donald Ritter, and Melvin Maury Jones.

    ◊ Ernest Laurel Jones (23 June 1913, Smith Center Ks., 26 Oct. 1983) Valley Center, Ks. m. 11 July 1938, Sedgwick Co. Ks. Geneva Arlene Mathias ch.: David Wesley, Joyce Arlene, and Lucy Lurene Jones.

    ◊ John Edward (Ted) Jones (7 Aug. 1915, Smith Center, Ks. 18 Jan. 1987 Valley Center Ks.) (World War II) m. 18 Jan. 1946 Valley Center, Ks. Juanita Ethel Keeler, (4 Sept. 1904-30 May 1980, Valley Center, Ks.

    ◊ Donald Ritter Jones, b. 23 Oct. 1917, Smith Center, Ks. m. 12 Dec. 1936, Garden City Ks. Anis Lucille Vanderee, d/o Frederick & Lillie Mae (Newton) Vanderee, ch.: Larry Lee Jones, and Gary Don Jones.

    ◊ Melvin Maury Jones b. 8 July 1920 Smith Center, Ks. m. 20 Nov. 1940 Phillis Grantine Robertson (d. 7 Apr. 1943), ch.: Mary Maureen Jones, and Melvin Maury Jones Jr.

  ♦ George Lee Jones (6 Feb. 1896 Henderson Co. Ill. 10 Apr. 1982, Wamego, Pottowatomea Co. Ks.) (World War I) Co.-G.- 313 Aef. 88 Div. bur. Wabaunseo Township Cem. m. Dec.1919 Smith Center, Ks. Hazel Bliss (2 Feb. 1903, Rulo, Nebr. 12 Jan. 1983, Manhattan, Ks., d/o Ed & Mary Hannah (Jones) Bliss, ch.: Gerry Lee Jones, and Ray Wayne Jones,

- ◊ Gerry Lee Jones m. Wayne Glen Wilson ch.: Deane Elaine Wilson, Jill Rayna Wilson & Julie Faye Wilson.
- ◊ Ray Wayne Jones m. Majel Elaine Hyres, ch.: Cynthia Lee Jones & Casey Wayne Jones.
- ♦ Homer Clarence Jones (24 July 1898, Cora Smith Co. Ks. 6 Aug. 1938), Los Angles, Calif. m. 20 June 1918 Smith Center, Ks. Etta Watson (18 Dec. 1895, Womer Smith Co. Ks. 26 Jan. 1985) Littleton Colo d/o David & Emma Amelia (Steffen) Watson, ch.: Crystal V. Jones, (see Watson Family)
- ♦ Harry Hector Jones (21 Jan. 1904, Cora, Smith Co., Ks. 9 Apr. 1971) Fairview Cem. Smith Center, Ks. m. 5 Jan. 1925 Smith Center, Ks. Esther Violet Martin, (3 Dec. 1905, Downs, Ks. 30 Dec. 1951), Smith Center, Ks. d/o Lem Martin & Clara (Yorgenson) Martin. ch.: Harry Hectar Jr. & Phyllis Joan Jones.
  - ◊ Harry Hector Jones Jr. m. Patricia Wiehl ch.: Harry Hector Jones III, & Sherri Jones.
  - ◊ Phyllis Joan Jones m. Richard Coulson, ch.: Ritchie Ronn Coulson, Jeffory Gene Coulson, Lauri June Coulson & Martin Joel Coulson.
- ♦ Mary Elizabeth Jones b. 26 Dec. 1921 Smith Center, Ks. m. Estel Alonzo Morford (1 Feb. 1915 Smith Co. Ks. 14 July 1984), Casper Natrona Co. Wyo. s/o Alonzo Washington Morford & Belle Isabell (Riley) Morford.

Most of the early Jones family was buried at Ceder Hill Cem. Cora, Smith Co. Ks. Other Jones buried there:
- Oliver Jones (1860-1919).
- Hattie Jones (1872-1906), son Wilber C. Jones (8 May 1892-28 May 1892).
- Nicholas J. Jones d. 16 Dec. 1893 ae 57 y. 11 m. 15 d. (b. 1 Jan. 1836). This could be the son Nicholas ae. 13 ys. in 1850 s/o Oliver & Rachel Jones of DeKalb Co. Ind.

Four generations of The Jones Family
John Jones, Glen Jones, Oliver Jones Jr., and Oliver Jones Sr.

George Scott

Giles Co. was created in 1806 mostly from Montgomery Co. bordered on the north by Monroe Co. and later giving up the western area for Monroe Co.

George Scott m. 29 Jan. 1816, Giles Co. Va. Cynthia Pool (1797-Dec. 1870-Boone Co. W. Va.) bondsman John Pool.

In 1830 George Scott Personal Property Tax on 7 1/2 acres Clover Bottom of Sinking Creek, adj. to Philip and Michael Harless. (Giles Co. Va.)

I find no record of George Scott in 1850 census. But by 1858 their son Simpkins R. Scott (b. 1838) marries in Roane Co. s/o George and Cynthia.

In 1870 Cynthia (Pool) Scott ae. 73 (wid.) was at the home of Charles W. Scott, Paw Paw twp. Marion Co. W. Va. She died Dec. 1870, Boone Co. W. Va.

Some of their children:
- Jane Scott, m. 1 Sept. 1840, Giles Co., Abram Collins.
- Judy Scott, m. 11 Feb. 1842, Giles Co. Anthony Harless.
- Dorenda Scott, m. 18 Apr. 1842, Giles Co. Absolem Collins.
- Isabel Scott, m. 27 Feb. 1833, Giles Co. John Sanders.
- Simpkins Rieley Scott, m. 20 Jan. 1858, Roane Co., (W) Va. Catharine A. Fairburn, d/o James A. and Elizabeth Fairburn.
- Isaac J. Scott, m. 20 Jan. 1859, Roane Co. Julia A. Patton, d/o Elizabeth B. Patton.
- Mary Scott, m. 29 Dec. 1859, Boone Co. (W) Va. Samuel B. Taylor, (b. 1836 Kanawha Co.) s/o George W. and Elizabeth Taylor.

- Cynthia Scott, m. 22 Feb. 1859, Boone Co. Samuel Scragg (wid) (b. 1824, England) s/o Richard and Lydia Scragg. In 1880 Samuel Scragg was in Boone Co. W. Va.

The Parents of Catharine (Fairburn) Scott:

James A. Fairburn, b. 1815 Virginia was in Lewis Co. in 1850 and Roane Co. in 1856. He m. Elizabeth, (perhaps Tole) as in 1850 a Catherine Tole ae. 55 yrs. (b. ca. 1795) Va. was living with them.

The Children of James A. & Elizabeth Fairburn:

1. Eliza Jane Fairburn b. ca. 1835 Lewis Co. m. 10 Apr.1856 Roane Co., Reuben P. Holbert (wid) b. 1824, s/o Aaron & Elizabeth Holbert.

2. Harriet E.Fairburn, b. ca. 1840.

3. Sarah A. Fairburn, b. ca. 1842.

4. Rebecca E. Fairburn b.ca. 1845 Lewis Co.

5. Catharine Ann Fairburn (28 Apr. 1838 Lewis Co. (W) Va. d. ca. 1924 Warren Co. Ill., (living with dau., Emma Jane (Scott) Million) m. 18 Mar. 1855, Roane Co. (W) Va. Simpkino Rieley Scott, (22 Sept. 1837, Giles Co. Va. 1 Dec. 1912, ae. 75 yrs. Warren Co. Ill.) s/o George and Cynthia (Pool) Scott.

Their children:

- James Delaze Scott (25 May 1859-1 June 1865 (W) Va.
- George Clarence Scott (14 Oct. 1863 (W) Va.-30 Apr. 1950, Bloomfield, Iowa) m. Francis ch.: 1 & 2 (twins) Lawrence Scott and James Scott, 3. Betty Scott and 4. Dora E. Scott (m. Glen Frichie, Wisconsin)
- Lucy Ellen Scott, (12 Apr. 1868, Monmouth, Warren Co. Ill. 4 Feb. 1951) Oberlin, Kans. m. (1st) John Blickenstaff, m. (2nd) Tom McKay. ch.: of (1st) family, 1. Glenn, 2. Edith m. Boyde Love, California. 3. Burnice, Kalsmith Falls, Oregon, 4. Grace California, 5. Eunice m. Huey - Oregon.
- Emma Jane Scott, b. 1 Aug. 1871-Warren Co. Ill. m. Frank Millian lived in Rush Center, Rush Co. Ks. ch.: 1. Alfred Millian, 2. Dean Million, 3. Charlie Million, 4. Fern Million, 5. Catharine Million, 6. Dare Million, 7. Laura Million, 8.-9. (twins) Murel Million and Burel Million, 10. Dale Million.
- John L. Scott b. 19 Feb. 1881 Warren Co. Ill.

- Elizabeth Cora Scott (twin) b. 20 May 1875, Warren Co. Ill m. Benjamin Barron lived Canton, Mo., ch.: Clarence and Eddie.
- Dora Esmeralda Scott (twin) (20 May 1875-Warren Co. Ill, -3 Mar. 1965) Smith Center, Kansas. m. 24 Dec. 1891 Monmouth, Warren Co. Ill. John Clarence Jones (24 May 1871-Kirksville, Wapello Co. Iowa-23 Feb. 1959) Smith Center, Smith Co. Kans. (Fairview Cemetery) s/o Hulbert Jones and Martha Jane Boyle. (see Boyle line later)

Their children; Earnest Orlando, George Lee, Homer Clarence, Harry Hector, and Mary Elizabeth Jones. (see Jones Line)

David Watson
(1806-1889)

David Watson was born 16 Aug. 1806 in Shaftsburg, Bennington Co. Vermont, both of his parents were born in Rhode Island. Records say he went to Chantauqua Co. New York in 1833, was m. there, 6 Oct. 1836. Ellington, N.Y. Betsey Biggs (25 Jan. 1816 Hancock, Berkshire Co. Mass. 29 Dec. 1896, Livingston Co. Ill.) d/o Frances (Frank) Briggs, on m. licence and 1850 in Brown Co. Ohio, Elizabeth Briggs ae. 62 yr. (b. ca. 1788) N.Y. was living with them.

History of Livingston Co. Illinois by LeBaron, David Watson, went to Brown Co. Ohio in 1839; to Woodford Co. Ill in 1851; to Peoria Co. Ill., in 1866; to Marshall Co. Ill., 1871; to Livingston Co. Ill., in 1876. David Watson died in Livingston Co. Ill. the 21 Apr. 1889 at the home of their son.

The only record of David Watson's parents, but really not proof, was the 1850 census of Ellington, Chautauqua Co. N.Y. David (or Daniel) Watson ae. 70 yrs. b. R. I. (b.ca. 1780) and Elizabeth ae. 65 yrs. R. I. (b. ca. 1785). listed ch.: Phebe L. 1814 and Mary A. Watson.

David & Betsey (Briggs) Watson Family.

1. Infant son (b. 25 Sept. 1837-d. 28 Sept. 1837) Ellingotn, Chautauqua Co. N.Y.

2. Edwin B. Watson b. 11 Apr. 1839, Ellington N.Y. s/o David & Betsey (Briggs) Watson, m. 22 Apr. 1867-Woodford Co. Ill. by Rev Wm Parker. Lucinda Kirby (b. Pa.). Their ch:

    - Jennie C. Watson, b. 4 July 1867, m. ___ Alfred lived near Alkinson, Henry Co. Ill.
    - William Watson b. 22 Feb. 1869, s/o Edwin B. & Lacinda (Kirby) Watson

- Elonedias Lon Leonadia Watson, b. 20 Oct. 1871 m. Lucy. They visited in Kansas around 1930 when they were moving to Portland, Oregon.

3. William L. Watson, b. 13 Sept. 1841-Ellington, Chautauqua Co. N.Y. s/o David & Betsey (Briggs) Watson served 3 years in the 108th Illinois Vols. from Woodford Co. Ill. recieved honorable discharge, P. O. Chenoa, Pike twp. Livingston Co. Ill., William L. Watson m. ca. 1877, Elizabeth, b. 15 Oct. 1862. ch.: Lucetta C. Watson b. 22 Dec. 1878; Lenna M. Watson b. 26 June 1880; Lafayett Watson b. 20 Jan. 1883; and William L. Watson b. 7 Apr. 1885.

4. Mary C. Watson, b. 3 Aug. 1844 Brown Co. Ohio, d/o David & Betsey (Briggs) Watson.

5. Infant daughter b. & d. 5 Oct. 1846, Brown Co. Ohio.

6. Lucetta C. Watson b. 11 June 1848 Brown Co. Ohio (d. before 1870) d/o David & Betsey (Briggs) Watson.

7. Francis Watson b. 29 May 1854 Chillicothe, Peoria Co. Ill. s/o David & Betsey (Briggs) Watson m. ca. 1872 Ellen b. 14 Oct. 1855 Indiana lived Woodford Co. Ill., ch.: Nettie E. Watson, b. 20 Sept. 1873; Charles Watson, b. 19 Dec. 1879; Nora Watson, b. 8 June 1882; Myrthe Watson b. 2 Nov. 1887; and Samuel Watson, b. 16 Jan. 1888.

8. Erastus L. Watson, (8 Aug. 1857-Chillicothe, d. by 1870) s/o David & Betsey (Briggs) Watson.

9. David Watson Jr. b. 27 July 1851-Chillicothe, Woodford Co. Ill. s/o David Sr. & Betsey (Briggs) Watson. m. (1) ca. 1872-3 Mary Ann Hunter (14 Apr. 1857-7 June 1883) ae. 26 yrs. bur. Womer Cemetery across the road from the Womer Church.

   They moved to Kansas in 1880 and lived in a sod house one mile west of the Womer community. Two children were born to this marriage. ch.: William Ellsworth Watson and Ida May Watson

   - William Ellsworth Watson (26 June 1875 Peoria, Peoria Co. Ill.- 29 Mar. 1948, Red Cloud, Webster Co. Ks.) s/o David Jr. & Mary Ann (Hunter) Watson. m. ca. 1909 Mrs. Belle Yeater of Lebonon, Ks. ch.: Four daughter by (1st) marrage: 6 children by (2nd) m. 5 living.
     - Mary Watson m. Marlion Mann.
     - Nellie Watson m. Albert Denton.
     - Elsie Watson

- ♦ Nettie Watson
- ♦ Willie Watson.
- Ida May Watson, (4 Sept. 1881 Cora, Smith Co. Ks. 8 Aug. 1919, ae. 38 yrs. Smith Co. Ks. d/o David & Mary Ann (Hunter) Watson, m. 12 Mar. 1901 Smith Co. Ks. Calvin Stoffer, (12 Aug. 1875, Spencerville DeKolb Co. Indiana, 8 June 1952, ae. 76 yrs. Womer, Smith Co. Ks.) s/o William Stoffer, b. 1841, Ohio and Sarah b. 1841, Indiana (maybe 2nd wife). (Their children, other than Calvin, William. 1864; Ellsworth Stoffer, 1869; Roy Stoffer ca. 1875; & Marion Stoffer 1880.). William Stoffer & Sarah Stoffer are buried near Tocoma, Washington.

Calvin & Ida May (Watson) Stoffer are bur. in the Womer Cem. Smith Co. Ks.

Their children:
- ♦ Myrtle Stoffer, b. 15 July 1904 Smith Co. Ks., m. Ray Arment, family of 8 children.; Verl, 23 June 1926; Gene, 2 Oct. 1927; Duane, 21 May 1929; Frank, 14 Oct. 1933; Kenneth, (25 May 1930 15 Apr. 1980, Aberdeen S. D.); Gary, (19 Mar. 1943; Virginia, 15 Oct. 1957); Thelma, 7 May 1940, m. Glassman.
- ♦ Loirn Stoffer, b. 13 May 1906, Smith Co. Ks., m. (1st) Freda Bliss b. 11 Sept. 1905 d/o Michael & Emma (Moede) Bliss. ch.: Delphin Loren, 18 Mar. 1925; Ida Orvilla, 28 Oct. 1932; & Ilona Louise, 10 Mar. 1940.
- ♦ Erma Stoffer, b. 27 July 1910 Smith Co. Ks. (1st) m. Everal Devlin, (29 Dec. 1906, 21 Nov. 1969) Smith Co. Ks. s/o Joseph & Estelle (Barnes) Devlini . m. (2nd)____Roberson, ch.: Arden Devlin, b. 18 Aug. 1937, Jewell Co. Ks. m. 1962 Lynne Ayers, b. 8 Sept. 1942, Smith Co. Ks. ch.: Lane Devlin m. Jan., Karen Devlin m. Gilbert Frieling.
- ♦ Irene Stoffer, 18 Mar. 1914, Smith Co. Ks., m. Fred Buss. Ch. 1 daughter.

David Watson (1851-1909) buys land in Pawnie twp., Smith Co. Ks.

The 14 Aug. 1886 David Watson bought from Newton Womer & Sarah Frances (Williams) for $1,325.00 E. ½ - S.W. ¼ of section No. 8 in Township One - South of Range 12 - West of 61b P.M.

Credit Eleanor Womer for this Womer & Hardman Line.

Newton Womer (1847 Center Co. Pa. & Aberdeen. Wa.) was a brother of Sylvester (Wes) Womer, (1848 Center Co. Pa.-1926 Smith Co.

Ks.) who m. 6 Feb. 1874 Franklin Co. Neb. Margaret Fender Mitchell, their son Leonard Edward Womer (1 Aug. 1882 Smith Co. Ks. 24 Sept. 1971 Phillipsburg Ks.) m. 31 Mar. 1909 Phillipsburg Ks. Lesley Hardman (14 Jan. 1882, Downs, Osborne Co. Ks.-10 Aug. 1974-Phillipsburg, Ks. d/o Nathaniel Marion Hardman (5 Feb. 1846 Ceder Co. Iowa-22 Sept. 1882) Downs Ks. and Ellen (Willford) Hardman (26 Dec. 1851-Beloit, Green Co. Wisc. -25 Mar. 1917) G/d of Cordes Hardman & Sarah Ann (Wise) Hardman, this line goes back to Peter and Margaret (Hacker) Hardman of Harrison Co, (W) Va. (see Hardman Line)

The Womer Cemetery was on land donated by the Womer Family and Sylvester & Margaret Womer, gave an acre of ground, across the road, south of the cemetery, for the new church, completed Sept. 1906 for The United Brethren in Christ Church, at Womer.

David Watson filed in Kerwin, Kansas before 1888, on the homestead of 20 May 1862 and was granted land at N.E. ¼ of Section # 17 in the township One, S. of Range 12, W. of the 6th Principal Meredian in Kansas. Containing 160 acres to David Watson and his heirs. Grover Cleveland was president, filed for record this 1 Nov. 1888 at 3 p.m. S. P. Simpson, Regestar of deeds.

Early Womer 1900. The south side of Womer's Main Street, Sam Null home and hardware store, Home and Office of Dr. Morrison, a photo gallery, millinery shop and barbershop and a few years later a general store, hotel, and restaurant and the Gould home.

On the north side of Womer's Main Street, the Mathe's home and their general store, and in later years the telephone office. (Local switchboard, where an operator rang your numbers 24 hours a day.)

The road going north had many houses, also a Creamery, blacksmith shop, livery barn, and the telephone office for a short time; the homes of Burwell Johnson, the Rask Family, also Dr. Jeffers. A little farther north was the home of David Watson. This road was known as Pig Alley.

After the Mathe's store was destroyed by fire, another store was built in replacement. Different merchants operated it, Everett Merriman, George Ormsbee, Orris Ring, and others. Another store was built on the south side of the street, some of the merchants being, Wylie Buchann, Harry Slade, Tom Moore, Chris Shennaman, <u>Charley Brown</u>, Bruce and Wyman Griffin, Harry Barnes and <u>Frank Million.</u>

At one time Eunice Campbell operated the telephone office and Jessie Million and others. Some Womer residents were Doctors

Morrison, Jeffers, and Watts, (all moved to Smith Center later), Burwell Johnson, who managed the livery barn, Cash Kersey, Mrs. Rask and son Nelse and daughter Jennie, David Watson and also Ed. Mathers.

Much of the above Information should be credited to *The Womer Church 100 years of Service (1885 to 1985)* Published by the Womer Church, Womer, South Co. Ks.

The membership of the Womer Church 1907-1927 grew, some of the people you will find in this list were family and neighbors of the Watson Family. Ed Mathes, Emma Mathes, Ella Robb, Will Lehr, James Cambpell, Dr. Victor Watts, Eva Watts, Retta Womer, Anna Wurster, Ida Lehr, Lola Ring, Lillie Campbell, Winnie Overmiller, Emmet and Grace Womer, Lee Pounds, Eunice Campbell, Will Campbell, Tillie Bliss, Herman Lehr and others.

The 6 Mar. 1900 William E. Watson (a single man) s/o David & Mary Ann (Hunter) Watson) sold to David Watson (his father) 160 acres for $1500.00 N.W. ¼ of Section 8 in township One, S. of Range 12, W. of 6th, P.M. of Kansas.

The 1895 state census of Kansas, Smith Co. Pawnee twp., Post Office Cora, provided the following information on David and Emma A (Steffen) Watson, Farmer, owner, 280 acres, cultivation 140 acres, Water well depth 45'- hand pump. Have 50 acres fenced, 230 acres not fenced, total of 280 acres. Farm improvement $1,500.00 wire 400, farm inptment $25.00

Crops: Corn 40 acres, fenced prarie 50 acres-Prarie hay cut 15 ton.

Sold in1895 - Eggs & Poultry $10.00, Butter 50 lb. Stock: horses 7, milk cows 6, other cattle 10, swine 20. Value of all animals $1,000.00 & dogs 2.

Schedule #5. Farm laborers, per month with board $14.00, Labor in City per day, housepainter $1.25 per day, Blacksmith $1.50 per day, Washwomen per day .50, domestic servents per week $1.50

Wheat per bu. .50¢, Corn per bu. .48¢, Fat Cattle per lb., 3.4¢, Stock Cattle per lb. .02¢, Milch Cows per head $14.00, Fat hogs per. pd..04¢.

David Watson (27 July 1851- Ill.-24 Apr. 1909) Womer, Smith Co. (ae. 58 y. 3 m. 3 d.) s/o David & Betsy (Briggs) Watson m. (2nd) 7 May 1885 Red Cloud, Webster Co. Nebr. Emma Amelia Steffen(12 May 1865, Cotton Hill, Sangamon Co. Ill. 29 Oct 1927 ae. 62 y. 5 m. 17 d. Womer, Smith Co. Ks.) d/o Charles Theador George Steffen & Maria (Mary) Dinghel. (see Steffen Family)

The David Watson Family
(Around 1906)

Nora, Frank

Edwin, David Watson Sr., David Jr., Ettie, Mary, Emma A. (Steffen) Watson, Ella, and Emma.

Both David & Emma Amelia (Steffen) Watson are buried at Womer Cem. along with the (1st wife) & members of the family. David & Emma (Steffen) Watson, had a family of 8 children.

1. Frances Lee Watson (9 June 1887 Womer 14 Mar.1954, ae. 67 y. Veterans Hosital, Grand Island, Nebr.) s/o David & Emma Amelia (Steffen) Watson World War I, m. 21 Mar. 1922 Smith Center, Esther Maria Bliss, (14 July 1899-Bladen, Webster Co. Nebr.-5 July 1976) Hastings, Adams Co. Nebr., d/o Michael & Emma (Moede) Bliss (Sister, Freda Bliss m. Loren Stoffer). Both buried Parkview Cem. Hastings, Nebr. Children:

- Doris Eldine Watson (31 Oct.1923-Flagher, Kit Carson Co. Colo- 12 Dec. 1986), Hastings, Nebr. m. 8 June 1941 Hastings Nebr. Raymond Charles Helms, (26 Mar. 1919 Hastings, Nebr.) s/o John Lewis & Mary (Afka) Helms. Children;
  - Marilee Laura Helms m. James Allen Jirkousky.
  - Susan Maria Helms, m David Allen Hoose.
  - John Raymond Helms m. Karen Larie Henthoron.
- David Adna Watson (28 Dec. 1924 Flagler, Colo. m.12 Apr. 1947- Hastings, Nebr. Dixie Hawthorne (26 Apr. 1929 Trumball, Adams Co. Nebr.) d/o Henry Andrew & Addie (Grigsby) Hawthorne.
  - Tom Dennis Watson, m. Lynda Enger.
  - Michelle Watson.

2. Nora Ellen Watson (5 Sept. 1891-Smith Co. 13 Aug.1930) Womer Cem. Smith Co. d/o David & Emma A (Steffen) Watson.

3. Mary Watson (19 April 1894-Smith Co.-26 Aug. 1988) d/o David & Emma Amelia (Steffen) Watson m. 10 Apr. 1922 Smith Co. Henry Andrew Lehr, (25 July 1883, Caroll Co. Ill. 3 Dec. 1935, Smith Co. Ks.) (ae. 52 y. 4 m. 9 d.) bur. Womer Cem.) s/o George Lehr (8 Jan. 1841 Germany-19 Aug. 1919 Smith Co. Ks. and Anna Marie Lehr (10 Mar. 1853 Germany-28 Jan. 1918 Smith Co.)

George Lehr emmigrated 1867 to Carroll Co. Ill. m. Anna Maria, ca. 1877 in Carroll Co. Ill. who emmigrated with her parents in 1868, when she was 15 yrs. old. Children of George & Anna Maria Lehr:

- The 3 small daughter d. in infancy.
- Willie Lehr b. Nov. 1880 Carroll Co. Ill.
- Henry Andrews Lehr 6 June 1883.
- Herman Lehr b. June 1888 Smith Co. Ks.

- Ida Lehr b. Dec. 1889, Smith Co. Ks.
- Oscar Lehr (twin), b. Oct. 1896, Smith Co. Ks.
- Otto Lehr (twin), b. Oct. 1896, Smith Co. Ks.
- Mrs. C. L. (Lohr) Benson.
- Charles Lehr of Walla Walla, Wa.

Henry Andrew & Mary (Watson) Lehr had these children:

- Anna Marie Lehr (21 Jan. 1922 Smith Co. Ks. 1 Oct. 1969 bur. Union Cem. Malta Bend, Mo.) m. 10 Jan. 1943 Sgt. Archie Hillebrande. Children:
    - Joe Henry Hillebrande.
    - Eugene Allen Hillebrande.
- Kenneth Dean Lehr, b. 3 Sept. 1929 Smith Co. Ks. U.S. Army.
- Velma Lucille Lehr (19 Dec. 1933 Smith Co. 15 Sept. 1949-bur. Womer Cem. with parents.

4. Ettie Watson (18 Dec. 1895 Smith Co.-26 Jan. 1985 ae 90 y, 1 m, 8 d, Littleton, Colo) d/o David & Emma A (Steffen) Watson m. 20 June 1918 Smith Center, Ks (by J. Jarvis), Homer Clarence Jones (24 July 1898 Cora, Smith Co. 6 Aug. 1939). (see Jones Family)

- Crystal Violet Jones (7 Sept 1919 Smith Co. Ks.), m. Marvin Lee Wagoner. (see Wagoner Family)

5. Edwin Watson (12 Apr. 1898, Smith Co., 6 Oct. 1973 Littleton, Jefferson Co. Colo. s/o David and Emma Amelia (Steffen) Watson, m. 30 Apr. 1922 Red Cloud, Webster Co. Nebr., Elizabeth Drew (5 Sept. 1903-19 June 1990 Littleton, Colo.) d/o Joseph & Harriet (Ball) Drew.

Joseph Drew (May 1861 Norfork, England-29 Nov. 1945 Thornburg, Smith Co. Ks.) Immegrated in 1879 s/o Robert Drew (who immigrated in 1892) m. ca. 1886 Harriet Ball (25 Oct. 1864 Gardner, Grundy Co. Ill. 8 Apr. 1941 Smith Co. Ks.) d/o Robert & Eliza C (Reed) Ball both born England. (ch.: George Ball 1854 Eng., Martha Ball 1857, Eng., Harriet Ball 1865 Ill., Robert Ball 1869 Ill.)

Joseph & Harriet (Ball) Drew had 5 sons & 1 daughter all b. Smith Co. Ks. (ch.: Robert DrewDec. 1890, John DrewOct. 1892, Herny Drew Feb. 1899 & twin, Herbert Feb. 1899, Joseph Drew 1902, Elizabeth Drew 1903)

Ettie Jones - Ella Brown - Mary Lehr - David Watson - Emma Pierce - Norma E. Watson
Edwin Watson   Emma A. Watson   Frank Watson

Ormald Watson - Ivan Pierce - Lavon Brown - Anna Marie Lehr - Crystal V. Jones - Adna Watson
Doris Watson - Edwin Watson Jr - Emma A. Watson - Bernard Watson - Violet Brown

Grandmother's Garden

Edwin & Elizabeth (Eliza) (Drew) Watson had 3 sons & 1 daughter, moved to Englewood Colo in 1944.:

- Ornold Watson b. 14 Apr.1923 Smith Co. Ks.
- Edwin Jr. Watson b. 12 May 1924 Smith Co. Ks. m. 5 Sept. 1946 Denver, Beatrice Arlene Harmon.
- Bernard Lee Watson, b. 4 Mar. 1927 Smith Co. m Beverly Ann Hemple b. 3 Mar. 1935.
- Melberta Watson m. Erven Braddy, (d. 21 Apr., 1991) s/o Arthur & Susan Braddy.

6. Emma Watson b. 17 May 1901, Smith Co. Ks. d/o David & Emma Amelia (Steffen) Watson m. ca. 1926. Edwin Pierce they had 4 sons;

- Ivan Eugene Pierce, b.3 Jan. 1927.
- Aubrey Dale Pierce, b. 30 Jan. 1931.
- Melvin Wayne Pierce, b. 30 Mar. 1932.
- Donald L. Pierce, b. 16 Apr. 1934.

7. David Watson b. 24 June 1903 Womer, Smith Co. s/o David & Emma Amelia (Steffen) Watson m. 10 Oct.1928, Smith Center, Ks. Alice Clemmison, (4 Oct. 1904, Smith Co., 25 Feb. 1962 Monrose, Colo.) d/o William & Elfie (McAlpin) Clemmison. Children:

- Lloyd Eldon Watson, b. 7 May 1930 m.Jackie Lou Wright.
- David Jr. Watson, b. 1 Apr. 1932 m. Ann Gruick.
- Kathryn Alice Watson, b. 9 Aug. 1934 m. Jaye Lloyd Bruce.
- Florence May Watson, b. 15 May 1936 m. Hugo John Frigetto.
- Clarence Lee Watson, b. 29 June 1938 Smith Co. Ks.
- Clifford Kay Watson, b. 4 May 1941 Montrose Co. Colo.

8. Ella Watson, b. 11 June 1905 Womer, Smith Co. Ks. d/o David & Emma Amelia (Steffen) Watson, m. 28 Sept. 1923 Charley Brown (1 June 1900 Smith Co., 29 June 1974) Smith Co. bur. Red Cloud Cem. Red Cloud, Webster Co. Nebr. s/o Howard Brown (b. Oct. 1858 Iowa) & Fannie M. Brown (b. Apr. 1859 Iowa) (They had 4 sons, Alfred K. Brown Apr. 1893; Erle H. Brown June 1894; (Guy) Bryano Brown July 1897; & Charley June Brown 1900).

Charley & Ella (Watson) Brown had 2 sons & 2 daughters:

- Violet Amelia Brown m. Lee L. Crowder Jr.
- Orris LaVon Brown m. May _____.
- Sharon Kay Brown
- Roy Charles Brown m. Peggy Ann Randolph.

Philip Dunkel

Philip Dunkel (ca. 1806 Baden, Germany-29 Mar. 1856 Sangmon Co. Ill. Emmigrated some time late 1846 (maybe Dec.).

Ref: Historical Encyclopedia of Ill. by Paul Selby edited by Newton Bateman L.L.D. Vol 2-pt.2.

Philip & Catharine (Spangler) Dunkle, had one child born on the vogage, whom they called Mary after the ship, on which she was born. The ship was blown off coruse and took over four months to make the trip, docking at New Orleans, La. having been 18 weeks on the water, belated by storms & nearly starved, as a consequence of running out of food.

The Dunkle family proceeded to St. Louis, Mo. and came from there to Springfield with an Ox team. Philip had a brother, Adam Dunkel, living near Springfield, where he located on a farm four miles out of the city. In Germany he had learned the blacksmith trade, but once in the United States, donated the remainder of his life to farming in Sangamon Co. Ill.

Philip Dunkel was m. Germany & immigrated with wife Catharine (Spangler) Dunkel (1810 Baden, Ger. 30 Sept. 1880 ae. 77 yrs.) Springfield, Ill. Lived in Garden twp. Sangamon Co. Ill., members of the Trinity Evangelical Lutheran Church in Springfield with their 3 sons & 2 daug.(bur. Crowder Cem. Garden Twp.)

1. John Adam Dunkel (19 Sept. 1838 Baden, Ger. Emm. with parents (1847-) Philip & Catharine (Spangler) Dunkel, (served Civil War), m. 13 May 1865 Springfield, Elizabeth Stahl b. 26 Mar. 1847. In 1869 Sept. moved to Tallula, Ill. (funature mfg. & undertaker). 6 ch.: Elizabeth Dunkel, 13 Sept. 1867; Sophia Dunkel, (13 May 1870-31 Dec. 1874); John Dunkel, 31 Aug. 1872; Frederick Dunkel, 4 June

1875; (twins) George S. Dunkel & William W. Dunkel, 3 Oct. 1878 (Wm. d. 29 July 1879).

2. Catherine (Dunkel) Dinkel (21 May 1844-Baden, Ger. 1 Jan. 1861, Springfield) m. 1 Jan. 1861, Trinity E. Lutheran Ch. Springfield., George Baumann (21 Oct. 1835 Baden Ger.-Emm. in 1850 New Orleans La. came to St. Louis, Mo. by boat & then to Springfield. Learned the trade of tinner where he remained 9 yrs. In 1873 he embarked in the grocery business.

Children of George & Catharine (Dunkle) Baumann:
- George Edward Baumann 1863.
- Henry Albert Baumann 1867.
- Charles Karl Theadour Baumann, 1869,-Sponsored by Charles G. F. Steffen.
- Georgetta Baumann 1872.
- Noble Baumann 1874.
- Herman Wm. Baumann. 1877.
- Benjamin B. Baumann.
- Belle Baumann.
- Katy Louisa Baumann.

3. Philip Dinkel (1848 Springfield, 21 Sept. 1930) m. Mary E. (1849 Ger. 1920).

4. George (Charles) Dinkel b. ca. 1851 Springfield, Ill.

5. Mary (Maria) Dinkel (7 Nov. 1846 at sea) d. Colton Hill twp Sangamon Co. Ill. 24 Apr. 1878) (due to an accident) m. 6 July 1864, Trinity E. L. Ch. Charles Theodour George Steffen wit. George and Catharine (Dunkel) Baumann, signed by Rev. Wm. Barlting.

✤✤

Charles Steffen is listed as a land owner in Gardner twp, Sangamon Co. Ill. in 1866. Charles T. G. Steffen (b. 1 Apr. 1834-Mecklemberg. Hamburg, Germany) Emm. from Canada into the U.S.A. in 1847 age 11 years.(d. 16 Dec. 1927 ae. 93 y. 8 m. 16 d. Hastings Nebr.) The death record gives his father as Charles Steffen & mother Johana Hanna Felton (Family Bible gives her d. date as 4 June 1894 ae. 93 y. 6 m. 0 d.)

After Mary (Dinkel) Steffen's death, Charles T. G. Steffen packed up his daughter and 4 sons, and all they owned, and set out for Nebraska and free land.

Charles T. G. Steffen
(1836-1927)

We find **Charles Steffen** ae. 44 y. (widowed) b. Prussia, in Colton Hill twp., Sangamon Co. in 1880, with children: Emma 15 yrs; George 11; Charles 9; Henry 6; and Frederick 4.

By 1883 they were in Nebr., as Charles Steffen m. 15 Mar. 1883, Red Cloud, Webster Co. Nebraska, his second wife Augusta Carrie Walner (7 Mar. 1859 Berlin, Germany-17 Feb. 1954 ae. 93 yrs.).

Each time you find Charles Theador George Steffen he is using a different name, so I'll use them all. (1 Apr. 1836-Hamburg, Mechlinbury, Germany. 17 Dec. 1927, Hastings, Nebr.), m. (1st) 16 July 1864 Springfield Mary (Marie) Dunkel, d/o Philip & Catharine (Spangler) Dunkel.

1. Emma Amelia Steffen (12 May 1865-29 Oct. 1927) m. 7 May 1883 Red Cloud Nebr. David Watson (Note C. T. G. Steffen d. 17 Dec. 1927 Hastings Nebr, his daughter Emma Amelia (Steffen) Watson d. 29 Oct. 1927 Womer K. one month and 19 days apart.) Emma Amelia Steffen m. 7 May 1885, Red Cloud, Nebr-David Watson. (see Watson Family)
2. George Ad Edward Steffen (20 Mar. 1869 Ill.-9 May 1953 Nebr.) bur. Parkview Cem. Hastings Nebr.
3. Charles Theador Steffen (28 Feb.1871-Ill.-27 Aug. 1949 bur. Parkview Cem. Hastings Nebr., m. Maude "Lennie" Patterson (1879-1946).
4. Henry Albert Steffen (27 Feb. 1874 Ill.-16 Sept. 1924, bur. Parkview Cem. d. Red Cloud, Nebr.
5. (Fritz) Frederick William Steffen, 2 June 1876 Ill. 19 Oct. 1965-Hastings, Nebr. m. (1) Myrtle M. Barstods 16 Oct. 1905, m. (2) 17 Oct. 1913 Marie Rebecca Smith. ch.: June Elizabeth Steffen, m. Elwood W. Camp, Grace Steffen m. Henry W. Metz.

Charles Theador George Steffen & (2nd) m. Augusta Carrie Walner on this m. record the info. reads; "Charles Steffen 42 b. Mechlemburg, Germany, resides Judson, Smith Co. Ks. Father John Steffen, mother Fredrecka Rink, m. 15 Mar. 1883 by Rev. G. W. Hummell. Red Cloud,

Webster Co. Nebr., Gusta Walner ae. 18-Prussia. On Gusta (Walner) Steffen death reacord , the name of her father is Emil Wallner. (There children were, Ida L.; Carrie B. & Edward A.)

Emma Amelia Steffen (1865-1927)
Charles Theador George Steffen (1836-1927)
Mary (Dunkel) Steffen (1846-1878)

Part Eight

Early Settlers at Hartford Connecticut

Inez Lucille Solomon (17 June 1908)
Daughter of Christian Elmer and
Florance Laura (Burnham) Solomon

Thomas Burnham
(1617-1688)

This part of my book is decicated to a lovely lady, Inez Lucille (Solomon) Wagoner, daughter of Elmer Christian Solomon 1867-1940 and Florance Laura Burnham (1875-1959) of Ellis Co. Kansas, who has made a differance to many who's lives she has touched.

Genealogy Records of Thomas Burnham (the Emigrant who was among the early settlers of Hartford Conn. and his descendants) by Roderick H. Burnham, Hartford, Conn. This book, printed in 1884, has preserved so many records that would have otherwise been lost over the years.

The name Burnham can be traced to Walter deVentre who came to England at the Conquest (1066), with William of Normandy, in the train of his cousin-German Earl Warron and at the survey (1080), was made lord of the Saxon Village of Burnham (and of many other manors) from these manors he took his surname of DeBurnham. The coats of arms and seal can be seen and listed on pg. 29. and early history from 1086 to 1528.

The first we find record of Thomas Burnham Sr. (No.1) in America was in 1649 bondsman for his servant Rushmore; sworn as Constable for artford, 1656, Conn. He purchased a very extensive tract from the Indians at Potunke in 1660: Attorney for Abigail Bitts, 1662. His house at Potunke, in 1675 was fortified and garrisoned during the Indian War. Thomas Burnham Sr. was educated and practiced as a lawyer appears to have been of a very determined character.

Thomas Burnham, Sr. was a descendent from the Burnhams of Herefordshire England, he came to this country, less by religious scrupler than by the desire to improve his fortunes. (s/o William & Joan

Burnam). Thomas Burnham Sr. Emigrated 20 Nov. 1635 from Barbados (ae. 18 y.) from Gravesand England.

Thomas Burnham Sr. (b. 1617 Halfield Court, Herefordshire, England d. 28 June 1688 ae. 71 yrs.) Potunke, East Hartford, Conn. (Ipswich, Mass.) m. ca. 1639 Anna Wright (1620 England d. 5 Aug. 1703) Hartford Conn. "Potunke" Windsor Court. She lived 15 years after Thomas death and was a woman of courage & determanition, she did not produce his will when it was called for by the court; it was subsequently proven by the witnesses to the instrument, June 1690. Only a portion of the original land was held by the sons & heirs after Anna's death.

Their children. (of Thomas of Potunk)

1. Elizabeth Burnham (1640-2 Dec. 1720) East Hartford, Conn. m. 1665 Hartford, Conn. Nicholas Maricock of Boston.

2. Mary Burnham (ca. 1642-25 Jan. 1720) Hartford, Windsor, m. 21 Mar. 1670-Hartford, William Morton. children:
   - John Morton.
   - Ann Morton.
   - Mary Morton.

3. Anna Burnham (1644-29 Nov. 1722) Glastonbury, m. 7 Apr. 1665 Samuel Gaines. Children:
   - Nathaniel Gaines.
   - Henry Gaines.

4. Thomas Burnham Jr., (1646-19 Mar. 1726) E. Hartford. Conn. m. 4 Jan. 1676, Killingworth Middlesex Co. Comm. by Edward Greswold, Naomi Hull (17 Feb. 1657-15 Mar. 1727) d/o Josiah Hull of Killingworth, Conn.

5. John Burnham (12 Nov. 1648-20 Apr. 1721) Hartford, Conn. m. (2nd) 12 Nov. 1684 of Potunk, Windsor Conn. Mary Olcott (10 July 1666-13 Dec. 1730) d/o John Olcott & Mary Marshall who were m. 27 July 1665-.

6. William Burnham (1652-12 Dec. 1730) Hartford, Conn. m. (1st) 28 June 1681 Hartford Conn. Elizabeth Loomis (7 Aug. 1655-19 Nov. 1717) Wethersfield Conn. d/o Nathaniel Loomis m. (2nd) (wid.) Martha (Thompson) Gaylord (w/o Eliaza Gaylord.). Children:
   - Elizabeth Burnham.
   - William Joseph Burnham.

- Nathaniel Burnham.
- Jonathan Burnham.
- Mary Burnham.
- Abigail Burnham.
- David Burnham.

7. Richard Burnham (1654-28 Apr. 1731) Potunke Hartford, Conn. m. 11 June 1680 Hartford, Conn. Sarah Humphrey (6 Mar. 1659-28 Nov. 1726) Hartford, Conn. d/o Michael & Prescilla (Grant) Humphrey of Windsor. children:

- Sarah (Hannah) Humphrey.
- Rebecca Humphrey.
- Mercy Humphrey.
- Mary Humphrey.
- Richard Humphrey.
- Martha Humphrey.
- Esther Humphrey.
- Jupiter Humphrey.
- Charles Humphrey.
- Susanna Humphrey.
- Michael Burnham.

8. Rebecca Burnham b. 1656 Hartford Conn. m. 5 Apr. 1685 Wethersfield Conn. William Mann. (1671-1736).

9. Samuel Burnham (1650-12 Apr. 1728) Hartford, Conn. m. 8 Oct. 1684, Windsor, Conn. Mary Cadwell (8 Jan. 1659-19 Apr. 1738) d/o Thomas Cadwill and Mrs. Elizabeth Wilson (wid/o Robert Wilson) d/o Dec. Edward Stebbing.

Our line - Thomas Burnham Jr. (1646-19 Mar. 1726) Hartford, Conn., s/o Thomas Burnham and Anna (Wright) Burnham, m. 4 Jan. 1676-Killingworth, Naomi Hull (17 Feb. 1657-15 Mar. 1727) Hartford. She was born at Windsor, Conn., the records of the Colonial Particular Court say that Thomas Burnham Jr. was married to Naomi Hull of Killingworth 16 Jan. 1676 by Edward Griswold, but family records give the date 4 Jan. 1676, as above.

Naomi was the daughter of Josiah Hull, b. England, and, m. 20 May 1641, Elizabeth Bemis, d/o Joseph Bemis. The brothers and sisters of Naome were:

- Josiah Hull (1642-1670) m. Elizabeth Tahnage.
- John Hull (1644-1728) m. 3 Dec. 1668 Abigail Kelsey.
- Elizabeth Hull (1647-1689) m. 28 Nov. 1661 Israil Deble.

- Mary Hull (1648-1720/26) m. 2 Aug. 1666 (1st) John Grant. (1642-1684) m. (2nd) 3 Nov. 1686 John Cross.
- Martha Hull (1650   ) m. 29 May 1670 John Nettleton.
- Joseph Hull (1652-1709) m. Elizabeth (Farmham) Rocke.
- Sarah Hull (b. 1654) m. (1st) Nicholas Munger m. (2nd) Dennis Crampton.
- Rebecca Hull b. 10 Aug. 1659.
- George Hull b. 28 Apr. 1662-dy.
- Thomas Hull m. 10 Dec. 1685 Killingworth, Hannah Sheather.

Father of Naomi Hull, Josiah Hull was deputy of the General Court From Windsor in 1659-60-62, and from Killingworth, from 1667 to 1674.

Children of Thomas and Naomi (Hull) Burnham:

- Thomas Burnham (bp.-16 Apr. 1678-12 May 1726) m. 19 Nov. 1711 Elizabeth Strong (20 Feb. 1671-18 Apr. 1720) d/o John Strong. Children:
  - Thomas Burnham.
  - Elizabeth Burnham.
  - Esther Burnham.
- John Burnham b. 22 May 1681-dy.
- Elizabeth Burnham (bp-4 June 1684-7 Mar. 1758) other records (d. 1 June 1758 ae. 75 y.) Hartford, Conn. m., 4 Mar. 1702 Hartford, Richard Gilman (1680-1 Feb. 1761 ae. 81 yrs.) s/o Richard & Elizabeth (Adkins) Gilman (Families of Early Hartford Conn. by Bardour, pg. 264). ch.: Elizabeth, Richard, Samuel, and Naomi Gilman.
- Sarah Burnham (bp. 7 Mar. 1685-)m. ____Mulford.
- Naomi Burnham (bp 3 June 1688-1 Jan. 1762) m. 7 May 1713 Hartford Josiah Gaylord (Deacon).
- Charles Burnham (bp 16 May 1690-15 Nov. 1779) (will dated 29 Mar. 1761) Hartford, Conn. m. 7 Nov. 1727 Hartford. Lydia Williams (bp 2 Dec. 1705-12 Dec. 1780) d/o Jonas Williams & Mary ____.
- Mary Burham (bp. 12 Apr. 1692-30 Sept. 1757) m. 12 Apr. 1712 Potunk, Hartford Conn. Lt. John Anderson.
- Abigail Burnham (bp. 25 Mar. 1693-4-26 Sept. 1732) m. 12 Apr. 1712-13) Jonah Williams, eldest son of Jonas & Mary Williams, Grandson of William and Jane (Westover) Williams & brother to Lydia (Williams) Burnham.

Our Line, Josiah Burnham (bp. 6 Sept. 1696-1 Oct. 1763) Hartford, Conn. Youngest son of Thomas and Naomi (Hull) Burnham m.

12 Feb. 1730 East Hartford, Conn., Margaret Wood, b. 1 July 1705, d/o Obadiah Wood, d. 11 Apr. 1712, and Martha (King) Wood. *(Note-Obadiah Wood was a soldier wouned in Philips War late in 1695, for whose cure the Conn. Council made liberal payment).* He was of Hartford 1676, (and perhaps son of the preceedent Obadiah) and had there bp. Margaret (6 Nov. 1687) who died young, the children of Obadiah Wood and Martha (King) Wood.

- Abegail Wood, bp. 23 Apr. 1699.
- Margaret Wood, bp. 1 July 1705, m. Josiah Burnham.
- Obadiah Wood, bp. 8 Sept. 1706, m. Mehitable.
- John Wood.
- Mary Wood m. John Shaw.
- Martha Wood.
- Samuel Wood.

Josiah & Margaret (Wood) Burnham were bur. Montoque, Hampshire Co. Mass. Their children:

- Lt. Josiah Barnham (1731) m. 1777 Jerusha (Bissell) Cooley,
- Thomas Burnham (4 May 1732-d. May 1808) Mareau, N. Y. m. Elizabeth Harmon who d. 8 Mar. 1811.
- Hannah Burnham m. 11 Aug. 1768 Holliston, Mass. John Muzzy.
- James Burnham (1733-26 Jan. 1787) m. Dorothy ____, she m. (2nd) 20 Oct. 1796 Samuel Call.
- Irene Burnham.
- Sybil Burnham (26 Sept. 1736-bp 1763) Franklin Co. Mass.
- Martha Burnham (bp. 5 June 1737) Deerfield, Hampshire Co. Mass.
- Daniel Burnham (1745-11 Oct. 1785) Montaque, Mass. m. 1766,- Jemina ____ (1745-20 Apr. 1810), ch.: Daniel Burnham, Elager Burnham, Asenath Burnham.
- Charles K. Burnham.
- Obediah Burnham.
- Erastus Burnham.
- Sylvester Burnham.

Our line - James Burnham (1733-26 Jan. 1787) Montaque, Hampshire Mass., s/o Josiah and Margaret (Wood) Burnham m. Dorothy ____. All their children were born in Montaque, Hampshire Mass.:

- Sybil Burnham (18 Dec. 1760-4 Feb. 1846) m. 7 Nov. 1791-Eli Gum (1757-1837).

- Zelpha Burnham b. 7 Feb. 1762.
- Hannah Burnham (16 Jan. 1763-16 Mar. 1773).
- James Burnham (12 June 1765-15 June 1765).
- Abigail Burnham (25 July 1766-29 Dec. 1844, ae. 79 y.) m. 15 May 1787 Greenfield, Franklin Co. Mass., Aaron Field Wills (25 June 1767-12 Feb. 1826) s/o Joseph Wells.
- Judith Burnham b. 10 Mar. 1768 m. 24 Oct. 1786-Joseph Latham.
- Lydia Burnham b. 9 Feb. 1770.
- Reubin Burnham (b.-16 May 1774) m. 31 Mar. 1796-Belchertown, Hampshire Co. Mass. Sarah Shumway.
- Sylvanus Burnham (26 July 1776-30 Oct. 1870), m. Hepsibeth Pickett, N.Y.
- Ashbill Burnham b. 7 Feb. 1772.

Our line **Sylvanus Burnham** (26 July 1776-30 Oct. 1870) s/o James & Margaret (Wood) Burnham, m. 4 Mar. 1797, Greenfield Mass. Hepsibeth Pickett (1777-1858) (in 1826 Potsdam, N.Y.) d/o Daniel Pickett. Both Bur. in Hinman Cemetery, Potsdam, St. Lawrence Co.

- James Burnham (1799-4 Sept. 1803), s/o Sylvanus & Hepsibeth (Pickett) Burnham, (h/o Greenfield, Mass.).
- James M. Burnham (22 Mar. 1811, Greenfield-d. 1901, Potsdam, St. Lawrence Co. N.Y.), s/o Sylvanus & Hepsibeth (Pickett) Burnham, m. (1st) 1 Oct. 1836 Martha Buttolph, d/o Jonathan Buttolph. m. (2nd) 9 June 1839 Miranda Owens (d. 6 May 1840) d/o Abel Owens of Burlington, Vt. children:
    - Capt. Collins A. Burnham of Wimure, Nebr. m. (3rd) 3 Nov. 1840 Hannah Gillette (1823-1903).
    - Martha J. Burnham.
    - Mary P. Burnham.
    - Miranda H. Burnham.
    - Frances S. Burnham.
- George W. Burnham, b. Greenfield, Franklin Co. Mass, s/o Sylvanus & Hepsibeth (Pickett) Burnham.
- John Burnham, b. Greenfield, Franklin Co. Mass, s/o Sylvanus & Hepsibeth (Pickett) Burnham.
- Sylvanus Burnham Jr., b. 1820, s/o Sylvanus & Hepsibeth (Pickett) Burnham, m. 1836 Olive E. _____.
- Mary P. Burnham, d/o Sylvanus & Hepsibeth (Pickett) Burnham. In 1860, Potsdam N.Y. Mary P. Burham (ae. 36 y.)

was at home with her father Sylvanus Burnham (ae. 88 y. b. Mass).

Our line **Sylvanus Burnham Jr.** (1820 Greenfield, Franklin Co. Mass., s/o Sylvanus & Hepsibeth (Pickett) Burnham, m. ca. 1836, Potsdam, St. Lawrence Co.N.Y. Olive E. _____ (b. ca., 1822 N.Y.) Their children:

- Elena Burnham, b. 1837.
- Hepsibeth Burnham, b. 1839.
- Amelia Burnham, b. 1841.
- James Douglas Burnham, (1843-1880), m. America M. Fry.
- George W. Burnham, b. 1847.
- Rolla Albert Burnham (May 1846-Potsdam, N.Y.) m, ca, 1888 - Belle C. (Dec. 1867 Wisconson) Their ch.: 1. Truman E. (June 1889 , Ks.) 2. Homer E. (Nov. 1890- Ks.) 3. Libbie O. (July 1893 Ks.) 4. Clyde (Sept. 1894 Ok.) 5. Laura (June 1896, Ok.) 6. Althea (Oct. 1898, Ok.), 7. Clara (Mar. 1900, Ok.).

Our Line - **James Douglas Burnham** (1843-1880, ae. 37 y.) s/o Sylvanus Burnham Jr. Olive E. Burnham m. 1867 Vinton, Benton Co. Iowa, America May Fry (1851-1931 Hays Ks.) d/o William (Bill) Fry and Ann Lane Fry. (see William Fry line.)

William Fry (1833-1914) and
Annie (Lane) Fry (1834-1917)
Parents of America May (Fry) Burnham

William Fry

William Fry (Frey) (May 1833 Pa.. 1914) Venton, Benton Co. s/o German Emigrants, mothers name Anna Frey. In 1880 Soundex, Anna Fry (mother-in-law), ae. 69 yrs. b. Pressia ca. 1811, was living with David and Catherine Ake, Benton Co. Iowa. Catherine (Fry) Ake was a sister to William Fry. If Catherine (Fry) Ake was born in Prussia in 1831-2, than the Fry Family must have emigrated just before William was born in May 1833 in Pennsylvania. William Fry m. ca 1850 Venton, Benton Co. Iowa, Anne Lane (June 1834 Indiana-1917 Iowa). Both of Anne Lane's parents were b. in Ky. The only possible parents living near in 1880 Benton Co., were Frank Lane ae. 76, b. 1804, and Rebecca Lane ae. 69- b. 1811 Kentucky, living with John and Martha Lane in Benton Co. Iowa. Brothers & Sisters of:

- America May (Fry) Burnham.
- (Joshua) Henry W. Fry (1856-1927) Benton Co. Iowa m. Margaret Stephson (b. Ohio) ch.: William C. (1876) and Charley 1878).
- George W. Fry (Aug. 1858) m. Emma J. ch.: Nellie (Dec. 1883) & Jay W. (Dec. 1890).
- William E. Fry (1859).
- Grant B. Fry (1866-1917).
- John H. Fry (1873-1920).

James Douglas Burnham (1843-1880) and America May (Fry) Burnham (1851-1931) d/o William & Annie (Lane) Fry. Their children:

- Annie Burnham (1869-1925) b. Venton, Benton Co. Iowa m. Martin T. Shade (1864-1911) bur. Mt. Hope, Ellis, Ellis Co. Kans..
- Clark R. Burnham (July 1871-) Kans. m. Ellis Co. Kans., Mary Dume.
- Ellie George Burnham, (1873-1899), Ellis Co. Kans.

- Florance Laura Burnham (10 Oct. 1875 Elk Co, Kans. 25 Dec. 1959, Ellis Co. Kans) m. 12 Aug. 1902 Christian Elmer Solomon.(see Solomon Family).
- James D. Burnham (9 Nov. 1877-Rash Co., Kans. 10 Dec. 1942) Hays City Cem., Ellis Co. Kans.
- Inez America May Burnham (25 Nov. 1879-23 May 1966) (was 8 mo. old when her father James Douglas Burnham died), she m. Berne Fitzpatrick.

The Soloman Family

We have the Hon. Raymond Drake to thank for the two German lines of the Solomon's & Selbitz's. In 1985 Ray spent a month in Germany, in & around the Gorsleben area. The minister, Adolf Hoffmann, of the Lutheran Church at Gorsleben, tanslated old church records of the two families. Ray's report is as follows:

"The furthest back that I have traced the Solomon line is to a Jens Lorenz Salomon, born about 1680 probable at Orebro (Narke province) Sweden, JLS was a shoemaker and was the father of Erich (Eric?) Salomon, born about 1700 at Orebro, ES was a soldier in the army of Sweden during the Great Northern War (1697-1717) and held the rank of Corporal, he also served as a mercenary soldier to the Doge of Venice, having seen service fighting the Turks in Constaninople, in Greece and lastly was severely wounded at the siege of Corfu (c. 1730) after which he settled at Gorsleben, province of Thuringa, Germany. I might mention that I have been unable to locate any records of any families named Salomon or Solomon in the Orebro area during the late 1600's or early 1700's, it was suggested, by a genealogist in Orebro, that the name could have been Salmon, and later was mis-spelled into Salomon (the spelling used during Erich Salomon's lifetime). The surname Salmon or Salmonson is common to the Orebro region while the name Salomon is almost nonexistant in Sweden. Anyway Erich Salomon married Catharina Fröbsen (daughter of Johann Lorentz Fröbsen) on 10, April 1731 on 10, April 1731 at Gorsleben, he died 2, Feb. 1772 and she on 13, April 1748, both at Gorsleben. They had three children; 1. Adam Wilhelm (our ancestor) born 23, Jan. 1735 2. Juliane Sophia, born 1, July 1740 (died 28, June 1756) 3. Phillippine Christiane, DOB unknown, married _____Hildenhagen.

Our line continues with Adam W. Solomo (note the spelling) who married on 31, October 1762, Sophia Mioffsky (b. 24, Nov. 1732-d. 30, Dec. 1771) he died 15, March 1818. They had five children; 1. Friedrich Wilhelm, born 25, Sept. 1763, 2. Susanne Elenore, born 29, Aug. 1764, 3. Christiane Sophia , born 15, Oct. 1766 (died following day) 4. Jakob (our ancestor) born 20, Feb. 1768, 5. Johann Friedrich , born 28, Dec. 1770.

Our line continues with Jakob Salomo who married on 10, June 1794, Maria Katharina Peininger (daughter of Christopf Peininger- who was from Vilach, province of Carinthia, Austria) she was born 1768 in Bretleben (see enclosed map) and died 18 Aug. 1828, he died 7, Nov. 1829. They had three children; 1. Johann Wilhelm, born 26, Feb. 1793, 2. Johann Christoph (our ancestor) 2, Feb. 1799 3. Johann Friedrich, (lived in Brussels Belgium) born 18, Jan. 1808.

Our ancestor Johann Christoph married on 29, Dec. 1822, Marie Sophie Steinacker (daughter of Georg Steinacker) born 12, Nov. 1805 - died 28, Jan. 1832, they had three daughters, Sophia Dorothea Christoph b. 1824, Maria Elizabeth Christoph b. 1828, Hanna Dorothea Christoph b. 1831. Johann C's second wife was Maria Dorothea Jessing (daughter of Christoph Jessing) she was born in 1809 at Bilzingleben (see map) and died 15, Nov. 1880,he died 10, Mar. 1859, they were married 15, Mar. 1832 in Bilzingleben. They had eight children; 1. Marie Christiane born 14, Oct. 1833 - died 22, Feb. 1888, wife of Georg Schwabe - one child, 2. Christian Friedrich (our ancestor) born 21, Aug. 1835, married Sarah Jane Silbitz on 26, July 1865 at Hollidaysburg (Blair Co.) Pa (see enclosure) 3. Friedrich Wilhelm b. 1, Sep. 1837 d. 14, Sep. 1837 4. Friedrich Wilhelm b. 23, Sep. 1838 5. Christiane Friedericke b. 23, Jan. 1840 6. Amalie Dorothea b. 6, Oct. 1844 (emigrated with her brother, Christian F. our ancestor) to Canada in 1860, she married a man she met on the voyage to the new world. His last name was Fisher (Fischer?) and they lived in Canada. 7. Carl Christopf born 9, Mar. 1847 8. Augusta Marie Dorothea, born 26 Oct. 1853, died 2, April 1935 married to Eduard Kreitel in 1877 had three children 1. Johane Christiane Anna born 10, Jan. 1878 (married 8, April 1901 to Karl Otto Gephardt) one son Richard Erich. 2. Friedrich Karl, born 8, May 1883 (soldier in S.W. Africa in W.W.1) lived at Zwickau (Saxony) one daughter living 1985 named Hanna. 3. Berta Amalie Emilie, born 21, Jan. 1892, died 11, Dec. 1974 in Erfurt Germany, one daughter Ursurla, married to Dieter Henkel, live in Erfurt at Schlachthofstrasse 4.

Virtually all the Solomon men were either shoemakers or saddle makers. All the death, birth and marriage locations listed in the foregoing, unless otherwise stated, were at Gorsleben."

Christian Friedrich Solomon (1835-1914)

Christian Friedrich Solomon (21 Aug. 1835, Gorsleben, Germany, 9 June 1914, Hays, Ellis Co., Ks.), s/o Johann Christoph (Salomo) Solomon. & (2nd) m. Maria Dorothea Jessing Emigrated through Canada in 1860 to Hollidaysburg, Blair Co. Pa. Came over with Christoph Andreas Selbitz. (was a 1st cousin of Sarah Jane Selwitz) who settled at Altoona where he owned a grocery store.

Christian Friedrick Solomon arrived in America at the beginning of the Civil War and was a soldier with a year enlisted 18 July 1861.

Civil War Record of
Frederick Solomon

Enlisted: 18, July 1861, at Pittsbugh Pa., in Company 'B' of the 9th Pennsylvania Reserve Voolunteer Corps.

Fought: 21, July 1861, at 1st Manassas (1st Bull Run)
4, April 1862, Peninsular Campaign
6, April 1862, Battle of Shiloh.
26, June through 2, July 1862, Seven Days Battle, Gaines Mill and Malvern Hill Battles.
30, August 1862, 2nd Battle of Bull Run
17, September 1862, Antietam (Battle of Sharpsburg) - severely wounded.
13, December 1862, Battle of Fredericksburg.
23, January 1863, "Mud March" Campaign.
2, May 1863, Chancellorsville Battle
1-5, July 1863, Battle of Gettysburg.

Re-enlisted: November 1863 in Company 'K' 190th Pennsylvania Reserve Veteran Volunteers.
Fought: 5-7, May 1864, Wilderness Campaign.
10-12, May 1864, Spotsylvania Battle.
Mustered out: 3, July 1865, at Arlington Heights Va.
Pensioner of United States by certificate no. 686962

On one Civil War record, Friedrich Solomon was described as: "born in Germany, 29 years of age, 5 feet 7 inches high light complexion, blue eyes, light hair, occupation was enrolled_____Union Army."

Note: Friedrich Solomon mustered out 3 July 1865 at Arlington Heights, Va.

Friedrich Solomon m. 26 July 1865, Hollidaysburg, Alleghany twp., Blair Co., Pa. Miss. Sarah Jane Selbitz, d/o Johann Christian Selbitz & Anna (Hanna) Maria Seyferth, by Michael Wolf Preacher at Altoona, Pa. Their children, William E., Annie E., Christian Elmer, Bertha A., Charles F., Annetta M. (Nellie), Emma Elizabeth, Friedrich W., Lucille Alma, Ida Belle, Henry Frank, & Infant d.y. Solomon. Moved to Ks. in 1876 Wheatland twp Ellis Co., Ks. (see Selbitz Family)

Christian Frederick Solomon (1835 Ger - 1910), and Sara Jane (Selbitz) Solomon (1846-1932)

1. William E. Solomon (19 June 1866 Altoona, Pa. 14 Sept. 1945, Mt. Allen Cem.) Hays, Ks., m. 31 Jan. 1893, (home of George Palmer, Ellis, Ks.) Mennie M. Sessin (14 Oct. 1868, Germany -5 May 1957, Mt. Allen Cem.). (Mennie M. Sessin, became a U.S. Citizen -1884) ch.: Rose B. Solomon, William E. Solomon, Ida B. Solomon, and Lawrence Solomon.

2. Annie E. Solomon (Oct. 1867, Altoona, Pa.,-21 Oct. 1924, Mt. Allen Cem.) Hays, Ks. m. George A. Palmer, (13 Apr. 1842-29 May 1917)

3. Christian Elmer Solomon (30 Dec. 1869, Altoona, Pa., 5 Dec. 1940, Mt. Hope Cem.) Ellis, Ks. m. 12 Aug. 1902, Florance Laura Burnham, (10 Oct. 1875, Elk Co. Ks 25 Dec. 1959, Ellis Co. Ks.) d/o James Douglas & America May (Fry) Burnham. ch.: Inez Lucille Solomon, Frank Fredrick Solomon, & Florance America Solomon.

- Inez Lucille Solomon (17 June 1903, Ellis Co. Ks.) m. 17 Sept. 1921, Wakeeney, Trego Co. Ks. Lee Elias Wagoner (5 Mar. 1899, Trego Co. Ks. -13 May 1988 Rogers, Ark.) Their children Elvena Blanche Wagoner, Marvin Lee Wagoner, Anna Lee Wagoner, Robert Dale Wagoner, Norman Leroy Wagoner, & Darrel Eugene Wagoner. (see Waggoner Family)
- Frank Friedrich Solomon (10 Dec. 1904-21 Dec. 1988, Mt. Hope Cem.) Ellis Co. Ks.
- Florance America Solomon (25 Feb. 1907, Ellis Co., Ks.-20 Feb. 1988, Arlington, Tx) m. Hugh Burnett s/o Richard Burnett (4 Jan. 1901-6 Dec. 1966) Hays, Ks. ch.: Richard E. Burnett & Donald Hugh Burnett.

Obit. for Elmer Solomon ae. 74 y. a pioneer resident of Ellis Co. Ks. d. at his home 7 mi. southeast of Ellis. Dec. 5, 1940. Mr. Solomn had lived in this county the past 65 years, comming here when a boy in 1876. Surviving Mr. Solomon; are his widow Mrs. Solomon, dau. Mrs. Lee Wagoner, Arkansas & Mrs. Hugh Burnett of Hays, and one son Frank Solomon of the Lome. Sisters, Mrs. H. H. King & Mrs. Frank King of Hays, Mrs. Ida Riser, Manhattan Beach, Calif. & Brothers, Will Solomon of Zurich & Fred Solomon, of Hays, Ks.

4. Bertha A. Solomon, (12 Apr. 1872 Altoona, Pa. 7 June 1924 Denver, Colo.) bur. Mt. Allen Cem. Hays, Ks.

5. Charles F. Solomon. b. Dec 1872, Altoona, Pa. m. Emma Stegman, lived Kansas City, Mo.

6. Annetta M. (Nellie) Solomon, (28 Apr. 1874, Altoona, Pa. -1936) Ellis Co. Ks. m. 25 Dec. 1898,

7. Emma Elizabeth Solomon, (1 Sept. 1880, Wheatland twp., Ellis Co., Ks. 7 June 1964), Hays, Ellis Co. Ks., m. 20 Sept. 1903, Frank King (29 Jan. 1878-23 Nov. 1951) ch.: Gretchen Lucinda King (1908-1920).

8. Friedrick W. Solomon (7 Jan. 1883, Wheatland twp., 29 Oct. 1955 Mt. Allen Cem.) Hays, Ks. m. Elizabeth (Lizzie) Troth.

9. Lucille Alma Solomon, (27 Jan. 1885, Ellis Co. Ks. 21 Apr. 1961) Hays Ks., m. 12 Sept. 1905, Ellis, Ks. Harry H. King (1883-1958)

10. Ida Belle Solomon (7 Oct. 1889-Ellis Co. Ks. 28 May 1985) Manhattan Beach, Ca. m. 10 Sept. 1917 Alma, Harlan Co. Nebr, Raymond Lawrence Riser. ch: Betty Irene Riser b. 19 Feb.1919 m. 1943 Wilmer Lester Drake--ch.: Raymond Lawrence Drake, Larry Alan Drake, Don Wayne Drake, & Diane Marie Drake.

11. Henry Frank Solomon, (16 Sept. 1878-20 Oct. 1879) Ellis Co. Ks.

12. Another son died in infancy.

Fredireck & Sarah Jane (Selbitz) Solomon had a family of 6 sons & 6 daughters. He was wounded at battle near Sharpsburg 17 Sept. 1862- (severely wounded) Antietam and recieved a pension of $30.00, which was dropped because of death 9 June 1914 and Sarah J. Solomon recieved a widows pension of $12.00 per month to commence June 15, 1914.

The Hays Free Press, Hays, Ellis County, Kansas, June 13, 1914

"Christian Frederick Solomon, soldier, citizen and churchman, after being a long time an invalid sufferer passed away Tuesday morning June 9th. The brief facts of his life were read at the furnel, from his own handwriting. Born in Gorsleben, Prussia, August 21, 1835. Came to America in June 1860 and enlisted in the Union Army in Company B. 9th Penn. Reserve Corps, July 18, 1861 at Pittsburgh, Pa. He re-enlisted in November 1863 in Company K, 190th Penn. Reserve Veteran Volunteers. Mustered out of service July 3, 1865. Thus showing that he served throughout the war and from the records we know that he was in many of the hottest battles.

He came to Kansas in September 1876 and made his home in Hays where he reared his family of ten children, four sons and six daughters, two boys living died in infancy. His wife who survived him and the ten children are well-known to the people of the community. He was one of the pioneers of Kansas and as he served in many battles and long marches, so he battled with the frontier conditions so well known to the early settlers of Kansas.

Mr. Solomon was of a Lutheran lineage, baptised in infancy, confirmed at the age of fourteen, and has lived a communicant member of the Lutheran church all his life. He was aged 78 years, 10 months, 13 days. His furneral was from the Lutheran church, Rev. H. P.

Alexander preaching the sermon in the absence of the pastor, who is on his vacation.

He was a member of the Hays Post. His comrades gave him the full ritual service and military burial at the grave, assisted by the Sons of Veterans, who also marched in column and uniform. The casket was decorated with national colors and many floral tributes."

OBITUARY

"Sarah Jane Solomon was born July 20, 1846 in Holidaysburg, Penn. Her parents were Mr. and Mrs. Johann Christian & Anna (Hanna) Maria (Seyferth) Selbitz. She was one of seven children. During her childhood she attended the public schools of her time. At the age of 19 years she was united in marriage with Frederick Solomon at Altoona, Pa., on July 26, 1865. Their union was blessed with eleven children-three have entered eternity--and the following eight are surviving her viz: William Solomon and Elmer Solomon of Ellis county, Nettie Gerken Solomon, Ellis; Charles Solomon, Kansas City, Mo.; Emma King Solomon, Hays; Lucille King Solomon, Hays; Fred Solomon, Hays ; Ida Reiser Solomon, Los Angeles, Calif. There also survive 29 Grandchildren - five dead; 14 great-grandchildren-two dead.

She was instructed in Luther's Catechism and at the proper age she was confirmed a Lutheran. She knew what her church taught and was proud in the knowledge that she was permitted here in her western home to worship her Lord in the faith of her Fathers.

Together with her husband and family she came to Ellis county in 1876, 56 years ago, and settled on a homestead near the Phillip's ranch. They were amongst, the earliest pioneers in Kansas, enduring, suffering, hoping, working, winning. She was the last of her family.

Hers was a long and useful life, she had reached the great age of 85 years; 7 months; 4 days.

The declining years of her life were spent at the home of her daughter and son-in-law, Mr. and Mrs. Harry H. King

St. Bonifacius Church
Gorsleben, Germany

Selbitz Family

Please credit The Hon. Raymond Drake for the German Research.

Selbitz Family-Church Records- Gorsleben, Germany.

The Selbitz research in Germany was also in Gorsleben, and records in St. Bonifacius Church, Pastor Adolf Hoffmann.

The first record of this line:

Hanns Georg Selbitz b. ca. 1625 in Kannawurf, Germany,

- His son; Hanns Caspar Selbitz, b. ca. 1650, Kannawurf.
  - His son, Hanns Nicholas Selbitz-b. ca. 1675 in Kannawurf, m. 1697 in Gorsleben, Magdelena Borns.
    - Their son, Johann Samuel Selbitz b. ca. 1700-wife, Sophia Eckhardin.
      - Their son. Johann Gottfried Friedrich Selbitz b. 3 Oct. 1738, Gorsleben, Germany wife Anna Dorothea Kaorper in Esperstodt. ST. Bonifacius Church records: Gorsleben, Germany.
        - Their son: Johann Adam Selbitz b. 1764, Esperstedt, Thuringa, Germany d. 26 Mar. 1823, Gorsleben, Thuringa, Germany, Laborer, Lutheran.

First Family of Johann Adam Selbitz:

1st (wife) Maria Elizabeth Krauthaus (Commonlaw)

Children:

1. Johann Gottlieb Conrad Selbitz (22 Sept. 1795-18 Nov. 1870) Gorsleben. m. 7 July 1822-Gorsleben, Dorothea Henrietta Kuhnast. (b. 1802 d/o Johann Gottlieb Kuhnast and Elizabeth Andrain. ch.: Andreas Selbitz (13 May 1825-29 Jan. 1828) Johann Friedrich Selbitz-b. 18 July 1827, Maria Dorothea Selbitz, b. 30 Oct. 1829. Johann Gerog Gottlieb Selbitz b. 22 Apr. 1833, Christoph Andreas Selbitz, b. 5 Apr. 1835. He emmigrated to America ca. 1860 with Friedrich Solomon. There are still decendents of Christian Selbitz living in Blair Co. Pa.

2. Johann Christian Selbitz (1 Apr. 1798 Gorsleben, d. 25 Dec. 1875, Carson Valley Blair Co. Pa.) m. 1 Aug. 1826, Gosleben, Germany. Friederike Wilhelmina Seyferth, (27 June 1794, Gunzerode, Province of Thuringa, Germany. d. 13 Oct. 1880, Carson Valley, Blair Co. Pa. (see this Family in Pa.)

Second Family of Johann Adam Selbitz:

Johann Adam Selbitz m. 18 Jan. 1799 Gorsleben, Christianan Sophia Krauthaus b. 1764-Esperstedt, Thuringa, Germany d. 30 Mar. 1826, Gorsleben, Germany.

Children:

3. Anna Maria Catharine Selbitz-(24 Dec. 1799),

4. Johann Gottfried Christoph Selbitz (27 May 1802-2 June 1802),

5. Johann Gerog Andreas Selbitz (1 May 1807, Gorsleben,) m. 5 Jan. 1834-Dorotha Maria Huffnagle, Gosleben. They emmigrated to America where Johann Gerog Andreas Selbitz died in 1885, Carson Valley, Blair Co. Pa.

Family of Johann Christian Selbitz:

This family must have emmigrted between, 1842 and 1846, because the first five children were born in Gorsleben, Germany and their birth records are in the St. Bonifacius Church there. Two children were born in Pa.

Johann Christian Silbitz (1798-Ger. 1875-Blair Co. Pa.) s/o Johann Adam Selbitz & Maria Elizabeth Krauthaus. m. Friederike Wilhelmina Seyferth (1794 Ger., 1880 Blair Co. Pa.) In census Anna (Hanna) Maria Selbitz. Both spellings of the name Selbitz and Selwitz are found in the Blair Co. Pa. records.

Children of Johann and Friederike Wilhelmina (Seyferth) Silbitz:

- Christian Gottlieb Selbitz, b. 21 Feb. 1827 Gorsleben, Ger. d. 4 Jan. 1895, Carson Valley Cem. Carson Valley, Blair Co. Pa.
- Anna Maria Selbitz, (20 Apr. 1830 Ger., -3 Jan. 1892 Altoona, Blair Co. Pa.) m. 10 Apr. 1849 Hollidaysburg, Pa. William Christian Brenneke.
- Carl Friedrich Selbitz b. 17 Mar. 1832, Ger. Carl's name is shown as Charles Selwitz, b. ca. 1833, Ger. so we show this record in the <u>Beographical & Partrait Cyclopedia of Cambria Co. Pa.</u> by Southwest Pa. Gen. Services pg 452.

  Dr. John Murphy b. 23 Sept. 1855, Edensbury, Cambria Co. Pa. s/o John & Lucenda (Todd) Murphy (Irish descent). m. 14 April 1879, Miss Annie Selbitz, a daughter of Charles Selbitz of Gallitzen, Pa.

  Their children; Marie, Katie (dec.), Maggie, Nillie & Charles (dec.) Murphy.

Credit Lloyd Keckler of Florida, who helped research this family in Pa.
- Andreas Julius Selbitz (20 Apr. 1834-Gorsleben, Ger. d. 5 Apr. 1909 Allegany twp. Blair Co. Pa. bur. Carson Valley Cem. m. 1 Dec. 1859 Newry, Blair Co. Pa. Mary Stom (25 Jan. 1839-5 Nov. 1916 Carson Valley Cem.) Blair Co. Pa. d/o George Stom-b. Ger., possibly Wortenburg and Catherine Grows. Andreas Julius had a name change to Anthony V. Selbitz. Their children:
  - Anna Selwitz b. ca. 1860 m. Elmer (?Yingring) lived Altoona Pa.
  - Sarah Elizabeth Selwitz, b. 10 Nov. 1861, Altoona, Pa. m. 26 Mar. 1938, John J. Glaichert. Rose Hill Cem.
  - Christian M. Selwitz-(3 Dec. 1863, Muleshee, Allegheny twp. Blair Co. Pa., 7 June 1939). Carson Valley Cem. Blair Co. Pa. m. 10 Jan. 1884, Emma Jane Brubaker (14 Nov. 1865-5 Feb. 1940) Blair Co. Pa. d/o Ephraim Brubaker & Lydia (Hart). ch.: Mary C. Selwitz (6 July 1884-d. 1884), and Lydia C. Selwitz (26 May 1885-d. 21 Dec. 1888).
    - Grover Selwitz (28 Oct. 1887-12 Apr. 1913) killed by train P.R.R. Altoona Pa. m. Clarissa Wilt Ch. Viola & Margarita Selwitz.
    - Flora Selwitz (1 Jan. 1890-2 Nov. 1964) Duncansville, Blair Co. Pa. m. Roy K. Davis (son of Roy) Kenneth Davis. bur. Carson Valley Cem.

- ◊ Grace Ella Selwitz-(15 Sept 1892-23 Nov. 1973 Wickliffe, Coyahoga Co. Ohio) m. Harry Lloyd Keckler_ bur. Crown Hill Cem. ch.: Lloyd Harry Keckler, Donald Arthur Keckler, and Carl Raymond Keckler.
- ◊ Rhoda Selwitz-b. 3 Jan.1895 Blair Co. Pa. m. Frank E. Biser ch. Madaline Biser, and William Biser.
- ◊ Albert Selwitz (3 June 1897-24 Aug. 1973- Alto Reste Cem. Altoona, Blair Co. Pa. m. Ethel Forsht, ch.: Hugh Selwitz & Francas Selwitz.

- ♦ John R. Selwitz b. ca. 1864-5 Carson Valley. m. Ida _____ (2 daughters)
- ♦ Mary E. (Mollie) Selwitz (1 Jan. 1869-30 Jan. 1962) Altoona, Pa. m. Samuel Brubaker.
- ♦ Margaret (Maggie) G. Selwitz (1875-1950) m. Charles Campbell, Carson Valley Pa.
- ♦ Emma Selwitz b. 1872-Blair Co. Pa. m. L. A. "Ollie" McConnell.
- ♦ Clara Selwitz-28 Mar. 1877-16 Jan. 1935) Blair Co. Pa. m. Elmer Turnbaugh, 18 Oct. 1901.
- ♦ William C. Selwitz b. Aug. 1879-Blair Co. Pa. m. Dorothy.

- Maria Augusta Selwitz, (b. 29 Dec. 1841, Gorsleben, Ger. m. 9 Feb. 1860 Newry Pa. Charles Caltaraugh.
- Sarah Jane Selwitz, (20 July 1846, Blair Co. Pa.-24 Feb. 1932, Hays, Ellis Co., Ks. m. 26 July 1865 Altoona, Pa. Christian Friedrick Solomon. (see Solomon line)
- Susan E. Selwitz b. ca. 1848 Blair Co. Pa.

The Blair Co. Pa. records show the names Christian Selintz (Selwitz) and wife refered to as Anna Maria, the dates are right and one finds the American spelling mostly Selwitz. The stones in the cemeteries all show Selwitz.

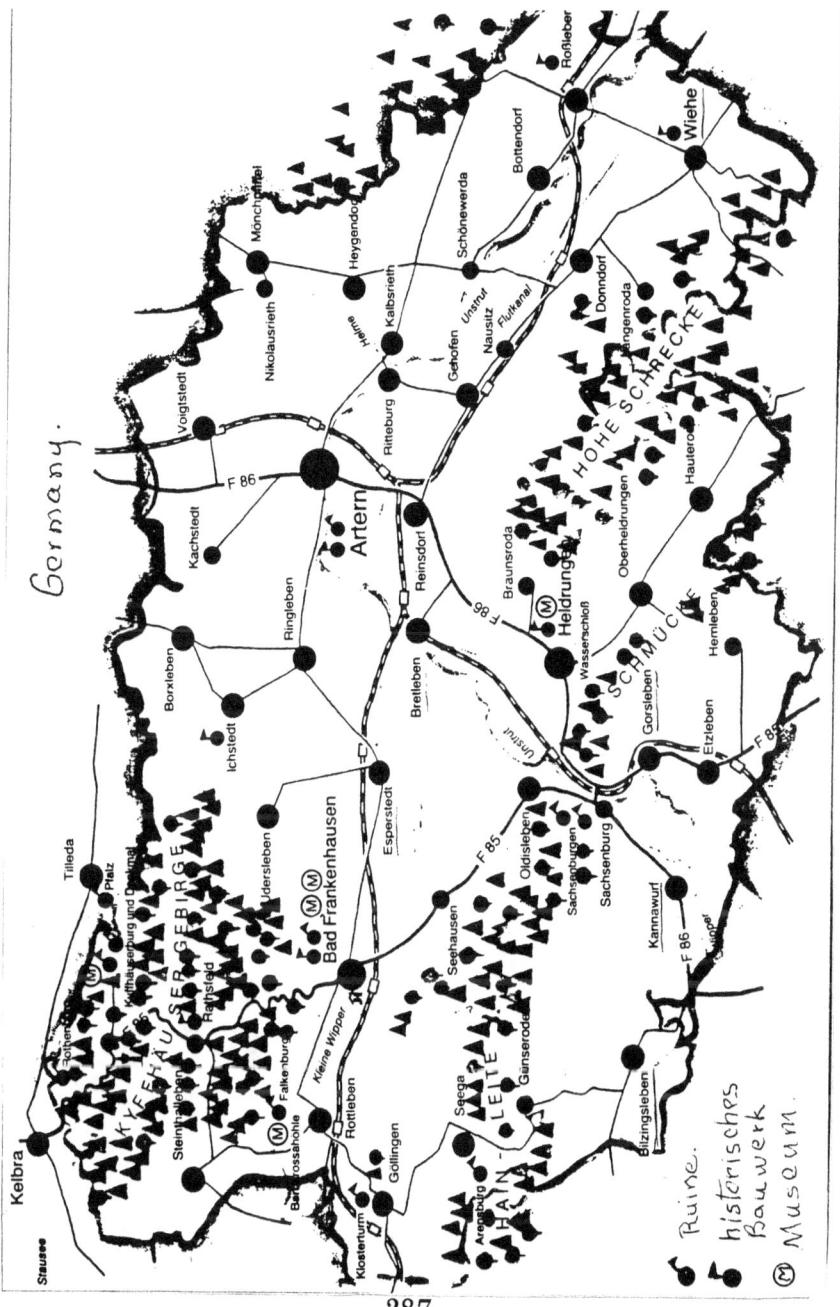

Index

Abbott, Biven, 220
Abbott, Nancy A., 220
Adair, Kenneth, Sr., 215
Ake, Catherine (Fry), 273
Ake, David, 273
Alexander, Wm., 145
Alkire, Benjamin, 66
Alkire, Elizabeth, 59, 107
Alkire, George Washington, 59
Alkire, John, 59, 64
Alkire, Margaret, 59
Alkire, Margaret V., 63
Alkire, Martha, 59, 107
Alkire, Mary, 59
Alkire, Nancy, 182
Alkire, Nicholas, 58
Alkire, Nicholas D., 59
Alkire, Nicholas Jr., 59
Alkire, Samuel, 59
Alkire, William Harrison, 59
Allen, Susan, 161
Allman Family in West Virginia, 199
Allman, Abraham, 217, 219, 222, 223, 224, 225
Allman, Abraham (Abram) Junior, 225
Allman, Abraham, children, 226
Allman, Abraham, Will of, 226
Allman, Albert Morgan, 208, 209
Allman, Alexander Simpson, 220
Allman, Alfred Wesley, 221
Allman, Alice M, 205
Allman, Alice May, 213
Allman, Alice Vertenice, 226
Allman, Alma B., 209
Allman, Amrose Kittorah, 211
Allman, Anna B., 209
Allman, Arrilius, 225
Allman, Aubra Roscoe, 209

Allman, Aurilla, 219, 222
Allman, Barbara, 217, 219
Allman, Bertie Cleveland, 206
Allman, C. R., 26, 55
Allman, Catharine, 106
Allman, Catherine, 216, 219, 233
Allman, Catherine A., 207
Allman, Christopher C., 203
Allman, Clyde Dale, 209
Allman, Cornelius J. D., 226
Allman, Daisy Florence, 209
Allman, David Alonso, 213
Allman, David Day, 228
Allman, David S., 201, 208, 213, 216
Allman, David S. (Stanton), 211, 214
Allman, David Thomas, 210
Allman, Davisson Gaston, 205
Allman, Desky Virginia, 206
Allman, Eber P., 205
Allman, Eddy C. (female), 207
Allman, Edward L., 70
Allman, Edward Lee, 228
Allman, Eleanor (Cleanor), 217
Allman, Eliza, 208
Allman, Eliza Irene, 210
Allman, Elizabeth, 67, 208, 217, 225, 226, 228
Allman, Elizabeth (Bonnett) & Madison children, 205, 206, 207
Allman, Elizabeth Jane, 204
Allman, Elizabreth (Weatherholt), 233
Allman, Ella M., 204
Allman, Elva Vetra, 222
Allman, Emery V., 205
Allman, Emma Jane, 228
Allman, Ernestine Ann, 204
Allman, Eva Casto, 219
Allman, Evert F., 205

Index

Allman, Fernando Wood, 205
Allman, Flora Aldine, 213
Allman, G. W., 218
Allman, Geo. W., 208
Allman, George, 217, 218, 219, 223
Allman, George A., 207
Allman, George McClellum, 213
Allman, George W., 207, 208
Allman, George William, 217
Allman, George, Commission Certificate, 222
Allman, Gillette Andrew, 222
Allman, Harold, 209
Allman, Harrison T., 222
Allman, Harrison Theodore, 221
Allman, Harvey Ugena, 204
Allman, Hendrix, 200
Allman, Henrich, 200
Allman, Henry Irvin, 206
Allman, Ida M., 207
Allman, Ida N., 215
Allman, Isaac, 219, 234
Allman, Isaac Marion, 226, 227, 228
Allman, Isaac Newton, 204
Allman, Isaac Upton, 206
Allman, J. M., 218
Allman, Jacob, 200, 216, 222, 234
Allman, Jacob 'Jake' Marion, 218
Allman, Jacob Marion, 218
Allman, Jacob Presley, 211
Allman, Jake, 215
Allman, James David, 205
Allman, James J., 208
Allman, James Madison, 203, 206
Allman, James Robert, 228
Allman, Jannattah May, 215
Allman, Jasper Sylvester, 206
Allman, Jefferson, 220
Allman, Jesse Lee, 214
Allman, John, 200, 201, 216
Allman, John Columbus, 205
Allman, John E., 204
Allman, John K., 214
Allman, John L., 199, 219
Allman, Joseph B., 206
Allman, Kasper Kimball, 209
Allman, L. M., 204
Allman, Lenora May, 206
Allman, Lewis (Louis) Madison, 205
Allman, Lloyd Manor, 212
Allman, Lloyd Samuel, 204
Allman, Lon V., 208
Allman, Lucinda, 225
Allman, Lurana, 221
Allman, Lydia Elizabeth, 205
Allman, M. (Mascena), 223
Allman, Madison, 70, 204, 208
Allman, Madison & Elizabeth (Bonnett) children, 205, 206, 207
Allman, Margaret, 204
Allman, Margaret E, 205
Allman, Mariam, 204
Allman, Martha Catherine, 206
Allman, Martha E., 204
Allman, Martin Post, 203
Allman, Mary, 216, 233
Allman, Mary Catherine, 206, 209, 210
Allman, Mary Elizabeth, 217, 219, 224
Allman, Mary Ellen, 207
Allman, Mary J. (Bean), 224
Allman, Matilda Fay, 206
Allman, Michael, 219, 223
Allman, Mildred, 213
Allman, Myrtle Belle, 215
Allman, Nancy Elizabeth, 207
Allman, Nancy Jane, 226
Allman, Nathan, 218, 219, 225
Allman, Nathan and Elizabeth Bligh children, 220, 221

Index

Allman, Nettie C., 207
Allman, Nicholas, 217, 229, 234
Allman, Novel Evans, 211
Allman, Ola, 215
Allman, Orion Francis, 203
Allman, Orval Lee, 227
Allman, Paul McPherson, 212
Allman, Peter, 106, 203, 208, 226
Allman, Peter Cecil, 212
Allman, Peter David, 202, 216
Allman, Peter Elihu, 209
Allman, Peter T., 203
Allman, Phillip Madison, 204
Allman, Phoebe, 220, 226
Allman, R. C., 205
Allman, Roscoe C., 227
Allman, Samuel B., 203
Allman, Sarah, 208
Allman, Sarah A., 205
Allman, Sarah Catherine, 208, 212, 224
Allman, Sarah E., 205, 223
Allman, Sarah Jane, 207
Allman, Sarah Margaret C., 204
Allman, Susannah L., 208
Allman, Sylvanius Columbus, 205
Allman, Talitha Jane, 210
Allman, Theodore Sylvester, 211
Allman, Thomas M., 221
Allman, Vada Columbia, 207
Allman, Valentine, 219
Allman, Virgil Henry, 227
Allman, Virginia Olive, 212
Allman, Wade E., 209
Allman, Wade Hampton, 207
Allman, William, 70, 200, 201, 202, 208, 209, 218, 219, 224, 229, 233
Allman, William (1), 216, 217, 222
Allman, William (1838), 224

Allman, William and Margaret Jane Echard children, 209
Allman, William Columbus, 214
Allman, William Francis, 211
Allman, William Franklin, 223
Allman, William Jefferson, 221, 226
Alman, Cora, 224
Alman, John, 200
Alman, William, 201
Almon, Catharine, 234
Anderson, John, 61
Anderson, Lt. John, 268
Andrain, Elizabeth, 284
Andrew, John F., 204
Andrews, Enoch W., 204
Anna, Johane Christiane, 276
Arbogast, Mary, 83
Arbogast, Peter, 83
Arbogast, Sarah, 83
Archer, Stephen, 52
Arlene, Joyce, 240
Arment, Ray, 249
Armstead, John B., 217
Armstrong, Catharine, 98
Armstrong, Mary Margaret, 71
Armstrong, Maxwell, 98
Arnold, Elijah, 146
Arnold, George, 81
Arnold, Robert, 163
Atkins, Catharine (B. W.), 183
Atkins, John, 182
Atkins, John G., 183
Atkins, Louisa, 182
Atkins, Richard N., 181, 182, 183
Atkins, Samuel M., 183
Atkins, William H., 182
Ayers, Lynne, 249

Babcock, John, 83
Bailey, Alstopius, 215
Bailey, B. T., 204

Index

Bailey, Benjamin Franklin, 176
Bailey, Bernard, 214
Bailey, Blackwell T., 215
Bailey, Blackwell Taylor, 215
Bailey, Bryon Pitt, 212
Bailey, Cordelia, 215
Bailey, Edward D, 68
Bailey, Florance B., 164
Bailey, Gladys, 214
Bailey, Guy, 209
Bailey, Nancy Cordelia, 215
Baily, Wm. J., 144
Baird, Adam, 73
Baird, Barbara (Wilhelm), 73
Baird, Mary, 73
Baker, James, 71
Baker, Nemimce, 50
Ball, Eliza C. (Reed), 254
Ball, George, 254
Ball, Harriet, 254
Ball, Jas., 109
Ball, M., 109
Ball, Martha, 254
Ball, Nancy Ann, 107, 109
Ball, Robert, 254
Ball, Sarah Jane, 112
Ballard, Edward H., 100
Bancroft, Mark, 41
Banet, Ludwig, 48
Bankhead, Euphemia, 215
Barb, Abraham, 214
Barb, Jessie Mae, 214
Barb, Lillie Mae, 214
Barb, Margaret Esther, 213
Barb, Philip E., 212, 213, 214
Barb, Sarah Ellen, 212
Bargerhuff, James, 158
Bargerhuff, Abner, 112, 158
Bargerhuff, Letisia, 158
Bargerhuff, Margaret (Reger), 112
Bargerhuff, Romeo, 112

Barlting, Wm., Rev., 260
Barnes, Harry, 250
Barnes, Jacob, 49
Barnes, James, 202
Barnes, Joseph, 249
Barnes, Rosanna, 49
Barnham, Josiah, 269
Barr, Mary K., 162
Barron, Benjamin, 245
Barstods, Myrtle M., 261
Bartholmew, Roy, 154
Barton, Rose, 176
Batten, Ara, 106
Batten, David, Rev., 208, 212
Batten, Kitturah, 210
Batten, Lydia, 209
Batten, Mary, 68
Batten, Richard, 212
Batten, Richard L., 207
Batten, Thomas, 182, 209, 210
Batten, Virginia L., 207, 208
Batton, Caroline, 67
Batton, Margaret (Mary), 176
Batton, Richard, 67
Baumann, Belle, 260
Baumann, Benjamin B., 260
Baumann, Catharine (Dunkel), 260
Baumann, George, 260
Baumann, George Edward, 260
Baumann, George Karl Theadour, 260
Baumann, Georgetta, 260
Baumann, Herman Wm., 260
Baumann, Katy Louisa, 260
Baumann, Noble, 260
Bean, Andrew, 224
Bean, Arminda, 224
Bean, Henry I., 224
Bean, Mary Jane, 224
Beanas, Polly (Mary), 239
Beatrice, F. Skinner, 215

Index

Beaty, Barbara A., 238
Beech, John, 167
Beeghley, Barl, 113
Beeghley, Caroline Norris Hall, 113
Beeghley, Cora, 212
Beeghley, Ethel, 113
Beeghley, Evelyn, 113
Beeghley, John, 113
Beeghley, Richard H., 113
Beeghley, Wirt, 113
Bell, Martha E., 206
Belt, Jamie, 107
Bemis, Elizabeth, 267
Bemis, Joseph, 267
Bender, Maria Margaretha, 45
Benderin, Apollonia, 12
Benderin, Christina, 12
Benderin, Margaretha, 11
Benderin, Maria Margaretha, 11, 12
Benderin, Marian Johanne, 11
Bennett, Anna, 177
Bennett, Charity, 179
Bennett, Jacob, 177, 185
Bennett, Martha, 177
Bennett, Richard, 177
Benson, Mrs. C.L. (Lohr), 254
Bent, George, 107
Berry, Andrew Jackson, 221
Berry, Connie Golden, 221
Berry, Ephran A., 85
Berry, G. A., 221
Berry, Hannah Loverna (McCray), 103
Berry, Mary Melessa, 103
Berry, William D., 103
Bibbee, Joseph, 58
Biers, Bessie, 151
Biers, Frank, 151
Biers, Maxie, 151
Biggs, Betsey, 247
Bird, Ella, 113

Biser, Frank E., 286
Biser, Madaline, 286
Biser, William, 286
Bishop, Clifford, 152
Bitts, Abigail, 265
Black, Abe, 222
Blankenship, George P., 178
Blankenship, Millie, 178
Bleigh, Elizabeth, 220, 225
Blickenstaff, John, 244
Bligh, James, 220
Bliss, Ed, 240
Bliss, Emma (Moede), 249, 253
Bliss, Esther Maria, 253
Bliss, Freda, 249, 253
Bliss, Hazel, 240
Bliss, Mary Hannah (Jones), 240
Bliss, Michael, 249, 253
Bliss, Tillie, 251
Bockstruck, Lloyd DeWitt, 35, 119
Bogard, Cornellius, 233
Bogart, Mary Ann, 233
Bolton, Mary A., 209
Bond, Mary, 203
Bonet, Jaques (Jacob), 16
Bonnet, Barbara, 42, 43
Bonnet, Benjamin, 43
Bonnet, Elizabeth, 43, 47
Bonnet, Eva, 43
Bonnet, Jacob, 15
Bonnet, John, 42, 43
Bonnet, Lewis, 41, 42, 43
Bonnet, Lewis Jr., 42
Bonnet, Lewis, Will of, 42, 43
Bonnet, Mary, 42
Bonnet, Simon, 43
Bonnett, Addy Maude, 211
Bonnett, Ann, 68
Bonnett, Anna Elizabeth (Waggoner), 26, 32
Bonnett, Azariah S., 68

Index

Bonnett, Barbara, 41, 72
Bonnett, C. M., 215
Bonnett, Caroline Y., 68
Bonnett, Catharine, 8, 18, 67, 141, 155
Bonnett, Catherine, 62, 181
Bonnett, Charlathy, 80
Bonnett, Charlotta (Hyde), 60
Bonnett, Christina, 7, 17
Bonnett, Daniel R., 66
Bonnett, David, 67
Bonnett, David S., 67, 68
Bonnett, Deannah, 70
Bonnett, Deborah (Debby), 70
Bonnett, Delilah, 60
Bonnett, Edgar H., 67
Bonnett, Eli M., 211
Bonnett, Elias, 106
Bonnett, Elias H., 107
Bonnett, Elias Hughes, 68
Bonnett, Elisabetha, 48
Bonnett, Eliza, 61
Bonnett, Eliza Louise, 71
Bonnett, Elizabeth, 8, 16, 18, 20, 40, 41, 57, 58, 60, 64, 65, 72, 73, 80, 106, 203, 204
Bonnett, Elizabeth (Betsy), 70
Bonnett, Elizabeth (Waggoner), 40, 41, 42
Bonnett, Elizabeth W., 71
Bonnett, Elmira, 60
Bonnett, G. H., 71
Bonnett, George W., 68
Bonnett, Grace, 60
Bonnett, Granville N., 60
Bonnett, Greenberry C., 69
Bonnett, H. R., 157
Bonnett, H. R., Rev., 205
Bonnett, Harriet, 60, 69, 80
Bonnett, Harriet A., 68
Bonnett, Henrietta V., 68

Bonnett, Henry, 57
Bonnett, Henry Harrison, 69
Bonnett, Henry R., 84, 123, 124, 179, 191, 193, 195, 206
Bonnett, Henry Radcliff, Rev., 68, 107
Bonnett, Ida, 72
Bonnett, Isabelle, 41
Bonnett, Jacob, 17, 18, 19, 20, 58, 74, 80
Bonnett, Jacob H., 60, 80
Bonnett, Jacob Wesley, 63
Bonnett, Jacque (Jacob), 7, 17, 56
Bonnett, Jane, 41, 70
Bonnett, Joel M., 68
Bonnett, Johan Semon, 17
Bonnett, John, 41, 42, 57, 67, 90, 142
Bonnett, John A., 71
Bonnett, John C., 68
Bonnett, John K., 69
Bonnett, John Simon, 7, 56
Bonnett, John T., 66
Bonnett, L. C., 72
Bonnett, Lewis, 7, 18, 21, 26, 27, 34, 35, 39, 41, 55, 58, 61, 63, 65, 92, 93, 95, 106
Bonnett, Lewis B., 70
Bonnett, Lewis Barzilla, 69
Bonnett, Lewis Capt., 40
Bonnett, Lewis Jr., 31, 41
Bonnett, Lewis Jr., Maj., 8, 18, 19, 20, 26, 27, 28, 32, 39, 41, 55
Bonnett, Lewis M., 69
Bonnett, Lewis Sr., 20, 55
Bonnett, Lewis Sr., Capt., 27
Bonnett, Louise, 71
Bonnett, Lucenda, 41
Bonnett, Lucinda, 60, 63
Bonnett, Lydia Ann, 68
Bonnett, M. Florence, 72

Index

Bonnett, Mansfield, 60, 80
Bonnett, Margaret, 7, 55, 62, 65, 73, 78
Bonnett, Margaret (Linger), 61, 65, 99
Bonnett, Margaret (Peggy), 57, 89
Bonnett, Margaret A., 68
Bonnett, Margaret E., 66
Bonnett, Margaret M., 67
Bonnett, Margareth Catharine, 18
Bonnett, Margarit, 71
Bonnett, Margret, 17
Bonnett, Margt (Margaret), 99
Bonnett, Marietta, 71
Bonnett, Martha, 61, 67, 70, 72, 106
Bonnett, Martha (Hughes), 80
Bonnett, Martha (Radcliff), 70, 155, 181
Bonnett, Martha Belinda, 69
Bonnett, Mary, 7, 8, 16, 18, 19, 20, 41, 62, 64, 65, 73, 74, 94, 100
Bonnett, Mary (Polly), 65
Bonnett, Mary A., 66
Bonnett, Mary D., 59
Bonnett, Mary Elizabeth, 58, 65, 67, 72, 73, 74, 89, 90
Bonnett, Mary L., 67
Bonnett, Matilda, 59, 67, 71
Bonnett, Matilda H., 68
Bonnett, Mifflin, 70
Bonnett, Minerva, 67
Bonnett, Mitilda, 71
Bonnett, Nancy J., 71
Bonnett, Nathan, 60
Bonnett, Nathan S., 80
Bonnett, Newton John, 66
Bonnett, Nicholas, 62
Bonnett, Nicholas H., 72
Bonnett, Nicholas L., 66
Bonnett, Nicholas M., 73
Bonnett, Otho, 69

Bonnett, Peregrine, 60
Bonnett, Periguine, 80
Bonnett, Perry G., 80
Bonnett, Perry Green, 59
Bonnett, Peter, 61, 65, 66, 74, 99
Bonnett, Philip, 73, 177
Bonnett, S. A., 72
Bonnett, Sally (Sarah), 71
Bonnett, Samual, 58
Bonnett, Samuel, 18, 35, 41, 55, 56, 57, 59, 65, 67, 69, 70, 71, 72, 73, 74, 89, 90, 144, 155, 181, 203
Bonnett, Samuel Baxter, 68
Bonnett, Samuel H., 60, 80
Bonnett, Samuel Jasper, 62
Bonnett, Samuel Jr., 67, 146
Bonnett, Samuel L., 66
Bonnett, Sarah, 41, 60, 63, 66, 69, 72, 80
Bonnett, Sarah Jane, 68
Bonnett, Serina, 68
Bonnett, Susan, 155
Bonnett, Susanna, 7, 17
Bonnett, Susannah, 20
Bonnett, Thomas Jefferson, 68
Bonnett, William, 41, 67, 71
Bonnett, William G., 60, 80
Bonnett, William Granville, 67
Bonnett, William Jr., 71
Bonnett, William M., 66, 72
Bonnett, William R., 69
Bonnett, William T., 71
Bonnett, Zillah, 70
Booth, James, Capt., 120
Boram, Elizabeth A. (Hinzman), 180
Boram, Pronetta, 180
Boram, Thomas Mrs., 67
Boram, William, 180
Boran, Etta Mae, 115
Boran, Jane Bonnett, 106

Index

Boran, Thomas, 106
Borem, George W., 123
Borem, L., 123
Borem, Mary (Hinzman), 123
Boren, Almira, 70
Boren, Angeline, 70
Boren, Margaret J., 70
Boren, Martha E., 70
Boren, Mary C., 70
Boren, Thomas, 70
Boren, Thomas J., 70
Borns, Magdelena, 283
Bosley, Julia A., 224
Bosworth, A. S., Dr., 121
Bott, Jacob, 65
Bott, Washington E., 65
Botts, John, 62
Bouher, John, 175, 177
Bowden, Kieth, 152
Bowen, Emma, 187
Bowen, F. L., 187
Bowen, Tho's Barth, 34
Bowers, Vencen, 238
Bowman, John, 47
Bowman, Nathaniel, 231
Boyd, Pearl, 153
Boyle, Amarinza, 238
Boyle, Anna, 238
Boyle, Artemus, 236
Boyle, Artenas, 238
Boyle, Christiana, 237
Boyle, Elizabeth, 237, 238
Boyle, Elnora, 238
Boyle, Emma, 236, 238
Boyle, Ephriam, 237
Boyle, Ephriam J., 237
Boyle, Frank, 237
Boyle, Hannah, 237
Boyle, Ida, 237
Boyle, James, 237
Boyle, Jefferson, 237

Boyle, John, 236, 237
Boyle, John Jr., 237
Boyle, Jonathan, 237, 238, 239
Boyle, Margaret (Maggie), 238
Boyle, Martha J., 236
Boyle, Martha Jane, 239, 245
Boyle, Mary, 237
Boyle, Merranda, 237
Boyle, Moses, 237
Boyle, Nancy C., 236
Boyle, Nancy Catharine, 238
Boyle, Newton, 236, 238
Boyle, Rhoda, 237
Boyle, Samuel Jr., 237
Boyle, Sarah, 237
Boyle, Sarah L., 237
Boyle, Thomas, 237
Boyle, William, 236, 237, 238
Boyles, John, 235
Boyles, Jonathan, 234
Boyles, Martha Jane, 238
Boyles, Nancy (Merritt), 235
Bozarth, John, 200, 217
Braddy, Arthur, 258
Braddy, Erven, 258
Braddy, Susan, 258
Bradford, Charlotte, 49
Bradford, Jacob, 49
Bradford, Sarah, 49
Bradford, Susan, 51
Bradley, Bernice Marie, 110
Brake, Granville, 84
Brake, Jacob, 200
Brake, Laura V., 213
Brake, Laura Virginia, 84
Brake, Pamilia (Hall), 84
Brannan, Nancy, 178
Brannan, William, 178
Brazea, Ramah, 152
Brener, Augusta Dorthea, 127
Brenneke, William Christian, 285

Index

Briggs, Elizabeth, 247
Briggs, Frances (Frank), 247
Brinkley, Chas. B., 168
Brinkley, Chas. Brooks II, 168
Brinkley, Fleming K., 207
Brinkley, Janet Louise, 168
Brinkley, Katherine Jane, 168
Brinkley, Majorie Anne, 168
Brinkley, Margaret A., 207
Brinkley, Thaddeus Waldo, 207
Brissey, Mayrie Lou, 210
Brock, Eleanor, 165
Brohard, Estelle, 164
Brooks, James, 152
Brown, (Guy) Bryano, 258
Brown, Alfred K., 258
Brown, Charley, 250, 258
Brown, Charley June, 258
Brown, Ella (Watson), 258
Brown, Erle H., 258
Brown, Eunice, 165
Brown, Fannie M., 258
Brown, Henry, 235
Brown, Howard, 258
Brown, Isaac, 235
Brown, Margaret, 162
Brown, Mary Jane, 217
Brown, Mildred C., 217
Brown, Orris LaVon, 258
Brown, Robert David, 163
Brown, Roy Charles, 258
Brown, Sarah E., 214
Brown, Sharon Kay, 258
Brown, Truman, 213
Brown, Violet Amelia, 258
Brubaker, Emma Jane, 285
Brubaker, Ephraim, 285
Brubaker, Lydia (Hart), 285
Brubaker, Samuel, 286
Bruce, Jaye Lloyd, 258
Buchann, Wylie, 250

Bucher, Clayton D., 227
Buckalew, James, 71
Bucklew, Galvin Larry, 227
Budd, Aaron, 129
Budd, Daniel, 129
Budd, Henry Marvin, 129
Budd, Kenneth Robert, 128, 129
Budd, Kennith Robert, Jr., 130
Budd, Margaret Lucille (Hughes), 129
Budd, Margaret Roberta Moore, 128
Budd, Nancy Kay, 128, 129
Budd, Sandra Lee, 130
Budd, William, 129
Burch, G. W., 212
Burham, Mary, 268
Burkholder, Mary, 220
Burl, Bertha, 213
Burnam, Joan, 266
Burnam, William, 265
Burnett, Donald Hugh, 279
Burnett, Hugh, 279
Burnett, Mrs. Hugh, 279
Burnett, Richard E., 279
Burnham, Abigail, 267, 268, 270
Burnham, Amelia, 271
Burnham, America May (Fry), 273, 279
Burnham, Anna, 266
Burnham, Anna (Wright), 267
Burnham, Annie, 273
Burnham, Asenath, 269
Burnham, Ashbill, 270
Burnham, Charles, 268
Burnham, Charles K., 269
Burnham, Clark R., 273
Burnham, Cpt. Collins A., 270
Burnham, Daniel, 269
Burnham, David, 267
Burnham, Elager, 269
Burnham, Elena, 271

Index

Burnham, Elizabeth, 266, 268
Burnham, Ellie George, 273
Burnham, Erastus, 269
Burnham, Esther, 268
Burnham, Florance Laura, 265, 274, 279
Burnham, Frances S., 270
Burnham, George W., 270, 271
Burnham, Hannah, 269, 270
Burnham, Hepsibeth, 271
Burnham, Hepsibeth (Pickett), 270, 271
Burnham, Inez America May, 274
Burnham, Irene, 269
Burnham, James, 269, 270
Burnham, James D., 274
Burnham, James Douglas, 271, 273, 274
Burnham, James M., 270
Burnham, Jasiah, 269
Burnham, John, 266, 268, 270
Burnham, Jonathan, 267
Burnham, Josiah, 268, 269
Burnham, Judith, 270
Burnham, Lydia, 270
Burnham, Lydia (Williams), 268
Burnham, Margaret (Wood), 269, 270
Burnham, Martha, 269
Burnham, Martha J., 270
Burnham, Mary, 266, 267
Burnham, Mary P., 270
Burnham, Michael, 267
Burnham, Miranda H., 270
Burnham, Naomi, 268
Burnham, Naomi (Hull), 268
Burnham, Nathaniel, 267
Burnham, Obediah, 269
Burnham, Olive E., 271
Burnham, Rebecca, 267
Burnham, Reubin, 270
Burnham, Richard, 267
Burnham, Roderick H., 265
Burnham, Rolla Albert, 271
Burnham, Samuel, 267
Burnham, Sarah, 268
Burnham, Sybil, 269
Burnham, Sylvanus, 270, 271
Burnham, Sylvanus Jr., 270, 271
Burnham, Sylvester, 269
Burnham, Thomas, 265, 268, 269
Burnham, Thomas Sr., 265, 266
Burnham, Thomas, Jr., 266, 267
Burnham, William, 266
Burnham, William Joseph, 266
Burnham, Zelpha, 270
Burnside, Charles Richard, 164
Burnside, Elizabeth, 164
Burnside, Ethel Blanch, 162
Burnside, Eugene Lee, 162
Burnside, James Lynn, 162
Burnside, James William, 162
Burnside, John Kent, 162
Burnside, John Lee, 162
Burnside, Joseph E., 162
Burnside, Lloyd, 164
Burnside, Robert Bland, 164
Burnside, Stella Blanch, 162
Burnside, Willard R., 164
Burnside, William, 164
Burr, John, 232
Burton, Lurana, 176
Bush, Adam, 144, 178
Bush, Alice, 206
Bush, Helen E. (Langford), 182
Bush, Jacob, 182
Bush, Leonard, 35
Bush, M. Scott, 206
Bush, Martha E. (Jackson), 115
Bush, Mary, 178
Bush, Mary A., 182
Bush, Maude, 206

Index

Bush, Nathaniel, 115
Bush, Ola Lena, 115
Bush, Zina, 182
Buss, Fred, 249
Butcher, Christiana (Alkire), 61
Butcher, Elizabeth C., 61
Butcher, Elizabeth L., 183
Butcher, Harold E., 163
Butcher, Henry, 144
Butcher, Ison Duane, 215
Butcher, Jesse, 61
Butcher, Jesse Ray, 214
Butcher, John, 61
Butcher, Mary L., 183
Butcher, Michael E., 215
Butcher, Milton, 63
Butcher, Nancy, 61, 63
Butcher, Paul T., 166
Butcher, Sarah, 99
Butcher, Septembeus O., 61
Butcher, Thomas L., 183
Butcher, Violet, 171
Butcher, Virginia, 61
Butcher, Virginia Bertie, 214, 216
Butcher, William, 61
Buttolph, Jonathan, 270
Buttolph, Martha, 270
Butts, Henry, 65
Byerley, Windell, 162

Cadwell, Mary, 267
Cadwill, Thomas, 267
Caldwell, Grace, 154
Caldwell, Louisa E., 223
Caltaraugh, Charles, 286
Calvert, Jesse, 162
Cambpell, James, 251
Camp, Elwood W., 261
Campbell, Brenda Darlene, 127
Campbell, Charles, 71, 286
Campbell, Edgar Cleulin, 127

Campbell, Eunice, 250, 251
Campbell, Freda, 214
Campbell, Lillie, 251
Campbell, Pemelia, 227
Campbell, Steve, 240
Campbell, Warren, 240
Campbell, Will, 251
Campbell, Wilma Beatrice (Nicholson), 127
Cane, Verba, 152
Carathers, John J., 66
Carder, E. F., 214
Carney, Thomas, 200
Carpenter, John, 71
Carpenter, Lucritia J., 71
Carper, Abraham, 200, 232, 233
Carson, Blanche Maybury, 77, 93, 94
Carson, Dr. Edwin, 78, 94, 98
Cartwell, Christopher, 114
Cartwell, Rachel, 114
Cartwell, Sinai, 114
Cartwright, Samuel, 35
Casto, Charles, 72
Casto, David B., 99
Casto, Eva, 218
Casto, George, 200
Casto, Mary J., 63
Casto, Paris, 218
Casto, W. M., 72
Casto, Whetzel B., 186
Channel, Joseph, 121
Channel, Nancy, 121
Chapman, Ruth, 72
Charles II, King, 3
Chenowith, John, 121
Chenowith, Mary, 121
Chew, Beth Ann, 162
Chew, John W., 162
Chittum, Eli Alexander, 213
Christian, Johann, 281

Index

Christiane, Marie, 276
Christiane, Phillippine, 275
Christopf, Carl, 276
Christoph, Hanna Dorothea, 276
Christoph, Johann, 276
Christoph, Maria Elizabeth, 276
Christoph, Sophia Dorothea, 276
Clark, Barbara (Helmick), 62
Clark, Cornelius, 202
Clark, Emily J., 62, 85
Clark, Gedian, 62
Clark, Harriet, 62, 86
Clark, Jacob, 221
Clark, John, 65, 85
Clark, John J., 62
Clark, John R., 62
Clark, Levi, 62
Clark, Lucinda, 62
Clark, Lucitta, 62
Clark, Mallory T., 221
Clark, Margaret, 62, 65
Clark, Margaret (Bonnett), 65, 85
Clark, Marie B., 213
Clark, Marshall, 62
Clark, Matilda, 50
Clark, Nathan, 62
Clark, Rebecca, 99
Clark, Robert H., 86
Clark, Susannah (Rains), 86
Clark, William, 62, 99, 229, 232
Clark, William. M., 1st Lt., 218
Claypole, Eliza J., 64
Clayton, Maria, 84
Clegg, Alexander, 52
Clemmison, Alice, 258
Clemmison, Elfie (McAlpin), 258
Clemmison, William, 258
Climer, Martha, 153
Climer, Mary A., 154
Climer, Minerva, 151
Clinger, William, 168

Coats, Septimus, 31
Cobb, Tom, 152
Cockran, James, 50
Coen, Delilah, 49
Coen, Francis, 51
Coen, John, 51
Coff, Henderson, 178
Coffield, Mary, 20
Coffman, Sue Ann, 228
Coger, Daniel, 178
Coger, Peter, 178
Coger, Phoebe, 178
Cohener, Jacob, 46
Collins, Abram, 243
Collins, Absolem, 243
Collins, Samuel F., 51
Colorado, Mamie Malia, 100
Combs, Mary Jane, 63
Comer, Mary, 186
Conley, George A., 210
Conley, Howard Davis, 110
Conlin, John A., 85
Constant, Alfred H., 154
Constant, Harold Waggoner, 154
Cookman, 1853 Samuel E, 68
Cookman, Amanda, 211
Cookman, Angeline, 69
Cookman, Elizabeth, 68, 106, 107, 161
Cookman, George, 68
Cookman, Harriet, 161
Cookman, Jeremiah, 161
Cookman, Mary (Mitchell), 68
Cookman, Parker B., 140
Cooley, Jerusha (Bissell), 269
Coon, Gilbert, 222
Coon, Lenora E., 112
Coon, William, 222
Cooperbarger, Elizabeth, 149
Cooperbarger, Joe, 149
Cooperbarger, Mary Ellen, 149

Index

Corathers, Eva, 100
Corathers, Nancy J., 62
Cory, Rhoda Jane, 153
Corzinne, Sarah, 48
Cosner, Adam, 123
Cosner, Susanna, 123
Costlow, Wilma Jo, 228
Cottrell, Melinda, 187
Cottrill, Andrew, 193
Cottrill, Elizabeth, 193
Cottrill, Gilbert, 193
Cottrill, Lucetta, 193
Cottrill, Malinda J., 193
Cottrill, Manerva J., 194
Cottrill, Mariah, 140
Cottrill, Nancy, 193
Cottrill, Rachel, 193
Cottrill, Susan, 193
Cottrill, Sylvester, 193
Cottrill, Virginia, 213
Cottrill, William, 193
Coulson, Dale, 240
Coulson, Eunice, 240
Coulson, Harry A., 239
Coulson, Jeffory Gene, 241
Coulson, Keith, 240
Coulson, Lauri June, 241
Coulson, Martin Joel, 241
Coulson, Richard, 241
Coulson, Ritchie Ronn, 241
Coulter, George, 153
Cox, Charles T., 85
Cox, Philip, 177
Cozad, Jacob, 71, 92, 176
Craft, Edward Joe, 162
Craig, Christopher W., 71
Crampton, Dennis, 268
Critchfield, William E., 111
Crites, Abram, 223
Crites, Jacob, 35
Crites, John D., 223

Crites, Michael, 219
Crites, Susanna M., 221
Crites, Winifred, 219, 222, 223, 224, 225
Cromerston, Elizabeth, 16
Crose, Martin, 153
Cross, John, 268
Crutchfield, J. C., 212
Culbertson, Joseph, 49
Cumberledge, Alexander, 51
Cumberledge, Andrew J., 51
Cumberledge, Barbara, 51
Cumberledge, Dililah, 51
Cumberledge, Elizabeth, 51
Cumberledge, George, 50, 51
Cumberledge, George Fielding, 50
Cumberledge, Jacob, 51
Cumberledge, John, 51
Cumberledge, Margaret, 51
Cumberledge, Mary, 51
Cumberledge, Nancy, 51
Cumberledge, Rachel (Barker), 50
Cumberledge, Rachel Priscilla, 51
Cumberledge, Sara, 51
Cumberledge, Simon, 51
Cumberledge, William, 51
Cummings, Mary E., 103
Cumpston, Myra, 164
Cumpston, Willis, 164
Cunningham, Francis M., 205
Cunningham, George H., 205
Cunningham, George P., 205
Cunningham, Julia, 205
Cunningham, Katherine, 213
Cunningham, Laura, 205
Cunningham, Perry, 205
Cunningham, Perry Green, 205
Cunningham, Temperance, 205
Curry, Grover, 114
Curry, Harold, 114
Curry, Mrs., 109

Index

Curtis, Bailey B., 169
Curtis, Charlotte Ann, 169
Curtis, Henry L., 227
Curtis, Janet, 164
Curtis, Joanna Samantha, 225
Curtis, Mary Helen, 169
Curtis, Olive Malissa, 227
Curtis, Robert lee, 169
Curtis, Sandra Laverne, 169
Cutright, Abraham, 232
Cutright, Ann, 225
Cutright, Barbara, 217, 225
Cutright, Barbara, children, 226
Cutright, Charlie, 226
Cutright, John, 226, 232
Cutright, Peter, 217, 225
Cutright, W. B., 200

Dalany, Daniel, 15
Dammerin, Anna Elisabeth, 10
Dammeron, Florence Hedley, 129
Dammeron, Zechariah, 129
Danbury, Clarissa, 121
Daniels, Jonathan, 233
Dantzler, Rudolp, 72
DarbyWilliam, 41
Darnall, Sue (Sutton), 124
Darnall, Thomas A. Jr., 124
Davey, Owen, 142
David, Slater, 213
Davis, Aletha, 84
Davis, James, 119
Davis, John David, 140
Davis, Marcellus, 111
Davis, Roy K., 285
Davis, Roy Kenneth, 285
Davisson, C. H., 215
Davisson, Caroline, 208
Davisson, Edgar, 208
Davisson, Elizabeth, 165
Davisson, George, 208

Davisson, Granville W., 208
Davisson, John, 208
Davisson, Jonathan, 208
Davisson, Mary, 208
Davisson, Sarah, 208
Davisson, William Edgar, 208
Dawson, Glenn Smith, 163
Day, Festus Ithameur, 228
Day, Freda Mae, 228
Day, John Wesley, 228
Dean, Adalade Victoria, 210
Dean, Alice Virginia, 210
Dean, James, 210
Dean, Kitturah (Batten), 209, 210
Dean, Leanoh, 210
Dean, Oleta, 218
Dean, Richard, 85
Dean, Thomas, 210
Deans, Betty Love (Darlington), 128
Deans, Jonathan Craig, 128
Deans, Leroy Ray, 128
DeBarr, Sarah Jane, 211
Deble, Israil, 267
deGruyter, Charles Conrad, 110
deGruyter, Elizabeth Eileen, 110
deGruyter, Etha Doris, 110
deGruyter, Ferdinand, 110
deGruyter, Margaret Louise, 110
deGruyter, Noel Kent, 110
deGruyter, Olin Ferdinand, 110
deGruyter, Otto, 110
deGruyter, Paul Arnold, 110
deGruyter, Rhonda Jane (Hill), 110
deGruyter, Roberta Gail, 110
Dennison, Hezekeah, 179
Denton, Albert, 248
Depriest, Louise A., 85
Depriest, Robert E., 85
Depriest, William A., 85
Dern, John P., 17
deVentre, Walter, 265

Index

Dever, Margaret, 202
Devlin, Arden, 249
Devlin, Everal, 249
Devlini, Estelle (Barnes), 249
Dicks, Mary, 63
Dinghel, Maria (Mary), 251
Dinkel, Catherine (Dunkel), 260
Dinkel, George (Charles), 260
Dinkel, Mary (Maria), 260
Dinkel, Philip, 260
Ditson, Martha A., 66
Divers, John W., 182
Dix, Isaac, 62
Dix, Jemina, 62
Dix, Stephen, 62
Dixon, Armissa, 224
Dixon, Armissa (Massa), 223
Dixon, Asa P., 223
Dixon, Mary, 223
Dobson, Anna, 186
Dobson, Catharine, 185
Dobson, Catherine, 140
Dobson, Charley, 186
Dobson, Elliott, 186
Dobson, G. W., 144
Dobson, George, 185
Dobson, George Wallace, 185
Dobson, Harmon, 186
Dobson, Ida, 186
Dobson, John, 185
Dobson, Mariah (Maria), 185
Dobson, Marjorie, 186
Dobson, Mary, 185
Dobson, Mary A., 185
Dobson, Minnie, 186
Dobson, Nancy Rebecca, 186
Dobson, Oliver, 186
Dobson, Onie, 186
Dobson, Sarah, 186
Dobson, Susan, 185
Dobson, William S., 186

Dobson, Wirt, 186
Dodson, Elizabeth, 67
Dodson, Joseph, 67
Dodson, Philip W., 67
Doke, Susan Frances, 130
Doke, Thomas Jefferson, 130
Doll, Jacob, 78
Dommick, Daniel, 237
Donely, Betsy, 48
Dormer, Arminta T., 221
Dorothea, Amalie, 276
Dorothea, Augusta Marie, 276
Dougherty, Carrie L., 169
Douglas, James, 279
Drake, Raymond, Hon., 275, 283
Drake, Wilmer Lester, 280
Draper, Lyman C., 26, 27, 55
Drew, Elizabeth, 254
Drew, Harriet (Ball), 254
Drew, Herny, 254
Drew, John, 254
Drew, Joseph, 254
Drew, Robert, 254
Duke, Lucy Ann, 129
Dume, Mary, 273
Dunkel, Adam, 259
Dunkel, Catharine (Spangler), 261
Dunkel, Elizabeth, 259
Dunkel, Frederick, 259
Dunkel, George S., 260
Dunkel, John, 259
Dunkel, John Adam, 259
Dunkel, Mary (Marie), 261
Dunkel, Philip, 259, 261
Dunkel, Sophia, 259
Dunkel, William W., 260
Dunkle, Catharine (Spangler), 259
Dunkle, Philip, 259
Duvall, Greenberry, 107
Duvall, Serena A., 69

Index

Eagle, Daniel Monroe, 115
Echard, Jacob, 209, 211
Echard, Janetta, 211
Echard, Jannetta, 216
Echard, Margaret Jane, 209
Echard, Sarah, 209, 211
Eckers, Martha Ann, 182
Eckhardin, Sophia, 283
Edge, George D,, 83
Edge, Jesse, 83
Edge, Obediah, 83
Edge, Sarah (Adams), 81, 83
Edmonds, John, 72, 144
Eiseman, Thomas, 167
Eldridge, Billie, 212
Elenore, Susanne, 276
Ellensworth, William, 82
Ellis, Fred, Sr., 213
Ellis, Gay Allman, 201
Ellison, Messouri, 80
Ellison, Missouri, 60
Ellison, Samuel, 80
Ellison, Sarah, 80
Emilie, Berta Amalie, 276
Enger, Lynda, 253
Erickson, Ronald Ray, 163
Estes, Frank, 151
Estes, Gary, 151
Estes, Jerry, 151
Estes, Ronnie, 151
Evans, Aden, 153
Evans, Willard, 163

Fairburn,, 244
Fairburn, Catharine A., 243
Fairburn, Catharine Ann, 244
Fairburn, Eliza Jane, 244
Fairburn, Elizabeth, 243
Fairburn, James A., 243, 244
Fairburn, Rebecca E., 244
Fairburn, Sarah A., 244

Family, Rask, 250
Farnsworth, D.D.T., 232
Felton, Johana Hanna, 260
Ferguson, Thomas, 166
Fernandez, Joanne, 212
Fernandez, Juan, 213
Ferrell, Mary, 176
Ferrell, William, 50
Fields, Walter, 164
Fink, Henry, 200
Fink, Sylvia, 214
Finley, Indiana Hannah C., 102
Fisher, Adam, 144
Fisher, Scott, 206
Fitzgerald, Eva, 218
Fitzpatrick, Berne, 274
Fitzpatrick, Donald Thomas, 151
Fitzpatrick, Lalia, 151
Fitzsimmons, Harold Irwin, 110
Flaherty, Annie Maria, 195
Flaherty, John P., 195
Flaherty, Synthia A., 195
Flanigan, Alice, 183
Flanigan, James, 183
Flanigan, Mary, 183
Flechtner, Johann Christian, 133
Fleischer, Anna Catharine, 11
Fleischer, Anna Elisabeth, 11
Fleischer, Anna Maria, 11
Fleischer, Balthasar, 11
Fleischer, Johann Henrich, 11
Fleischer, Johannes, 11
Flescher, John, 145
Flesher, Barbara, 73
Flesher, Elizabeth, 73
Flesher, Henry, 73
Flesher, Margaret (Peggy), 73
Flesher, Nancy, 73
Flesher, Peter, 73
Flesher, Polly, 73
Flesher, Rosanna, 67

Index

Fliescher, Baltzar, 9, 10
Fliesher, Baltzar, 28
Flint, Betty Jean, 228
Flint, Joseph, Rev., 217
Flint, Thomas Fred, 228
Floyd, John B., 222
Floyd, Lulu, 226
Foltz, Joshua, 100
Foltz, Reganah, 100
Foltz, Susan, 100
Forenash, Ann (Plant), 103
Forenash, Catharine (Kritz), 102
Forenash, Isaac, 103
Forenash, Jacob Sr., 102
Forenash, Malinda, 102
Forenash, William D., 103
Forinash, Elias P., 64
Forinash, Hannah (Paterson), 64
Forinash, Jacob Sr., 64
Forinash, Martha A., 66
Forinash, Oliver G., 69
Fornash, Mary Jane, 233
Forsht, Ethel, 286
Fort Buttermilk, 25
Fort Waggoner, 25
Fortney, Burl A., 167
Foster, Ethel J. (Thrash), 206
Foust, Job, 86
Fowler, Mell, 226
Fowler, Nancy, 86
Fox, Martin, 144
Francis, John R., 65
Frankboue, Betsie, 48
Franklyn, Michael, 5
Freeman, Betty, 215
Freeman, Edward, 142
Freeman, Katharan Ann, 72
Freeman, Orpha Grace, 162
Frey, Anna, 273
Frichie, Glen, 244
Friedericke, Christiane, 276

Friedrich, Christian, 276
Friedrich, Johann, 276
Frigetto, Hugo John, 258
Fröbsen, Catharina, 275
Fröbsen, Johann Lorentz, 275
Fry, America May, 271
Fry, Ann Lane, 271
Fry, Annie (Lane), 273
Fry, George W., 273
Fry, Grant B., 273
Fry, Henry W. (Joshua), 273
Fry, John H., 273
Fry, William, 273
Fry, William (Bill), 271
Fry, William E., 273
Full, Elizabeth, 192
Full, Lewis, 192
Full, Ruben, 192
Fultz, Amanda Belle, 228
Fultz, William Scott, 228
Funk, Florence E., 215
Funk, John Henry, 213
Fury, Columbia Laverne Marion, 217
Fury, Harrison H., 217
Fuschain, Adam, 40, 47
Fuschain, Clara, 40, 47
Fuschon, Clara, 40

Gaines, Henry, 266
Gaines, Nathaniel, 266
Gaines, Samuel, 266
Gains, Susan Harrison, 130
Garrison, Nancy, 195
Garten, Edna, 166
Garton, John W., 212
Gaston, Minnie, 182
Gautchia, Lillian, 215
Gay, Adiain, 114
Gaylord, Josiah, 268
Gaylord, Martha (Thompson), 266

Index

Geiben, Margaretha Johanna, 133
George, Elizabeth, 185
George, Henry, 185
George, Nancy, 192
Gephardt, Karl Otto, 276
Gerwig, Edith, 171
Gibson, Granville, 66
Gillette, Hannah, 270
Gilman, Elizabeth (Adkins), 268
Gilman, Richard, 268
Glaichert, John J., 285
Goff, Mary Ellen, 186
Goff, Susannah (George), 186
Goff, Thomas R., 186
Golden, Rose Rhealina, 113
Goldsmith, George W., 84
Goodnight, Margaret E., 149
Goodrich, Nathan, 20
Goodwin, Emily C., 71
Goodwin, Vida, 167
Gorden, Joseph F., 205
Gordon, Olive B., 205
Gould, Waldo G., 180
Goven, John, 9
Gower, Karl K., 155
Gower, Karl L., 141
Grabner, Jakob Nikol, 134
Graham, Jess, 151
Grant, George W., 169
Grant, Joe, 126
Grant, John, 268
Grant, Zelda L., 169
Green, John, 33, 34
Green, Perry, 125, 126
Greswold, Edward, 266
Gribble, Cornelius, 99
Griffin, Bruce, 250
Griffin, Wyman, 250
Grim, Martha J., 51
Griswold, Edward, 267
Grose, Clyde Ballard, 218

Grose, George Washington, 220, 226
Grose, John Andrew, 226
Grose, Lucinda, 225
Grose, Phoebe Allman, 226
Grose, Roberta May, 220
Grose, Samuel, 226
Grows, Catherine, 285
Gruick, Ann, 258
Gum, Anthony, 163
Gum, Eli, 269
Gum, Leslie Jennings, 162
Gum, Mary Kathleen, 162
Gum, Otterbein, 162
Gunn, Jesse, 48
Gunn, Mary M., 48

Hacker, Elizabeth, 84
Hacker, John, 67, 81, 82, 84, 92
Hacker, John T. Rev., 106
Hacker, Lydia, 81
Hacker, Margaret, 81, 82
Hacker, Margaret (Sleeth), 84
Hacker, Margaret (Steeth), 81
Hacker, Marget (Margaret), 81
Hacker, Martha, 57
Hacker, Mary Ann, 82
Hacker, Susannah (Smith), 67
Hacker, Thomas, 80
Hacker, Thos. L., 60
Hacker, William, 107
Hackney, W. L., 186
Hadden, Elizabeth, 121
Hadneck, Frank, 166
Hall, Asa Warren, 166
Hall, C. I., 212
Hall, Christine, 166
Hall, Gertrude Melvina, 214
Hall, J. S., 212
Hall, Jacob A., 62
Hall, James M., 212
Hall, Juanita, 166

Index

Hall, Julea V., 166
Hall, Madge V., 166
Hall, Marvin, 153
Hall, Morgan Minor, 212
Hall, Nancy Louella, 212
Hall, Nancy S. (Law), 166
Hall, Pearl, 166
Hall, Peyton R., 214
Hall, Robert, 166
Hall, Sobisca Stalnaker, 166
Hall, Warren, 166
Hall, William D., 166
Halterman, Clarence, 162
Halterman, Virginia, 167
Hammack, Catharine, 193
Hammack, Martin, 193
Hammack, St. Clair, 193
Hammer, Howard R., 212
Hamrick, Alice Faye, 163
Hamrick, Barbara Jean, 163
Hamrick, Dorsey Frazier, 163
Hamrick, Elizabeth Carol, 163
Hamrick, Janet Rose, 163
Hamrick, Junior, 162
Hamrick, Tina Louise, 163
Hamrick, Vickie Lynne, 163
Hamrick, William Everett, 163
Hanks, Joseph, 78
Hann, Mary, 58
Hannah, Martha, 239
Hannigan, Genevine, 114
Hanshaw, Ira Lee, 111
Harbaugh, Margaret, 154
Hardman , Jacob Wolf, 78
Hardman, Able, 100
Hardman, Abraham, 86
Hardman, Ada May, 165
Hardman, Alcinda, 84
Hardman, Alonzo C., 165
Hardman, Amanda E., 85
Hardman, Ann, 100

Hardman, Anna Mabia, 85
Hardman, Anthony, 100
Hardman, Catharine, 79
Hardman, Catharine V., 103
Hardman, Catherine, 82
Hardman, Charlotte, 84
Hardman, Charlotte (Lazier), 78, 81, 97, 107
Hardman, Chas. L., 84
Hardman, Cora Adaline, 99
Hardman, Cordes, 250
Hardman, Cordis, 83
Hardman, Cynthia J., 103
Hardman, Daniel, 79, 86, 103
Hardman, David, 86, 100, 103
Hardman, Delilah, 84
Hardman, Della, 84
Hardman, Edgar Bruce, 99
Hardman, Eliza, 83
Hardman, Elizabeth, 81, 83, 100, 101
Hardman, Elizabeth (Waggoner), 78, 93, 94
Hardman, Ellen (Willford), 250
Hardman, Foster, 165
Hardman, George Washington, 85
Hardman, Hanna, 86
Hardman, Hanna Matilda, 103
Hardman, Hattie, 84
Hardman, Henry, 82, 84, 85
Hardman, Henry (Dexter), 98
Hardman, Henry D., 99
Hardman, Ida, 101
Hardman, Imogene H., 101
Hardman, Ira S., 165
Hardman, Jacob, 60, 80, 83, 86, 100
Hardman, Jacob M., 102
Hardman, Jacob W., 102
Hardman, Jacob Wolf, 94, 98
Hardman, Joe (John), 82

Index

Hardman, John, 77, 84, 85, 97, 98, 100, 105, 106
Hardman, John C., 63, 103
Hardman, John Columbus, 100
Hardman, John Dexter, 84
Hardman, John G., 102
Hardman, John Wolf, 94
Hardman, John, Rev., 77, 78, 79, 94
Hardman, Jonathan, 83
Hardman, Joseph, 100
Hardman, Josephine, 78, 94
Hardman, Joshua A., Jr., 101
Hardman, Joshua W., 99, 100
Hardman, Lee Adam, 84
Hardman, Lesley, 250
Hardman, Leslye, 83
Hardman, Louisa, 86
Hardman, Louise, 85
Hardman, Marcellus L., 99
Hardman, Margaret, 79, 81, 83, 85
Hardman, Margaret (Hacker), 250
Hardman, Margaret Lilly, 99
Hardman, Margaret M., 103
Hardman, Marshall, 100
Hardman, Martha, 83
Hardman, Martha Ann, 102
Hardman, Mary, 100
Hardman, Mary (Molly), 100
Hardman, Mary (West), 99
Hardman, Mary Elizabeth, 84, 99, 103
Hardman, Matilda J., 99
Hardman, Melvenia, 101
Hardman, Nancy, 100
Hardman, Nancy Jane, 84
Hardman, Nathan, 100
Hardman, Nathaniel Marion, 83, 250
Hardman, Nelson, 83
Hardman, Nicholas, 78, 79
Hardman, Paul, 77, 98
Hardman, Perry G., 213
Hardman, Perry Green, 84
Hardman, Perry Worthington, 103
Hardman, Peter, 60, 78, 79, 80, 81, 82, 83, 97, 107, 250
Hardman, Peter Ellis, 84
Hardman, Peter Jamison, 102
Hardman, Peter Jr., 81
Hardman, Peterman (Peter), 200
Hardman, Porter, 165
Hardman, Rebecca, 101
Hardman, Salathiel B., 99
Hardman, Sam, 65, 77, 78
Hardman, Sam W., 98
Hardman, Samuel, 100
Hardman, Samuel Baxter, 99
Hardman, Samuel J., 77, 98
Hardman, Samuel M., 103
Hardman, Samuel W., 99
Hardman, Sarah, 82, 86
Hardman, Sarah Ann (Wise), 250
Hardman, Sarah Ella, 103
Hardman, Sarah Matelda, 100
Hardman, Sevilly, 86
Hardman, Stephen, 84
Hardman, Susan (Foltz), 100
Hardman, Susan Elizabeth (Summers), 165
Hardman, Thomas M., 99
Hardman, Thomas R., 85, 165
Hardman, Valentine E., 101
Hardman, Virginia, 100
Hardman, W. M., 84
Hardman, Weese, 213
Hardman, William, 99
Hardman, William Edward, 77
Hardman, William Henry, 102
Hardman, William Roper, 84
Hardman, Wm. Edward, 98
Hardmon, John, Rev., 78
Harless, Anthony, 243

Index

Harmon, Beatrice Arlene, 258
Harmon, Elizabeth, 269
Harness, John, 35
Harness, John, Capt, 141
Harness, John, Capt., 39
Harpold, Barbara, 71
Harpole, Adam, 71
Harpole, Margaret Cunning (Dunkle), 71
Harres, Cora Kaser, 133
Harris, Charles, 188, 193
Harris, J. H., 193
Harris, Julina E., 188
Harris, Nancy, 188, 193
Hartley, Amanda, 220, 221
Hartley, Florence, 211
Hartley, H. E., 209
Hartley, Jacob K., 209
Hartman, A. M., 223
Hartman, Josephine, 98
Hartman, Margaret, 78
Harvey, Robert, 153
Haskett, Martha, 128
Hatcher, J. B., 106
Hawkins, Caroline B., 208
Hawthorne, Addie (Grigsby), 253
Hawthorne, Dixie, 253
Hawthorne, Henry Andrew, 253
Hay, Arena J., 238
Hayes, Beatrice, 214
Hayes, Edman, 50
Haymond, Henry, 92
Hays, Martha R., 218
Hearting, Louis, 126
Heavner, Dorothy, 124
Heck, William S., 103
Heckart, Peter, 141, 155
Heffner, Elizabeth, 167
Hefner, Agnes Lee, 167
Heinzman, Matilda, 106
Heinzman, Matilda (Bonnett), 125

Heir, Clara, 216
Heizman, Isaac M., 125
Helmick, Barbara, 229
Helmick, Elizabeth, 217, 229
Helmick, Isabel A., 66
Helmick, Joana, 66
Helmick, John H., 66
Helmick, Mary, 225
Helmick, Mary Ann (Hacker), 66
Helmick, Sarah J., 64
Helms, John Raymond, 253
Helms, Marilee Laura, 253
Helms, Mary (Afka), 253
Helms, Raymond Charles, 253
Helms, Susan Maria, 253
Hemple, Beverly Ann, 258
Hempleman, Littlie J., 83
Henderson, Amy, 48
Henkel, Dieter, 276
Hennen, Dorothy T., 50
Henry, Ruth, 111
Henthoron, Karen Larie, 253
Henzman, Abram, 144
Henzman, Minerva, 68
Herl, Ellen, 133
Herrod, James, 235
Hershman, C. L., 204
Hershman, George P. W., 204
Hershman, Isaac B., 204
Hershman, M. S., 204
Hershman, Margaret, 68
Hershman, Margaret L., 204
Hershman, Mark, 68
Hershman, Marshall, 204
Hershman, Polly, 68
Hershman, William Bruce, 204
Hersman, Alexander Morrison, 109, 111
Hersman, Alice Faye, 111
Hersman, Alma Kate, 111
Hersman, Bertha Hattie, 110

Index

Hersman, Bruce Ireland, 110
Hersman, Charles E., 207
Hersman, Elizabeth Gertrude, 111
Hersman, Elmer Earl, 111
Hersman, Esta M., 207
Hersman, Ethel Grace, 125
Hersman, George, 125, 208
Hersman, Harry B., 125
Hersman, Harvey Harrison, 110
Hersman, Ina, 114, 121
Hersman, John, 124
Hersman, John Clark, 125
Hersman, John, Rev., 106
Hersman, Margaret Ann (Morrison), 109
Hersman, Mark, 125
Hersman, Mark Jr., Rev., 109
Hersman, Mark Kenneth, 111
Hersman, Maude Margaret, 110
Hersman, Romie Dale, 110
Hersman, Stanley B., 125
Hersman, Thelma Inez, 111
Herssman, Harold (Bill) Sutton, 125
Hess, Abraham, 60
Hess, Clark, 60
Hess, Eliza, 60
Hess, Emily, 60
Hess, Javon, 60
Hess, Marion, 60
Hess, Nancy, 60
Hess, Newton, 60
Hess, Vinton, 60
Hickerson, Albert R., 154
Hide, James, 79
Hier, Leonard, II, 216
Hier, Mary (House), 216
Hill, Gertrude (Peterson), 181
Hill, Henry, Rev., 239
Hill, Permelia, 130
Hillebrande, Archie, 254
Hillebrande, Eugene Allen, 254

Hillebrande, Henry, 254
Hillies, Oscar, 213
Hinkle, Elvina, 228
Hinkle, Lorina, 171
Hinkle, Mary Ellen (Radcliff), 215
Hinton, Harry L., 214
Hinzman, Alta, 166
Hinzman, Anne Sarah, 210
Hinzman, Charity, 71, 179
Hinzman, Columbia A. (Moore), 125
Hinzman, Henry, 71, 179
Hinzman, Isaac, 68
Hinzman, Isaac M., 68
Hinzman, Jacob, 176
Hinzman, James M., 71
Hinzman, John, 71
Hinzman, Louisa, 176
Hinzman, Martha J. (Bonnett), 68
Hinzman, Martha M., 71
Hinzman, Mary, 205, 210
Hinzman, Olive Rebecca, 125
Hinzman, P. G., 211
Hinzman, Robert, 68
Hinzman, Samuel B., 71
Hinzman, Stilla, 125
Hinzman, Thomas Columbus, 179
Hinzman, William C., 125
Hinzman, William Marcellous, 70
Hisey, Hannah, 130
Hitt, Mary E., 212
Hitt, Ruth M., 212
Hitt, William D., 212
Hodges, Leona L., 70
Hoffman, Johann, 134
Hoffmann, Adolf, 275
Holbert, Aaron, 244
Holbert, Elizabeth, 244
Holbert, Reuben P., 244
Holswide, Christian F., 59
Holt, Mary K., 140
Hood, T. M., 227

Index

Hoofman, John, 55
Hooks, Lewis, 43
Hooper, H. R., 223
Hooper, J. J., 223
Hoose, David Allen, 253
Hoover, Lea, 212
Hoover, Polly (Mary), 226
Hopkins, Martha, 60
Hopkins, Martha A. (Stalnaker), 80
Hopkins, Menerva S., 80
Hopkins, Minirva S., 60
Hopkins, Robert, 60, 80
Horner, Amanda, 61
Horner, George M., 61
Horner, Harriet, 61
Horner, Joseph M., 61
Horner, Louisa, 61
Horner, Lucinda, 61
Horner, Marinda, 61
Horner, Martha J., 61
Horner, Monterville, 61
Horner, Samuel, 61, 106
Horner, William H., 61
Hornor, Carl Edwin, 228
Hornor, Mary Kathleen, 228
Hough, Gertrude, 214
Hoult, Milenisa Ann, 51
Houston, Geneviena, 167
Hove, Lucinda Fitzhugh, 59
Howes, Andrew, 223
Howkins, Sarah, 106
Howland, June Jane (Cowan), 128
Howland, Patricia Ann, 128
Howland, William McKenley, 128
Hudson, Almina (Elmira), 101
Hudson, Commodore Perry, 102
Hudson, George Washington, 102
Hudson, Hosea M., 102
Hudson, Ilasca, 102
Hudson, Jacob, 101
Hudson, Jacob W., 101

Hudson, Marion, 102
Hudson, Matilda, 101
Hudson, Parthena, 101
Hudson, Regina Victoria, 102
Hudson, Reginia (Foltz), 101
Hudson, Thomas J., 102
Hudson, William Worth, 102
Huffman, Rachel Smith, 20
Huffman, Weeden, 146
Huffnagle, Dorotha Maria, 284
Hughes, Deborah, 178
Hughes, Ellis (Elias), 58
Hughes, Grace (Tanner), 58
Hughes, Jesse, 56, 58, 78, 82, 91, 203
Hughes, Job, 58
Hughes, John Cargyle, 129
Hughes, Margaret Lucille, 129
Hughes, Martha, 58
Hughes, Mary Baker, 178
Hughes, Richard Adolphus, 129
Hughes, Thomas, 178
Hughes, Thomas Jr., 58
Hughes, Thomas, Sr., 58
Hull, Betty Dell, 162
Hull, Carolyn, 163
Hull, Elizabeth, 267
Hull, Emmett, 162
Hull, George, 268
Hull, Ishmael, 162
Hull, John, 267
Hull, John Harley, 162
Hull, Joseph, 268
Hull, Josiah, 266, 267, 268
Hull, Martha, 268
Hull, Mary, 268
Hull, Mary Kemper, 163
Hull, Naomi, 266, 267, 268
Hull, Rebecca, 268
Hull, Robert, 162
Hull, Rose Mary, 162

Index

Hull, RuthAnn Bette, 163
Hull, Sarah, 268
Hull, Thomas, 268
Hummell, G. W., .Rev., 261
Humphery, Elizabeth, 112
Humphery, William Pelham, 112
Humphrey, Charles, 267
Humphrey, Esther, 267
Humphrey, Jupiter, 267
Humphrey, Martha, 267
Humphrey, Mary, 267
Humphrey, Mercy, 267
Humphrey, Michael, 267
Humphrey, Prescilla (Grant), 267
Humphrey, Rebecca, 267
Humphrey, Richard, 267
Humphrey, Sarah, 267
Humphrey, Sarah (Hannah), 267
Humphrey, Susanna, 267
Hunt, Jonathan, 237
Hurst, Whiston H., 176
Hushman, Marshall, 67
Hushman, William George, 179
Hyar, John, 35
Hyde, Catharine (Hardman), 60, 77, 106, 107
Hyde, Charlotta, 60, 80
Hyde, Daniel, 60, 79, 80
Hyde, Isaac, 60, 79, 80
Hyde, James, 80
Hyde, James Jr., 60, 79, 106
Hyde, James Sr., 79
Hyde, James, Estate Settlement of, 80
Hyde, John, 60, 79, 80
Hyde, Sarah, 79
Hyer, Catherine, 219
Hyer, John, 216
Hyer, Patience, 216
Hyre, Catharine (Kesting), 99
Hyre, Jacob, 200

Hyre, Mahala A., 99
Hyre, Martin, 99
Hyre, Noah, 99
Hyres, Majel Elaine, 241

Irey, Annie M., 203

Jack, Catharine, 193
Jack, John, 193
Jack, Sarah J., 193
Jackson, Alice, 133
Jackson, Cecilia (McNulty), 65
Jackson, Cecilia Ann, 65
Jackson, Cecilice B., 102
Jackson, Edward, 200
Jackson, Eliza, 161
Jackson, George, 92
Jackson, George R., 65
Jackson, George W., 102
Jackson, Henry, 200
Jackson, Jacob J., 102
Jackson, Margaret D., 102
Jackson, Parmalia(Watson), 102
Jackson, Pernillia (Watson), 101
Jackson, Stonewall, 102
Jardine, Bill, 152
Jeffers, Dr., 250
Jeffries, James, 179
Jenkins, Lucretia (Lucy), 120
Jenkins, Lyda Jane, 227
Jennings, Ray J., 166
Jessing, Christoph, 276
Jessing, Maria Dorothea, 276, 277
Jirkousky, James Allen, 253
Johannes Lantz, 45
Johns, Ronnie, 153
Johnson, Burwell, 250, 251
Johnson, Joseph, 146
Johnson, Mary E., 237
Johnson, Sallie, 93
Johnson, Sally, 92

Index

Johnson, Sarah (Van Baskirk), 41
Johnson, William, 41
Johnston, Macel, 114
Jones , Rachel, 241
Jones, Calvin, 239
Jones, Casey Wayne, 241
Jones, Catherine, 239
Jones, Clarence Homer, 128
Jones, Crystal V., 128, 241
Jones, Crystal Violet, 254
Jones, Cynthia Lee, 241
Jones, Donald Ritter, 240
Jones, Earnest Orlando, 240
Jones, Elizabeth Catherine, 239
Jones, Ernest Laurel, 240
Jones, Ettie (Watson), 128
Jones, Gary Don, 240
Jones, George Lee, 240
Jones, Gerry Lee, 240, 241
Jones, Hannah, 210
Jones, Hannah Telitha, 209
Jones, Harry Hector, 241
Jones, Harry Hector III, 241
Jones, Harry Hector Jr., 241
Jones, Hattie, 241
Jones, Homer Clarence, 241, 254
Jones, Hulbert, 238, 239, 245
Jones, John Clarence, 240, 245
Jones, John Edward (Ted), 240
Jones, Larry Lee, 240
Jones, Laura (Cunningham), 205
Jones, Limuel, 239
Jones, Lucy Lurene, 240
Jones, Luther, 239
Jones, Mary Elizabeth, 241
Jones, Mary Maureen, 240
Jones, Melvin Maury, 240
Jones, Melvin Maury Jr., 240
Jones, Nancy, 239
Jones, Nicholas, 239
Jones, Nicholas J., 241

Jones, Oliver, 239, 241
Jones, Phyllis Joan, 241
Jones, Rachael, 239
Jones, Ray Wayne, 240, 241
Jones, Rose, 239
Jones, Sherri, 241
Jones, Thomas, 239
Jones, Veala R., 239
Jones, Wilber C., 241

Kaiser, Irene Gladys, 133
Kaorper, Anna Dorothea, 283
Karl, Friedrich, 276
Keckler, Carl Raymond, 286
Keckler, Donald Arthur, 286
Keckler, Lloyd, 285
Keckler, Lloyd Harry, 286
Keeler, Juanita Ethel, 240
Keener, Howard N., 171
Keith, Anna Jean, 215
Keller, John Raymond, 227
Kelley, David S., 70
Kelley, Edgar M., 70
Kelley, Elizabeth J., 70
Kelley, Halzen, 70
Kelley, James W., 222
Kelley, John, 70
Kelley, Marcenia, 223
Kelley, Margaret, 70
Kelley, Mary Ann, 70
Kelley, Matilda, 70
Kelley, Menter B., 70
Kelley, Samuel, 70
Kelley, Weeden H., 70
Kelley, William, 70
Kelley, William Henry, 70
Kelley, William W., 222
Kelly, Deborah (Bonnett), 67
Kelly, Harmonetta, 67
Kelly, Helzen, 67
Kelly, Icie, 112

Index

Kelly, James W., 225
Kelly, Mary A., 175
Kelly, Mary Ann, 175
Kelly, Mascena, 222
Kelly, Minter B., 67
Kelly, Sarah, 222, 223
Kelly, Wilda, 77
Kelly, William, 144
Kelly, William W., 223
Kelly, Wm., 175
Kelsey, Abigail, 267
Kemper, John, 164
Kemper, Rev. Reuben, 162
Kemper, Rosamond, 162
Kemper, Rose May, 162
Kent, Elizabeth (Odenbaugh), 50
Kent, Minerva, 50
Kent, William, 50
Kidd, Cletus R., 221
Kidd, Virginia, 165
Killingsworth, John, 224
King Charles II, 3
King, Cornelius, 72
King, Daniel Webster, 69
King, Elijah, 69
King, Frank, 279
King, Gretchen Lucinda, 279
King, Harry H., 280
King, Margaret Mary, 168
King, Mrs. Frank, 279
King, Mrs. H. H., 279
King, Nancy, 69
King, Ross Lauden, Jr., 215
King, Sarah, 69
King, Sarah A., 69
King, William, 69
Kirby, Lucinda, 247
Kirby, Vance, 126
Kirkpatrick, Mary, 48
Kirkpatrick, Phebe, 48
Kittle, Chas., 169

Kittle, Grace Dell, 169
Kittle, Mary J., 64
Knicely, Daniel Albert, 213
Knight, David, 236
Knight, Michael, 236
Knoedler, Leland Frederick, 110
Kolb, John, 155
Kolbaugh, William Wooden, 163
Konrad, Johann, 126
Krauthaus, Christianan Sophia, 284
Krauthaus, Maria Elizabeth, 283, 284
Kreitel, Eduard, 276
Kuhnast, Dorothea Henrietta, 284
Kuhnast, Johann Gottlieb, 284

LaFayette, Genl., 143
Lanam, Mary, 154
Lane, Anne, 273
Lane, Frank, 273
Lane, John, 273
Lane, John W., 204
Lane, Martha, 273
Lane, Rebecca, 273
Lane, Roxie A., 204
Lane, Spenser S., 204
Lanneny, Francena, 48
Lantz, John and Barbara (Waggoner) Family, 48
Lantz, Alexander, 25, 41, 49, 50, 52
Lantz, Amassa (Massy), 50
Lantz, Andrew, 46, 47
Lantz, Anna Maria (Mary), 48
Lantz, Barbara (Waggoner), 25, 26, 45, 47, 48, 49, 50
Lantz, Catharine, 47
Lantz, Clara (Fuschain), 47
Lantz, Delilah, 50
Lantz, Delilah (Coen), 49
Lantz, Elias, 50
Lantz, Elizabeth, 40, 42, 43, 50

Index

Lantz, Elizabeth (Bonnett), 40
Lantz, Georg, 46
Lantz, George, 40, 45, 46, 47
Lantz, George, Will of, 45, 46
Lantz, Hans George, 45
Lantz, Henry, 47
Lantz, Jacob, 9, 41, 45, 46, 47, 49, 50, 52
Lantz, Johannas, 10
Lantz, Johannes, 9, 12, 28, 40
Lantz, Johannes (John), 47
Lantz, John, 40, 45, 46, 47, 48, 49, 50, 51, 52
Lantz, John (Launce), 48
Lantz, John George, 49
Lantz, John Jr., 40, 47
Lantz, John Sr., 40
Lantz, John, Will of, 51
Lantz, Joseph, 47
Lantz, Lewis, 40, 49, 50
Lantz, Lot, 50
Lantz, Margaret, 50
Lantz, Margaret 'Peggy', 40
Lantz, Margaretha, 46, 47
Lantz, Maria, 46, 47
Lantz, Maria Margaretha, 12
Lantz, Marian, 47
Lantz, Mary, 40, 47, 48, 50
Lantz, Nancy, 41
Lantz, Philip, 47
Lantz, Samuel, 50
Lantz, Sarah, 41
Lantz, Simon, 50
Lantz, Susanna, 50
Lantz, Thomas L., 50
Lantz, Wilhelm, 49
Lantz, William, 41, 47, 49, 50
Larance, John, 33
Larentz, Jacob, 121
Latham, Joseph, 270
Launce, John (Lantz), 48

Launtz, Johannes, 45
Laurence, John, 34
Law, Catharine, 106
Law, Dora Vi, 212
Law, Fred D., 106
Law, Gertie, Mrs., 210
Law, Newton, 206
Law, Thomas, 106
Lawless, Dorothy (Roper), 127
Lawless, J. C., 127
Lawless, Peggy Jo, 127
Lawman, Barnard, 227
Lawman, Emma Jane, 227
Lawman, William Henry, 227
Lawrence, Alexander, 208
Lawrence, Daniel, 208
Lawrence, Noah, 208
Lawrence, Peter, 208
Lawrence, Rebecca, 208
Lawson, Ailsy V., 205
Lawson, Cecelia, 205
Lawson, Rulena Pearl, 115
Laymons, Stephen, 153
Lazier, Charlotte, 78, 79
Lee, Henry, 92
Lee, Ronald, 171
Lee, Ruth, 169
Legget, Elizabeth Ann, 62
Leggett, Francia, 177
Leggett, John, 177
Lehr, Herman, 251
Lehr, Anna Marie, 253, 254
Lehr, Charles, 254
Lehr, George, 253
Lehr, Henry Andrew, 253, 254
Lehr, Henry Andrews, 253
Lehr, Herman, 253
Lehr, Ida, 251, 254
Lehr, Kenneth Dean, 254
Lehr, Mary (Watson), 254
Lehr, Oscar, 254

Index

Lehr, Otto, 254
Lehr, Velma Lucille, 254
Lehr, Will, 251
Lehr, Willie, 253
Lemley, Barbara, 47
Lemmons, A. W. C., 223
Lemmons, John, 52
Lemons, Goff, 180
Lentz, Jacob, 72
Lentz, Johannes, 11
Lentz, Maria Christina, 72
Leonard, Zeba, 237
LePori, Willis, 130
Lewis, John, 253
Lewis, Minerva, 204
Life, John, 84
Life, Laura B., 167
Life, Mary, 84
Life, Mary (Wimer), 84
Linger, Eliza, 59
Linger, Inez, 166
Linger, John, 180
Linger, John D., 65
Linger, Lewis, 59
Linger, Lucina (Curtis), 65
Linger, Margaret, 65
Linger, Margaret (McNemar), 61, 62, 64, 65
Linger, Mary, 61, 106
Linger, Matilda, 100
Linger, Nicholas, 61, 62, 65
Linger, Nicholas D., 64
Linger, Nicholas F., 65
Linger, Roy W., 221
Linger, Susan, 73
Linn, Eliza, 48
Linton, William, 57
Lively, David, 50
Livingston, John, 84
Lockhart, M. Adean, 214
Lockhart, Thomas Hanson, 73

Loomis, Elizabeth, 266
Loomis, Nathaniel, 266
Looney, George W., 84
Lorance, Elizabeth (Larantz), 57
Lorance, John, 57
Lorance, Mary, 57
Lorentz, J. W., 218
Lorentz, Jacob, 200, 202, 219
Lorentz, Johannes, 34
Lorentz, Kent, 221
Lortow, Mary Ellen, 212
Lough, Evelyn, 214
Lough, George F., 85
Lough, Matilda S., 85
Lough, P. J., 215
Lough, Rachel (Wimer), 85
Lough, Ray R., 213
Louk, Ralph E., 169
Lountz, George, 46
Love, Boyde, 244
Lovett, Catherine E., 212
Lowe, Arthur Waitman, 111
Lower, Christian, 31
Lowhead, Ellen (Eleanor), 237
Lowrentz, Oma Gray, 110
Lowther, Col., 57
Lowther, Dorris, 164
Lowther, Jonathan, 58
Lowther, Sudna (Hughes), 58
Lowther, Wilham, Col., 58
Lowther, William Col., 142
Lucas, Virginia, 173
Lucinda A. Bonnett, 61
Lucus, Will B., 238
Luetge, Anton Urich, 49
Lunsford, A. J., 182
Lunsford, Andrew, 101
Lunsford, Oscar, 182
Lunsford, Ruth, 166
Lutts, Agnes, 33, 34
Lutts, Agnes (Waggoner), 21, 34, 47

Index

Lutts, Barbara, 33
Lutts, Conrad, 21, 32, 33, 34, 45, 89, 90
Luzader, Sida H., 113
Lyons, Philip, 234

Mace, Edna, 111
Mace, Elizabeth, 217
Mace, Isaac, 178
Mace, John, 111
Mace, Rebecca, 178
Mace, Webster, 111
MacIntyre, Milo Arol, 112
Mack, John, 73, 90
MacKlinberg, Genl., 143
MacLemasters, Cerilda, 163
Madara, Matilda, 67
Mahnyn, Christina, 72
Malcom, Alexander, 219
Malcom, Dorothy, 219
Malcom, John, 219
Mall, Joseph, 141
Mann, Lacy Andrew, 227
Mann, Louise, 214
Mann, Marlion, 248
Maricock, Nicholas, 266
Marion, Isaac, 219
Marks, Amanda B., 111
Marks, Elizabeth, 216
Marks, J. O., 218
Marley, Ben, 152
Marple, A. J., 201
Marple, Emma O., 112
Marrow, John, 66
Marsh, Albert J., 66
Marsh, Aramantha, 66
Marsh, Catharine E., 65
Marsh, Eliza, 66
Marsh, Emily J., 65
Marsh, Flanivs A., 66
Marsh, George Irwin, Rev., 66

Marsh, George W., 66
Marsh, Gilbert M., 66
Marsh, Hiram, 66
Marsh, John, 62
Marsh, John C., 65
Marsh, Lucinda, 65
Marsh, Margaret, 65
Marsh, Mary (Bonnett), 62
Marsh, Nathan N., 62
Marsh, Nathan Newton, 65
Marsh, Rheuhana, 66
Marsh, Salathiel, 66
Marsh, Sally (Curtis), 65
Marsh, Sarah J., 66
Marsh, Sarah L., 65
Marsh, Spencer, 65
Marsh, William G., 66
Marshall, Mary, 266
Marstella, Charles, 233
Martha, Gates, 223
Martin, Charles Col., 142
Martin, Clara (Yorgenson), 241
Martin, Elizabeth, 201, 213, 222
Martin, Enoch E., 224
Martin, Esther Violet, 241
Martin, Joaquin F., 215
Martin, John, 50
Martin, Lem, 241
Masson, Philip, 33, 34
Mathers,, 251
Mathes, Ed, 251
Mathes, Emma, 251
Mathews, Lucinda, 63
Mathews, Lucinda (Bonnett), 61
Mathews, Mary, 62, 63
Mathews, William W., 62, 63
Mathias, Geneva Arlene, 240
Mauck, John, 74
Maxon, James, 83
Maxon, Ora B., 212
Maxwell, Luie, 144

Index

Mayberry, Blanche, 98
Mayberry, Hiram, 98
Maybury, Blanche, 78, 94
Maybury, Herman, 78
Maybury, Hiram, 94
Mays, Richard Allen, 128
Mays, Ronald F., 128
McAvoy, Francis C., 157
McAvoy, Jane, 157
McAvoy, John, 157
McCalley, Mary (McCullough), 48
McCallough, John, 177
McCay, Jim, 151
McCay, Wm. Albert, 151
McClain, Jane, 41
McClain, Melissa Carolyn, 214
McClaskey, May, 149
McClendon, Natalie, 110
McCollough, John, 175
McConnell, Ollie, 286
McCormick, Margaret, 50
McCoy, to Nancy E., 204
McCroskey, James, 191
McCue, Charles F., 180
McCue, Charles Franklin, 101
McCue, Dorothy, 180
McCue, Firth, 180
McCue, Frances, 101
McCue, French, 180
McCue, Ora, 180
McCue, Parthinia, 180
McCue, Thelma, 180
McCue, William B., 101
McCue, William Henry, 180
McCullough, Catharine, 48
McCullough, Mary, 48
McCullough, Rebecca, 49
McCullough, William, 49
McCurdy, Bill, 152
McDade, Polly, 185
McDonald, Alexander, 176, 179

McDonald, Elizabeth, 176, 179
McDonald, Frank, 113
McGlothan, Elizabeth, 228
McIntire, Presley, 144
McIntosh, John, 71
McIntyre, Toni, 168
McKay, Tom, 244
McKeever, Loretta, 212
McKinney, Pheobe Ellen, 70
McKinney, Roy, 214
McLaughton, May, 98
McMahan, William B., 71
McMullen, Margaret, 166
McNeamer, Elizabeth (Liloy), 99
McNeamer, Rebecca A., 99
McNeamer, William, 99
McNeill, John, 57
McNemar, Margaret, 64
McNutt, Lillian, 40, 47, 50
McVaney, Anna Mary, 110
McVaney, Josiah, 64
McWhorter, Eliza (Alkire), 208
McWhorter, Elizabeth, 109, 121, 164
McWhorter, Emma, 165
McWhorter, Emma A., 167
McWhorter, Grace, 218
McWhorter, Henry, 91, 144
McWhorter, John M., 208
McWhorter, L. V., 93
McWhorter, Levi, 208
McWhorter, Lucullus Virgil, 93
McWhorter, Margaret (Hurst), 109, 121, 164
McWhorter, Mary L., 158
McWhorter, Sarah Elizabeth, 157
McWhorter, Walter Fields, 121
Means, Isaac, 35, 107
Means, Margaret, 69
Means, Otho, 107, 179
Means, Robert, 69

Index

Meridith, Sherrie Lynn, 127
Merrill, Phillip H., 128
Merrill, Stephanie Maria, 128
Merriman, Everett, 250
Merrit, Mathew, 237
Merritt, Moses, 235, 237
Merritt, Nancy, 237
Metz, Henry W., 261
Meyer, Edwin, 133
Michael, Margaret, 123
Miles, A. Ross, 166
Miles, Beatrice, 203
Miles, Thomas E., 166
Mill, Hites Col., 34
Miller, Edith M., 223
Miller, Harriet, 84
Miller, James W., 223
Miller, Tobias, 146
Miller, William H., 213
Millian, Alfred, 244
Millian, Frank, 244
Million, Emma Jane (Scott), 244
Million, Burel, 244
Million, Catharine, 244
Million, Charlie, 244
Million, Dale, 244
Million, Dare, 244
Million, Dean, 244
Million, Fern, 244
Million, Frank, 250
Million, Jessie, 250
Million, Laura, 244
Million, Murel, 244
Mills, Artie Mishie, 224
Mills, John, 237
Minere, Adam H., 208
Minor, Margaret, 50
Minor, Menerva, 41
Minor, Permilia (Lancaster), 41
Minor, Samuel, 40, 41, 50
Minor, Susan (Clegg), 40

Minor, Theophylas, 40
Minor, William, 40
Mioffsky, Sophia, 276
Mitchel, Henderson D., 69
Mitchel, John, 81
Mitchel, John E., 69
Mitchel, Prudence (McCully), 69
Mitchell, Amelia Jane, 147
Mitchell, John, 74, 144, 147, 161, 233
Mitchell, John, Rev., 106, 107, 202, 216, 217, 219, 225
Mitchell, Margaret E., 187
Mitchell, Margaret Fender, 250
Mitchell, Mary O., 187
Mitchell, Peggy (Snider), 187
Mitchell, Thomas, 187
Mithcell, Margaret Fender, 83
Mock, Elizabeth, 74
Mohler, Mary Margaret, 62
Mooney, Glen, 151
Mooney, Nancy, 151
Moore, Alexis Evanda, 128, 129, 130
Moore, Dollie Lee, 129
Moore, E., 195
Moore, Edward Gleason, 130
Moore, Indemion Benjamin, 130
Moore, J. H., 195
Moore, James R., 106
Moore, Lucy, 59
Moore, Margaret E., 149
Moore, Margaret Roberta, 129
Moore, Roberta Benedict (Surbaugh), 128, 129
Moore, Tom, 250
Moore, Willie, 206
Morford, Alonzo Washington, 241
Morford, Belle Isabell (Riley), 241
Morford, Estel Alonzo, 241
Morford, Hanna (Taylor), 111

Index

Morford, John, 111
Morford, Priscilla Victoria, 111
Morgan, David Col., 143
Morgan, Parker, 231
Morgan, Sarah, 143
Morgan, Stephen, 143
Morris, Adra, 180
Morris, Allen J., 180
Morris, Aubra, 180
Morris, Davies Allen, 180
Morris, Gidion, 113
Morris, Gratice, 180
Morris, Hannah (Lawson), 180
Morris, Hartford Clyde, 111
Morris, Isaac, 146
Morris, Joseph, 189
Morris, Ottis, 180
Morrison, Albert N., 205
Morrison, Alexander, 68, 69
Morrison, Bridget, 67
Morrison, Elizabeth (Keagle), 68
Morrison, Elizabeth Frances, 113
Morrison, Fannie, 113
Morrison, George A., 113
Morrison, Gidion, 113
Morrison, H. R., 103
Morrison, Harriet Jane, 69
Morrison, Ida E., 205
Morrison, James M., 102
Morrison, James Monroe, 68
Morrison, John Brake, 176
Morrison, Lewis C., 205
Morrison, Margaret, 107
Morrison, Margaret (Brake), 69
Morrison, Marshal Dexter, 70
Morrison, Mary, 207, 210
Morrison, Minnie R., 205
Morrison, Verta Layola, 205
Morrison, William, 207
Morrison, William Dexter, 207
Morrison, William J., 178

Morton, Ann, 266
Morton, John, 266
Morton, Mary, 266
Morton, William, 266
Mowery, George, 46
Mullins, Pauline V., 111
Mundy, Nimrod, Capt., 218
Munger, Nicholas, 268
Murin, Nicholas, 163
Murphy, Anna (Dempsey), 129
Murphy, Dr. John, 285
Murphy, James, 129
Murphy, John, 285
Murphy, Josephine, 129
Murphy, Lucenda (Todd), 285
Murrow, Levina A., 66
Musser, Mary B., 211
Muzzy, John, 269
Myers, Charles, 34
Myles, David, 35

Neal, John, Capt., 142
Neal, Thomas, 142
Neely, Joseph Allen, 223
Neely, Libbie, 223
Neely, Teter, 224
Nestor, Lillie, 209
Nettleton, John, 268
Nichols, Nancy Jane, 178
Nichols, Samuel, 177
Nichols, Sarah, 111
Nickles, James N., 194
Nickles, John, 194
Nickles, Nancy, 194
Nickols, Samuel, 175
Norman, Arden, 114
Norman, Forest A., 200
Norman, Shumate, 114
Norman, Victoria, 114
Null, Sam, 250
Nutter, Elizabeth, 178

Index

Olcott, John, 266
Olcott, Mary, 266
Oliver, Aaron, 231
Oliver, Abegail, 231
Oliver, Anna, 231
Oliver, Benjamin, 231
Oliver, Catharine (Allman), 234, 237
Oliver, Catherine (Alman), 235
Oliver, Deborah, 232
Oliver, Elesha, 232
Oliver, Elizabeth, 216, 231, 232, 234, 235, 237, 239
Oliver, Gallaudett, 232
Oliver, Gillaudott, 232, 233
Oliver, Hanna, 86
Oliver, Jane, 231
Oliver, Jane (Jenny), 231
Oliver, John, 216, 233
Oliver, Joseph, 231
Oliver, Levi, 231
Oliver, Lydia, 216, 233, 234
Oliver, Mary, 231, 232, 233
Oliver, Rachel, 231
Oliver, Reuben, 216, 231, 232
Oliver, Samuel, 200, 231, 232, 233, 235
Oliver, Samuel Jr., 233
Oliver, Samuel, Jr., 216, 234
Oliver, Samuel, Sr., 216, 234
Oliver, Thomas, 232
Oliver, William, 233
Olson, Erik Michael, 128
Olson, Gordon Harold, 128
Olson, Helen Kathryn (McKuskie), 128
Ormsbee, George, 250
Osborn, Sophia, 61
Osburn, Howard, 70
Osburn, Philip, 70
Osburn, Ruth (Ware), 70
Osburn, Wilson, 179
Ostrowske, John, 218
Ours, Almira, 226
Ours, Iva, 226
Overmiller, Winnie, 251
Owens, Abel, 270
Owens, Miranda, 270
Owens, William, 177
Owens, Wm., 175

Palmer, George, 278
Palmer, George A., 278
Pancake, John, 57
Park, Della, 153
Parker, Mary Elizabeth, 218
Parker, Wm., Rev., 247
Parson, Annis, 62
Parsons, Evaline Amanda, 63
Parsons, Isaac, 35
Parsons, Victoria S., 111
Patterson, Maude "Lennie", 261
Patterson, Stout, 49
Patterson, William T., 64
Patton, Elizabeth B., 243
Patton, Julia A., 243
Paugh, Mary L., 114
Paxton, Hannibal, 186
Payne, Ella Mae, 152
Payne, Janet, 153
Payne, Layman, 152
Payne, Lynn, 152
Peck, Adam, 164
Peininger, Christopf, 276
Peininger, Maria Katharina, 276
Pendleton, Manley Richards, 82
Penn, William, 3
Penn, William, Charter of Liberties, 4
Penninger, Henry, 73
Perkins, Murl, 215

Index

Perry, Catherine, 227
Peters, Christian S., 193
Peters, Mary S., 193
Peters, Nancy E., 193
Peterson, Blanche, 182
Peterson, Clara, 182
Peterson, Eliza, 182
Peterson, Grant, 182
Peterson, Gretrude, 182
Peterson, Hannibal, 182
Peterson, Howard G., 181
Peterson, Jasper, 181
Peterson, Jasper N., 181, 182
Peterson, John P., 181
Peterson, John Peterson, 182
Peterson, John Waggoner, 182
Peterson, Joseph, 182
Peterson, Kate, 182
Peterson, Laura, 182
Peterson, Lenura, 182
Peterson, Lewis, 182
Peterson, Maggie, 182
Peterson, Martha O. (Waggoner), 182, 183
Peterson, Newton, 182
Peterson, Samantha, 182
Phillips, Israel, 81
Pickerill, A. J., 192
Pickerill, Levi, 192
Pickerill, Mariah, 192
Pickett, Daniel, 270
Pickett, Hepsibeth, 270
Pickrill, Ann E., 191
Pickrill, Levi, 191
Pierce, Aubrey Dale, 258
Pierce, Donald L., 258
Pierce, Edwin, 258
Pierce, Ivan Eugene, 258
Pierce, Melvin Wayne, 258
Plasman, Bertha, 133
Pletcher, Nellie Clayton, 218

Pockrus, Ralph, 124
Pohlman, Adam Frederick, 133
Pohlman, Adam Henry, 133
Pohlman, Alma Emma, 133
Pohlman, Irene, 130
Pohlmann, Adam Hunrich, 134
Pohlmann, Anna Margaretha, 133
Pohlmann, Elizabetha Margaretha, 134
Pohlmann, Johann Adam, 134
Pohlmann, Johann Georg, 133
Pohlmann, Johann Konrad, 133
Pohlmann, Katharina Christiana, 134
Pohlmann, Katharina Margaretha, 133, 134
Pohlmann, Konrad, 130
Pohlmann, Margareta Christina, 126
Pohlmann, Margareta Johanna, 126
Pohlmann, Margaretha (Maggie) Christinna, 134
Pohlmann, Margarita Christiana, 126, 130
Pohlmann, Margaritha Johanna, 130
Pohlmann, Nicholas, 126, 130
Pool, Cynthia, 243
Pool, John, 243
Port of Philadelphia Pennsylvania, 3
Porter, Faiery V. Slacum, 171
Porter, John, 171
Post, C. C., 205
Post, Charles, 207
Post, Eber E., 68
Post, Eber. E., 205
Post, Elizabeth, 59
Post, Ida Rachel, 207
Post, Jane, 207
Post, John, 59, 205
Post, Julia Ann, 207
Post, Martha Jane, 70
Post, Mary L., 59

Index

Post, Samantha, 59
Post, Sarah Olive, 205
Post, Sophia, 205
Post, Sophia S. (Cookman), 59
Post, Verdie M., 205
Post, William Lowther, 207
Postlethwait, H. J., 214
Potter, Ruth Jane, 129
Pounds, Lee, 251
Powell, Sophia, 206
Powers, William, 177
Powers, Wm., 140
Price, Sarah C., 191
Price, Susan, 192
Price, William, 192
Price, William P., 192
Pringle, Cecil, 115
Pringle, Clarence Wm., 115
Pringle, Ella May, 115
Pringle, John, 114, 232
Pringle, Mildred, 121, 179
Pringle, Mildred (Gould), 114
Pringle, Millard A. Earl, 115
Pringle, Millard Fillmore, 114
Pringle, Moss Monroe, 115
Pringle, Reta Ariella, 115
Pringle, Samuel, 232
Pringle, Wealthy, 223
Pringle, William, 232
Pritchard, Amanda, 64
Pritchard, Benjamin, 64
Pritchard, Charles, 64
Pritt, Joan, 213
Pritt, Joanne Fernandez, 214
Probst, William Brooks, 211
Propst, Dora, 103
Pugh, Joseph, 46
Purgate, Jacob, 78
Putman, Pauline, 162
Putman, Peter, 78

Queen, Armstead, 179
Queen, Boyd, 167
Queen, Merna, 114

Radcliff, Deborah (Hughes), 67, 175
Radcliff, Debra (Hughes), 121
Radcliff, Jane (Jenny), 175, 178
Radcliff, Jenny, 106
Radcliff, Martha, 67, 203
Radcliff, Susannah, 121
Radcliff, William, 67, 121, 175, 178
Radcliffe, Albert Lewis, 215
Radcliffe, Anna, 215
Radcliffe, Henry, 215
Rader, Jackson, 195
Rader, Mariah, 191
Rader, Nancy, 195
Rader, Saphronia, 195
Raines, Anna, 62
Raines, Frances (Fanny), 179
Raines, Frances (McDonald), 179
Raines, John, 179
Rainey, Brad, 169
Rains, Frances (McDonald), 176
Rains, John, 176
Rains, Martha Frances, 176
Ramsburg, Hugh, 212
Ramsburg, Retta, 214
Ramsbury, Caroline, 183
Ramsbury, John W., 183
Ramsbury, Sarah A., 183
Randall, Abel, 35
Randolph, Peggy Ann, 258
Ratcliff, Stephen, 35
Reed, Agnes, 214
Reed, Daniel, 71
Reed, Elijah, 231
Reed, Martha J., 71
Reed, Mary Belle, 173
Reed, Susan, 71
Reeder, Otto, Rev., 206

Index

Reeder, Thomas A., 206
Reger, Anthony, 124
Reger, Eva Grace, 124
Reger, Frank, 221
Reger, Hazel, 113
Reger, Henry, 157
Reger, Ida (Lewis), 113
Reger, John S., 157, 158
Reger, Linda E., 158
Reger, Margaret, 158
Reger, Margaret E., 158
Reger, Mary (Lynch), 124
Reger, Mary Elizabeth, 59
Reger, Philip, 157
Reger, Philip E., 70
Reger, Phillip, 200, 233
Reger, Romulus S., 113
Reger, Sally, 233
Reger, Virginia A., 124
Regester, Arthur R., 115
Regester, Frank W., 115
Regester, Nettie M., 115
Remley, James F., 124
Remmell, Owen William, 238
Reuben, Levi, 231
Reynolds, Nancy, 188
Reynolds, Reuben, 188
Reynolds, William, 188
Rhinehart, Juliana, 85
Rhinehart, Juliana A., 84
Rhodes, Beecher, 164
Rhodes, John, 28
Rhyner, Elizabeth, 189
Rich, Charles, 213
Richards, Arnold, 139
Richards, Margaret (Matthews), 79
Richards, Mary, 79
Richards, Paul, 139, 147
Richards, Susannah, 95, 139
Richards, William, 79
Richardson, Harvy, 126

Richardson, Pam, 128
Richardson, Virginia (Kraft), 128
Richardson, William, 128
Rickey, Laura, 154
Riddle, Col., 141
Rieger, Johannes Bartholomew, 5
Riely, Simpkin, 240
Riffee, Minnie B., 164
Riffle, Barbara, 234
Rinehart, Abraham, 112, 113
Rinehart, Alice C., 113
Rinehart, Arthur J., 211
Rinehart, Burtie, 113
Rinehart, Cora Virginia, 221
Rinehart, Elizabeth A., 113
Rinehart, Fernando, 112
Rinehart, Gladstone Addison, 113
Rinehart, Isaac C., 220, 221
Rinehart, Jefferson Leo, 175
Rinehart, John, 113
Rinehart, Noah H., 112
Rinehart, Orlando, 112
Rinehart, Rachel Lavernia, 220
Rinehart, Reta B., 112
Rinehart, Richard, 68
Rinehart, Sarah (Eckard), 113
Rinehart, Susannah, 207
Ring, Lola, 251
Ring, Orris, 250
Rink, Fredrecka, 261
Riser, Betty Irene, 280
Riser, Ida, 279
Riser, Raymond Lawrence, 280
Ritchier, Eunice, 163
Ritter, Lois Mary, 240
Roan, Margaret (Peggy) Clark, 229
Roan, Peggy Clark, 229
Roan, T. C. H., 229
Roan, Thomas C. H., 229
Robb, Ella, 251
Roberts, Hannah, 31, 32

Index

Roberts, John, 162
Robertson, Phillis Grantine, 240
Robinson, Carol Dean, 152
Robinson, Dan, 152
Robinson, Jorene, 152
Roby, Burton, 204
Rocke, Elizabeth (Farmham), 268
Rodefer, Phillip, 41
Rodeffer, John, 41
Rodeffer, Philip, 42, 43
Rodman, Alexander, 98
Rodman, Maria, 78, 94
Rodman, Marion, 98
Rogers, Eliza, 86
Rogers, Joan, 223
Rogers, Philip, 176
Rogers, William, 223
Rohrbough, Bertha, 218
Rohrbough, David A., 102
Ross, Reese, 178
Roth, Larry, 152
Roth, Rosena, 32
Rowan, E. Howard, 224
Rowe, Allie, 111
Rucker, Margaret Willis, 129
Rummel, Susan, 236
Rummell, Susanna, 238
Runge, Mary Leone, 128
Runge, Neal H., 128
Runge, Robert Neal, Jr., 128
Runyon, Elijah, 97, 98, 177
Runyon, John, 139, 140, 145
Runyon, Susannah, 140
Ruse, Howard, 153
Russell, John, 110
Rutan, Clemma Mae, 154
Rutherford, Robert, 46
Ryneheart, Daniel, 39

Saint Michael's Evangelical Lutheran Church, 10

Salomo, Jakob, 276
Salomon, Erich, 275
Salomon, Jens Lorenz, 275
Saltner, George, 16
Sanders, J. Clarke, Professor, 17
Sanders, John, 243
Santee, John L., 112
Sayler, Jeanne Marie, 228
Schiefer, John T., 64
Schoolcraft, Leonard, 82
Schwabe, Georg, 276
Scott , Betty, 244
Scott, Alfred, 237
Scott, Catharine Ann (Fairburn), 240
Scott, Charles B., 72
Scott, Charles W., 243
Scott, Cynthia, 244
Scott, Cynthia (Pool), 244
Scott, Dora E., 244
Scott, Dora Esmeralda, 245
Scott, Dora Esmerilda, 240
Scott, Dorenda, 243
Scott, Eliazabeth, 237
Scott, Elizabeth Cora, 245
Scott, Emma Jane, 244
Scott, George, 243, 244
Scott, George Clarence, 244
Scott, Henry, 237
Scott, Isaac J., 243
Scott, Isabel, 243
Scott, James, 244
Scott, James Delaze, 244
Scott, Jane, 243
Scott, John L., 244
Scott, Judy, 243
Scott, Lawrence, 244
Scott, Lucy Ellen, 244
Scott, Mary, 243
Scott, Simpkino Rieley, 244
Scott, Simpkins R., 243
Scott, Simpkins Rieley, 243

Index

Scragg, Lydia, 244
Scragg, Richard, 244
Scragg, Samuel, 244
Searle, Mary, 82
Selbitz, Andreas, 284
Selbitz, Andreas Julius, 285
Selbitz, Anna (Hanna) Maria (Seyferth), 281
Selbitz, Anna Maria, 285
Selbitz, Anna Maria Catharine, 284
Selbitz, Annie, 285
Selbitz, Carl Friedrich, 285
Selbitz, Charles, 285
Selbitz, Christian, 284
Selbitz, Christian Gottlieb, 285
Selbitz, Christoph Andreas, 277, 284
Selbitz, Hanns Caspar, 283
Selbitz, Hanns Georg, 283
Selbitz, Hanns Nicholas, 283
Selbitz, Johann Adam, 283, 284
Selbitz, Johann Christian, 278, 284
Selbitz, Johann Friedrich, 284
Selbitz, Johann Gerog Andreas, 284
Selbitz, Johann Gerog Gottlieb, 284
Selbitz, Johann Gottfried Christoph, 284
Selbitz, Johann Gottfried Friedrich, 283
Selbitz, Johann Gottlieb Conrad, 284
Selbitz, Johann Samuel, 283
Selbitz, Maria Dorothea, 284
Selbitz, Sarah Jane, 278
Selintz, Christian, 286
Selwitz , Lydia C., 285
Selwitz, Albert, 286
Selwitz, Anna, 285
Selwitz, Charles, 285
Selwitz, Christian M., 285
Selwitz, Clara, 286
Selwitz, Emma, 286
Selwitz, Flora, 285

Selwitz, Francas, 286
Selwitz, Grace Ella, 286
Selwitz, Grover, 285
Selwitz, Hugh, 286
Selwitz, John R., 286
Selwitz, Margaret G., 286
Selwitz, Maria Augusta, 286
Selwitz, Mary C., 285
Selwitz, Mary E. (Mollie), 286
Selwitz, Rhoda, 286
Selwitz, Sarah Elizabeth, 285
Selwitz, Sarah Jane, 277, 286
Selwitz, Susan E., 286
Selwitz, William C., 286
Sessin, Mennie M., 278
Seyferth, Anna (Hanna) Maria, 278
Seyferth, Friederike Wilhelmina, 284
Shade, Martin T., 273
Shafer, Charles S., 186
Shafer, David Lee, 186
Shafer, Ezra, 186
Shafer, George B., 186
Shafer, John, 186
Shafer, John Wesley, 186
Shafer, Maria (Dobson), 186
Shafer, Mary (Cox), 186
Shafer, Mary A., 186
Shafer, Matilda, 166
Shafer, Sarah C., 186
Shafer, Viola V., 186
Shall, Peter, 140
Shanet, Elizabeth, 161
Shapiro, Norma, 128
Shaver, John Wesley, 185
Shaw, John, 269
Sheather, Hannah, 268
Shelton, Annabell, 152
Shelton, Clarence, 152
Shennaman, Chris, 250
Sheppard, Diana, 191

Index

Sheppard, Henry, 191
Sheppard, Sarah K., 191
Sheppard, Winifred Cline, 171
Shoulders, Catharine, 208
Shoulders, David, 208
Shoulders, Edward, 208
Shoulders, Joseph, 60, 208
Shoulders, Laban, 60
Shoulders, Laben, 208
Shoulders, Mattie Jane, 218
Shoulders, Rosa E., 218
Shoulders, Susan, 60
Shoulders, W. M., 60
Shoulders, William, 208
Shouldes, Joseph, 80
Shouldes, Laban, 80
Shouldes, Susan, 80
Shouldes, W. M., 80
Shumway, Sarah, 270
Shurtliff, James, Rev., 219
Shurtoff, Mary, 99
Shurts, Philitus A., 238
Sicks, John, 89
Silbitz, Sarah Jane, 276
Simms-Allman, Catherine, 203
Simpson, J. L., 225
Simpson, John, 35
Sims, Catherine, 202, 208
Sims, Claudius W., 191
Sims, Edward J., 191
Sims, Granville, 191
Sims, Henry M., 191
Sims, John W., 191
Sims, John Wesley, 191
Sims, Leonard D., 145
Sims, Louvernia C., 225
Sims, Lucy C., 191
Sims, Martin, 144, 191
Sims, Martin Luther, 192
Sims, Mary (West), 191
Sims, Mary Louisa, 192
Sims, Minton B., 192
Sims, Okey J., 191
Sims, Olive M., 191, 192
Sims, Perry G. (Perigrine), 192
Sims, Susan, 144
Sims, Susan B., 191
Sims, Susanna, 140, 202
Sims, Susanna Elizabeth, 192
Sims, Thomas, 107
Sims, William, 202, 225
Singleton, E. I., Mrs., 210
Sisemore, Arlis, 127
Sisemore, Janie, 127
Sisemore, Mildred, 127
Six, Barbara (Knotts), 19
Six, Barbara (Selsor), 49
Six, Barbara Selsar, 19
Six, Catharine, 19
Six, Catharine (Bonnett), 19
Six, Catharine Lemley, 19
Six, Christina (Munger), 19
Six, Daniel, 19
Six, Edward, 19
Six, Henrick, 49
Six, Henry, 19
Six, Jacob, 19
Six, John, 18, 19, 40
Six, John Conrad, 18, 19
Six, Lewis, 19
Six, Mary (Garrison), 19
Six, Phillip, 19
Skeens, Thomas P., 111
Slabaugh, Charles E., 213
Slade, Harry, 250
Sleath, Elizabeth C., 192
Sleeth, Amelia, 82
Sleeth, David, 56, 74
Sleeth, David M., 142
Sleeth, Henry W., 146
Sleeth, Miss Jane, 58
Slover, John T., 127

Index

Small, Harvey K., 163
Smith, 1853 Rulina M, 70
Smith, Adelina L., 64
Smith, Amanda, 64
Smith, Artenia S., 64
Smith, Augustine J., 216
Smith, Cabel, 81
Smith, Calvin N., 69
Smith, Catharine (Fench), 64
Smith, Catherine, 205
Smith, Clark, 167
Smith, David, 81, 144
Smith, David H., 68, 107
Smith, David P., 69
Smith, Edwen Lee, 65
Smith, Eliza, 167
Smith, Ellis Lee, 101
Smith, Emily B., 206
Smith, Ermine, 79
Smith, Floyd O., 102
Smith, Gedion G., 69
Smith, George, 64, 73, 182
Smith, George Lewis, 207
Smith, Gordon Ross Jr., 128
Smith, Granville, 64
Smith, Hanson H., 64
Smith, Harriet K., 64
Smith, Henry R., 69, 207
Smith, Jacob, 64
Smith, Jane, 64
Smith, Jesse, 64
Smith, John, 64, 133
Smith, John William, 213
Smith, John, Rev., 106
Smith, Lydia, 229
Smith, Lydia (Ball), 81
Smith, Lyle, 167
Smith, Marcelia, 64
Smith, Marcellus, 64
Smith, Margaret, 206
Smith, Margaret (Talbott), 101

Smith, Marie Rebecca, 261
Smith, Mark, 64, 144
Smith, Martha Margaret, 204
Smith, Martin J., 101
Smith, Mary C., 64
Smith, Mary Pence, 64
Smith, Matilda C., 205
Smith, Mrs. John, 126
Smith, Nancy, 69, 212
Smith, Nancy Ann, 207
Smith, Reta Elizabeth, 215
Smith, Rheuhanna, 64
Smith, Robert B., 81, 146, 155
Smith, Samuel B., 69
Smith, Samuel R., 64
Smith, Sarah, 68
Smith, Sarah (Hacker), 68
Smith, Sarah J., 69
Smith, Solomon, 229
Smith, Stephen, 69
Smith, Stephen L., 70
Smith, Waitman E., 212
Smith, Weeden H., 64
Smith, William, 69
Smith, William H., 69
Smith, William H. Harrison, 64
Smith, Willis, 215
Snodgrass, Nola, 207
Snodgrass, Winfield, 207
Snyder, Bertie, 100
Snyder, Dorsey Stanton, 214
Snyder, Ellen F. Lewis, 204
Snyder, Nora, 212
Snyder, Orpha, 164
Solomo, Adam W., 276
Solomon, Annetta M. (Nellie), 279
Solomon, Annie E., 278
Solomon, Bertha A., 279
Solomon, Charles, 281
Solomon, Charles F., 279
Solomon, Christian Elmer, 274, 279

Index

Solomon, Christian Frederick, 280
Solomon, Christian Friedrich, 277
Solomon, Christian Friedrick, 286
Solomon, Elmer, 279, 281
Solomon, Elmer Christian, 127, 265
Solomon, Emma Elizabeth, 279
Solomon, Emma King, 281
Solomon, Florance America, 279
Solomon, Florance Laura
   (Burnham), 127
Solomon, Frank, 279
Solomon, Frank Fredrick, 279
Solomon, Frank Friedrich, 279
Solomon, Fred, 279, 281
Solomon, Frederick, 277, 281
Solomon, Friedrich, 284
Solomon, Friedrick W., 279
Solomon, Ida Belle, 280
Solomon, Ida Reiser, 281
Solomon, Inez Lucille, 127, 279
Solomon, Johann Christoph
   (Salomo), 277
Solomon, Lucille Alma, 280
Solomon, Lucille King, 281
Solomon, Nettie Gerken, 281
Solomon, Sarah Jane, 281
Solomon, Will, 279
Solomon, William, 281
Solomon, William E., 278
Sophia, Christiane, 276
Spangle, Robert Burl, 168
Spangler, Jane Ellen, 168
Spangler, Sarah Kathleen, 168
Spaur, Abel, 63
Spaur, Almirah, 63
Spaur, Anthony R., 63, 100
Spaur, Dafina, 63, 100
Spaur, David N., 63
Spaur, Gidion D., 63
Spaur, Gilbert, 63
Spaur, Greenbury C., 63

Spaur, John, 63
Spaur, Lafayette, 63
Spaur, Nancy, 63, 100
Spaur, Sarah (Bonnett), 100
Spaur, Virginia, 63
Speagle, Michael, 74
Spencer, Col., 236
Spivey, Joe Glenn, 153
Spivey, Stanton, 153
Spivey, Ward, 153
Springer, Cornelius, Rev., 106
Sprouse, Arnette Wayne, 162
Sprouse, Eliza (Bonnett), 69
Sprouse, Fleming, 61, 69
Sprouse, Garley, 162
Sprouse, George, 61
Sprouse, Leonard S., 61
Sprouse, Lucinda, 61
Sprouse, Martha, 61
Sprouse, Martha E., 69
Sprouse, Ruth Ann, 162
Sprouse, Sarah, 61
Sprouse, Washington, 61
Staats, Abraham, 176
Staats, Ann, 176, 177
Staats, Ann E., 186
Staats, Catharine, 72
Staats, Elijah, 72
Staats, Isaac, 186
Staats, Sarah E., 72
Staats, Squire, 186
Staggers, W. F., 51
Stahl, Elizabeth, 259
Stalnaker, Adam, 118, 119, 120
Stalnaker, Albert V., 167
Stalnaker, Andrew, 121, 165
Stalnaker, Anna G., 166
Stalnaker, Bailey, 101
Stalnaker, Bassel, 165
Stalnaker, Charles, 165
Stalnaker, Charles Burton, 167

Index

Stalnaker, Christina Victoria, 166
Stalnaker, Claude Festus, 112
Stalnaker, Clyde E., 166
Stalnaker, Dessi Julia, 111
Stalnaker, Edna Mable, 167
Stalnaker, Eleanor (Reeder), 64
Stalnaker, Elizabeth, 165
Stalnaker, Elizabeth (McWhorter), 112, 165
Stalnaker, Elizabeth Ann, 109
Stalnaker, Elizabeth Rebecca, 165
Stalnaker, Ellen T., 64
Stalnaker, Elwood (Bud) A., 111
Stalnaker, Emma Louisetta, 112
Stalnaker, Emma Merly, 167
Stalnaker, Ernest Ross, 167
Stalnaker, Ethel, 166
Stalnaker, Eula, 165
Stalnaker, Eunice Virginia, 111
Stalnaker, George, 119, 165
Stalnaker, George Washington, 112, 121
Stalnaker, George Whitman, 111
Stalnaker, George William, 166
Stalnaker, Guy, 111
Stalnaker, Harold, 165
Stalnaker, Haroldine, 63
Stalnaker, Henry W., 167
Stalnaker, Hobart C., 167
Stalnaker, Hobert, 165
Stalnaker, Ida Mae, 111
Stalnaker, Ira Alonzo, 167
Stalnaker, J. W., 121
Stalnaker, Jacob, 119, 121
Stalnaker, John, 121, 165
Stalnaker, Julia (Hall), 114
Stalnaker, Julia Ann, 165
Stalnaker, Kenneth, 63, 165
Stalnaker, Laura H., 166
Stalnaker, Leda Verona, 167
Stalnaker, Lelia R., 167
Stalnaker, Levi, 165
Stalnaker, Marcellus Elias, 165
Stalnaker, Mary (Peterson), 101
Stalnaker, Mary E., 167
Stalnaker, Mary Oliva, 111
Stalnaker, Mary Olive, 165
Stalnaker, Mary P., 166
Stalnaker, Mary Phyliss, 114
Stalnaker, Matthew C., 167
Stalnaker, Maude, 111
Stalnaker, Meryl, 165
Stalnaker, Minter L., 101
Stalnaker, Nancy, 120
Stalnaker, Rebecca, 86, 121
Stalnaker, Rita, 167
Stalnaker, Robert Hughes, 112
Stalnaker, Roy S., 166
Stalnaker, Ruth Ann, 111
Stalnaker, Sabisco, 165
Stalnaker, Samuel, 109, 112, 118, 119, 120, 121, 164, 165
Stalnaker, Samuel Elijah, 165
Stalnaker, Sobisca, 164
Stalnaker, Spencer Cleber, 111
Stalnaker, T. E., 114
Stalnaker, Thaddeus, 166
Stalnaker, Thomas Brooks, 166
Stalnaker, Thomas Curl, 166
Stalnaker, Thomas Edward, 166
Stalnaker, Torcia, 167
Stalnaker, Val, 121
Stalnaker, Valentine, 120
Stalnaker, Vesta, 166
Stalnaker, Walter, 121, 165, 166
Stalnaker, Walter (Watt), 109
Stalnaker, Walter Everett, 111
Stalnaker, William P., 64
Stalnaker, William Paul, 167
Stangley, Jacob, 35
Stanley, John W., 187
Staracher, Hannah, 178

Index

Starcher, Abraham, 178
Starcher, Adam, 178
Starcher, Amanda C., 176
Starcher, Anna, 175, 177, 179
Starcher, Arnold, 178
Starcher, Barbara, 178
Starcher, Catherine, 179
Starcher, Daniel, 178
Starcher, Deborah, 179
Starcher, Elizabeth, 176, 178
Starcher, Emma Cornelia, 168
Starcher, Francis, 176
Starcher, George W., 176
Starcher, Henry, 178
Starcher, Isaac, 178
Starcher, Jacob, 175, 176, 177, 178, 179
Starcher, Jacob Jasper, 176
Starcher, Jacob Jr., 177
Starcher, Jacob Sr., 177
Starcher, Jane, 176, 179
Starcher, Jane (Jenny) (Radcliff), 179
Starcher, Jean, 177
Starcher, Jesse, 178
Starcher, John, 106, 175, 176, 177, 179
Starcher, John T., 168, 176
Starcher, Joseph P., 178
Starcher, Manuel, 176
Starcher, Martha, 179
Starcher, Martha Ann, 176
Starcher, Mary, 176, 178, 179
Starcher, Mary (Waggoner), 175
Starcher, Mary Ann (Ferrell), 168
Starcher, Mary Bush, 178
Starcher, Mifflin, 176
Starcher, Nancy, 179
Starcher, P., 178
Starcher, Phillip, 178
Starcher, Purdy F., 175

Starcher, Quincy Oliver, 176
Starcher, Rebecca A., 175
Starcher, Samuel, 177
Starcher, Sarah, 125, 178, 179
Starcher, Stephen, 179
Starcher, Susanna, 179
Starcher, William, 176
Starcher, William (Billy Bluehead), 178
Starcher, William B., 178
Starcher, William Elmore, 176
Starcher, William R., 175, 176, 179
Starn, Frederick, 119
Stasel, Christopher, 145
Statur, Phillip, 176
Statzer, Jacob, 177
Staurcher, John Fairlee, 70
Stebbing, Dec. Edward, 267
Steelman, Lear D., 66
Steffen, Charles, 260, 261
Steffen, Charles G. F., 260
Steffen, Charles T. G., 260
Steffen, Charles Theador, 261
Steffen, Charles Theador George, 251, 261
Steffen, Charles Theodour George, 260
Steffen, Emma Amelia, 251, 261
Steffen, Frederick William, 261
Steffen, George Ad 'Edward', 261
Steffen, Grace, 261
Steffen, Henry Albert, 261
Steffen, John, 261
Steffen, June Elizabeth, 261
Steffen, Mary (Dinkel), 260
Stegman, Emma, 279
Steinacker, Georg, 276
Steinacker, Marie Sophie, 276
Stephens, Alfred William, 128
Stephens, Mary Lore, 128
Stephson, Margaret, 273

Index

Stevens, Earnest, 152
Stevens, Edward, 142
Steward, Margaret, 84
Steward, Martha, 220
Stewart, David, 20
Stewart, Hezekiah, 20
Stewart, Jacob, 20
Stewart, Jesse, 20
Stewart, Robert, 224, 225
Stewart, Susannah, 20
Stiles, Isaac, 51
Stiles, Jonathan, 48
Stiles, Mary, 52
Stine, Arva, 147
Stine, Charles, 147
Stine, Charles W., 151
Stine, Terry, 151
Stine, Tom, 151
Stoats, Annie, 71
Stofer, William, 239
Stoffer, Calvin, 249
Stoffer, Ellsworth, 249
Stoffer, Erma, 249
Stoffer, Ida May (Watson), 249
Stoffer, Irene, 249
Stoffer, Loirn, 249
Stoffer, Loren, 253
Stoffer, Marion, 249
Stoffer, Myrtle, 249
Stoffer, Roy, 249
Stoffer, Sarah, 249
Stoffer, William, 249
Stokes, John C., 168
Stom, George, 285
Stom, Mary, 285
Stone, Nelson, 71
Strader, Ethel May, 114
Strader, Julia A., 114
Strader, Willis I, 114
Straley, Anna, 95
Straley, Caroline, 161

Straley, Christian, 72
Straley, Christina, 72
Straley, Elias, 161
Straley, Elizabeth, 72, 147
Straley, Elizabeth (Bonnett), 147, 161
Straley, Geo. Presley, 161
Straley, George, 106, 147, 161
Straley, George Jr., 72
Straley, George Sr., 72
Straley, Hannah, 72
Straley, Jacob, 72, 161
Straley, James, 161
Straley, Joseph, 161
Straley, Mary, 72, 107, 161
Straley, Nancy, 72
Straley, Samuel B., 161
Straley, Simmons, 161
Straley, Thomas S., 107
Stringer, William G., 73
Strong, Elizabeth, 268
Strong, John, 268
Stuber, Chas., 168
Styles, Andrew, 48
Styles, Deborra, 48, 49
Styles, Eliza, 49
Styles, George, 48
Styles, Jacob, 48
Styles, John, 48
Styles, Jonathan, 49
Styles, Lewis, 49
Styles, Margaret, 49
Styles, Mary, 48
Styles, Mary (Lantz), 49
Styles, Simon, 48
Styles, Stephen, 48
Styles, Thomas, 48
Summers, Alvin, 165
Summers, Lucy Eugenia, 124
Summers, Rose, 165
Summers, Washington, 218

Index

Sumner, Elizabeth, 85
Sumner, George, 85
Sumner, Susan Elizabeth, 85
Surbaugh, Henry Clay, 130
Surbaugh, Roberta Benedict, 130
Surbaugh, William, 130
Sutton, Alcinda Margaret
  (Waggoner), 125
Sutton, Amanda A., 126
Sutton, Andrew Elias, 125
Sutton, Andrew N., 125
Sutton, Auagistine, 166
Sutton, Audrey R., 125
Sutton, Dinah, 125
Sutton, Dorothy Lee, 124
Sutton, G., 125
Sutton, George Ralph, 124
Sutton, Goodloe, 108
Sutton, Goodlow (John G.), 124
Sutton, Henry A., 126
Sutton, Jacob, 124, 125
Sutton, Jacob G., 125
Sutton, James W., 126
Sutton, Jo Ann, 124
Sutton, John A., 124, 125
Sutton, John Abernathy, 124
Sutton, John Hayward, 124
Sutton, Luverna Catharine
  (Waggoner), 124
Sutton, Margaret C., 125
Sutton, Mary Sue, 124
Sutton, Mary V., 125
Sutton, Maude Florance, 124
Sutton, Rachel A., 125
Sutton, Roy C., 124
Sutton, Samuel C., 125
Sutton, Synthia J., 125
Sutton, Virginia A. (Reger), 125
Sutton, William E., 124
Swaney, Thomas, 236
Swecker, Eddy M., 207

Swecker, Minerva J., 207
Swecker, Samuel, 207
Swecker, to John E., 207
Swisher, Alfred Washington, 210
Swisher, Ardelia Maud, 180
Swisher, Bertha A., 205
Swisher, Clay, 212
Swisher, David, 207
Swisher, David Rinehart, 206, 207
Swisher, Dora, 206
Swisher, Dora Ethel, 210
Swisher, Eda A., 211
Swisher, Edwin C., 205
Swisher, Elizabeth, 113
Swisher, Floe, 180
Swisher, George, 180
Swisher, Hannah, 79
Swisher, Ira Erwin, 211
Swisher, Isaac Columbus, 209, 210
Swisher, Isaac M., 206
Swisher, Isaac R., 211
Swisher, James Blain, 210
Swisher, James Lee, 210
Swisher, John B., 205
Swisher, Juliana, 179
Swisher, Lewis D., 204, 207
Swisher, Lydia E., 207
Swisher, Martha, 207
Swisher, Mary (Boram), 180
Swisher, Mary (Post), 203
Swisher, Mary Marcelia, 209
Swisher, Meade, 207
Swisher, Nancy C., 204
Swisher, Peter, 179
Swisher, Peter Jr., 207
Swisher, Rella May, 210
Swisher, Rocky, 210
Swisher, Samantha M., 206
Swisher, Sara A., 206
Swisher, Sarah J., 211
Swisher, Stella M., 205

Index

Swisher, Stokes, 166
Swisher, Susanna, 179
Swisher, Thomas E., 182
Swisher, Willard D., 207
Swisher, Zora, 206

Tahnage, Elizabeth, 267
Tanner, Grace, 58
Tanner, Jesse, 178
Tanner, Nancy, 178
Taubald, Emma, 133
Taubald, Emma Margaret (Maggie), 133
Taylor, Edward Oliver, 180
Taylor, Elizabeth, 243
Taylor, Erma Augusta, 114
Taylor, Francis, 179, 181
Taylor, Francis Edward, 180
Taylor, George W., 243
Taylor, Howard, 173
Taylor, Hustus, 166
Taylor, J. O., 114
Taylor, James Smith, 111
Taylor, Margaret, 179
Taylor, Mary Margaret, 180
Taylor, Nettie, 110
Taylor, Purdy (Waggoner), 180, 181
Taylor, Ray, 173
Taylor, Sadie V., 114
Taylor, Samuel B., 243
Taylor, T. S., 86
Taylor, Thomas, 179
Tecumseh, 90, 142
Templeton, Nancy, 130
Tennev, Ethel Addie, 227
Tenney, Ina Beatrice, 125
Tenney, John S., 225
Tenney, Jonathan, 225
Tenney, Jonathan Milroy, 225
Tenney, Peter, 227
Tenney, Rosa Lee, 222

Tenney, Rufus, 227
Terry, George, 78
Teter, Rebecca A., 176
Thomas, Albert, 152
Thomas, Arva, 151
Thomas, Carol Sue, 152
Thomas, Earl, 152
Thomas, Frank, 151
Thomas, Irene, 152
Thomas, Juanita, 152
Thomas, Junetta, 151, 152
Thomas, Lois, 151
Thomas, Lucy, 50
Thomas, Ralph, 151
Thomas, Ray Wesley, 152
Thomas, Ruth, 152
Thomas, Sarah, 41
Thomas, Verl, 152
Thompson, Martha A., 166
Thorn, Caroline, 195
Thorn, Elizabeth, 195
Thorn, Jehu, 195
Thorne, Adrian Upton, 173
Thorne, Frederick Wilhelm, 171
Thorne, Myrdith Evelyn, 171
Thorne, Orie Eugene Wilson Rev., 171
Thorne, Paul Eugene, 171
Thorp, William, 149
Thrash, Benjamin F., 206
Thrash, E. J., 212
Thrash, Mary Christine, 211
Thrash, Michael, 211
Throckmorton, Joseph R., 213
Tibbetts, Al, 149
Tibbetts, Cordelia Olive, 149
Tillman, Teresa, 85
Tillman, Thomas W., 85
Tillman, Zachariah Taylor, 85
Timms, Catherine, 213
Tinney, John S., 225

Index

Tinney, Lavina, 225
Tinney, Peter, 225
Tole, Catherine, 244
Tole, Elizabeth, 244
Tracey, Grace L., 17
Treece, Eugene, 128
Treece, Gregory Gene, 128
Troth, Elizabeth (Lizzie), 279
Truby, Elizabeth, 121
Truby, John, 121
Truman, William, 178
Trustin, Albonus, 212
Turnbaugh, Elmer, 286
Turner, Byron Jarvis, 110
Turner, Elizabeth, 179
Turner, Elizabeth (deGruyter), 121
Turner, John Mark, 110
Tutwiler, Ina, 214
Tygart, Eagon, 41

Upton, Elizabeth, 187
Utter, Briant, 185
Utter, Bryant, 185
Utter, Elizabeth, 185
Utter, William, 185

Van Meter, Major Corroll, 141
Vanderee, Anis Lucille, 240
Vanderee, Frederick, 240
Vanderee, Lillie Mae (Newton), 240
Vandine, Laura Ann, 71
Vandle, John, 185
Vandle, Rachel, 185
Vandle, Wm. J., 185
Vannoy, John, 195
Vannoy, Lelita, 195
Vannoy, Susan, 195
Vassar, Ruth, 214
Vetra, Mayo Elva, 221
Vincent, Joseph Israel, 211
Vincent, Viola Victoria, 211

Wade, Mary J., 64
Wagener, Wilhelm, 12
Wagener, William, 11
Waggoner, Adran, 168
Waggoner, Agnes, 21, 25, 28, 48, 90
Waggoner, Agnesa, 11, 12, 89
Waggoner, Agnisa, 139
Waggoner, Alcinda Margaret, 125
Waggoner, Alda M., 114
Waggoner, Alice Ruth, 163
Waggoner, Alonzo, 167
Waggoner, Alvin, 169
Waggoner, Alvin L., 157
Waggoner, Amazith, 167
Waggoner, Amelia Jane, 147
Waggoner, America C., 147
Waggoner, Amos, 145
Waggoner, Anderson Erwin, 123
Waggoner, Anna Elisabeth, 10, 12
Waggoner, Anna Elizabeth, 25, 26, 28, 32, 34
Waggoner, Annie, 107, 109
Waggoner, Arthelia G., 180
Waggoner, Auaugustine, 167
Waggoner, Ava, 168
Waggoner, Baltas, 32
Waggoner, Barbara, 25, 28, 33, 45, 47
Waggoner, Belle, 153
Waggoner, Bess, 152
Waggoner, Carrie M., 154
Waggoner, Carus Jennings, 163
Waggoner, Casey Catharine, 112
Waggoner, Catharine, 107, 141
Waggoner, Catharine (Bonnett), 182
Waggoner, Catharine (Hardman Hyde), 80, 123, 126
Waggoner, Catharine (Troxel), 155
Waggoner, Catherine, 140, 185

Index

Waggoner, Catherine (Hardman Hyde), 79, 108
Waggoner, Caty, 155
Waggoner, Charles, 154
Waggoner, Charles G., 123
Waggoner, Charles Garland, 169
Waggoner, Charles O., 187
Waggoner, Christina, 164, 165
Waggoner, Clements P., 123
Waggoner, Columbia A., 157
Waggoner, Columbia D., 180
Waggoner, Daniel Voorhees, 149
Waggoner, Dempsey F., 195
Waggoner, Earnest Gale, 164
Waggoner, Edna D., 164
Waggoner, Edward Burl, 114, 166
Waggoner, Edwin, 168
Waggoner, Eleanor, 171
Waggoner, Elias Marion, 126
Waggoner, Elias Straley, 154
Waggoner, Elias W., 161, 164
Waggoner, Elijah, 72, 141, 145, 146, 161, 164, 165, 167, 187
Waggoner, Elijah H., 187
Waggoner, Eliza J., 187
Waggoner, Eliza Kathleen, 168
Waggoner, Elizabeth, 18, 21, 33, 41, 42, 78, 84, 94, 97, 149
Waggoner, Elizabeth (Straley), 147, 149, 151, 153
Waggoner, Elmer, 153
Waggoner, Emily E. (Amy), 151
Waggoner, Emma C. (Starcher), 171, 173
Waggoner, Emma Pearl, 162
Waggoner, Ermgne, 151
Waggoner, Ermyne, 152
Waggoner, Eugene, 114
Waggoner, Everett, 114
Waggoner, Fernando, 113
Waggoner, Florence, 154

Waggoner, Frances Ruie, 157
Waggoner, Francis, 145
Waggoner, Frank M., 149
Waggoner, Fred, 167
Waggoner, G. L., 195
Waggoner, Geneva, 169
Waggoner, George, 107, 113, 144, 145, 149, 167, 187, 188, 195
Waggoner, George Burl, 167
Waggoner, George Columbus, 124
Waggoner, George Kemper, 163
Waggoner, George S., 167
Waggoner, George T., 113, 187
Waggoner, George W., 188
Waggoner, George Washington, 162
Waggoner, George Wilson, 163
Waggoner, Georgia, 153, 173
Waggoner, Geraldine, 114
Waggoner, Gertrude D., 112
Waggoner, Glen, 169
Waggoner, Grace, 162
Waggoner, Harriet (Cookman), 164
Waggoner, Harriet Ella, 164
Waggoner, Harriet Lucinda, 114
Waggoner, Harriet Rose, 162
Waggoner, Harvey P., 114
Waggoner, Harvey W., 167
Waggoner, Helen, 154
Waggoner, Henry, 95, 141, 144, 146, 155, 157
Waggoner, Henry E., 157
Waggoner, Henry Wilks, 113
Waggoner, Herbert E., 123
Waggoner, Howard W., 123
Waggoner, Ida A., 154
Waggoner, Ida Dirah, 113
Waggoner, Ira S., 154
Waggoner, Irene, 167
Waggoner, Iris, 114
Waggoner, Ishmael (Eddie), 164
Waggoner, J. D., 77

Index

Waggoner, Jack Elias, 163
Waggoner, Jackson, 171
Waggoner, Jacob, 140, 141, 145, 155, 181, 182
Waggoner, James E., 188
Waggoner, James Edwin, 163
Waggoner, James M., 154
Waggoner, James Miflin, 157
Waggoner, James R., 149
Waggoner, Jefferson, 147
Waggoner, Jessie, 152
Waggoner, Joann, 114
Waggoner, Joanna Pifer, 149
Waggoner, Johan Georg, 155
Waggoner, Johannes, 12, 25, 28, 45
Waggoner, Johannes Peter, 31
Waggoner, John, 11, 12, 26, 33, 34, 35, 39, 40, 55, 57, 72, 77, 78, 89, 90, 92, 94, 95, 97, 100, 105, 108, 139, 140, 141, 142, 143, 144, 145, 146, 155, 157, 161, 175, 179, 181, 185, 187, 188, 189, 191, 193, 195
Waggoner, John (Johannes), 89
Waggoner, John Andrew, 169
Waggoner, John C., 169
Waggoner, John C. B., 149
Waggoner, John Calhoun, 168, 171, 173
Waggoner, John E., 180
Waggoner, John H., 188
Waggoner, John Peter, 25, 28, 31, 32, 33
Waggoner, John Straley, 147
Waggoner, John W., 195
Waggoner, Joseph, 146, 153
Waggoner, Joseph Clinton, 163
Waggoner, Junetta, 151
Waggoner, Kathryn Ann, 163
Waggoner, Laura 'Lewey', 112
Waggoner, Leo, 154

Waggoner, Leora, 113
Waggoner, Lina, 153
Waggoner, Lloyd Bascom, 157
Waggoner, Lola, 152
Waggoner, Lucille Winifred, 114
Waggoner, Luther Everett, 114
Waggoner, Luverna Catharine, 124
Waggoner, Lydia, 152
Waggoner, Malinda, 188
Waggoner, Malissa, 153
Waggoner, Marella, 162
Waggoner, Margaret, 91, 140, 141, 155
Waggoner, Margaret (Bonnett), 40, 55, 77, 89, 94, 97, 105, 141
Waggoner, Margaret M., 187
Waggoner, Margaret Ruhana, 157
Waggoner, Margarita Christiana Pohlmann, 130
Waggoner, Mariah, 140, 193
Waggoner, Martha O., 181
Waggoner, Martin Green, 112
Waggoner, Mary, 12, 25, 28, 95, 149, 175, 179, 185, 195
Waggoner, Mary (Straley), 161, 164, 165, 167
Waggoner, Mary A. (Kelly), 179
Waggoner, Mary Columbus, 113
Waggoner, Mary E., 187
Waggoner, Mary Elizabeth, 169
Waggoner, Mary L. (Kelley), 179
Waggoner, May, 153
Waggoner, Maybelle, 153
Waggoner, McClellen, 149
Waggoner, Melinda (Cottrell), 188
Waggoner, Mildrid, 169
Waggoner, Minerva (Climer), 152
Waggoner, Nancy Ann (Ball), 109, 112, 113, 114, 165
Waggoner, Nancy N., 112
Waggoner, Nellie Mae, 164

Index

Waggoner, Nervy J., 188
Waggoner, Olive C., 195
Waggoner, Olive Majorie, 168
Waggoner, Oliver, 180
Waggoner, Oliver Eugene, 114
Waggoner, Oliver H. P., 153
Waggoner, Oliver M., 149
Waggoner, Oliver Ray, 149
Waggoner, Orville Clarence, 171
Waggoner, Paul, 72, 140, 146, 147, 149, 151, 153, 169
Waggoner, Pauline, 169
Waggoner, Peggy, 95, 155
Waggoner, Perry Green, 123, 126
Waggoner, Pete, 152
Waggoner, Peter, 12, 31, 32, 60, 77, 79, 89, 92, 94, 105, 106, 107, 108, 113, 123, 126, 140, 141, 145, 146, 151, 152
Waggoner, Peter G., 164
Waggoner, Peter M., 147
Waggoner, Purdy, 179
Waggoner, R. E. Bland, 164
Waggoner, Rachel, 188
Waggoner, Raleigh Benton, 154
Waggoner, Rasabell, 187
Waggoner, Rebecca, 180
Waggoner, Rhuelina L., 109, 165
Waggoner, Robert Bess, 153
Waggoner, Robert M., 187
Waggoner, Sadie JoAnn, 114
Waggoner, Samual, 145
Waggoner, Samuel, 113, 144, 146, 188, 195
Waggoner, Samuel B., 157
Waggoner, Samuel C., 157
Waggoner, Samuel L., 123
Waggoner, Sarah, 112
Waggoner, Sarah E., 157
Waggoner, Selma Gay, 169
Waggoner, Seymour, 151

Waggoner, Sherman, 112
Waggoner, Stella, 153
Waggoner, Stella (Estella), 162
Waggoner, Stephen, 149
Waggoner, Susan (Bonnett), 157
Waggoner, Susan Jane, 157
Waggoner, Susan M., 187
Waggoner, Susanna, 140, 146, 188
Waggoner, Susanna (Cosner), 125, 126
Waggoner, Susanna (Richards), 72
Waggoner, Susanna A., 195
Waggoner, Susannah, 140, 151, 157, 191
Waggoner, Susannah (Richards), 137, 139, 140, 145, 147, 155, 161, 175, 181, 185, 187, 189, 191, 193, 195
Waggoner, Thelma, 153
Waggoner, Thelma May, 169
Waggoner, Thomas, Capt., 26
Waggoner, Verona Alda, 114
Waggoner, Virginia, 112, 187
Waggoner, Virginia Catharine, 153
Waggoner, Virginia Elizabeth, 149
Waggoner, Voarhees, 154
Waggoner, Waifferd A., 167
Waggoner, Wesley, 151
Waggoner, Wilhelm, 7, 9, 10, 11, 12, 25, 28, 45, 48, 89, 139
Waggoner, Wilhelm, life on the South Branch, 28
Waggoner, Wilheln, 25
Waggoner, Willa Ruth, 162
Waggoner, Willard, 154
Waggoner, Willhelm, 26
Waggoner, Willhelm, tragedy of, 26, 27
Waggoner, William, 11, 107, 109, 112, 113, 114, 165, 188, 189
Waggoner, William Burl, 161, 169

Index

Waggoner, William Carus, 164
Waggoner, William Milton, 153
Waggoner, Wm., 140, 146
Waggoner, Wm. B., 72
Waggoner, Wm. Burl, 109
Wagner, Miflin, 157
Wagner, Peter, 31
Wagner, Wilhelm, 10
Wagnerin, Anna Elisabeth, 10, 11
Wagnerin, Anna Elizabeth, 28
Wagoner, Alcinda May, 126
Wagoner, Anna Lee, 279
Wagoner, Annalee, 128
Wagoner, Charles Dean, 128
Wagoner, Cris, 229
Wagoner, Cynthia Lucille, 128
Wagoner, Darrel Eugene, 279
Wagoner, Darrell Ann, 128
Wagoner, Darrell Eugene, 128
Wagoner, E. M., Mrs., 133
Wagoner, Elias M., 134
Wagoner, Elias Marion, 126
Wagoner, Elvena Blanche, 127, 279
Wagoner, Ginger Lea, 128
Wagoner, Henry Grant, 126
Wagoner, Ida Mable, 126
Wagoner, Inez Lucille (Solomon), 265
Wagoner, James Franklin, 153
Wagoner, Jodi Maria, 129
Wagoner, John, 98
Wagoner, Juli Rene, 129
Wagoner, Lee Charles, 128
Wagoner, Lee Elias, 126, 127, 279
Wagoner, Lee, Mrs., 279
Wagoner, Marvin Lee, 128, 254, 279
Wagoner, Nancy Ann (Budd), 129
Wagoner, Norman Jr., 128
Wagoner, Norman Leroy, 128, 279
Wagoner, Ramona Danette, 128
Wagoner, Robert Dale, 128, 279

Wagoner, Terry Ann, 128
Wagoner, Tony Dale, 128
Wagoner, Wilhelm, 9
Wagoner, William Lynn, 128, 129
Walker, Marire, 191
Walker, Rebecca J., 49
Walker, Roseline, 191
Walker, Thomas, Dr., 118, 119
Wallace, Mattie, 152
Walls, Robert, 168
Walner, Augusta Carrie, 261
Walner, Gusta, 262
Walter, Clyde Lyman, 127
Walter, Daniel Robert, 127
Walter, David Roy, 127
Walter, Elvena (Wagoner), 130
Walter, James Stuart, 127
Walter, Lynda Deane, 127
Walter, Mark Lyman, 127
Walter, Robert, 130
Walter, Robert R., 127
Walter, Robert Roy, 127
Walter, Steven Michael, 127
Wamsby, Jonathan, 80
Wamsley, Isaac, 123
Ward, Emit K., 199
Ward, Ruskin, 167
Warner, Anna M., 195
Warner, Delia, 195
Warner, Elizabeth (Davis), 195
Warner, George G, 62
Warner, James F., 195
Warner, John W., 195
Warner, Nettie J., 195
Warner, Oren, 195
Warner, Ova E., 195
Warner, Thomas A., 195
Warner, William D., 195
Warron, Earl, 265
Washington, Genl. George, 143

Index

Waters, Catherine Ruth, 227
Waters, Ulysses Elsworth, 227
Watson, Bernard Lee, 258
Watson, Betsey (Briggs), 248
Watson, Betsy (Briggs), 251
Watson, Charles, 248
Watson, Clarence Lee, 258
Watson, Clifford Kay, 258
Watson, David, 241, 247, 248, 249, 250, 251, 253, 254, 258, 261
Watson, David (or Daniel), 247
Watson, David Adna, 253
Watson, David Jr., 248, 258
Watson, David Sr., 248
Watson, Doris Eldine, 253
Watson, Edwin, 254, 258
Watson, Edwin B., 247
Watson, Edwin Jr., 258
Watson, Elizabeth (Drew), 258
Watson, Ella, 258
Watson, Elonedias (Lon) Leonadia, 248
Watson, Elsie, 248
Watson, Emma, 258
Watson, Emma A. (Steffen), 251
Watson, Emma Amelia (Steffen), 241, 253, 254, 258
Watson, Erastus L., 248
Watson, Etta, 241
Watson, Ettie, 254
Watson, Florence May, 258
Watson, Frances Lee, 253
Watson, Francis, 248
Watson, Ida May, 249
Watson, James W., 107
Watson, Jennie C., 247
Watson, Kathryn Alice, 258
Watson, Lacinda (Kirby), 247
Watson, Lafayett, 248
Watson, Lenna M., 248
Watson, Lloyd Eldon, 258
Watson, Lucetta C., 248
Watson, Mary, 248, 253
Watson, Mary A., 247
Watson, Mary Ann (Hunter), 248, 249, 251
Watson, Mary C., 248
Watson, Melberta, 258
Watson, Melinda A., 111
Watson, Michelle, 253
Watson, Myrthe, 248
Watson, Nellie, 248
Watson, Nettie, 249
Watson, Nettie E., 248
Watson, Nora, 248
Watson, Nora Ellen, 253
Watson, Ornold, 258
Watson, Samuel, 248
Watson, Tom Dennis, 253
Watson, William, 145, 247
Watson, William E., 251
Watson, William Ellsworth, 248
Watson, William L., 248
Watson, Willie, 249
Watts, Dr. Victor, 251
Watts, Eva, 251
Waugh, Mary E. Corinna, 204
Wayne, Gen., 92, 93
Wayne, Genl. A., 143
Weatherhold, Nicholas, 201
Weatherhold, Peter, 201
Weatherholt, Elizabeth, 201
Weatherholt, Gary, 201
Weatherholt, Jane, 201
Weaver, Lucy M., 86
Webb, Flora Ellen, 215
Webb, Ray K., 215
Weber, Johann Wilhelm, 49
Weekley, Carol, 162
Weihrer, Arthur, Jr., 227
Welch, Mary, 69
Weley, Margaret, 51

Index

Wells, Elnora, 227
Welton, John, 35
Wenger, Mahlon, 227
Wesley, David, 240
West, Alexander, 142, 144
West, Charles, 98
West, Edmond Jr., 82
West, Edmond Sr., 82
West, Elizabeth, 80, 158
West, G. W., 168
West, George W., 158
West, James, 99
West, Janet Louise, 163
West, John, 158
West, Josiah, 60, 80
West, Mary, 98
West, Mary C., 218
West, Matilda, 62
West, Moses, 60
West, Sarah S., 69
West, Thomas, 80
Westfall, Albert S., 229
Westfall, Angelina, 188
Westfall, Ashbury, 193
Westfall, Barbara, 217, 229
Westfall, Barbara E., 113
Westfall, Cornelius, 217, 225, 226, 229
Westfall, Elizabeth (Smith), 193
Westfall, George, 113
Westfall, George W., 229
Westfall, Jacob, 193
Westfall, Joel, 200
Westfall, John, 202
Westfall, John H., 217, 226, 229
Westfall, John H. (or W.), 229
Westfall, Jonah L., 111
Westfall, Lorenzo Dow, 229
Westfall, Mary, 229
Westfall, Mary Ann, 113
Westfall, Nancy, 225

Westfall, Peter, 229
Westfall, Ruhama, 229
Westfall, Samuel, 226, 229
Westfall, Virginia, 229
Westfall, Zachariah, 200
Westzell, Martin, 39
Wetherholt, Christina, 226
Wetzel, Christiana, 20
Wetzel, David Jr., 62
Wetzel, David Sr., 101
Wetzel, George, 20
Wetzel, George Michael, 16
Wetzel, Hans Martin, 5
Wetzel, Hans Martin Jr., 5, 15
Wetzel, Hans Martin, Family, 5
Wetzel, Henry, 5, 15
Wetzel, Jacob, 20, 39
Wetzel, Johann Jacob, 16
Wetzel, John, 15, 16, 18, 19, 20, 39
Wetzel, John Capt., 39
Wetzel, John Friedrich, 16
Wetzel, John Jr., 20
Wetzel, Katharine, 5
Wetzel, Katherine, 15
Wetzel, Lewis, 20, 26
Wetzel, Lucy Webb, 215
Wetzel, Magdelena Elisabeth, 16
Wetzel, Maria Barbara, 5, 15
Wetzel, Maria Catharine, 16
Wetzel, Martin, 15, 16, 20, 39
Wetzel, Martin Jr., 16, 18
Wetzel, Martin Sr., 15, 16
Wetzel, Mary (Bonnett), 20, 39
Wetzel, Nicholas, 5, 16
Wetzel, Nicholaus, 15
Wetzel, Nicolaus, 16
Wetzel, Regina (Foltz) Hudson, 101
Wetzel, Susannah, 20
Wetzell, John, 39
Wggoner, John H., 157
Wheatley, Linda Lou, 163

Index

Whetsel, David D., 85
Whetzell, Martin, 16
White, Eula Dean, 162
White, Forrest A., 213
White, Levi, 179
White, Lisa, 163
Whitsel, Rebecca, 85
Wiehl, Patricia, 241
Wiemmar, Bernhardt, 15
Wiemmar, John Bernhardt, 15
Wietmannin, Hanna Catharine, 11
Wilhelm, Adam, 275
Wilhelm, Friedrich, 276
Wilhelm, Johann, 276
Wilhers, Alexander Scott, 74
Will, Florence, 212
Willford, Ellen, 83
Williams, Abraham, 186
Williams, C. H., 204
Williams, Eleanor, 20
Williams, Jane (Westover), 268
Williams, Joel, 186
Williams, Jonah, 268
Williams, Jonas, 268
Williams, Lydia, 268
Williams, Margaret Ellen, 163
Williams, Mary, 268
Williams, Mary A., 186
Williams, Mary Rebecca, 185
Williams, Sarah Frances, 249
Williams, William, 268
Wills, Aaron Field, 270
Wills, Della Mae, 152
Wills, Flossie, 151
Wilson, Amy Elizabeth, 115
Wilson, Archie, 206
Wilson, Benj., 98
Wilson, Deane Elaine, 241
Wilson, Elizabeth, 267
Wilson, Emily B. (Smith), 206
Wilson, Jane, 113

Wilson, Jill Rayna, 241
Wilson, John Capt., 39
Wilson, Julie Faye, 241
Wilson, Maria (Rinehart), 113
Wilson, Mildred H., 163
Wilson, Olive Malissa, 68
Wilson, Robert, 267
Wilson, Virginia Louisa, 206
Wilson, Wayne Glen, 241
Wilt, Clarissa, 285
Wimer, Christina, 107
Wimer, Earl, Rev., 212
Winemiller, Aaron L., 66
Winemiller, Dora, 100
Winemiller, Francis, 100
Winkle, Allen, 127
Winkle, Marsha, 127
Winkle, Ruth (Tarbox), 127
Wise, Jemina, 51
Wise, Sarah Ann, 83
Withers, Alexander Scott, 93, 94
Witsall, John, 39
Witsel, David, 100
Witzel, Alonza A., 85
Witzel, David D., 62
Witzel, George, 85
Witzel, Henry Bevin, 62
Witzel, Henry Bivan, 85
Witzel, John, 84
Witzel, Julia A., 85
Witzel, Margaret (Hardman), 62
Witzel, Mariah L., 85
Witzel, Marietta, 85
Witzel, Rheuhana, 85
Wolf, Eva, 42
Wolf, Jacob, 145
Wolf, Jacob Jr., 95
Wolf, Jacob M., 68
Wolf, Jacob Sr., 95
Wolf, James R., 72
Wolf, Jane, 179

Index

Wolf, Mary, 95
Wolf, Michael, 278
Wolf, Thomas, 179, 208
Wolfe, Jacob, 20
Wolfe, Joseph B., 59
Wolfe, Madge, 168
Womer, Eleanor, 249
Womer, Emmet, 251
Womer, Grace, 251
Womer, Leonard Edward, 83, 250
Womer, Margaret, 250
Womer, Newton, 249
Womer, Retta, 251
Womer, Sylvester, 83, 250
Womer, Sylvester (Wes), 249
Wood, Abegail, 269
Wood, James, 97
Wood, John, 269
Wood, Kurts, 165
Wood, Margaret, 269
Wood, Martha, 269
Wood, Martha (King), 269
Wood, Mary, 269
Wood, Obadiah, 269
Woodward, Florence, 176
Woodward, Sarah, 83

Woofter, Carrie, 209
Woofter, Nancy A., 68
Woofter, Oliver, 209
Workman, Edna (Dutch), 171
Wright, Anna, 266
Wright, F. Edward, 231
Wright, Jackie Lou, 258
Wurster, Anna, 251
Wust, Klaus, 31, 118
Wyant, Robert, 153

Yeager, Elizabeth A., 67
Yeater, Mrs. Belle, 248
Yingring, Elmer, 285
Yoke, Christopher C., 64
Young, Andrew, 33, 34

Ziegler, Leda, 126
Zinn, George W., 66
Zinn, Marion Bukey, 206
Zinn, Martha Della, 206
Zinn, Mary J., 66
Zinn, Sarah (Gray), 66
Zinn, Tensey Fay, 206
Zobrist, Mary, 209

www.ingramcontent.com/pod-product-compliance
Lightning Source LLC
Chambersburg PA
CBHW050331230426
43663CB00010B/1820